Microsoft Office In Concert

Other Prima Computer Books

Available Now!

WINDOWS Magazine Presents: Access from the Ground Up
Adventures in Windows
CompuServe Information Manager for Windows: The Complete Membership Kit & Handbook (with two 3½" disks)
Computers Don't Byte—The Absolute Beginner's Guide to Getting Started with the PC
CorelDRAW! 4 Revealed!
Create Wealth with Quicken
DOS 6.2: Everything You Need to Know
WINDOWS Magazine Presents: Encyclopedia for Windows
Excel 5 for Windows: The Visual Learning Guide
Free Electronic Networks
Improv for Windows Revealed! (with 3½" disk)
Lotus Notes 3 Revealed!
Making Movies with Your PC
Microsoft Works for Windows By Example
PageMaker 5 for the Mac: Everything You Need to Know
PageMaker 5 for Windows: Everything You Need to Know
Paradox 4.5 for DOS Revealed! (with 3½" disk)
PC DOS 6.1: Everything You Need to Know
WINDOWS Magazine Presents: The Power of Windows and DOS Together, 2nd Edition
PowerPoint: The Visual Learning Guide
Quattro Pro 4: Everything You Need to Know
Quicken 3 for Windows: The Visual Learning Guide
QuickTime: Making Movies with Your Macintosh
Smalltalk Programming for Windows (with 3½" disk)
Superbase Revealed!
Think THINK C (with two 3½" disks)
Windows 3.1: The Visual Learning Guide
Windows for Teens
WinFax PRO: The Visual Learning Guide
Word for Windows 6: The Visual Learning Guide
WordPerfect 6 for DOS: The Visual Learning Guide
WordPerfect 6 for DOS: How Do I . . .?
WordPerfect 6 for Windows: The Visual Learning Guide
Your FoxPro for Windows Consultant (with 3½" disk)

Upcoming Books

Making Music with Your PC: A Beginner's Guide
Migrating to Windows 4 (with 3½" disk)
Symantec C++: Programming Fundamentals for Macintosh
Visual Basic for Applications Revealed!

How to Order:

Individual orders and quantity discounts are available from the publisher, Prima Publishing, P.O. Box 1260BK, Rocklin, CA 95677-1260; phone: (916) 632-4400. On your letterhead include information concerning the intended use of the books and the number of books you wish to purchase. Turn to the back of the book for more information.

Microsoft Office In Concert

Professional Edition

John Weingarten

Prima Publishing
P.O. Box 1260BK
Rocklin, CA 95677

Prima Computer Books is an imprint of Prima Publishing, Rocklin, California 95677.

Executive Editor: Roger Stewart
Managing Editor: Neweleen A. Trebnik
Project Editor: Dan J. Foster and Steven Martin
Technical Reviewer: Heidi Purvis
Copy Editor: Betsy Ahl
Book Designer, Production Artist: Susan Glinert, BookMakers
Indexer: Mary Jane Mahoney
Cover Designer: Page Design, Inc.
Cover Production Coordinators: Kim Bartusch and Anne Johnson

Library of Congress Catalog Card Number: 94-66631

ISBN: 1-55958-640-0
Printed in the United States of America

94 95 96 97 CWO 10 9 8 7 6 5 4 3 2 1

For Dad and Cyrille

Contents at a Glance

Contents

Acknowledgments

I would like to thank the people who helped make this book a reality.

Roger Stewart, Executive Editor, was instrumental in getting this project off the ground. His ideas, suggestions, encouragement, and insights helped beyond measure.

Dan Foster and Steven Martin, Project Editors, made sure that this project went smoothly—no small feat! Their hard work, attention to detail, and constant support were invaluable.

Neweleen Trebnik, Managing Editor, keeps the wheels turning at Prima. She is a dynamo and model of efficiency and organization. And a nice person, too.

Diane Pasquetti, Prima Publishing's all-around cool person, made heroic efforts getting software to the right places. She managed to keep her cool when I lost mine.

Heidi Purvis, Technical Editor, helped to ensure the technical accuracy of this book. Her help and suggestions were greatly appreciated.

Susan Glinert, Book Designer/Typesetter, did a terrific job making this the wonderful-looking book that it is.

Betsy Ahl, Copyeditor, did a tremendous job ensuring that the words were just right.

Matt Wagner of Waterside Productions is more than just a great agent. I can't thank him enough for his encouragement and guidance.

Ron Varela, a great guy and a wonderful friend, whose grasp of the English language is more better than mine are. He took the time to read through the manuscript and point out the errors of my ways.

Finally, my wife, Pam, and children, Sarah and Joshua, provided love and encouragement. What more could I ask?

Introduction

Microsoft Office 4.3 has such a wide range of capabilities that you could spend months trying to digest all the details. Fortunately, you don't have to learn how to use every feature, function, and command to put Office to work for you. If you want to learn the essentials of Microsoft Office, this book is for you.

You'll find that all of the main Office programs are covered in enough depth to get you going and feeling confident but not so much depth that you'll be overwhelmed. You won't find detailed discussions of arcane and seldom-used features here. What you will find are clear explanations of how to get the most from Office in the shortest time.

The procedures in the book are general enough that you'll be able to apply them to your own requirements. The illustrations and examples are based on real-world situations and should provide you with practical ideas of how the programs can be used.

The tasks and concepts related to each program are presented in a logical order, progressing from orientation and navigation to more complex tasks. After learning the fundamentals of the individual Office programs, you'll learn to use them together to create compound documents incorporating data from multiple Office programs.

Don't worry about intimidating computer jargon in this book. All the terms and concepts are clearly defined and explained as you come to them.

The material is presented in a clear, concise, and friendly manner, without stilted, pretentious writing. What you'll find is writing that regards you as a real human being. Now there's a switch for a computer book.

Who Should Read This Book

If you've never used Windows or any of the Office programs before, don't worry. Everything you need to know to get started is carefully explained. I don't assume any previous computer experience. Even if you aren't yet sure what each of the Office programs can be used for, you'll find the answers you're looking for.

If you've worked with previous versions of any of the Office programs—or even other word processing, spreadsheet, or presentation programs—without ever feeling completely productive and comfortable, this book will help you learn to use the latest versions while providing a refresher on general concepts.

All the important new features of each program are described at the beginning of the first chapter that deals with that program. You won't have to hunt through the text to find the new goodies.

Summary

If you've been afraid of diving in and learning to use Office (its sheer size can be frightening), this book lets you put a few toes in the water. After finishing this book, I hope you'll feel comfortable not only using the features discussed in the book but also exploring the limitless possibilities of Microsoft Office.

Section I

Welcome to Microsoft Office

1

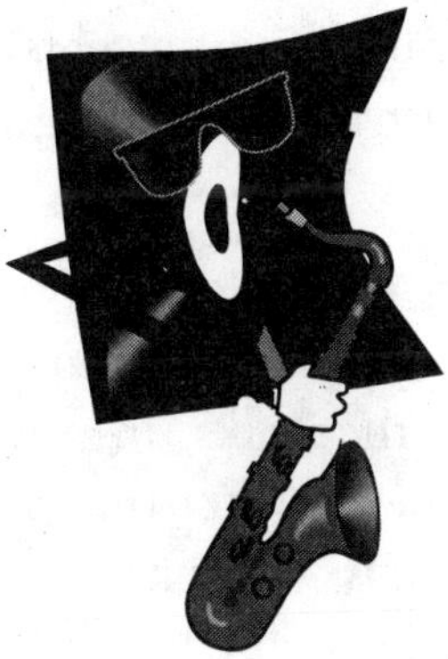

Why Microsoft Office?

You may have purchased Microsoft Office for its first-rate word-processing, spreadsheet, database, and presentation graphics programs. But the true power and elegance of Microsoft Office are found in the way the programs interact with one another to achieve a level of synergy that no other similar combination has yet achieved. As this book progresses, you'll learn how to use Office's programs in combination to perform business tasks that can't be accomplished with any of them individually.

Before you can use the programs together, however, you must learn to use each one by itself. Before getting to the specifics of using the programs, let me give you some perspective. I'll start with a little background about the programs and then discuss which is best for which type of task. Finally, I'll tell you how Windows makes the extraordinary integration of these programs possible.

Where the Programs Came From

The personal computers that run Microsoft Office are a far cry from the computers used as business tools just a few decades ago. Back then, computers weren't personal at all. They were huge hunks of machinery kept in special climate-controlled rooms with raised floors, and they were attended to by specialized staff (usually in white coats) trained in computer science. Information was distributed through printed reports requested by top management.

These computers were often designed to perform only a couple of business tasks, generally in the area of accounting—perhaps inventory control or accounts receivable and payable. If the folks in the accounting department had any interaction with the monster (mainframe) computer, it was through dumb terminals (screens and keyboards without processing capacity), which were useful for little more than remote data entry. If management wanted the computer to perform a new function, they had to put in a request to the programmers running the system.

In the early 1970s ordinary office workers got their first glimpse of personal computers with the advent of the dedicated word processor—not to be confused with word-processing *programs* like the Word for Windows program included with Microsoft Office. Dedicated word processors were complete computers small enough to fit on or next to a desk, but they could accomplish only one thing—creating and revising typed documents. While these devices were a boon to office productivity, they didn't do much to empower the user with tools that could be used creatively.

In the late 1970s, the first multipurpose personal computers arrived on the scene. They gave office workers much of the power of those early mainframe computers along with the flexibility to add programs for word processing and other tasks for almost unlimited expansion of the machine's power.

WordStar was the first popular word-processing program for personal computers. Users of the early versions of WordStar had a love/hate relationship with the program. It allowed the creation of almost any kind of document but was so awkward and required the memorization of so many arcane keyboard combinations and codes that many people, myself included, tore their hair out trying to get the program to create the documents they needed. I guess that accounts for the large number of bald computer users.

You could even create customized programs for those machines, though very few personal computer users acquired enough programming skill to create anything useful.

As wonderful as those early machines and programs were, it wasn't until the introduction of the first spreadsheet program, VisiCalc, in 1978, that businesses could justify putting personal computers on employees' desks.

Before spreadsheets, it was mainly accounting and bookkeeping types who created the budgets and forecasts for businesses, using data supplied by management. Perhaps this was because they were the only people who had the patience to perform the endless recalculations required when *actual* income and expenses collided with projections. If you are an accounting or bookkeeping type, you have my admiration. Of course spreadsheet programs help you too, alleviating the drudgery of many accounting tasks.

It was especially for the non-accountant and number-phobe that programs for turning numbers into charts and graphs were devised. A picture may not always be worth a thousand words, but it can sure make it easier to visualize the relationships and trends of the numbers they represent.

At first, if you wanted to create charts, you had to use a charting program that worked with the numbers generated by your spreadsheet program. The people at Personal Software, who brought us VisiCalc, later introduced a companion charting program with the charming name of VisiTrend/Plot.

The next generation of spreadsheet programs, ushered in by Lotus 1-2-3, added rudimentary charting capabilities within the program. The flexibility and capacity of the charting portions of current spreadsheet programs have expanded to surpass those of the early stand-alone charting programs. Even so, most spreadsheet programs lack at least a few important charting and graphics capabilities. For example, one category that is seldom covered adequately is presentation graphics.

Presentation-graphics programs, such as Office's PowerPoint, let you produce presentations including charts, speaker's notes, outlines, and slides that can be printed or displayed sequentially on-screen with sound for multimedia presentations.

Programs for managing complex data got off the ground with the introduction of a little program called dBase, which was originally designed to track horse-racing statistics to improve its author's odds of winning. Microsoft Access is light years beyond that original program, both in ease of use and power.

Power Windows

Microsoft Office for Windows runs on IBM-compatible computers. Your computer must have two programs installed and running before you can even install Office—DOS and Windows. DOS is the *disk operating system,* which provides your computer with the most fundamental instructions for communicating with some of its parts, including disk drives, memory, and files. It enables files to be copied, deleted, and backed up.

Until a few years ago, the vast majority of programs ran with just DOS and lacked several useful features found in programs running under Windows. Because DOS doesn't have any rules for the way you work with programs, each program has to start from scratch to create a bridge, or *user interface,* between you and the program. Therefore, some programs might require you to press the Esc key to cancel an operation while others might use the F1 key. To save a document, you might use F10 in one program and Ctrl-Shift-S in another.

This inconsistency of user interface made it more difficult to learn how to use software, because the commands that worked for one program were usually completely different from those required by the next. The practical effect was to cause most users to limit the number of programs they used to only those necessary to complete their tasks. This lack of consistency also prevented many users from trying new programs that might have improved productivity or allowed broader creative expression. It was just too much hassle to install and learn a new program.

Not only did DOS stifle software experimentation, it stifled the ability to share information among programs. Sure, there were (and still are) some DOS programs that provided ways to exchange data with other DOS programs, but the exchange was rarely smooth and easy. And, like the user interface, the methods for exchanging data lacked consistency. Knowing how to exchange data between two DOS programs did not guarantee that you would know how to move data to a third DOS program.

Windows makes a good stab at eliminating the data exchange and interface limitations of DOS. It even addresses a couple of other DOS weaknesses—memory management and multitasking.

Windows is a program that complements DOS by adding a graphical interface. With Windows, many tasks are easier and more intuitive. (Well, I should point out that some people who are already intimately familiar with the workings of DOS feel that Windows is counter-intuitive. I guess intuition is in the eye of the beholder.)

A Pretty Interface

Most DOS programs display only text on-screen and don't even show the fonts (type styles) that will appear on the printed page. Even those DOS programs that allow you to view graphic elements often require you to switch modes to see them. Windows, on the other hand, uses a *graphical user interface* or GUI (pronounced "gooey"). The advantage of a GUI is that your screen presents a reasonable facsimile of the printed page. This is called "what you see is what you get" (or WYSIWYG, pronounced "wizzywig").

The Windows GUI also lets you perform many tasks by manipulating graphical objects on-screen. For example, instead of typing a command, you may be able to use your mouse to click on an *icon* (a pictorial representation of a command or task).

Microsoft, the maker of Windows, suggests a set of user-interface guidelines for programs written to run under Windows. Most Windows programs follow these suggestions, which means users (that's you) no longer have to relearn everything each time they start using a new program.

The Great Exchange

One of the most dramatic ways Windows has made working with multiple programs easier is by providing a consistent approach to data exchange among Windows programs. From cutting or copying information from a Windows program and electronically pasting it into another, all the way to linking and embedding portions of data from one Windows program into another, Windows makes these exchanges a snap.

With each succeeding version, Windows has included increasingly sophisticated methods for exchanging data. But not all Windows programs support all the latest technologies. Of course, programs from Microsoft are usually among the first to support the latest methods, and the programs included with Microsoft Office 4.2 do. The latest Windows technology for exchanging data is called OLE (Object Linking and Embedding) version 2.0, but don't worry about the terminology now. I'll describe what it is and what it means to you in the last chapters of this book.

Juggling Virtuoso

Given this ease of use, consistent interface, and powerful data-exchange capability, you may find yourself wishing you could work in several programs at once. Windows grants your wish with its multitasking ability. Multitasking means running more than one program at a time. Windows can juggle as many programs as the memory and speed of your computer allow.

There are many reasons to run several programs at once. For example, you could let your huge Excel spreadsheet recalculate in the background while you work on a Word document. Or you could receive your electronic mail from corporate headquarters while you prepare a dazzling PowerPoint presentation. The possibilities are endless!

Frankly, most people run multiple programs so they can switch quickly from one to another. If you're working on the company budget in Excel and you get a call from a major customer asking to review the details of a proposal you created in Word, you don't have to exit Excel, start Word, and then reverse the procedure at the end of your conversation. With a couple of keystrokes or mouse clicks, you can switch to Word and open the proposal document; then, when you're finished talking to the customer, you can instantly switch back to your budget in Excel.

Multitasking can also make moving data between programs easier. By having the source program and the destination program in small windows on your screen at the same time, you can see what you're doing as you perform the data transfer.

Memory Master

To run, computer programs need memory, which is supplied on chips in your computer—and the more the better. Just having enough chips, however, doesn't guarantee that your programs will be able to use all the memory (Random Access Memory, or RAM) that they provide. Providing DOS programs with enough memory to run efficiently can be difficult at best and is often a nightmare. There are some clever ways to get around DOS memory limitations, but because different DOS programs take different approaches, setting up your computer properly for DOS programs that need different kinds of memory (no, there isn't just one kind of memory) can be intimidating.

Windows eliminates many of the memory problems associated with DOS. All Windows programs use the same kind of memory, called *extended memory*. Windows even manages memory allocations, supplying the current program with the memory it needs and then freeing that memory when the program no longer needs it.

Windows can actually let you use more memory than you have. Most computers aren't equipped with enough RAM to keep all your available Windows programs in memory. But you can still have them all running at once because of Windows' *virtual memory* capabilities. When Windows runs out of memory, it can use space on your computer's hard disk as though it were just more RAM.

Windows can even enable your computer to supply the correct kind of memory to the various DOS programs you may still use.

tip

Even though Windows will use your hard disk as virtual memory, you can't have too much real memory. Because they are mechanical devices, even the fastest hard disks are hundreds of times slower than RAM. The more often you run out of memory—requiring Windows to swap data to and from your poky old hard disk—the slower your overall Windows performance will be.

Depending on how fast your computer is and how much memory it has, you could get a bigger performance boost by spending a couple of hundred dollars for extra RAM than by spending several thousand for a faster computer. This is usually the case if you have less than 8MB of RAM in your computer. If you have only 4MB and you wish your computer were faster, get more RAM.

Harmony in the Office

At the beginning of this section, I mentioned that the beauty of Microsoft Office lies in the way the programs interact with one another. I also said that the programs use the latest data exchange technology. With Office, Microsoft has gone to great lengths to bring you an even more consistent user interface than a typical assortment of Windows programs.

As you work with the Office programs, you'll find that several major consistencies jump out at you. The menus for the programs are almost identical. Of course, the options within the menus are appropriate for the particular program you're working with.

Microsoft also ensures that *dialog boxes, toolbars, shortcut menus,* and program *help* all operate consistently. Don't worry if these terms are unfamiliar. I'll explain them all as we start using the programs that include them. There's even a consistent shortcut for switching between the Office programs. There are also hundreds of minor consistencies that give the group of programs a unified feel.

This consistency makes learning the second and third programs much easier than learning the first. After you've learned to use any one of the programs, you'll find yourself guessing, often correctly, about how to perform a task in one of the other programs. After a short while it will all start to feel natural and automatic.

Don't worry. Learning to use even the first of the Office programs will be painless. I won't make you suffer; I promise.

The Right Tool for the Job

Deciding which of the four Office programs to use for a particular task or project is the first—and often the most difficult—challenge. There is some overlap in capabilities, so many projects can be completed using any of the programs. Choosing the best one for the job, however, will make the job go more smoothly and give you greater flexibility to do it the way you want to.

Picking the correct program might seem to be a matter of common sense—working with words, use Word; manipulating numbers, use Excel; creating a presentation or a chart, use PowerPoint. Well, it's not quite that easy, because the Office ensemble shares a set of capabilities.

Word, for example, has a table feature for manipulating rows and columns and can even perform calculations just as Excel does. Word also has the ability to create charts. Excel, in addition to its extensive number-handling capability, can create dazzling charts. Both programs have the ability to create databases and to sort and select portions of the database that meet certain criteria. PowerPoint also lets you work with text and create charts.

The path to the best choice becomes even murkier when you take into account the ability to link portions of these programs to other programs. So how do you decide?

As a general rule, Word is the best choice for primarily text-oriented documents. When you need to work extensively with numbers and calculations, Excel is usually the preferred tool. Excel also makes the most sense for charts, especially those that reflect data in an Excel spreadsheet. Access is the tool to turn to for complex data management needs. PowerPoint is normally the tool you'll turn to for presentations that pull together elements from the other two programs.

Ultimately, the best advice I can give is to learn the capabilities, strengths, and weaknesses of all three programs. It also helps if you know what elements you want to include in your document. If you know what the programs can do and what you want to accomplish, choosing the right one can be as easy as picking the right socks to go with your shoes. Actually, I sometimes have more trouble with the socks.

The following examples will help you decide which program is best suited for a given type of task.

Word makes putting together almost any written document a breeze. From business and personal letters to book-length manuscripts, simple memos to annual reports to almost any legal document, Word has the tools to make any document appear just the way you want it to.

For number-oriented documents, from simple household budget worksheets to forecasts for multinational corporations, from a cash flow analysis for a sandwich shop to a portfolio analysis for a multi-million dollar pension fund, Excel provides tools for deftly manipulating the numbers to answer the questions you are posing and to find the best solutions when you are wondering "what if…?".

Excel is also the first place to turn when you want to transform the numbers from your Excel worksheets into charts. A column chart showing the relationship between income and expenses is a good way to clarify the numbers. A pie chart that shows the contribution each division is making to the company makes a stronger statement than numbers alone. A line chart showing the ups and downs of the various investments in the pension fund can help you make better choices than a bunch of numbers.

The word-oriented documents created in Word and the number-oriented worksheet documents created in Excel, as well as the related charts, can be combined in compelling presentations. The point of most documents created in Word and Excel is to persuade and enlighten, so it makes sense that by simply putting them together you can create a persuasive presentation. True enough. But if you want to use the right tool for the job (that is the heading of this section, after all), PowerPoint is probably the best choice.

Let's say you're making a presentation to the board of directors of a corporation in which you want to persuade them to recommend the acquisition of another company. You might use Word to create an analysis of the proposed acquisition, but you could also use salient portions of the analysis, as well as Excel charts, to create slides for the presentation. Within PowerPoint itself, you might add slides with bulleted lists of important points, as well as speaker's notes for you to use during the presentation.

PowerPoint lets you add music, digitized speech, and even video clips to create a multimedia presentation with the kind of production values you would expect to find in a Pepsi commercial. Uh huh. If you can't convince the board with all those tools at your disposal, maybe it's time to move on to the next project.

Section VII will present several real-world projects that use the Office programs in combination. Along the way, as you learn about each program, I hope you'll be inspired to think of many more uses for the both programs individually and in concert.

Section II

Windows—A Jump Start

2

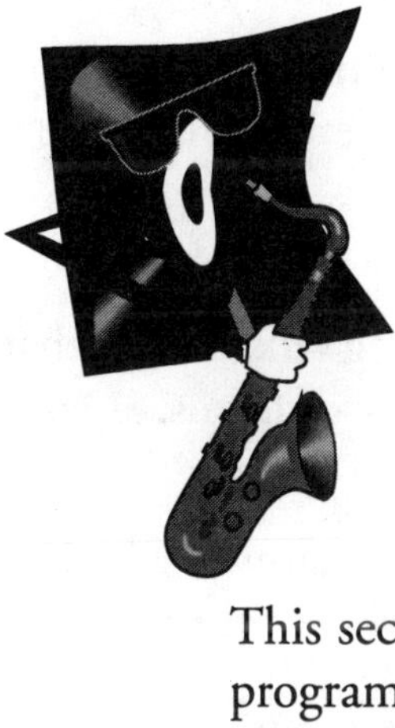

Starting at the Very Beginning

This section provides a solid foundation for working with the Office programs—and all other Windows programs for that matter. You can learn to use Word, Excel, and PowerPoint with only a rudimentary understanding of Windows. If you become comfortable navigating and manipulating the Windows environment, however, you'll find that working with all Windows programs is faster, easier, and less frustrating.

With Windows, you won't need to memorize hundreds of secret commands and codes to operate your software. You'll be able to see the available choices in menus, buttons, and other graphical devices that will lead you to your destination without much trauma. Because

Windows is so friendly and inviting, the best way to learn it is to dive right in and start exploring your new world.

Starting Windows

Many computers are set up to start Windows automatically. If this is the case with your system, you can skip this section. On second thought, at some point you could find yourself dumped out of Windows and needing a way to get back in, so follow along.

When you turn on your computer, the most common greeting you see on the screen is the DOS prompt that looks something like this:

```
C:\>
```

The reason I say the DOS prompt looks "something" like this is that the prompt can be customized to appear in a variety of forms. If your prompt looks a little different, don't worry.

The C indicates that you are currently working on drive C, which is normally the designation of your hard disk drive, where your program and document files are stored. If you have more than one hard drive or if your hard drive is divided into several partitions, their designations will usually be D, E, F, and so on.

note

Depending on how your computer was set up, your drive letters may be different. If your computer is part of a network (many computers connected together to share resources) and is using programs from the network drive, the drive letter will probably be F or a subsequent letter of the alphabet.

Your floppy disk drive is normally called drive A. If you have a second floppy drive, it is usually called drive B. If you have only one floppy disk drive, your drive designations skip from A to C.

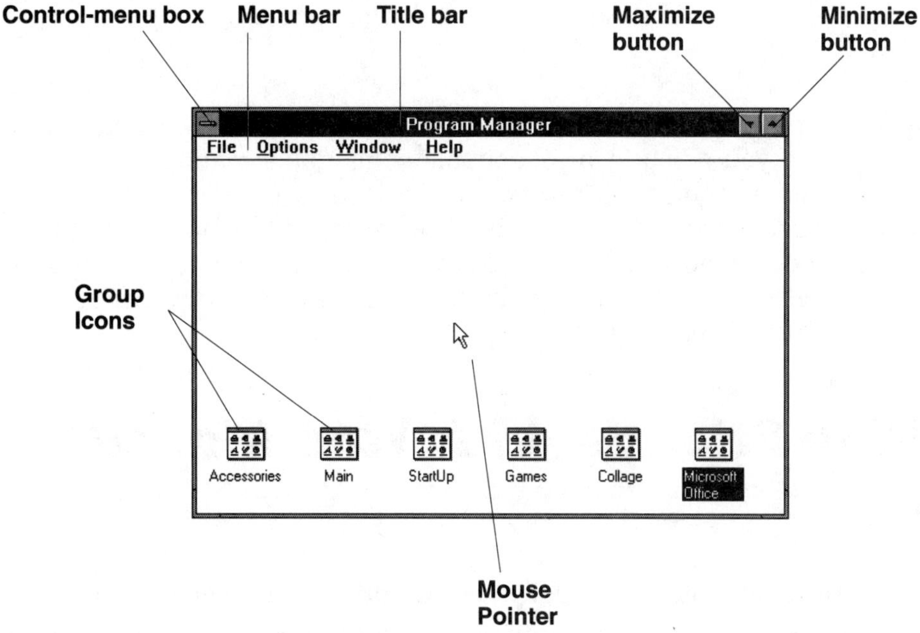

FIGURE 2–1 The opening Windows Program Manager window

Let's proceed with our Windows startup now.

1. Type: **WIN**.
2. Press the Enter key.

Shortly, the Windows Program Manager window appears as shown in Figure 2–1.

One of the things that makes Windows lovable but also confusing at first is how customizable it is. Because of this, your opening Windows screen may look very different from the one in Figure 2–1. If it does, you'll still be able to follow the procedures in the remainder of this section.

If none of the group icons shown in the figure are visible, see the section on moving windows later in this chapter to learn how to move and size windows so you can find what you're looking for, even if it's buried.

note In this book, you'll learn just enough about Windows basics to get you going in a reasonably comfortable manner. For more information on the ins and out of Windows, including many of the customization features, check out some of the many books that focus specifically on Windows. One of my favorite introductory Windows books is *Windows 3.1: The Visual Learning Guide* from Prima Publishing.

Making Friends with Your Mouse

Although you can actually get around in Windows by using just the keyboard, you'll find many tasks easier or more efficient if you use the mouse, which is probably attached to your computer and sitting on your desk next to your keyboard.

As you move the mouse on the surface of your desk, the on-screen mouse pointer moves correspondingly. In addition to moving the mouse pointer, there are three other basic mouse operations you'll need to master to use the mouse effectively: *clicking*, *double-clicking*, and *dragging*.

Clicking is quickly pressing and releasing the left mouse button while pointing at something on the screen. A double-click is two fast clicks. Dragging is pressing and holding the left mouse button while moving the mouse.

tip One of the areas of your Windows environment you may want to customize right away is the way your mouse operates. It can be modified so the pointer moves faster or slower on the screen and so its double-click speed matches your comfort level. You can even swap the left and right mouse buttons so you can use the mouse on the left side of your keyboard if you are left-handed.

See Chapter 3 for more information on customizing the mouse.

As we start working in the Office programs in the next section, you'll find occasions to use other mouse actions, such as right-clicking (clicking with the right mouse button), clicking while pressing the Ctrl or Shift key, and triple-clicking. But, once you have the basic mouse actions mastered, the others are a piece of cake.

You'll get a chance to use the basic mouse operations as you work through this chapter.

Working with Menus and Dialog Boxes

Two of the most common ways you communicate with Windows are through menus and dialog boxes. Every Windows program has a set of menus that you use for issuing commands and making choices. The primary menus appear on the menu bar. Some of the menu choices require additional information and display a *dialog box* or a *submenu.*

Choosing a menu item followed by an ellipsis (...) causes a dialog box to appear. A dialog box is a small window that lets you specify further information. Choosing a menu item followed by a right-facing triangle displays a submenu of additional choices. You'll learn more about submenus in Chapter 4. Office programs also have shortcut menus, which offer commands for specific elements of the screen. I'll cover these shortcut menus as we start working through the programs.

Let's use the mouse to choose a menu item and then work with a dialog box.

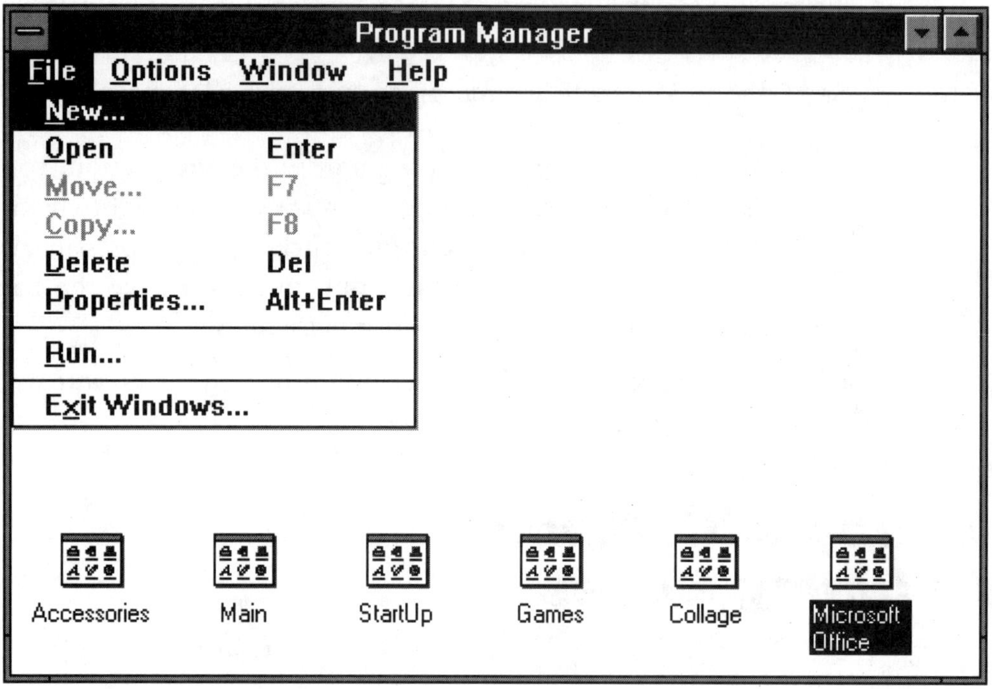

FIGURE 2–2 The Program Manager's File menu

1. Move your mouse so the pointer is on the word File in the menu bar and click (press and release the left mouse button) to display the File menu, as shown in Figure 2–2.
2. Click on New, the first choice on the menu (followed by an ellipsis), to display the New Program Object dialog box shown in Figure 2–3.
3. You could choose one of the dialog box's option buttons by clicking on it, but we don't want to add a new program object, so click on the Cancel button to remove the dialog box from the screen without performing any action.

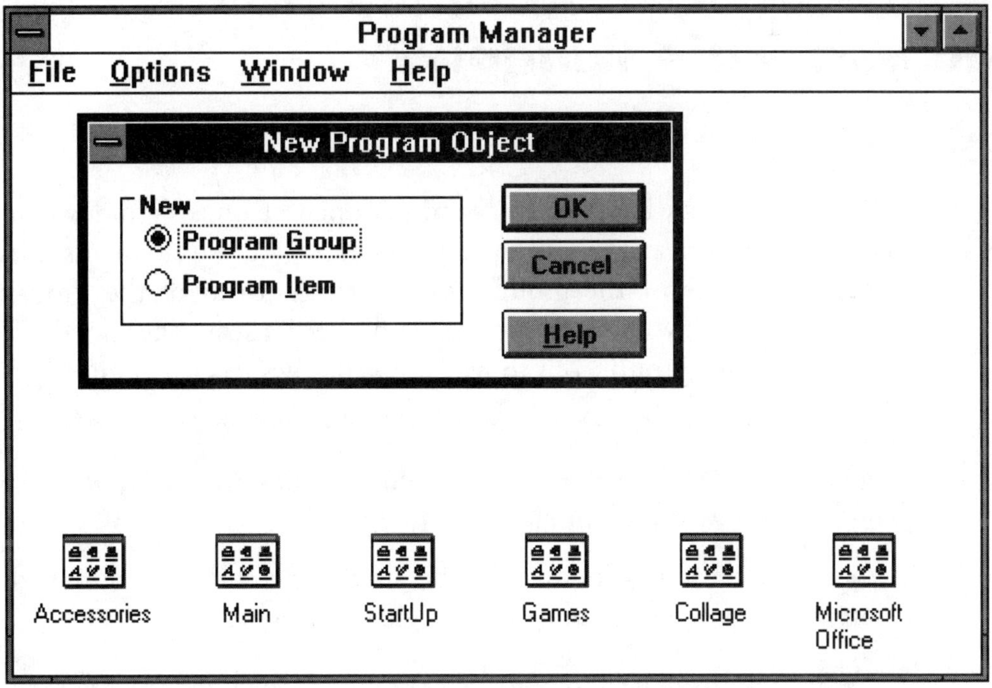

FIGURE 2–3 The New Program Object dialog box

note

You can choose menus from the keyboard by pressing Alt and the underlined letter in the menu name. For example, to open the File menu, press Alt-F. Once the menu is open, you can choose one of the menu items by just pressing its underlined letter (no need to press the Alt key).

You can also choose a menu item by using the ↑ or ↓ key to highlight the item and then pressing Enter.

You Mean I Can Actually Move and Size This Window?

Because you can have several windows open at once, Windows provides ways to arrange them to suit your taste and requirements. First, we'll open one of the group icons at the bottom of the Program Manager window, move it around, and alter its size. Then we'll open two additional group icons to see how Windows lets us arrange them.

The fastest way to open an icon is to double-click on it.

Point to the Main group icon and double-click to display the Main group window shown in Figure 2–4.

Your Main group window may be sized differently or contain different program icons. Don't worry. That's all right.

tip Here's an easy way to open a group if you can't find the group icon you are looking for: Choose Windows (click on the Windows menu) to display a list of the group icon names. Then just click on the name of the group you want to open.

We now have two window types on the screen. The Program Manager window is called an *application window.* This makes sense because the Program Manager is an application (program) that runs within Windows.

Although I've been calling the Main group window a group window, it is actually a *document window.* Every program (application) has an application window. Within an application window most Windows programs allow you to open several document windows. The term document window will probably make more sense when we are working in one of the Office programs where a document window contains a document instead of a group of icons.

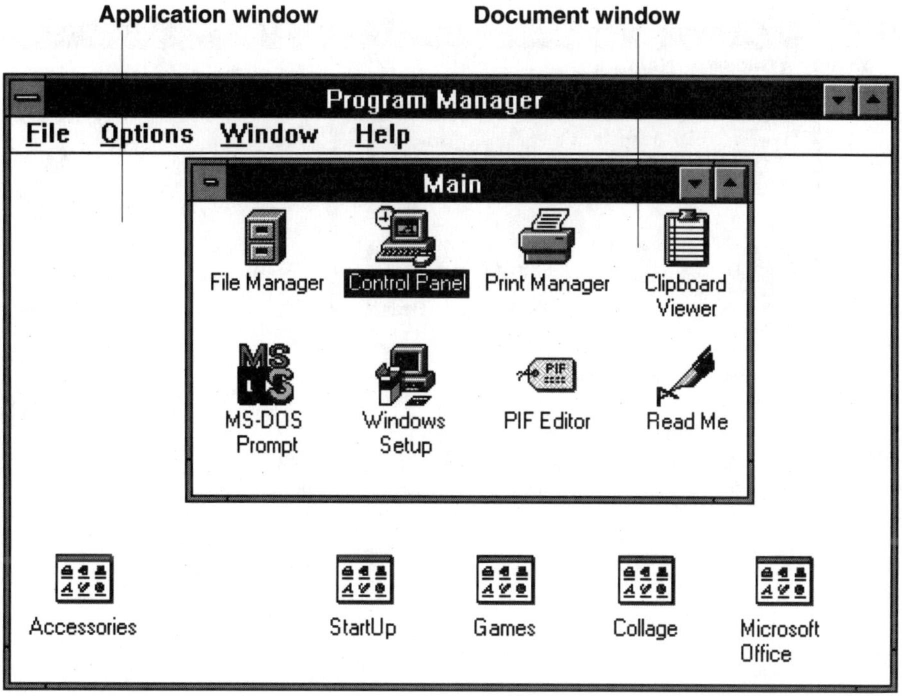

FIGURE 2–4 The Main group window

There is an easy way to differentiate between application and document windows. Application windows always have their own menu bars, while document windows are manipulated by using the menus from the application window. Notice that the Main group window has no menu of its own. This is a sure clue that this is a document window.

Before moving and sizing the Main group window, let's give ourselves more room to work in the Program Manager window by *maximizing* it. To do this, click on the Maximize button in the upper-right corner of the Program Manager window to maximize it, as shown in Figure 2–5.

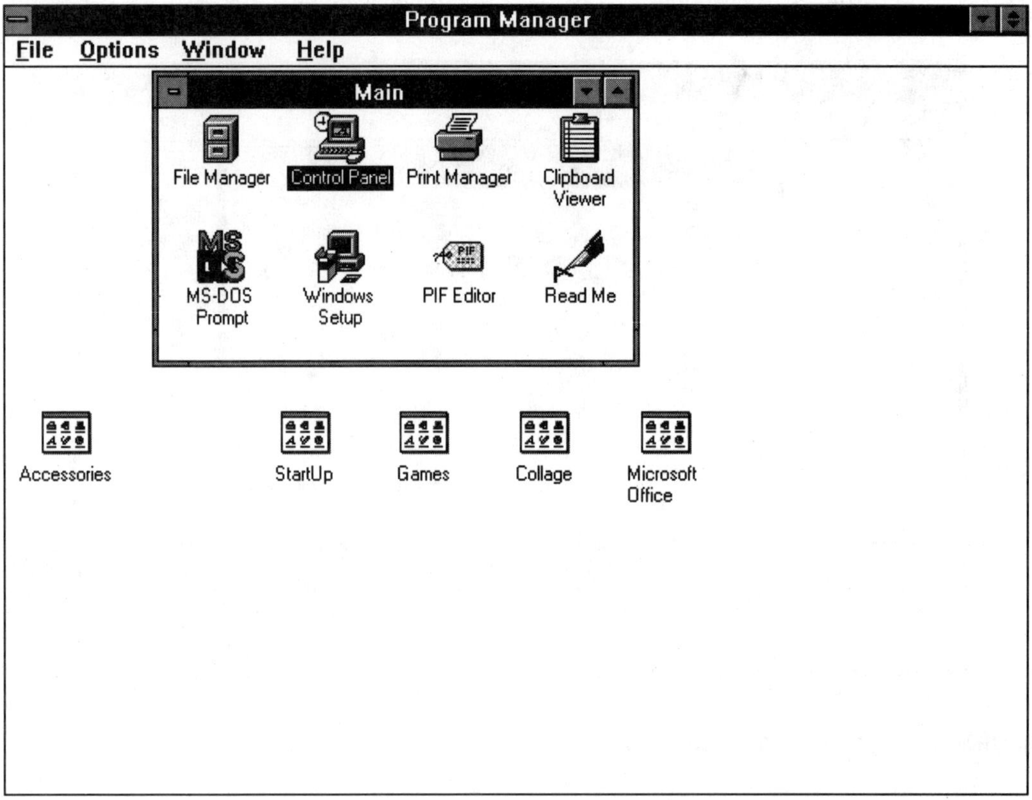

FIGURE 2-5 The maximized Program Manager window

The Maximize button is replaced by a *Restore button.* Clicking on a Restore button restores a window to its previous size.

The group icons are now too high in the window and would be less likely to get in the way if they were at the bottom of the window. You could just drag them to the bottom of the window, but that would require hauling each one down individually, and they probably wouldn't be aligned properly (unless you have a better eye for that sort of thing than I do). The easiest approach is to let Windows arrange the icons.

All we have to do is make sure one of the group icons is selected (its name highlighted) and then choose Arrange Icons from the Windows menu.

1. Click on any one of the group icons.

   A control menu will pop up. You can eliminate this menu by clicking on the menu's Close item, or just clicking on the group icon once more, but it's okay to leave the control menu open. The next step will remove it.

2. Choose Window➢Arrange Icons to arrange the group icons at the bottom of the Program Manager window, as shown in Figure 2–6.

   Now let's try moving the Main group (document) window. To move a window, point to its title bar and drag. Release the mouse button when the window's outline is where you want the window to appear.

3. Move the mouse so the tip of the pointer is inside the title bar and drag it down a couple of inches and to the right a couple of inches.

   Before you release the mouse button, an outline of the window appears, as shown in Figure 2–7.

4. Release the mouse button to accept the new window position, as shown in Figure 2–8.

   To size a window in one dimension (horizontally or vertically), position the mouse pointer on one edge of the window so it turns into a double-headed arrow, and then drag to increase or decrease the window's size. You can size a window both horizontally and vertically at the same time by positioning the mouse pointer over one of the window's corners so the pointer is a diagonal double-headed arrow.

   The Main group window displayed in the figure is large enough to display all its program icons. Let's reduce it so they aren't all visible.

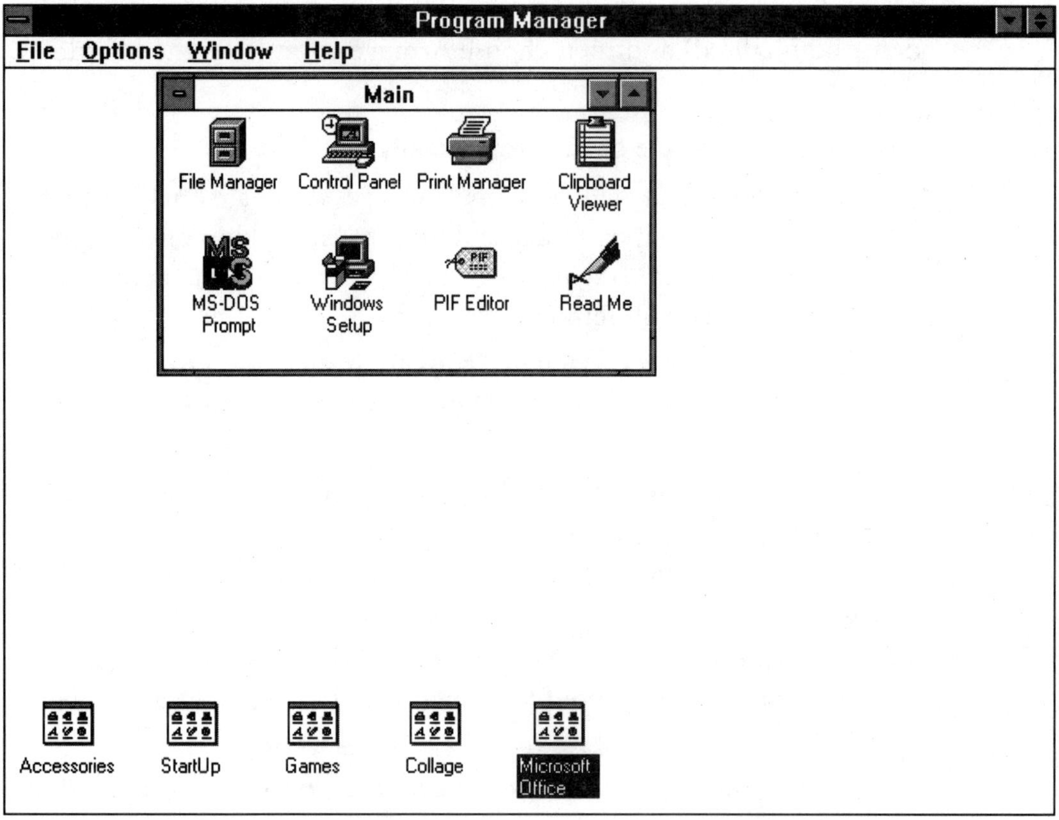

FIGURE 2–6 The group icons are arranged at the bottom of the Program Manager window.

5. Position the mouse pointer over the right border of the Main group window so it is a double-headed arrow and drag left a couple of inches so some of the program items are hidden; then release the mouse button.

   Figure 2–9 shows the resized Main group window. Notice that Windows automatically added a *scroll bar* at the bottom to allow you to view contents of the window that aren't currently visible.

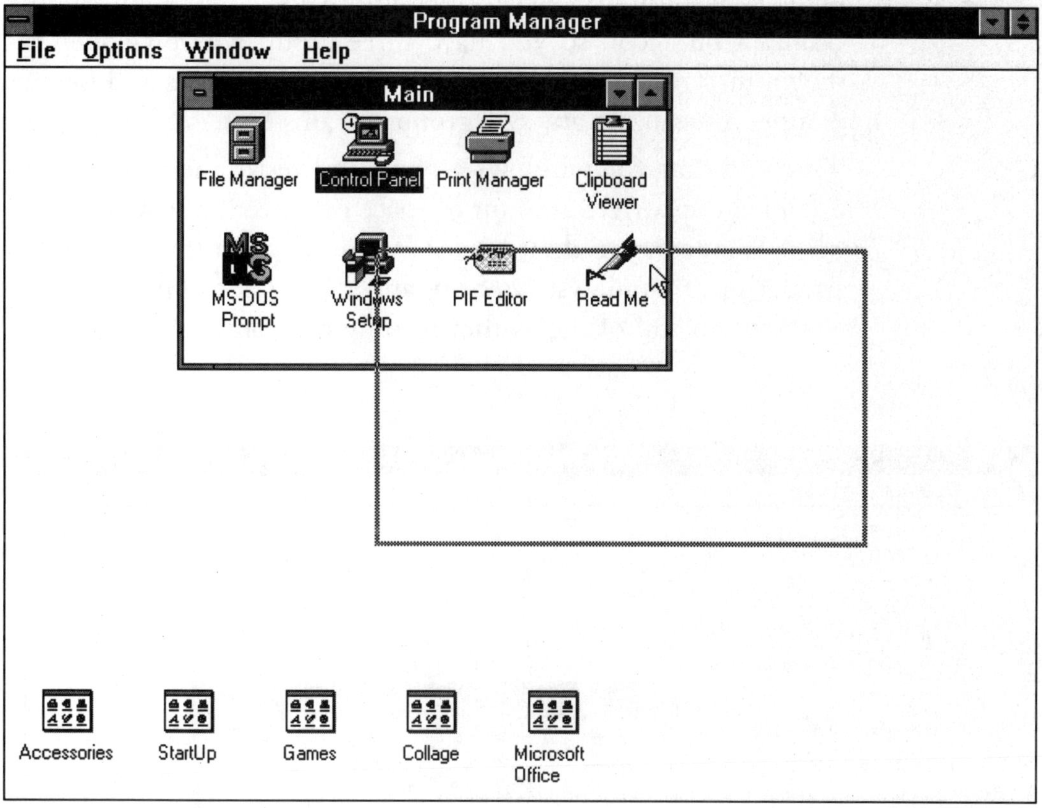

FIGURE 2–7 The outline of the Main group window

The scroll bar allows you to reposition a window's contents by clicking on one of the scroll buttons or by dragging the scroll box. The position of the scroll box indicates the relative position of the window's contents.

6. Try scrolling to the middle of the window's contents by dragging the scroll box to the middle of the scroll bar.

Now let's open two more group windows and see how Windows can help us arrange them.

7. Double-click on the Accessories group icon and then on the Games group icon so you have three group windows open, as shown in Figure 2–10. If you don't have Accessories and Games groups, you can use any two groups for this exercise.

   We could drag the windows around and resize them so they all occupied the correct amount of space on screen, but why bother when Windows can do it for us? Windows provides two ways to arrange open windows: *cascading* and *tiling*. Cascading stacks the windows on top of each other so only the contents of the front

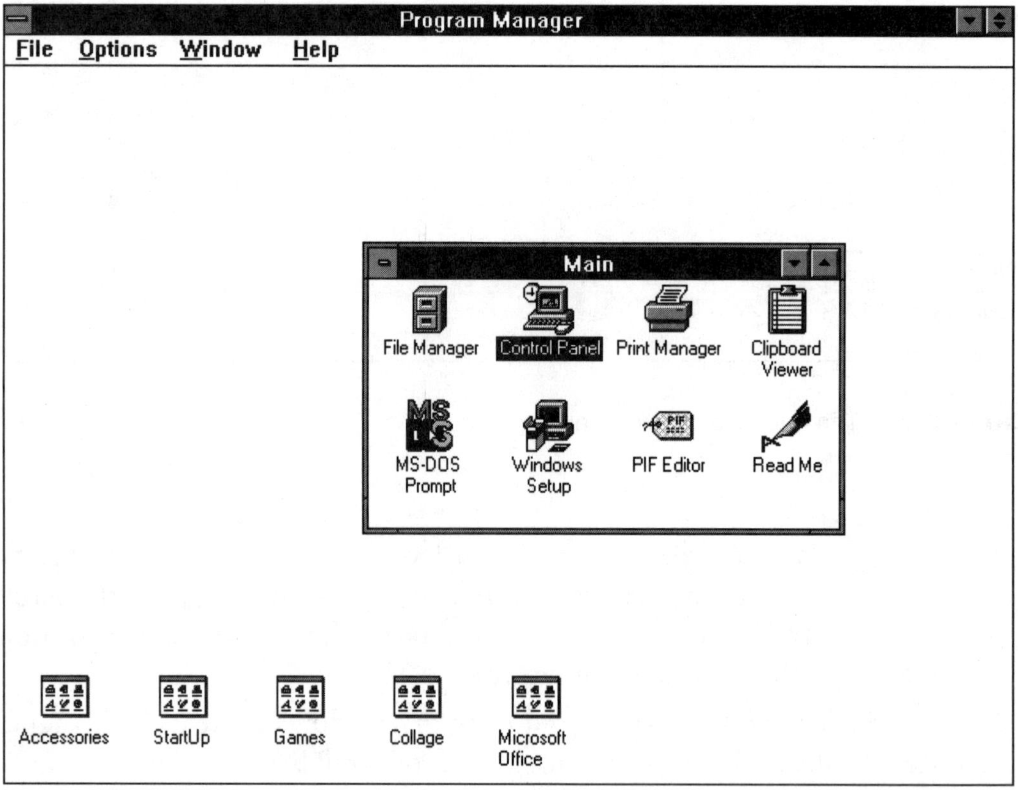

FIGURE 2–8 The repositioned Main group window

window are visible, but the title bars for all the other windows are visible. Tiling resizes all of the open windows, placing them side by side. We'll try both methods.

8. Choose Window➢Cascade to cascade the three open group windows, as shown in Figure 2–11.

   The active window is the one with the highlighted title bar. In Figure 2–11, the active window is the Games window. You can make an inactive window active by clicking on any visible portion. For example, you can make the Accessories window active

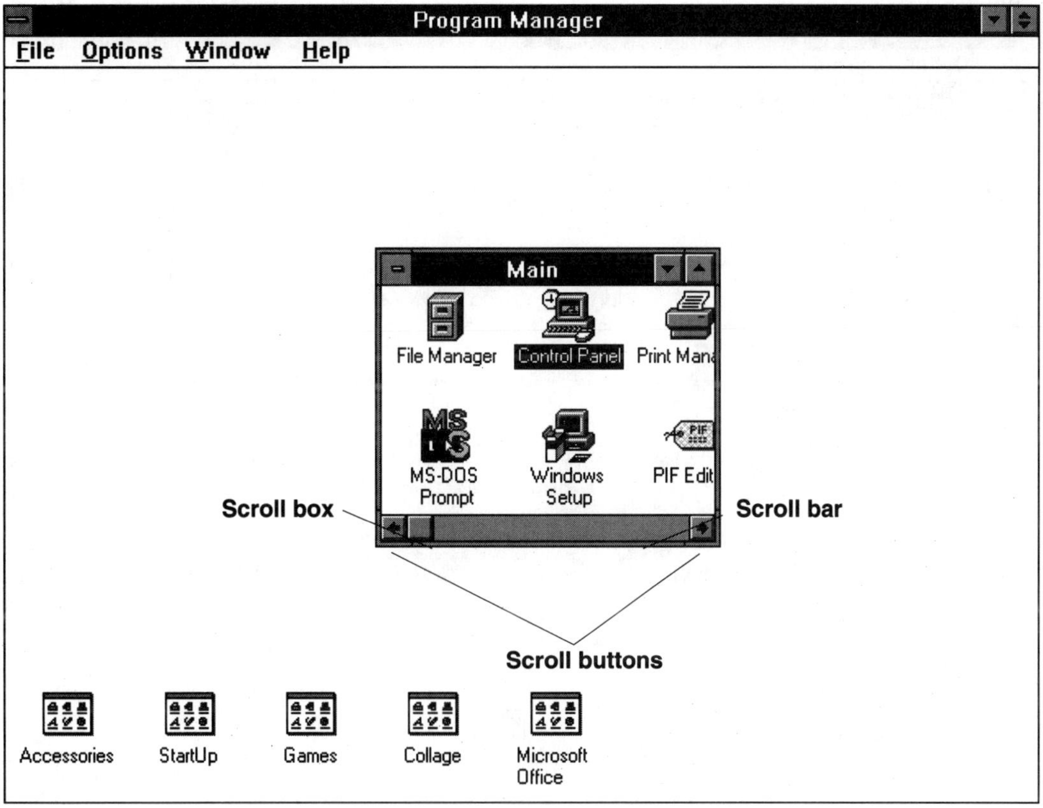

FIGURE 2–9 The smaller Main group window with a horizontal scroll bar

and bring it to the front by clicking on its title bar. After you do, you may want to cascade the windows again so they are neatly arranged.

Now let's tile the group windows.

9. Choose Window➢Tile to tile the windows, as shown in Figure 2–12.

   Notice that the Games window has no scroll bar because it's large enough to display all its program icons without scrolling. You

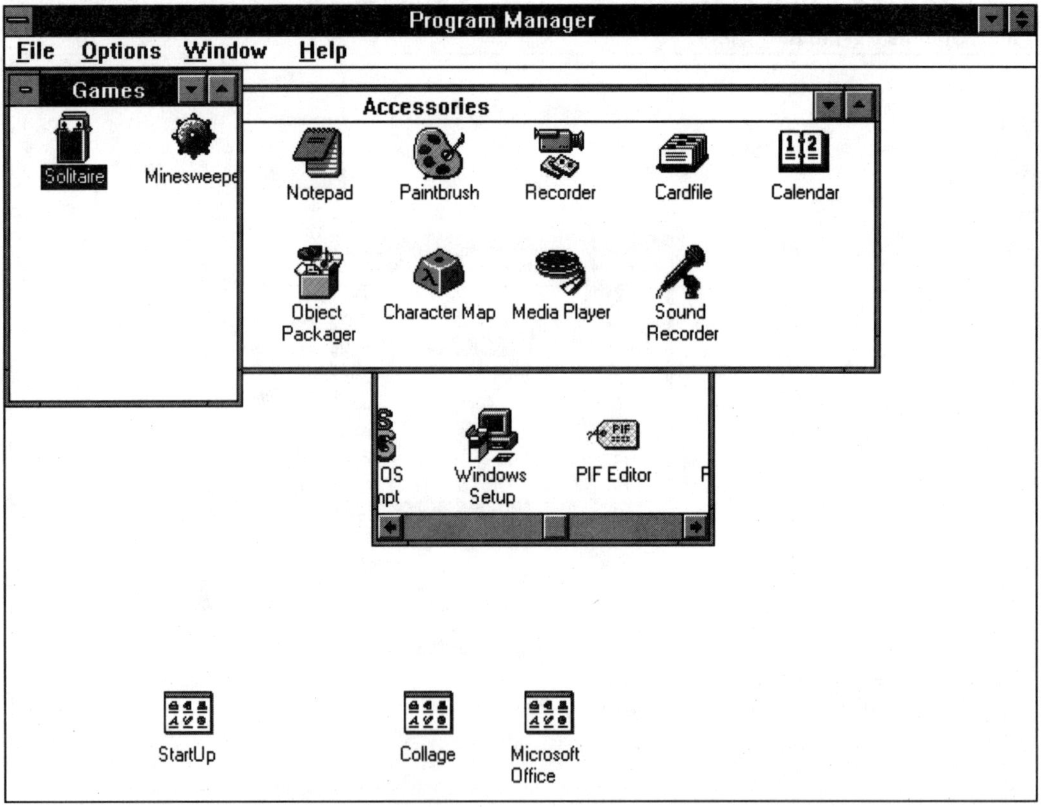

FIGURE 2–10 A cluttered Program Manager window with several group windows open

can resize, move, minimize, and maximize windows even when they are cascaded or tiled.

Help! What Do I Do Now?

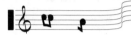

One of the most endearing features of Windows is its Help facility. It is endearing because it is consistent from program to program. I seem

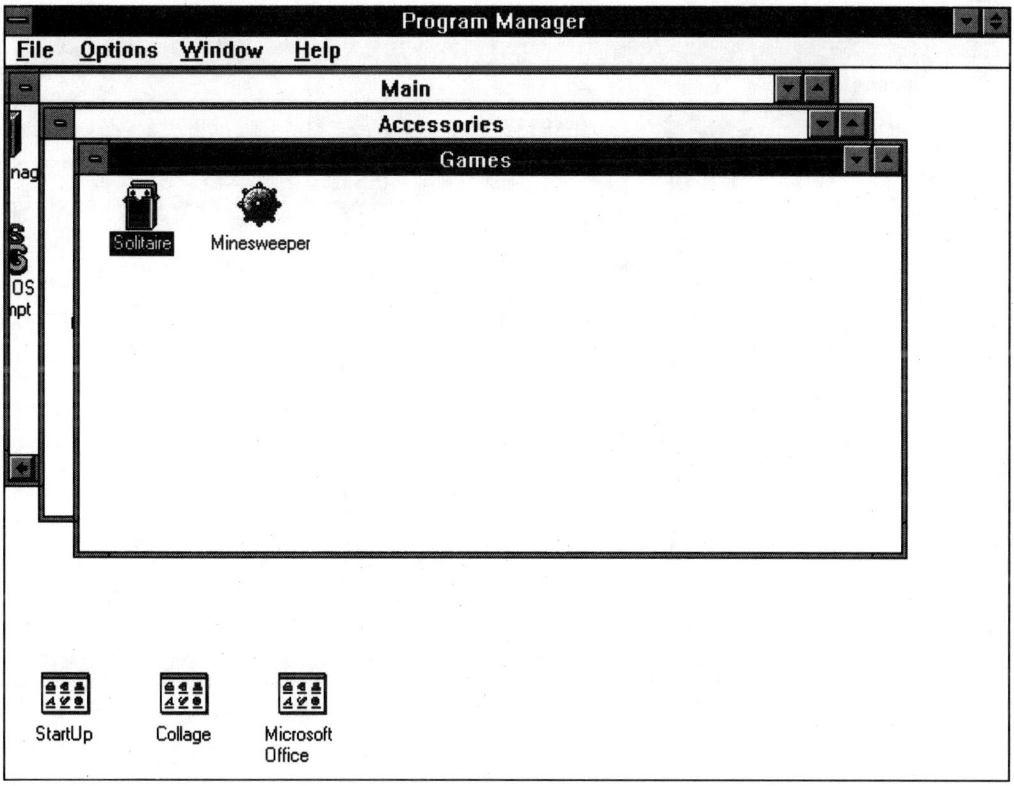

FIGURE 2–11 The cascaded group windows

to be harping on this consistency theme, don't I? Well, it's important, and nowhere more so than in Help. After all, perhaps the most important skill you can learn is how to get yourself unstuck when you run into difficulty.

We'll take a quick look at the Windows Help facility here and revisit the topic in the sections dealing with the Office programs because, as consistent as Help is, the programs have a few extra Help goodies.

You can display a *context-sensitive* help screen by pressing the F1 key while you are performing a task. For example, if the New Program Object dialog box was displayed and you pressed F1, a help screen

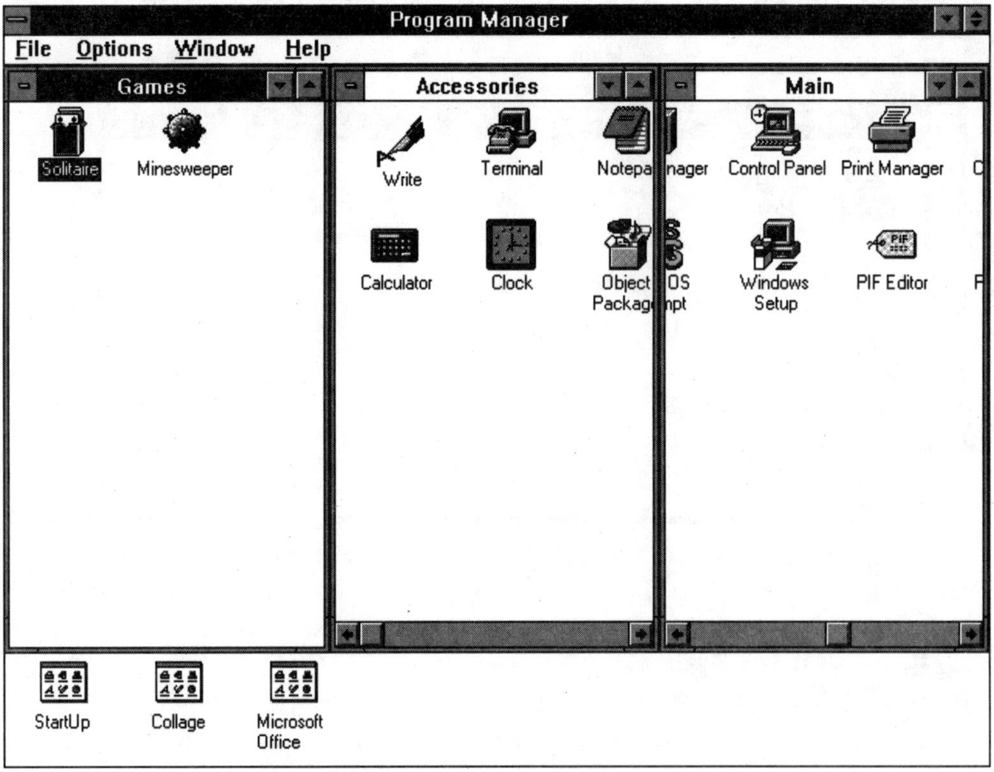

FIGURE 2–12 The tiled group windows

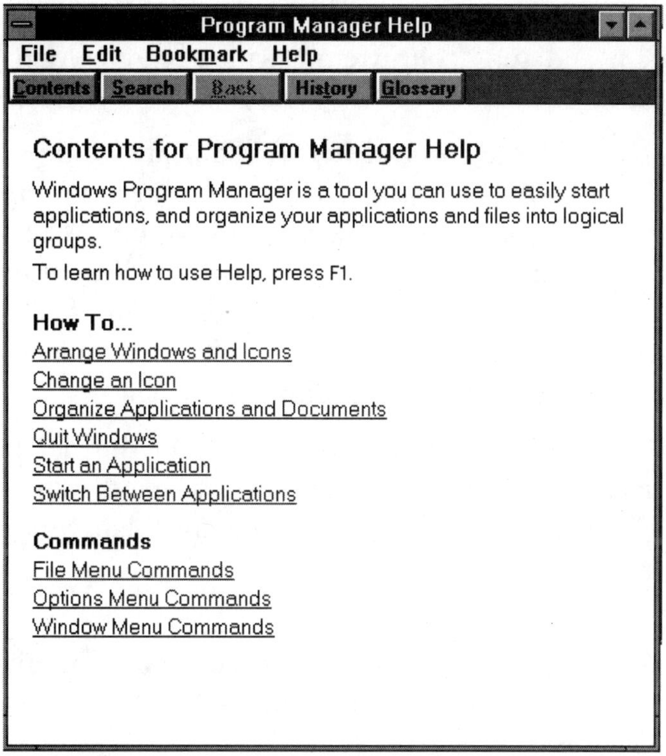

FIGURE 2–13 The Program Manager Help window with the contents displayed

for New Program Object would appear. Most dialog boxes have Help buttons that accomplish the same thing.

To find specific help information, you can choose from a list of topics or use a help dialog box to search for the help you need. Let's take a look at Program Manager's main contents help screen.

➡ Choose Help➢Contents to display the Program Manager Help window, as shown in Figure 2–13.

Once again, your Help window may be sized differently from the one in the figure. Notice that the Help window is an application window.

How can you tell? It has its own menu. Help is actually a separate program and runs concurrently with Program Manager and other programs.

Also notice the underlined items. (They are in green, if you have a color screen.) An item with a solid underline is a jump item that will take you to another help screen for that topic. When you move the mouse pointer over one of these items, the pointer turns into a hand. Let's jump to the File Menu Commands screen. If your Help window is sized so that you can't see the File Menu Commands topic, use the scroll bar to scroll down and bring it into view.

Position the mouse pointer over the underlined File Menu Commands topic and click to display a help screen that lists descriptions of the commands available from Program Manager's File menu, as shown in Figure 2–14.

Some help screens have items with dashed underlines. Clicking on one of these items displays a definition box. The File Menu Commands screen has one of these items—scroll bar.

Click on the words *scroll bar,* which are underlined with a dashed line, to display the scroll bar definition box shown in Figure 2–15.

Click anywhere to remove the definition box.

Now let's search for a specific topic. Let's say you forgot how to arrange your icons. We'll use the Help search facility to find the help screen we need.

Click on the Search button just below the Program Manager Help menu bar to display the Search dialog box shown in Figure 2–16.

You can also get to the Search dialog box by choosing Help➢Search For Help On when you first ask for help.

The flashing vertical line in the text box in the upper portion of the dialog box is called the *insertion point* and indicates where text will

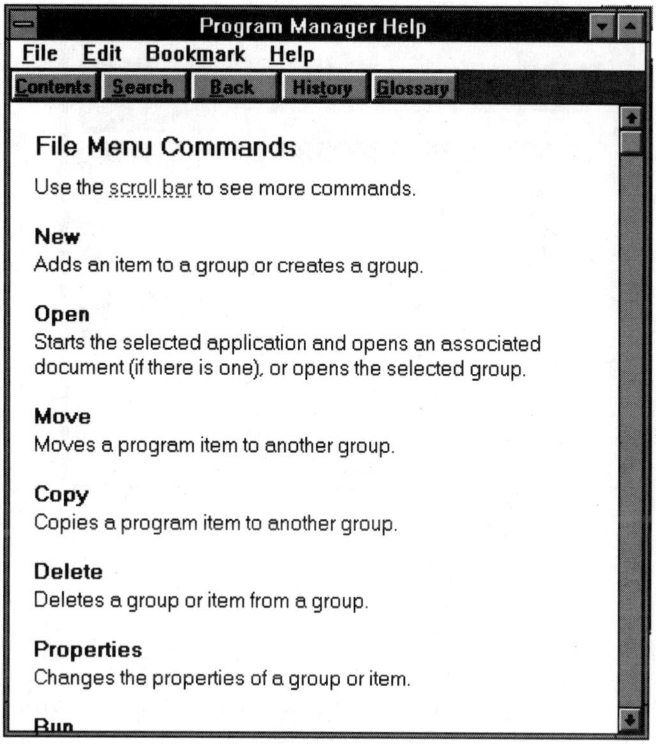

FIGURE 2–14 The Help screen for the File Menu Commands topic

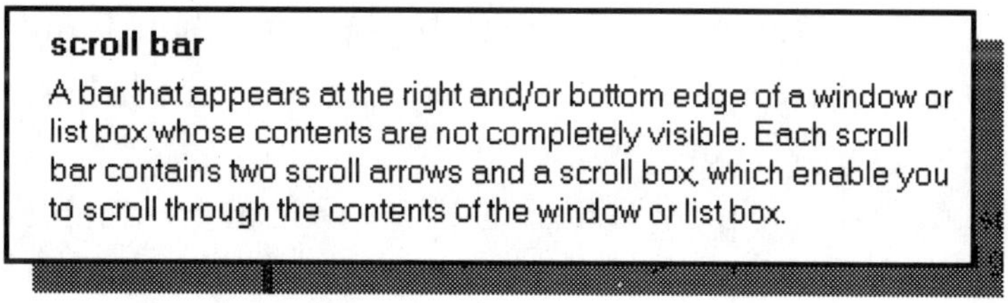

scroll bar
A bar that appears at the right and/or bottom edge of a window or list box whose contents are not completely visible. Each scroll bar contains two scroll arrows and a scroll box, which enable you to scroll through the contents of the window or list box.

FIGURE 2–15 The scroll bar definition box

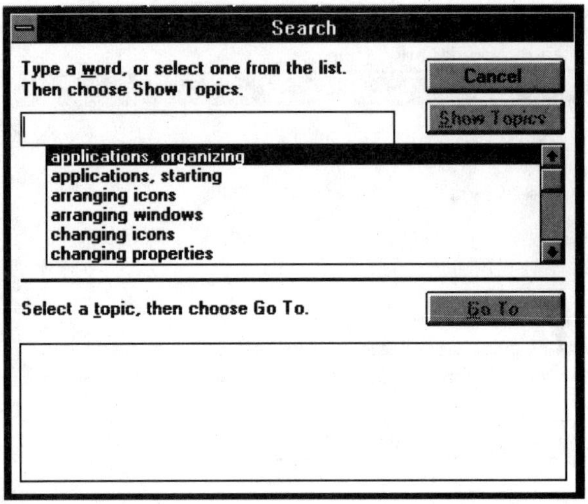

FIGURE 2–16 The Search dialog box

appear when you start typing. You can use the scroll bar to scan the list of help items or start typing the name of the item if you know it.

1. Type **ar**, the first letters of *arranging windows,* and notice that the highlighter moves to the first item that starts with these letters.

   The item we're looking for is now highlighted. If it was not, you could continue typing until it was, or click on it in the list.
2. Click on the Show Topics button to display the list of available help topics for this item. In this case, there is only one.
3. Click on the Go To button to display the help screen for Arranging Windows and Icons.
4. Exit Help by choosing File➢Exit or by double-clicking on the Control-menu box in the upper-left corner of the help window.

It's Time to Say Good-bye—Exiting Windows

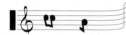

When you have finished using your computer and are ready to exit Windows, all you have to do is choose File ➢ Exit or double-click on the Control-menu box in the upper-left corner of the Program Manager window.

tip Before you exit Windows, you may want to save the changes, such as the group windows that are open and their arrangement, that you have made. To do this, choose Options and, if there is no check mark in front of Save Settings On Exit, click on Save Settings On Exit.

The next time you start Windows, you may wish to remove the check mark by choosing Options ➢ Save Settings On Exit again so you will retain the current settings the next time you exit Windows.

➡ Choose File ➢ Exit, or double-click on Program Manager's Control-menu box.

Windows displays the Exit Windows dialog box shown in Figure 2–17.

➡ If you really want to exit Windows, click on the OK button. Otherwise, click on the Cancel button to stay in Windows.

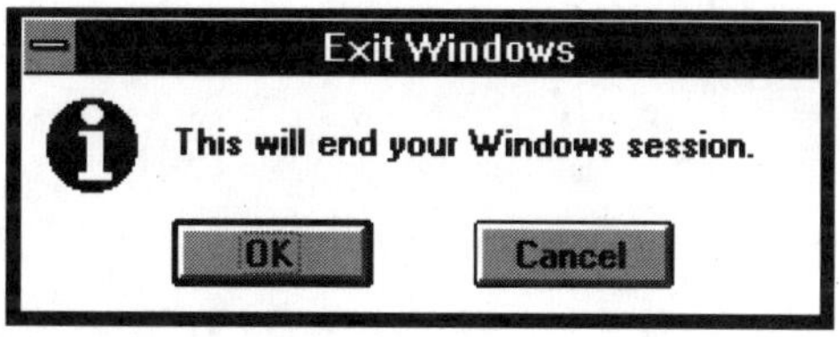

FIGURE 2–17 The Exit Windows dialog box

3

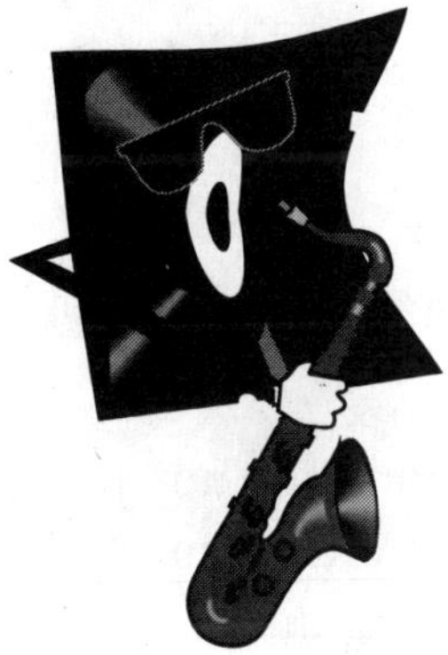

Customizing Windows

One of the fastest ways to increase your comfort level with Windows is to learn how you can customize it to make it meet your specific needs. There's no limit to the ways that you can modify Windows—entire books have been written on the subject. I'll show you how to perform some of the more common tasks for tailoring Windows to suit you.

Using the Control Panel

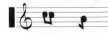

The Control Panel program, included with Windows, provides facilities for customizing a wide array of Windows attributes, such as the way the mouse and keyboard operate, the colors for various Windows elements, and desktop properties. The skills you learned in Chapter 2 are all you need to make full use of the Control Panel.

To start the Control Panel, simply double-click on the Control Panel icon, which is usually located in the Main program group. We'll start the Control Panel program now.

1. Start Windows, if it isn't already running.
2. Double-click on the Main group to open it.
3. Double-click on the Control Panel icon to start the Control Panel program.

You can tell that the Control Panel is an application and not just another group (document) window because it has its own menu bar (Figure 3–1). You work with the Control Panel by using dialog boxes

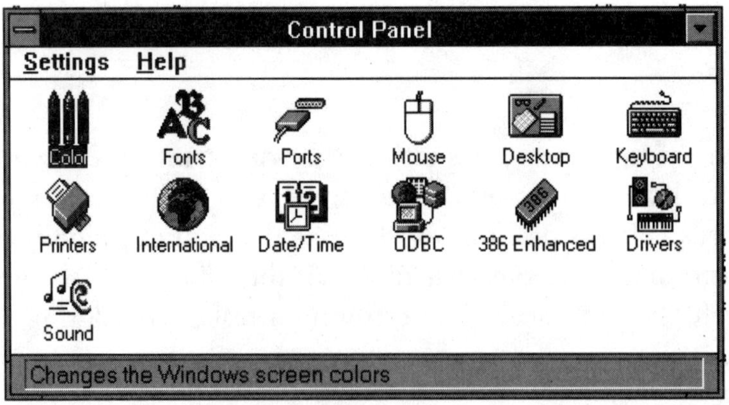

FIGURE 3–1 The Control Panel application window

to customize each facet of Windows. To open a dialog box, double-click on the appropriate icon.

Teach Your Mouse Some Manners

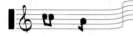

Of the various options we'll look at in the Control Panel, mouse customization can have the most profound effect on your ability to work comfortably with Windows, so that's what I'll start with. Because you spend so much of your time manipulating Windows and applications with the mouse, it's crucial that it be set up so you can use it comfortably. The Control Panel's Mouse icon opens a dialog box containing options that let you tailor mouse operations to your degree of dexterity.

Double-click on the Mouse icon in the Control Panel window to display the Mouse dialog box, as shown in Figure 3–2.

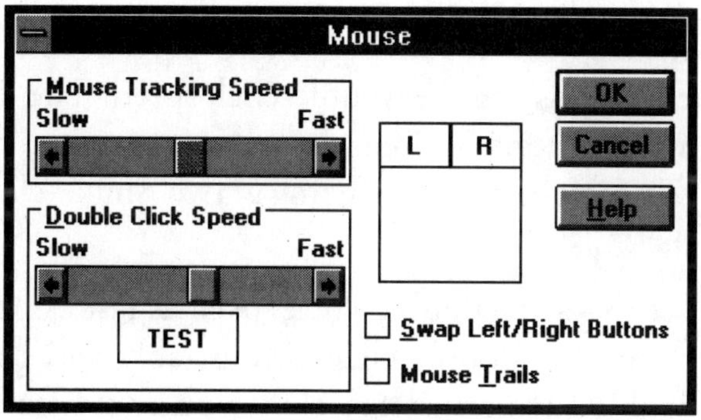

FIGURE 3–2 The Mouse dialog box

note Some versions of the Mouse dialog box include additional options that aren't shown in Figure 3–2. For example, you may have options for changing the shape of the mouse pointer. If you need instructions for using any of the options in your Mouse dialog box, click on the Help button to display a help screen with all the details.

The Mouse Tracking Speed portion of the dialog box lets you adjust how fast the on-screen mouse pointer moves in relation to the speed with which the mouse is moved on the desk. Adjust the tracking speed by moving the scroll box to the Slow (left) side or the Fast (right) side of the scroll bar. Give it a try now.

➡ Move your mouse back and forth on your desk and notice how fast the mouse pointer moves compared to how fast you move the mouse.

➡ Drag the scroll box in the Mouse Tracking Speed scroll bar all the way to the left; then move your mouse again and see how much slower the mouse pointer moves.

➡ Drag the scroll box all the way to the right and, once again, move the mouse and notice how quickly the pointer moves.

Now that you've seen how the extreme settings affect the tracking speed, you'll want to set it so it's just right for you.

➡ Position the scroll box for a comfortable tracking speed.

Just below the Mouse Tracking Speed portion of the dialog box is a scroll bar for adjusting the double-click speed. The double-click speed determines how much time can elapse between two mouse clicks before Windows interprets them as two single-clicks rather than a double-click.

The goal is to set the double-click speed as fast as possible, but not so fast that you can't double-click comfortably and consistently. If you set the double-click speed too slow, you could find yourself waiting between single-clicks, while Windows waits to see if you are going to click again.

Point to the Test box that appears below the Double Click Speed scroll bar and double-click.

If you double-clicked successfully, the Test box is highlighted, as shown in Figure 3–3.

Drag the scroll box in the Double Click Speed scroll bar all the way to the left and see how slowly you can double click.

Drag the scroll box all the way to the right and try double-clicking. Don't fret if you can't double-click at the fastest speed. I can't either.

Drag the scroll box to a position that allows you to double-click comfortably.

note If you are just getting started with the mouse, you'll find that your proficiency increases over time. For this reason, you may want to reset the Mouse Tracking Speed and the Double Click Speed after you've become more adept at mousing around.

Let's take a look at the Mouse dialog box options for swapping the left and right mouse buttons and adding mouse trails.

You may want to swap mouse buttons if you are left-handed and want to place the mouse on the left side of your keyboard. To swap the buttons, just click in the Swap Left/Right Buttons check box.

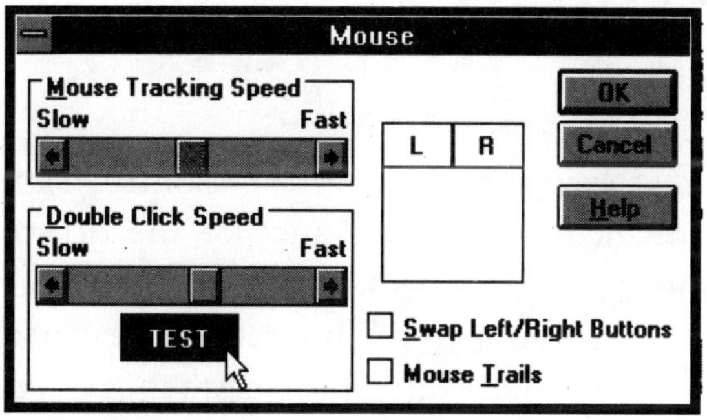

FIGURE 3–3 The highlighted double-click Test box

CAUTION

If you click in the Swap Left/Right Buttons check box and change your mind, you won't be able to undo your choice by clicking with the left button. The left button now acts like the right button and vice versa. Therefore, you must use the right mouse button to click in the Swap Left/Right Buttons check box to uncheck it.

You should also be careful not to use this option on a computer that others use, especially if one of the others is your boss. It can take other users quite a bit of time and frustration to figure out what's going on. Careers have been ruined for less.

Choosing the Mouse Trails option leaves a temporary trail of mouse pointer images as you move the mouse pointer. This feature is often useful for laptop computers with LCD (Liquid Crystal Display) screens. The mouse pointer on some LCD screens has a "submarine" effect, which can obscure the pointer as you move it from one place on the screen to another. Using the Mouse Trails feature can help you keep track of the mouse pointer in these situations. For standard desktop computer screens, this feature is usually more of an annoyance, though it can be amusing to try it for about two minutes.

After you are happy with all the mouse settings, click on the OK button to accept the changes and close the dialog box.

Desktop Designs

We'll look at several options in the Control Panel's Desktop dialog box for enhancing the appearance of the desktop, such as adding background graphic images, adjusting the spacing of icons and windows, and adjusting the blink rate of the cursor (insertion point). These options primarily affect the aesthetics of several Windows elements. But don't scoff. For many users, aesthetics are just as important as options that play a more functional role.

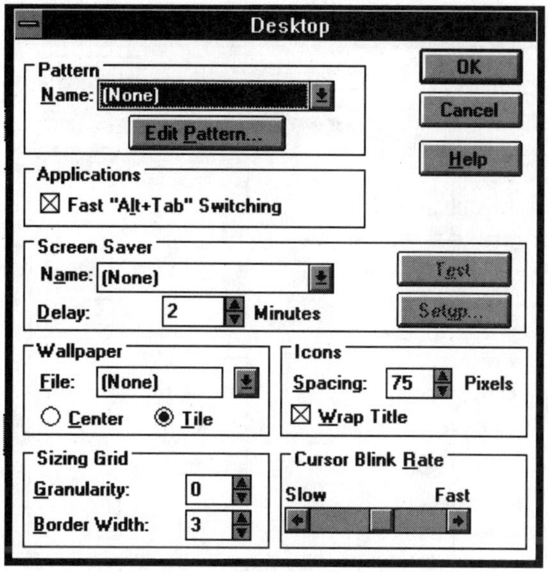

FIGURE 3–4 The Desktop dialog box

Let's take a look at these desktop options now.

Double-click on the Control Panel's Desktop icon to display the Desktop dialog box, as shown in Figure 3–4.

Adding graphic images can increase visual appeal when you are looking at a screen that isn't occupied entirely by application and document windows. You can add graphics with patterns or wallpaper.

Pattern lets you choose a pattern from a list of designs made up of dots. If you don't like the choices Windows provides, you can create your own pattern or edit one of the included patterns.

Follow these steps to apply a pattern to your desktop.

Click on the arrow next to the Name drop-down list to display the list of pattern names, as shown in Figure 3–5.

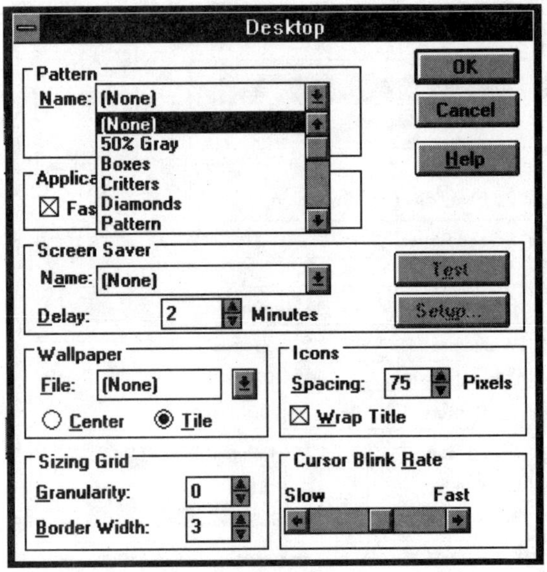

FIGURE 3–5 The list of pattern names

- Click on the name of your choice of pattern. You'll have to use the scroll bar to bring some of the names into view.

note The pattern won't be displayed until the Desktop dialog box is closed by clicking on the OK button.

- Click on the Edit Pattern button to display the Edit Pattern dialog box, and then use the mouse to add or remove dots. Click on the Help button for further instructions.
- Click on the OK button to accept the changes, or click on the Cancel button to return to the original pattern.

Wallpaper serves the same purpose as a pattern, but wallpaper can be much more intricate than patterns and can include color, which patterns can't. Wallpaper uses graphic files stored on your computer's

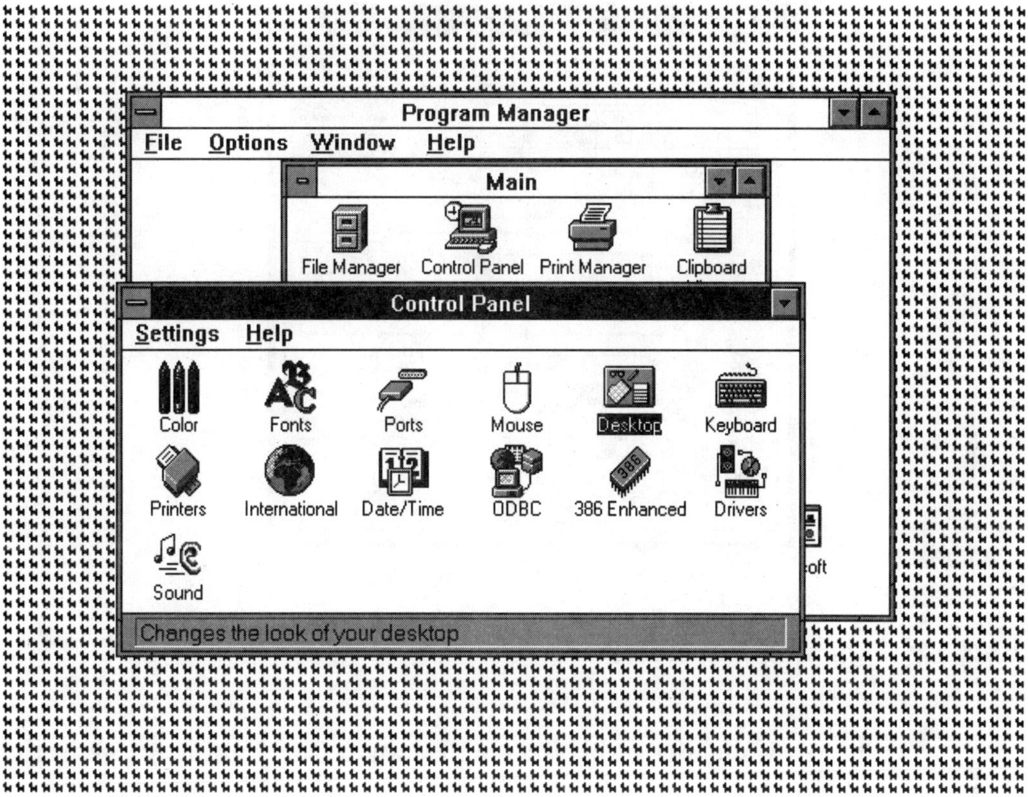

FIGURE 3–6 An example of a background pattern. This is the Scottie pattern.

hard disk. The graphic can be one of the supplied images, or you can design your own in a program like Paintbrush, which is included with Windows.

To add wallpaper, follow these steps.

➡ Click on the Center or Tile option button in the Wallpaper portion of the dialog box.

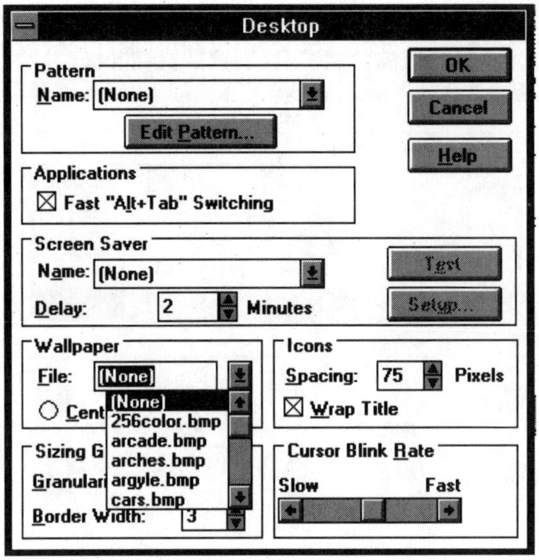

FIGURE 3–7 The list of wallpaper file names

Centered wallpaper displays a single copy of the graphic image in the middle of the screen. Depending on the size of the image and how other open windows are sized and arranged, you may not be able to see centered wallpaper. The solution is to choose the Tile option that displays as many copies of the image as are required to fill the screen.

Click on the arrow next to the File drop-down list to display the list of wallpaper file names, as shown in Figure 3–7.

Click on the name of the wallpaper file you want to use.

note Like the pattern you chose above, the wallpaper will be displayed only after the Desktop dialog box is closed by clicking on the OK button.

tip Windows performance can suffer if there isn't enough memory available, and using wallpaper uses memory. The more complex and larger wallpaper images use more memory than the smaller,

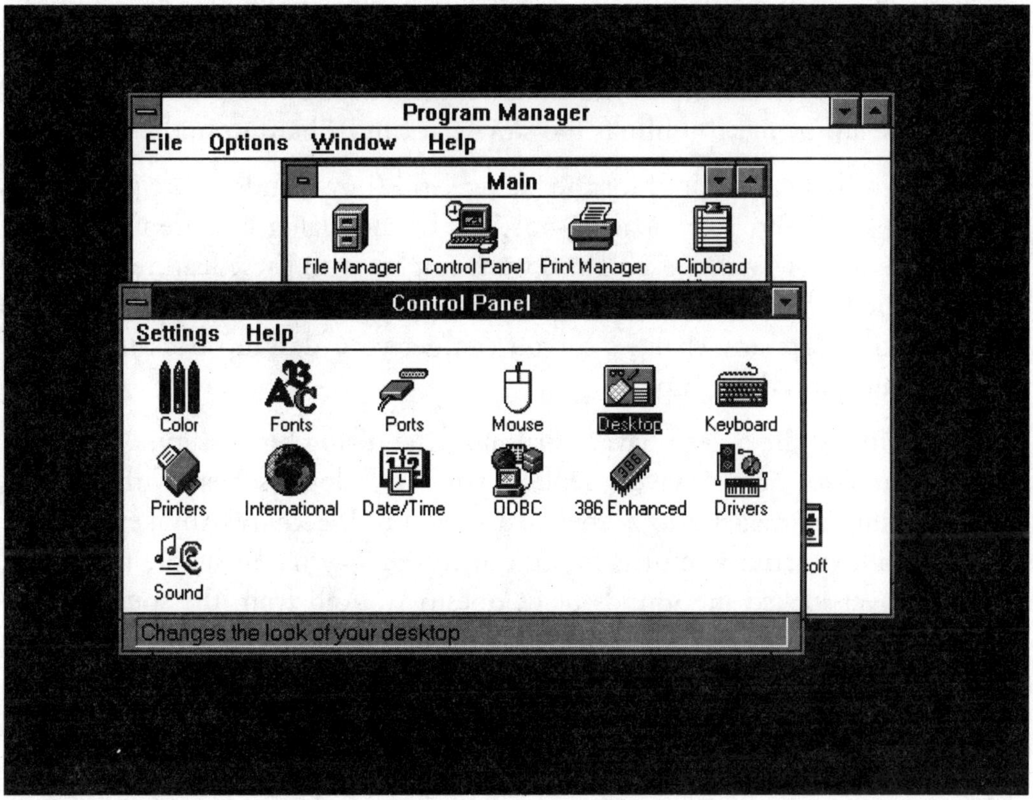

FIGURE 3–8 An example of a wallpaper. This is the Argyle wallpaper file.

simpler ones, but they all use memory. If you want to conserve as much memory as possible for your Windows programs and thus maximize performance, consider avoiding wallpaper.

The Applications portion of the dialog box has a check box for fast "Alt+Tab" switching. This check box is checked by default, and I strongly recommend that you leave it checked. This option allows you to switch among running applications by pressing Alt+Tab. I have no idea why anyone would want to turn this feature off.

The Cursor Blink rate scroll bar lets you determine how fast the cursor blinks. Where you set this option is completely a matter of personal choice. Keep in mind that, if the cursor blinks too rapidly, it can be annoying. If it blinks too slowly, it can be hard to find.

The default settings for the Sizing Grid (how windows are placed and spaced) and Icon Spacing portions of the dialog box are usually just fine the way they are. If you want to play with these features, click on the Help button, but be sure to write down the current settings before you make any changes so you can get your desktop back in order if you mess things up.

Finally, the Screen Saver portion of the dialog box deserves some discussion. Screen savers replace your Windows screen with moving graphic images after a specified period of inactivity. Any keyboard or mouse activity returns the screen to the way it was before the screen saver kicked in. Sounds okay, doesn't it? And from the sound of the name of the feature, you might think a screen saver could save your screen from something.

Older computer screens were susceptible to *burn-in* if the same image remained on screen for too long. This burn-in resulted in a ghost image that could be quite distracting. Newer screens, particularly VGA and super VGA screens, are virtually immune to burn-in. In fact, you could leave the same image on your screen for days or even weeks without causing any damage.

Because screen savers use some of your computer's processing power to monitor keyboard and mouse activity, they can affect performance adversely. If your computer is fast enough, you may not notice the performance decrease. But why not let your computer run at full speed? I know screen savers are cute and amusing, and I don't want to be a Scrooge, but my recommendation is to forget about screen savers. Bah! Humbug!

➡ If the Desktop dialog box is still open, click on the OK button to accept your changes and close it.

Color Counts

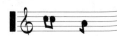

The Color dialog box permits you to choose from a variety of color schemes that apply different colors to various Windows elements. You can also create your own custom color scheme. This may seem a bit frivolous, but a comfortable and pleasing color combination can actually increase productivity by reducing eyestrain and fatigue. Well, at least I think that's a good enough rationalization for spending some time playing around with your colors.

Follow these steps to change color schemes.

Double-click on the Color icon in the Control Panel to display the Color dialog box, as shown in Figure 3–9.

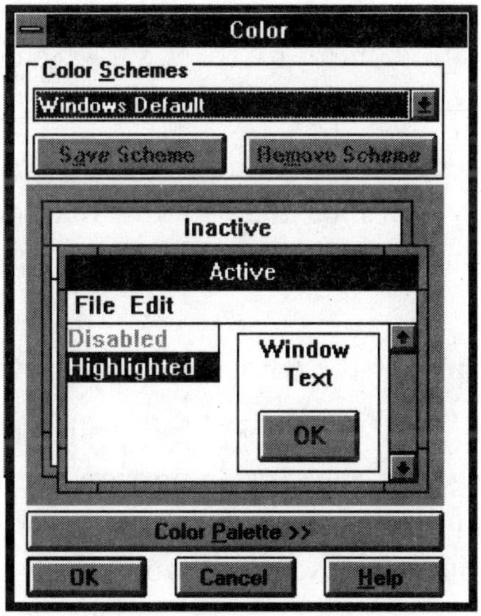

FIGURE 3–9 The Color dialog box

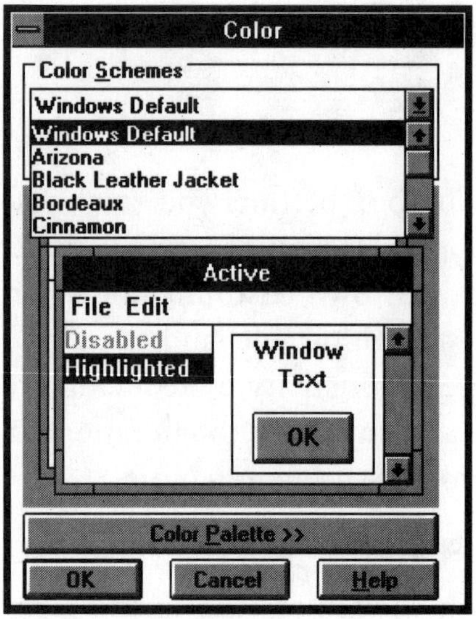

FIGURE 3–10 The list of predefined color schemes

Click on the arrow next to the Color Schemes drop-down list to display the list of predefined color schemes.

From the names Microsoft chose for the color schemes, it's hard to guess what they will look like, so you may have to do quite a bit of experimentation to determine which color schemes, if any, strike your fancy.

Click on the name of the color scheme you want to use.

A preview of the colors that will be applied to the various screen elements is displayed in the sample portion of the dialog box just below the Save Scheme and Remove Scheme buttons. Because the figures in this book are black and white, I won't show an example of the color schemes.

The color scheme is applied to the entire screen after the Color dialog box is closed by clicking on the OK button.

tip Even if you don't have a color monitor, the Color dialog box may provide some benefit. In fact, you may benefit more than those who have color, because it can be very difficult to discern certain screen elements on monochrome (single-color) screens. The predefined color schemes include several choices designed to optimize monochrome screens, especially the LCD screens common on laptop computers.

To create a custom color scheme, follow these steps.

- Click on the Color Palette button to display the expanded Color dialog box with the color palette, as shown in Figure 3–11.
- Click on the arrow next to the Screen Element drop-down list to display the list of Windows screen elements, as shown in Figure 3–12.
- Click on the name of the screen element whose color you want to change. You can use the scroll bar to bring additional elements into view.

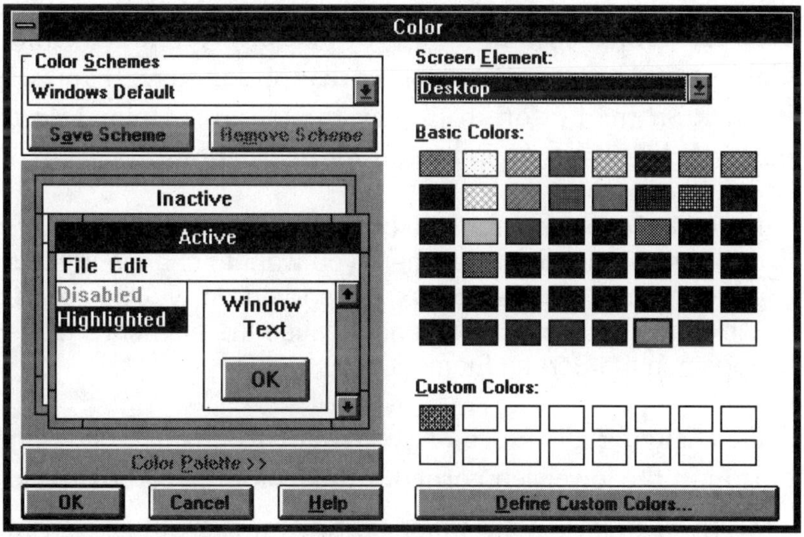

FIGURE 3–11 The expanded Color dialog box including the Color Palette

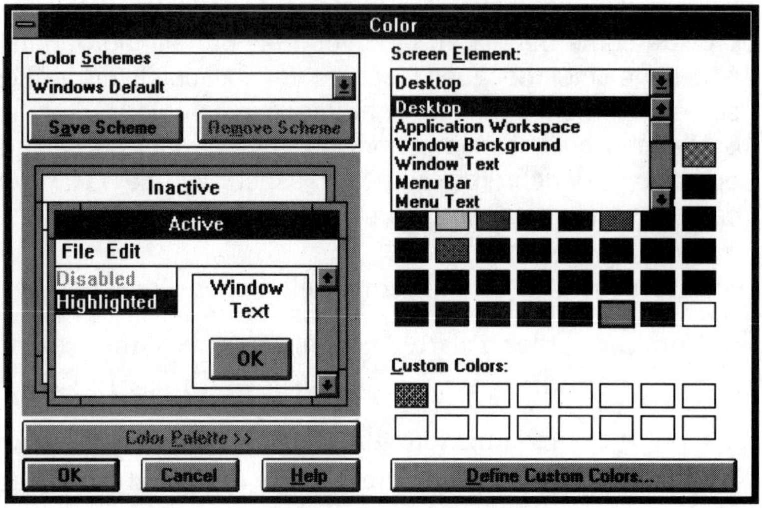

FIGURE 3–12 The drop-down list of screen elements

Click on one of the Basic Colors to change the element to that color.

You can create custom colors by clicking on the Define Custom Colors button, but we won't cover that option here. If you want to use it, click on the button to display the Custom Color Selector dialog box and click on its Help button for instructions.

tip Instead of choosing from the drop-down screen element list, you can simply click on the element you want to change in the sample portion of the dialog box. When you do, you'll know if you clicked on the correct element because the element's name will appear in the Screen Element box.

After changing all the colors you want to change, click on the OK button in the lower-left corner of the Color dialog box to close it.

The changes will remain in effect for future Windows sessions. But if you later choose a different color scheme, the colors you have just selected will be lost unless you save them with a color scheme name by clicking on the Save Scheme button and entering a unique name.

Double-click on the Control Panel's Control-menu box to close it.

Summary

In this chapter, you learned some of the more useful Windows customization techniques. Spend some time exploring these and the other options in the Control Panel. The more time you spend learning the ins and outs of Windows, the more comfortable you'll feel working with Windows and Windows applications, including Microsoft Office.

Section III

A Short Course in Word for Windows

4

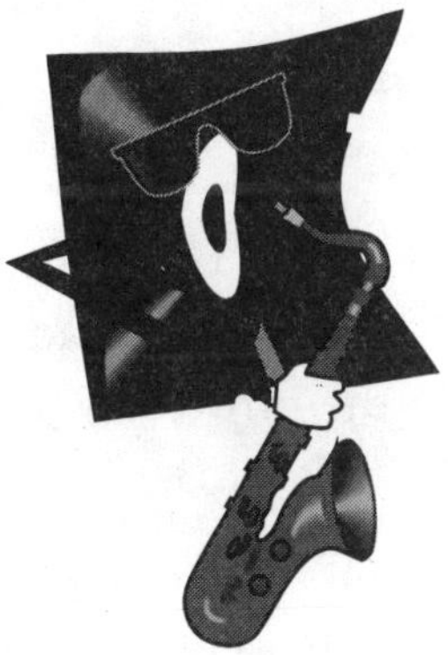

Word for Windows—The Basics

Word processing is the one activity performed by more computer users than any other. From simple memos to complex reports and even books, word processing programs provide the tools for entering, formatting, and editing text and printing documents.

When it comes to word processing programs, none has more capabilities—combined with incredible ease of use—than Word for Windows 6.0.

Overview of New Features in Word for Windows 6.0

If you've worked with previous versions of Word for Windows, you already know that Microsoft goes to great lengths to make the program as intuitive and automatic as possible. You don't have to be a computer nerd (and I use the term affectionately) to produce spectacular-looking documents. Version 6.0 provides a dizzying array of features to assist you in creating the perfect document. Here is a brief overview of some impressive new additions.

Almost Unlimited Undo

If you're as prone to mistakes as I am, this feature alone is worth the price of admission. In previous versions of Word, you could undo only the last thing you did, so if you didn't realize the error of your ways immediately, you were out of luck.

Version 6.0 keeps track of the last 100 actions, and you can undo any individual action or sequence of actions. You can also redo any series of actions if you change your mind.

AutoCorrect

This feature actually corrects your mistakes automatically as you type them. No human intervention is required, which suits me just fine. Suppose you have a nasty habit of typing *teh* instead of *the,* or *recieve* instead of *receive.* AutoCorrect automatically corrects these and many other common mistakes as soon as you press the spacebar.

AutoCorrect can also ensure that the first letter of each sentence and the names of days—Monday, Tuesday, etc.—are in uppercase. You can add your own mistakes to the list of items to be automatically corrected.

AutoText

This feature is similar to the Glossary feature in previous versions of Word. You can use AutoText to store text passages or graphics and then retrieve them with a mouse click or keystroke.

AutoFormat

Wouldn't it be great if you had your own personal design expert to format your documents tastefully? You do! AutoFormat can analyze your document and apply the formatting it thinks is best suited to the content. Of course, AutoFormat doesn't always make a good guess, so you have the opportunity to choose from several format templates or reject the changes altogether.

Shortcut Menus

Clicking the right mouse button on almost any object on the Word screen will display a shortcut menu of options for manipulating that object. This can be a tremendous time saver. Rather than forcing you to navigate a series of menus to find the appropriate options, this feature puts those options at your fingertips. The other Office applications also make use of shortcut menus.

Wizards

Wizards present a series of dialog boxes to aid you in creating different types of documents. You can create the structure for several types of letters, memos, newsletters, fax covers, and tables by simply answering questions in the Wizard's dialog boxes. With Wizards, you can create sophisticated documents, even if you don't know how to use the features involved in their creation.

Don't worry if some of these concepts seem a bit foreign to you now. As we progress through the next few chapters, you'll learn to use these and many other new features. Also, if you are familiar with the previous version of Word, you'll find that you can do almost everything just as you did it before. However, I promise it will be worth your time to learn to use the new features and shortcuts.

Starting Word for Windows

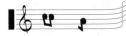

Starting Word for Windows is the same as starting any other program. In Chapter 3, you started the Control Panel program by double-clicking on the Control Panel icon in the Main program group. Use the same procedure to start Word.

To start Word for Windows, follow these steps.

- Start Windows, if it isn't already running.
- Double-click on the Microsoft Office group icon to open the Microsoft Office group windows, as shown in Figure 4–1.

note If your computer starts the Microsoft Office Manager (MOM) automatically, you'll see toolbar buttons in the Program Manager title bar. You can start Word by just clicking once on the Microsoft Word button. You can switch to and start any of the Office programs by clicking on the button for that program.

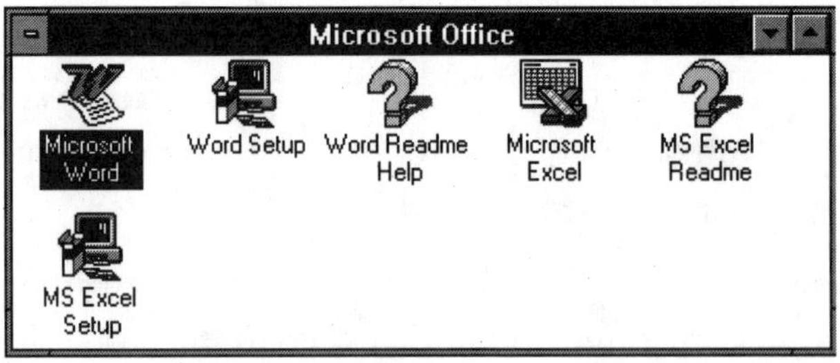

FIGURE 4–1 The Microsoft Office 4.2 group window

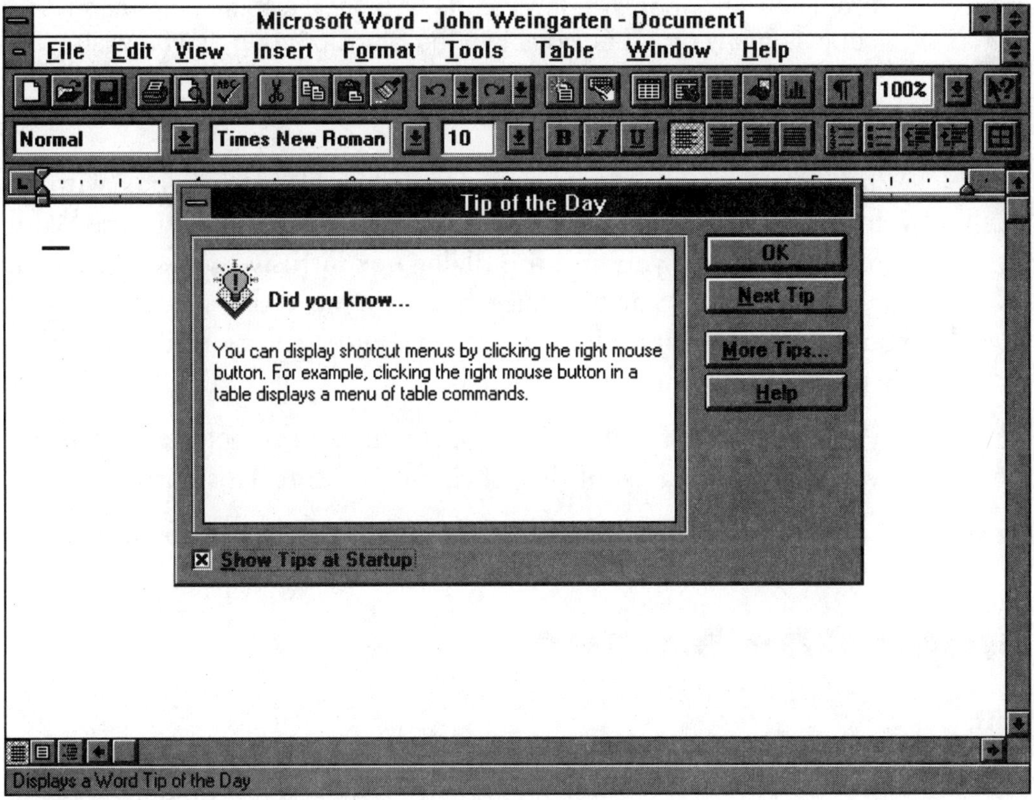

FIGURE 4–2 The Microsoft Word opening screen with the Tip of the Day dialog box

Double-click on the Microsoft Word icon to start Word and display its opening screen, as shown in Figure 4–2.

If you want to start Word or any other program automatically when Windows is started, you can copy its program icon into the StartUp group in the Program Manager. To copy the Word program icon to the StartUp group, press and hold down the Ctrl key and drag the Word program icon onto the StartUp group icon and release the mouse button.

From now on, when Windows starts, Word will also start. You can copy as many program icons into the StartUp group as you wish, but the more programs you start automatically, the longer you will have to wait before you can get to work when you start Windows.

When Word starts, it displays a Tip of the Day dialog box with an informative (or sometimes just amusing) hint about how to use Word more effectively. If you find this dialog box intrusive, you can click on the Show Tips at Startup check box to remove the check. I suggest you let Word display the tips, at least until you've read and either memorized or ignored all of them.

If you want to see another tip, you can click on the Next Tip button. If you want to see a list of tips, click on the More Tips button.

➡ Click on the OK button to close the Tip of the Day dialog box.

Touring the Screen

After the Tip of the Day dialog box is cleared, Word presents a blank document, ready to accept your text entry, as shown in Figure 4–3.

Many parts of the Word screen will seem familiar, since they are the same elements you'll find in most Windows applications. Among these are the title bar, menu bar, scroll bars, Control-menu box, and Minimize and Restore buttons. These elements work essentially the same way in Word as in Windows itself and other programs.

Let's discuss some elements you may not be familiar with.

- ✓ The buttons on the toolbars (the Standard and Formatting toolbars are shown here below the menu bar) provide shortcuts for accomplishing various tasks. Just click on a button to

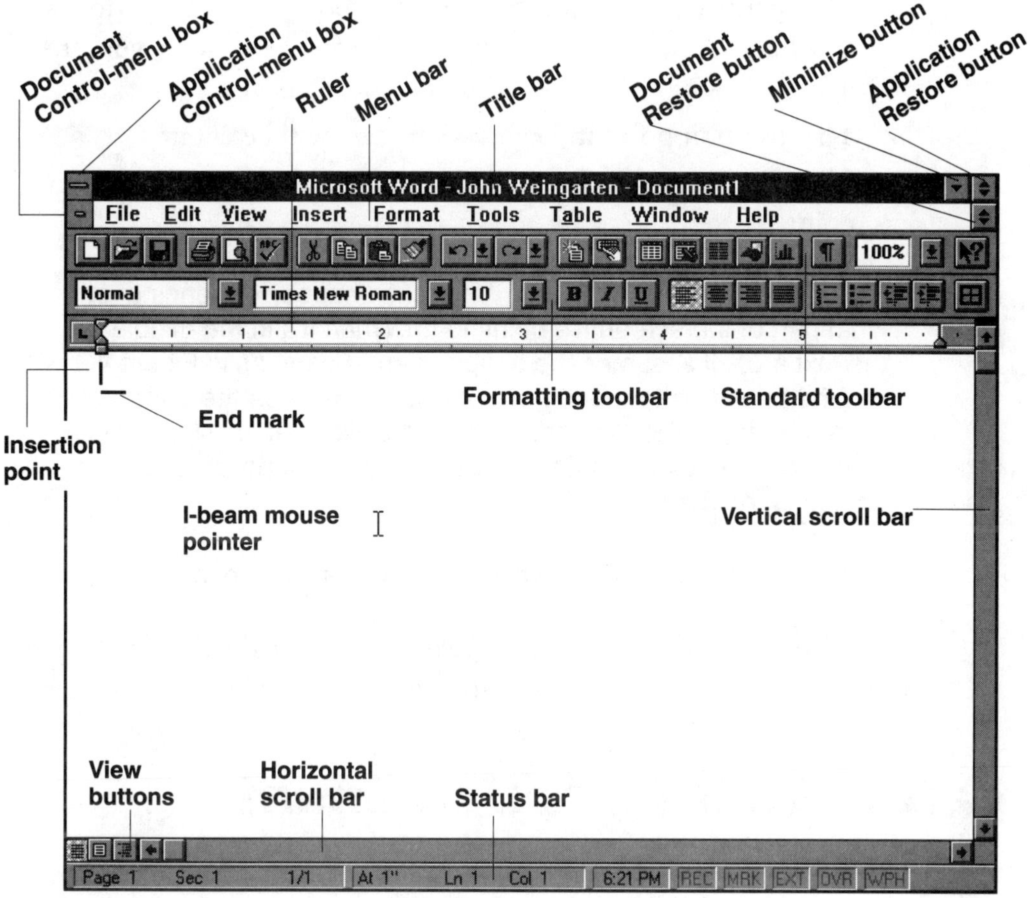

FIGURE 4–3 The Word screen elements

do what might take several keystrokes or mouse clicks using the menus.

- ✓ The Ruler shows you where you are entering text in your document and lets you change margins, indents, and tab stops.
- ✓ The View buttons provide shortcuts for changing the view of the document.

✓ The Status bar provides information about the current document and messages about the buttons or menu items you are using.
✓ The insertion point indicates where text will be entered.
✓ The I-beam mouse pointer lets you reposition the insertion point.

note The mouse pointer takes on different shapes, depending on what part of the screen it's pointing to. When it's in the middle of the text area, it assumes the shape of an I-beam, as in Figure 4–3. When pointing to menus or buttons, it assumes the shape of an arrow angled to the left. In the selection bar or style area, which will be covered later, it assumes the shape of an arrow angled to the right.

✓ The End mark indicates where the current document ends.

You'll see how all these elements work in Word documents as you progress through the next few chapters.

Creating Your First Document

There are several ways to start a new document. If you want to create a document that looks fancier than something that came off a typewriter and you don't know much about Word's formatting features, you might want to start with one of the document creation Wizards. We'll invoke some wizardry later. For now, if you just want to enter some text as quickly as possible, follow these steps.

1. Start typing.
2. Stop typing.

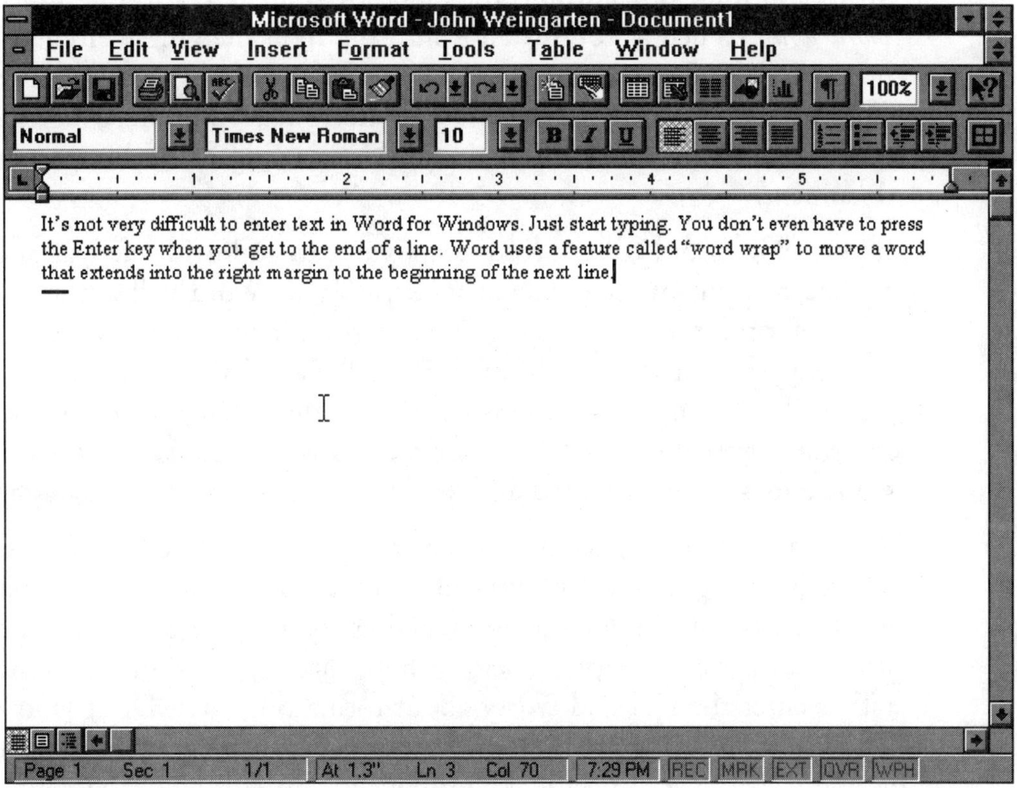

FIGURE 4–4 Text entered in a Word document

It's just that simple. After you stop typing, you'll have some text on your screen, as shown in Figure 4–4.

Okay, there are a few things you should know before you go charging off creating real documents. First, don't ever use the Enter key to move to the next line as you would on a typewriter. Press Enter only when you want to start a new paragraph or end a short line—when entering a name and address, for example.

Word and most other word processing programs use a feature called *word wrap*. When a word extends into the right margin, Word automatically moves the entire word to the beginning of the next line. This isn't just a nice feature. If you don't take advantage of this feature, you will have a difficult time formatting and editing your document.

If you allow Word to use word wrap, you can add or delete text and change margins or fonts (character styles) and Word will automatically reformat the text to accommodate the changes you have made. Pressing Enter at the end of each line tells Word that you want the line to break there, regardless of the editing changes you make. Pressing Enter also tells Word that the following line is a new paragraph and is to be formatted differently than lines within a paragraph.

With that caveat out of the way, let me give you some reassurance. There is no right or wrong way to create a document. Some people want to have all the formatting—such as margins, line spacing, and page numbering—in place before they start typing. Others would rather enter the text and worry about formatting later. Don't worry. The beauty of word processing, especially with a program as flexible as Word, is the ability to make formatting and editing changes after you enter your text. If you make mistakes or change your mind about formatting, you can always take care of it later.

Saving Your Work and Closing a Document

Before we go any further, we need to talk about what is perhaps the most important topic of all—saving your work. I know, it's pretty mundane stuff, but if you've ever lost an important document, you know just how important saving really is.

Let's face it, computers aren't infallible; neither is your local electric company. Things can and do go wrong. Just last week, a book fell off my bookshelf, landed behind my computer, and dislodged the power cord. Fortunately, I save my work regularly so, after plugging the computer back in, I was able to retrieve the document I was working on without too much inconvenience.

Until you save a document, it is stored in your computer's random access memory (RAM). Whatever is in RAM when the power goes out is history. If you save your work on your computer's hard disk (or a floppy disk) it will be there for you even if you accidentally turn off the computer.

So how often should you save? Often enough that, if the power went out just before you were about to save, you wouldn't lose so much work that it would ruin your day. Most folks find that saving every 10 to 20 minutes is sufficient. If you save that often, you'll never lose more than 10 or 20 minutes of work.

note Word provides an automatic save feature, which is discussed in Chapter 10. The feature is a nice safety net, but it doesn't take the place of saving your document frequently in the normal fashion.

Fortunately, saving is extremely easy. To save your document for the first time, follow these steps.

Choose File➢Save As to display the Save As dialog box shown in Figure 4–5.

Word assigns the filename doc1.doc to this document. Not very descriptive. You're generally better off entering a name that better describes the document. Since the name in the File Name text box is highlighted, you can just start typing to replace the existing name with a new one.

Filenames can have a maximum of eight characters followed by an optional period and an optional three-character extension. If you

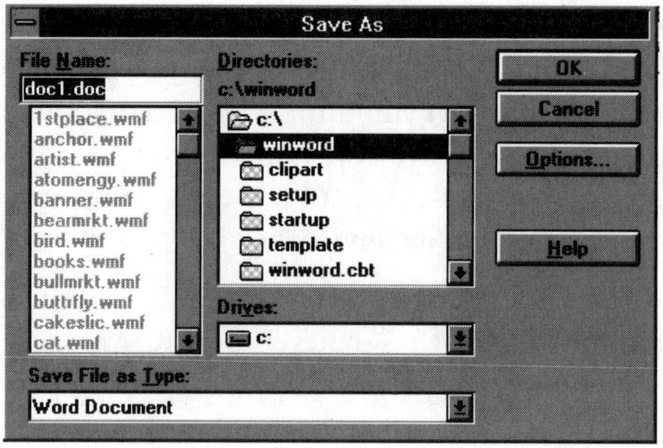

FIGURE 4–5 The Save As dialog box

don't add your own extension, Word will automatically add the .doc extension. It's usually best to let Word add the extension to make it easier to locate Word documents.

Enter a name—sample, for example.

If you want to save the document in a special directory that already exists on your computer's hard disk, double-click on the name of the directory in the Directories list. You may have to double-click on c:\ to move up one directory level and then double-click on the directory name you want. You may also have to scroll to bring the chosen directory into view.

If you want to save to a drive other than the one shown under Drives, click on the arrow next to the Drives drop-down list; then click on the drive letter you want to use.

note Directories are similar to file folders in a file cabinet. Just as you might organize your paper documents by type or project in your file cabinet, you may want to organize your Word documents in a similar fashion on your hard disk.

If you need more information about creating and using directories, take a look at the Windows File Manager documentation.

Word does provide a way to specify a default directory so you don't have to manually select the directory for your documents each time you save a new one. I'll cover that feature in the chapter on customization.

Click on the OK button to save the document.

The title bar displays the name you assigned to the document. In the next chapter, you'll learn some quick ways to save a document once it has been named.

CAUTION

Just because a document is saved on your computer's disk, don't assume that it is 100 percent safe. A variety of perils can befall your file. The computer could completely malfunction or be stolen. A fire or flood could wipe out your system. I hate to spread doom and gloom, but these things really can happen.

There is a way to protect your valuable information from even these horrible scenarios. The solution is to back up your important files onto floppy disks or tape (if you have a tape backup system). If you don't know how to back up your files, refer to your Windows and DOS documentation or to your tape backup system documentation.

Once you're on a prudent backup schedule, don't store the backup disks or tapes next to your computer, where they could be stolen or burned along with your computer. Put them in another location—perhaps a fireproof file cabinet in another room. It may be trite, but it really is better to be safe than sorry.

After saving a document, you may want to close it before beginning your next task.

Choose File➢Close or double-click on the document's Control-menu box.

note

If you have made any changes to the document since the last time it was saved, Word displays a dialog box asking you if you want to save the changes to your document. Click on Yes to save the changes or No to close without saving and lose any edits.

Opening a Document

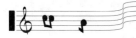

Word lists the last four files you used at the bottom of the File menu. The easiest way to open one of these file is to choose File and then click on the name of the file you want to open at the bottom of the menu.

If the file you want to open isn't one of the last four you used, follow these steps.

1. Choose File➢Open to display the Open dialog box, as shown in Figure 4–6.

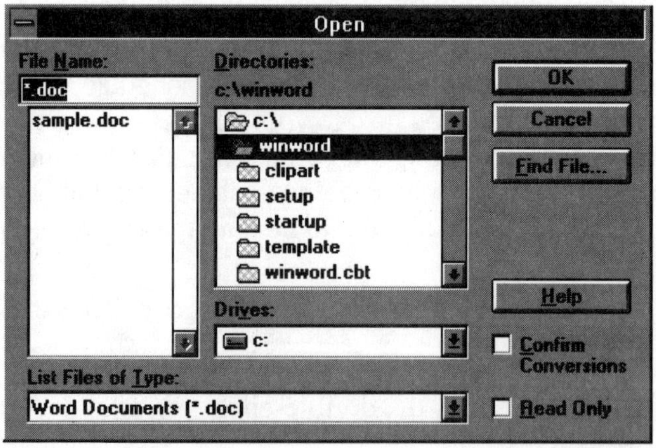

FIGURE 4–6 The Open dialog box

2. If the file you want is listed in the File Name list, click on it and then click on the OK button, or just double-click on the filename.

If the file you want is in a different directory, use the technique described in the section on saving your work to switch to the correct directory before you select the file.

note One of the greatest fears of new computer users, and sometimes even old computer users, is losing an important document. You know it's on your hard disk somewhere, but where? If you can't find the file, don't panic. Word provides a wonderful facility, called File Find, for locating lost files.

Summary

You now know enough to create, save, and open simple Word for Windows documents. In the next chapter, we'll start exploring Word's editing features. The fun is just beginning.

5

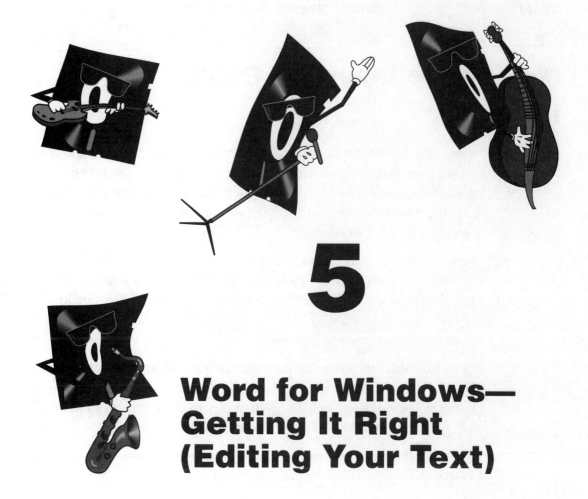

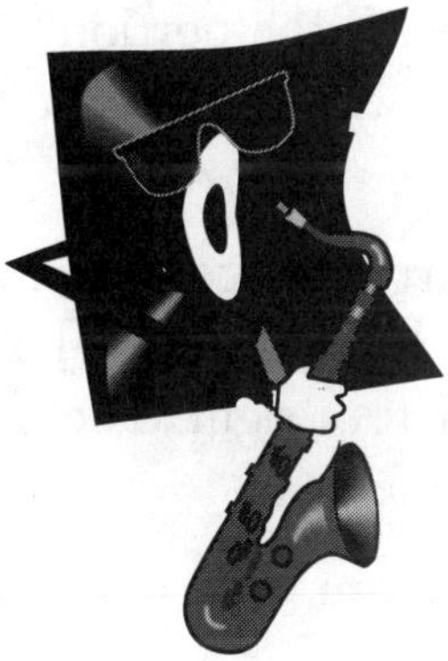

Word for Windows— Getting It Right (Editing Your Text)

Editing and formatting are the main reasons to use word processing programs. If you never make mistakes and don't care too much how your documents look, you may as well stick with a typewriter or a more primitive word processing program. If, like most Word users, you do care, read on. This chapter covers the editing part of the equation. You'll learn about formatting in the next chapter.

Moving the Insertion Point

Before you can edit a document, you must be able to get to the spot you want to edit. It's a common mistake to think you can move the I-beam pointer to a new location and start typing or deleting text there. Actually, the insertion point, not the mouse pointer, determines where you will begin editing.

You can move the insertion point using a variety of methods. If the location you want to move to is visible on the screen, you can simply move the mouse pointer to that position and click. If the portion of the document you want to move to isn't visible, you can use the scroll bar to bring that portion into view and then click.

If you just want to move the insertion point a short distance from its current location, the arrow keys may be your best bet. Pressing ← or → moves the insertion point one character to the left or right. The ↑ and ↓ move the insertion point up or down one line.

Here are a few keyboard shortcuts to get you where you want to go in a hurry.

- ✓ Press the Home key to move the insertion point to the beginning of the line.
- ✓ Press the End key to move to the end of the line.
- ✓ Press Ctrl-← or Ctrl-→ to move the insertion point a word at a time.
- ✓ Press Ctrl-Home to move to the beginning of the document.
- ✓ Press Ctrl-End to move the end of the document.
- ✓ Press Ctrl-↑ or Ctrl-↓ to move up or down a paragraph at a time.

Often the fastest way to move to a new location in your document is to use the Go To dialog box. You can display the Go To dialog box by

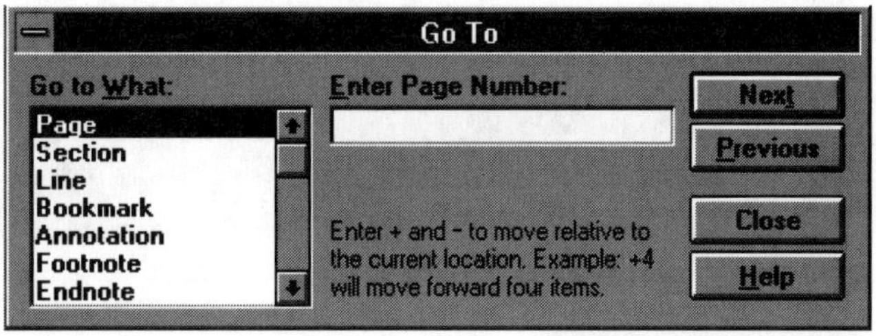

FIGURE 5–1 The Go To dialog box

choosing Edit➢Go To, by using the keyboard shortcut Ctrl-G, or by double-clicking on the left or middle portion of the status bar. Figure 5–1 shows the Go To dialog box.

In the Go To What list, click on the element you want to go to, then enter its name or number in the text box. For example, if you want to move to page 5, leave Page highlighted in the Go To What list, type 5 in the text box, and click on the OK button.

Once the insertion point is where you want it, you can begin typing to insert text, press the Backspace key to erase the character to the left of the insertion point, or press the Delete key to erase the character to the right of the insertion point.

Selecting Text

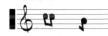

Before you can execute most editing and formatting tasks, you must first select the portion of the document you want to manipulate. For example, if you want to delete a sentence, select the sentence and then choose Edit➢Cut. The selected portion of the document appears highlighted, as shown in Figure 5–2.

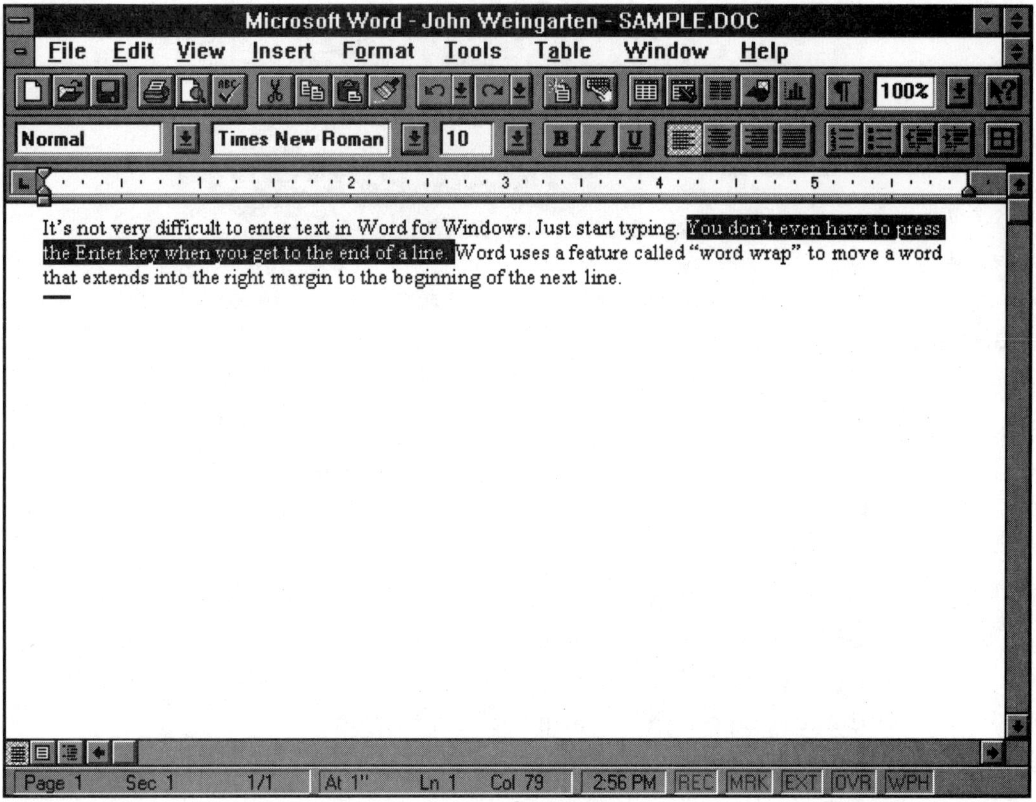

FIGURE 5–2 The third sentence is selected

You can select text by dragging the mouse over it. You can drag horizontally to select a character at a time or vertically to select a line at a time. There are several shortcuts you can use for selecting text.

For example, you can select an entire word by double-clicking on it. To select a sentence, including the space after the period, hold down the Ctrl key and click anywhere in the sentence. To select a paragraph, double-click in the selection bar next to the paragraph or triple-click in the paragraph. To select an entire line, move the mouse pointer into the selection bar on the left side of the line and click.

You can select from the insertion point to any portion of the document by pressing Shift and clicking on the place you want to be the end of the selection.

tip If you drag over a portion of two words, Word is smart enough to select all of both words automatically, including the spaces between and after the words. You can turn this feature off with the Options dialog box. You'll learn more about this feature in Chapter 10.

If you change your mind, you can cancel a selection by clicking anywhere outside the selection or by pressing an arrow key.

Working with Toolbars and Shortcut Menus

All the options for manipulating your document are available from the menus on the menu bar. However, Word and the other Office applications provide two additional methods that are usually more efficient—toolbars and shortcut menus.

Toolbars contain buttons you can click on to perform various tasks. Word provides a variety of toolbars you can display. Some appear automatically when you start to perform a particular task. For example, when you change to the Outline view of your document, Word automatically displays the Outline toolbar with buttons for working with outlines.

Toolbars can be moved to a convenient location on the screen, and their size can be changed as well. You can even create customized toolbars with just the buttons you want. I'll cover customizing toolbars in Chapter 10.

When you start Word, the Standard and Formatting toolbars are displayed between the menu bar and the horizontal ruler.

note The toolbars that were displayed on screen when you last exited Word appear in the same positions the next time you start Word. If you have different toolbars or your toolbars aren't located between the menu bar and the ruler, don't worry. You can easily move and display or hide them.

If you haven't worked with toolbars before, you may be wondering how in the world you'll ever learn and remember what all the little pictures on the buttons represent. You don't have to. All you have to do is move the mouse pointer over any button to display a ToolTip—the name of the button. The ToolTip is usually enough to clue you in to the button's function, but if you need a further explanation, just look at the status bar.

Figure 5–3 shows the mouse pointer pointing to the Italic button on the Formatting toolbar. Notice the ToolTip below the mouse pointer and the explanation of the button's function on the status bar.

The ToolTip displays the button name, Italic, which probably tells you what you need to know. The status bar explains that the button will make the selection italic. It also tells you it's a *toggle,* which means that if the selection is already italic, clicking the button will turn off the italic attribute.

Explore the buttons on the toolbars to get a feel for what's available. Some of the buttons that will save you time right away are the New, Open, and Save buttons. Instead of choosing File➢New, File➢Open, or File➢Save, you can just click on one of these buttons. As discussed in Chapter 4, you should be saving your document regularly, and clicking on the Save button now and then is a very painless way to do it.

A button that deserves special and immediate consideration is the Help button on the right side of the Standard toolbar. This button

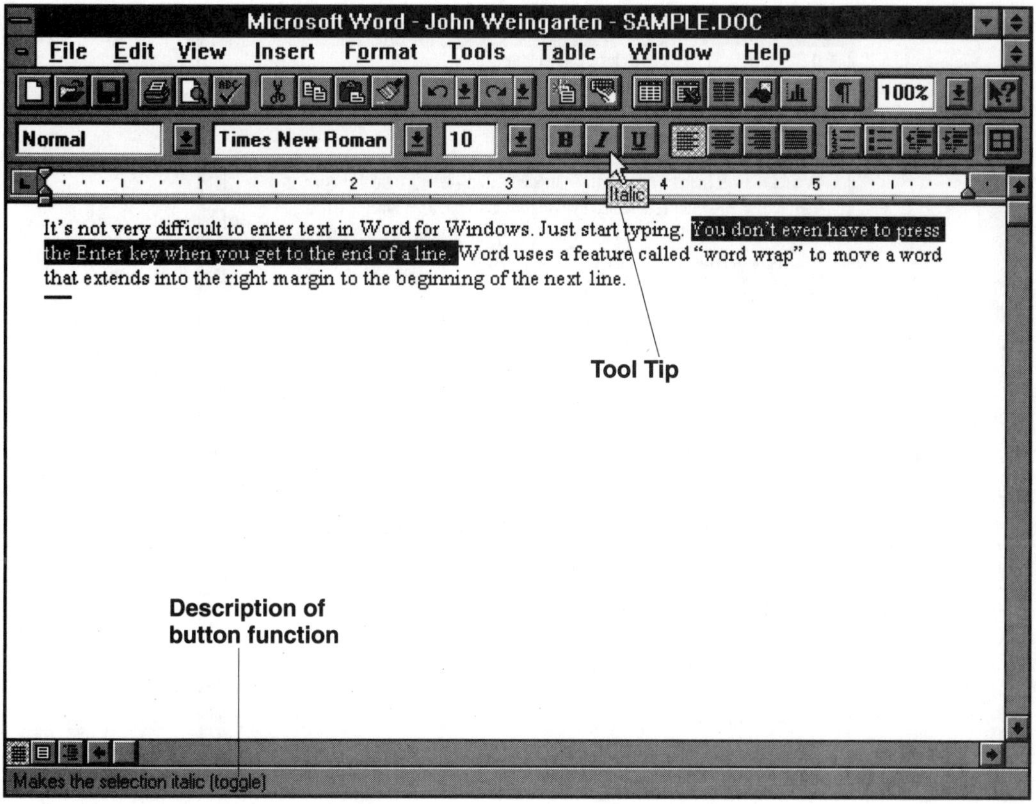

FIGURE 5–3 The mouse pointer on a button

lets you summon a help screen for any screen element or menu item you have questions about. This is a real gem. Simply click on the Help button; then move the mouse pointer (which now looks like an arrow with a question mark attached) to the element you need help with and click.

For example, suppose you don't remember how the scroll bar works. No problem. Just click on the Help button, point to the scroll bar and click. In a few seconds, a Scroll Bars help screen will appear, as shown

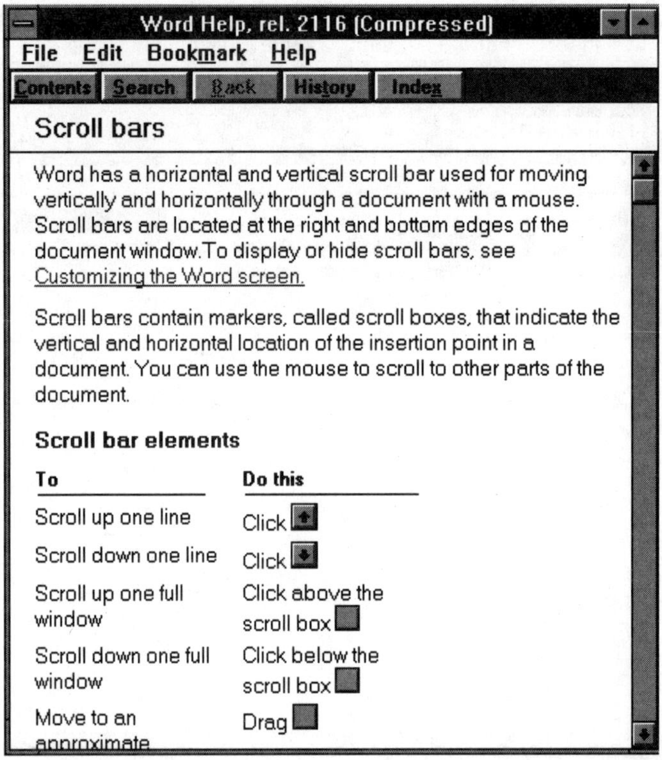

FIGURE 5–4 The Scroll Bars help screen

in Figure 5–4. To get back to Word from Help, click on the Word screen or choose File➢Exit from the Help menu bar.

If you want to display other toolbars or hide toolbars that are currently on the screen, you can choose View➢Toolbars to display the Toolbars dialog box, but this is the perfect time to use a shortcut menu.

To display an object's shortcut menu, just point to it and right-click (click the right mouse button). So, if you want to see the toolbar shortcut menu, point to a toolbar and right-click. We'll use other shortcut menus in the next chapter but, for now, this will show you how they work.

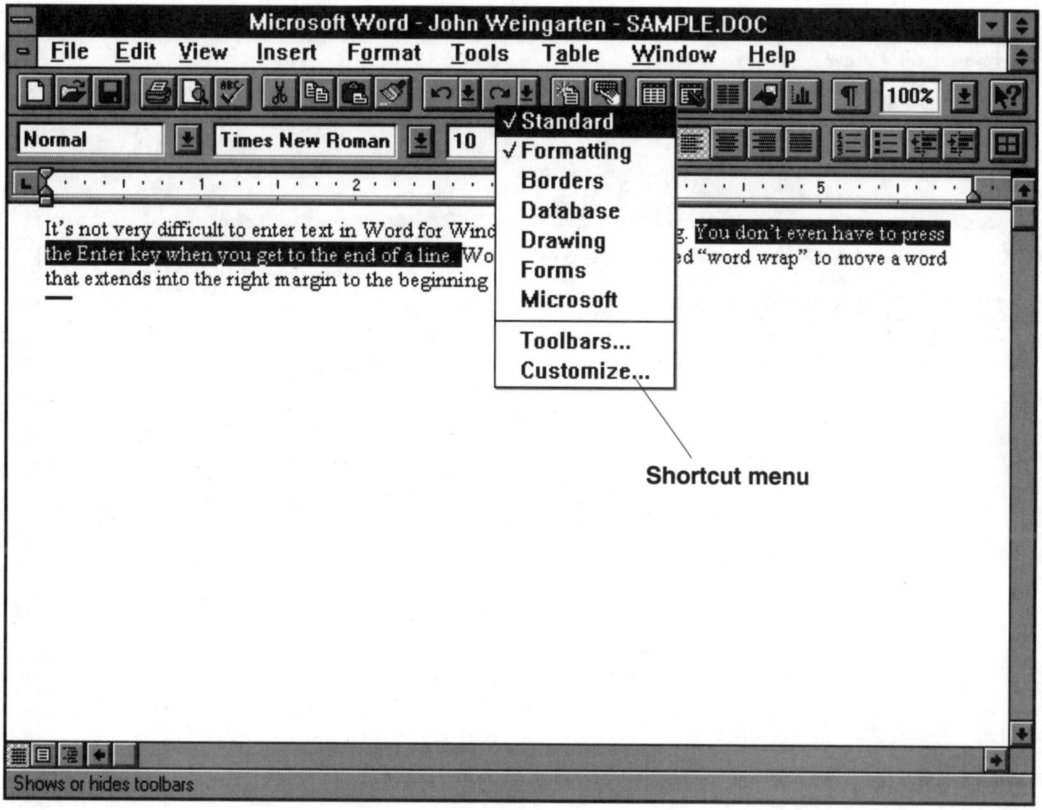

FIGURE 5–5 The toolbar shortcut menu

The toolbar names with check marks next to them are the ones that are currently displayed. To hide a toolbar that is checked, click on its name in the shortcut menu. To display a toolbar that isn't currently shown, click on its name; a check mark will appear next to it in the shortcut menu.

Figure 5–6 shows the screen with the Borders toolbar displayed.

You may decide that there are just too many toolbars and other screen elements at the top of the screen. You can decrease that clutter by

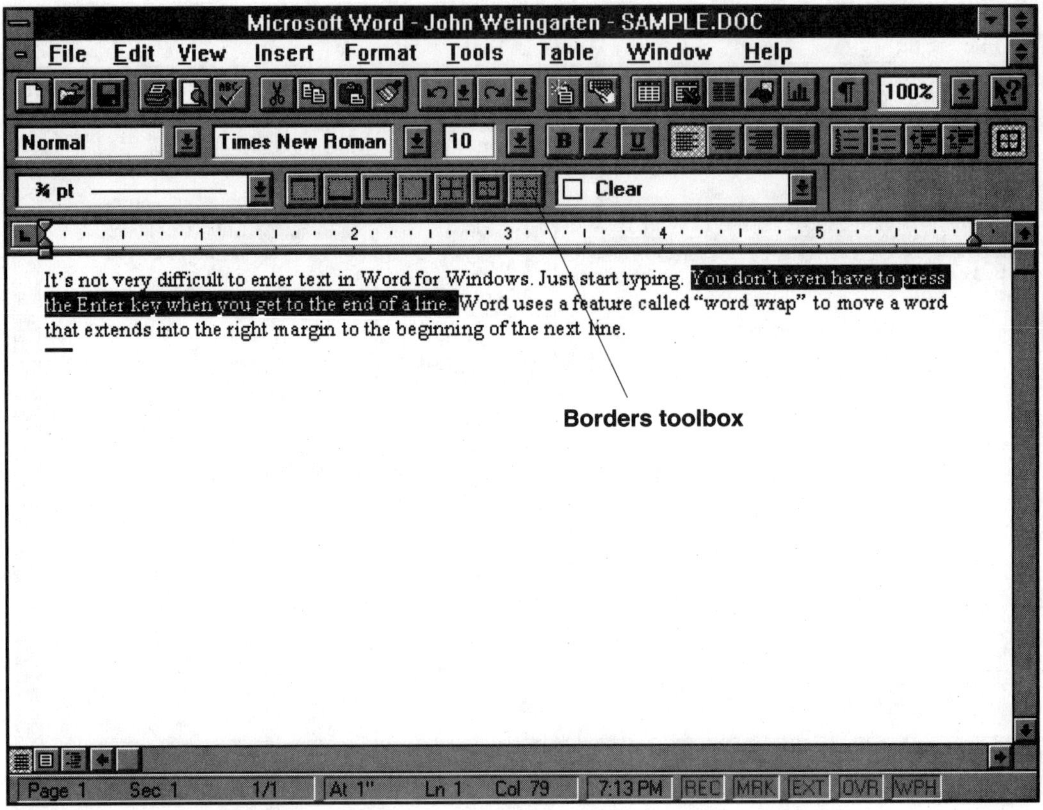

FIGURE 5–6 The Borders toolbar, used for applying borders to portions of a document

repositioning one of the toolbars. The three toolbars shown in Figure 5–6 are *docked,* or *anchored,* at the top of the screen. Toolbars can be anchored at the top, bottom, or either side of the screen. They can also "float" anywhere on the screen.

To reposition a toolbar, point to an empty area on the toolbar or between toolbar buttons and drag it to the new location. Figure 5–7 shows the Borders toolbar docked at the bottom of the screen. Figure 5–8 shows the Borders toolbar floating.

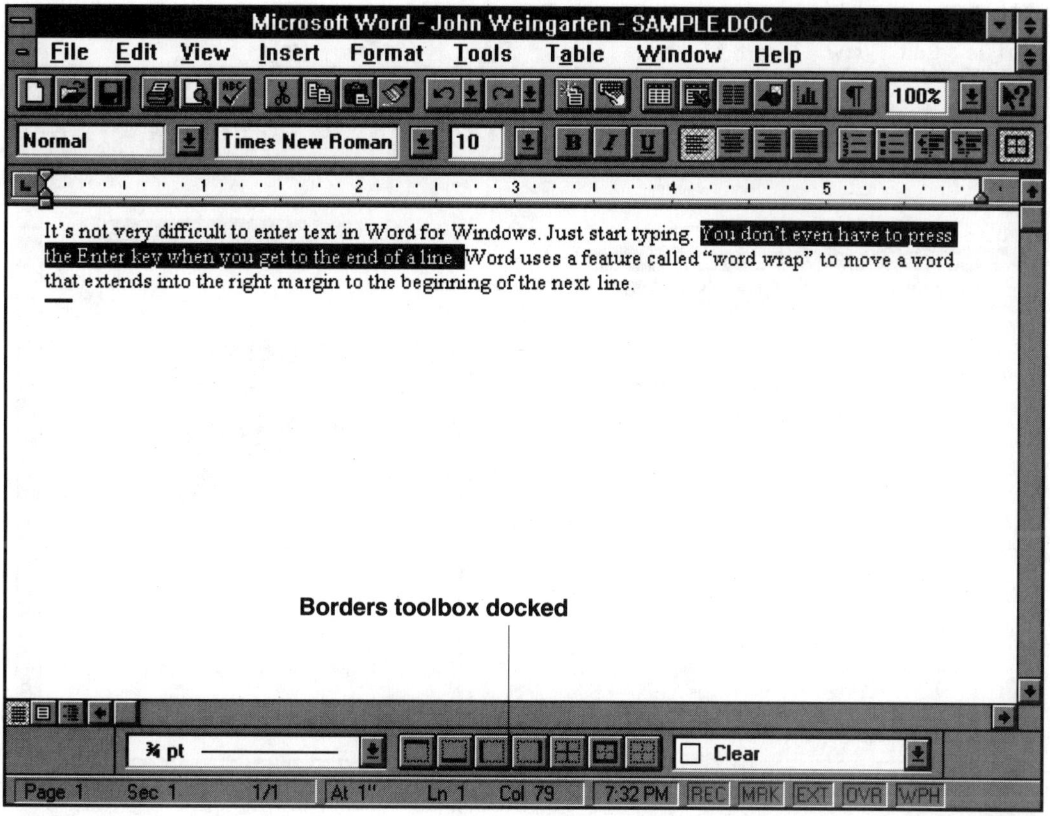

FIGURE 5–7 The Borders toolbar docked at the bottom of the screen

As you can imagine, displaying too many toolbars can add a lot of distracting clutter to the screen and reduce the amount of the document you can see. For this reason, you'll want to display as few toolbars as possible while keeping the really useful buttons available.

tip If you dock toolbars that have drop-down list buttons (such as the Formatting toolbar's Font Size button) on the left or right side of the screen, the drop-down list buttons will be replaced with potentially less efficient buttons that display dialog boxes. For

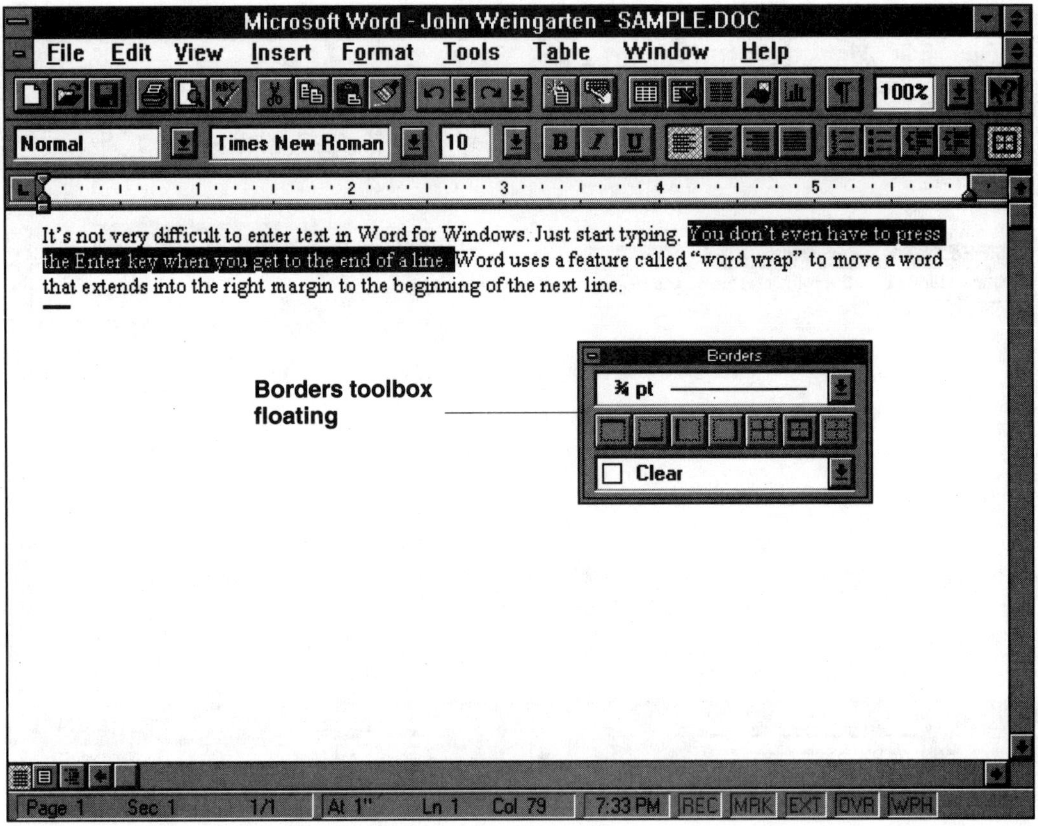

FIGURE 5–8 The Borders toolbar floating

this reason, it's usually best to have toolbars with drop-down list buttons at the top, at the bottom, or floating.

Cutting, Copying, and Pasting

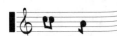

When you delete (cut) text or other objects, they are stored temporarily on the Windows Clipboard. The Clipboard is just a holding area for data that may need to be retrieved (pasted) into another location in the current document, in another Word document, or even in another application, such as one of the other Office programs. You can also send a copy of the data to the Clipboard if you want to use it somewhere else but don't want to remove it from its original location.

The first step, as with most tasks, is to select the text or objects you want to cut or copy. Having selected the desired text, you can cut the selection by choosing Edit➢Cut or clicking on the Cut button on the Standard toolbar. You can copy the selection by choosing Edit➢Copy or clicking on the Copy button on the Standard toolbar.

After you've cut or copied the selection, move the insertion point to the location at which you want to paste it and choose Edit➢Paste or click on the Paste button on the Standard toolbar.

note

You can paste the Clipboard contents as many times as you like. For example, if you had inserted a picture into a document and copied it to the Clipboard, you might want to paste the picture on several different pages of the document.

Keep in mind that the Clipboard holds only the last thing that was cut or copied. As soon as you cut or copy again, the contents of the Clipboard are replaced with the new data.

Another way to move or copy is with a technique called *drag and drop.* Particularly when you want to move or copy some data from one part of the current document to another, drag and drop can be the most efficient method. You can use drag and drop between documents or applications, but it can be cumbersome.

To move a selection to another part of the document with drag and drop, simply point to the selection, drag it to the new location, and release the mouse button. As you drag, the mouse pointer will have a small rectangle attached to let you know that you are, indeed, dragging.

To copy a selection with drag and drop, hold down the Ctrl key while dragging to the new location. The mouse pointer will have the rectangle attached and will also have a + next to it to indicate that you are copying.

Summary

In this chapter, you learned the skills necessary to do basic editing, including how to use toolbars, shortcut menus, cutting, copying, and pasting.

In the next chapter, you'll learn how to add some pizzazz to your documents with formatting and graphics.

6

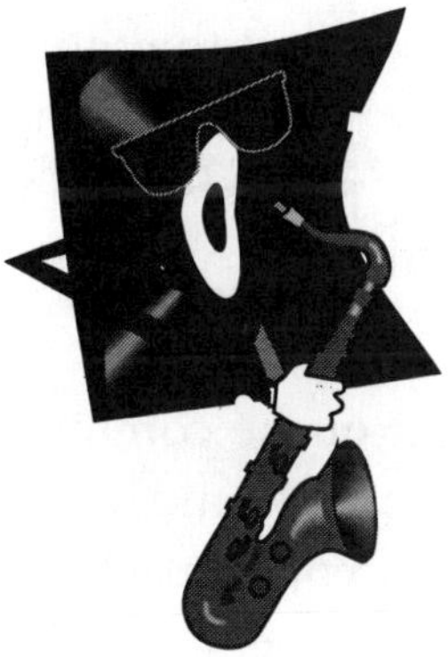

Word for Windows—Making It Pretty

The way a document looks can be as important as its content. The purpose of most documents is to convey information or persuade the reader to agree with the document's message. With improper or careless formatting, the document may look amateurish and, therefore, be perceived as inaccurate and unworthy of consideration.

Character Formatting

You can apply formatting to the entire document, selected paragraphs, or selected characters. We'll start the formatting discussion at the character level since that is often where you'll start.

Character formatting includes applying attributes such as bold, italic, and underline, as well as changing the font (typeface) and font size. To apply any of these attributes, select the text you want to change and specify the attribute you want from a toolbar button, keyboard shortcut, or dialog box. You can also specify an attribute without selecting text. If the insertion point is in a word, character formatting changes will affect only that word. If the insertion point isn't in a word, the text you type from that point will display the new attributes until you turn them off.

The Formatting toolbar provides buttons for several of the common character formatting attributes including bold, italic, and underline. For example, to apply bold to several words in a sentence, select the words and click on the Bold button on the Formatting toolbar. The keyboard shortcut for bold is Ctrl-B. You can also choose Bold from the Font Style list in the Font dialog box.

You can open the Font dialog box by choosing Format➢Font or by choosing Font from the shortcut menu (Figure 6–1) that appears when you right-click on the selection you want to change.

In the Font dialog box (Figure 6–2), you can also make multiple changes using the check boxes in the Effects portion of the dialog box, and the Font, Font Style, Size, Underline, and Color lists.

Until you are familiar with the ways in which various character formatting changes will affect your text, using the Font dialog box is the safest way to apply them. This is because, unlike the toolbar buttons

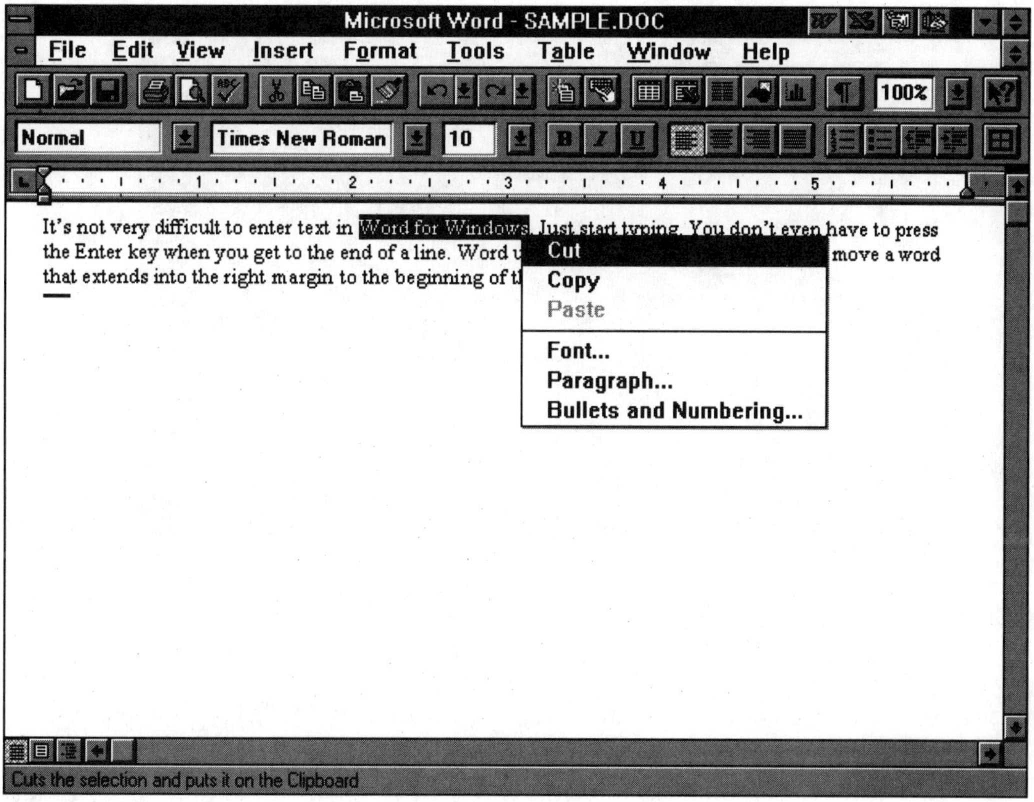

FIGURE 6–1 The shortcut menu for selected text

and keyboard shortcuts, the Font dialog box lets you see how your text will look before you accept the changes.

Using Fonts

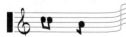

In Word terminology, a font is a set of characters, including letters, numbers, and symbols, that share a common design or typeface, and

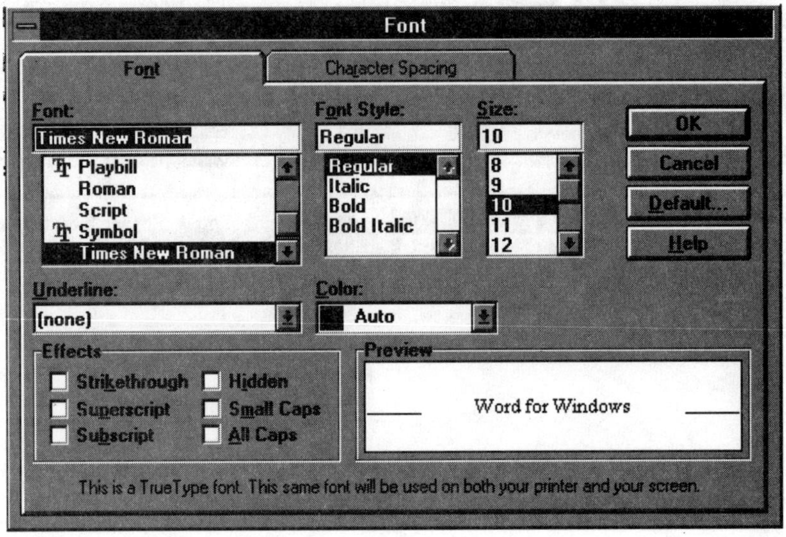

FIGURE 6–2 The Font dialog box

the same rules apply for changing fonts as for changing attributes. The subject of fonts occupies an important position in the realm of word processing and desktop publishing, however. There are, in fact, entire books devoted to teaching readers to choose the correct fonts for different types of material.

Using the correct font can make the difference between an effective, powerful document and one that has no visual impact or authority. When using more than one font in a document, it's also important to know which fonts look good together. Just as certain color combinations clash, some font combinations just don't work; they tell the reader that you are an amateur.

CAUTION

Unless you want your document to look like a ransom note, don't use too many fonts in a single document. One of the surest ways to signal your novice status is to overuse fonts. I think this happens to new users because they are unable to resist the temptation to use all the fonts at their disposal just because they're there. Resist the temptation.

If in doubt, use only one font. Your documents will look more professional with one nice font, perhaps in a couple of sizes and styles, than in two or more that don't go well together or are otherwise used improperly.

No discussion of fonts would be complete without a look at the various kinds of fonts. Some fonts reside in your printer. These are called, naturally enough, *printer fonts.* Some printer fonts have corresponding *screen fonts,* which are necessary if you want to be able to see on your screen what your printed fonts will look like. If your printer fonts don't have matching screen fonts, Windows will use substitute screen fonts, which may or may not resemble the printer fonts. If worrying about screen fonts and printer fonts sounds like more hassle than you want to deal with, there is a solution.

With the introduction of Windows 3.1, a new font technology called *TrueType fonts* was introduced. TrueType fonts have several advantages over other font technologies. All TrueType fonts have matching screen and printer fonts, so you don't have to worry about that problem anymore. Also, TrueType fonts work with almost any kind of printer, from inexpensive dot matrix printers to laser printers. Of course, the quality of the output differs according to the quality of the printer, but at least you can print the same fonts.

Also, all TrueType fonts are scalable, which means you can use them in virtually any size. A good selection of TrueType fonts is included with Windows 3.1, and you can purchase additional groups of TrueType fonts that can be easily added to Windows.

If your files will be edited by other people on other computers, TrueType fonts offer another advantage. They can be embedded in a document so that, even if the other computer doesn't have the fonts you used, the document will still print correctly.

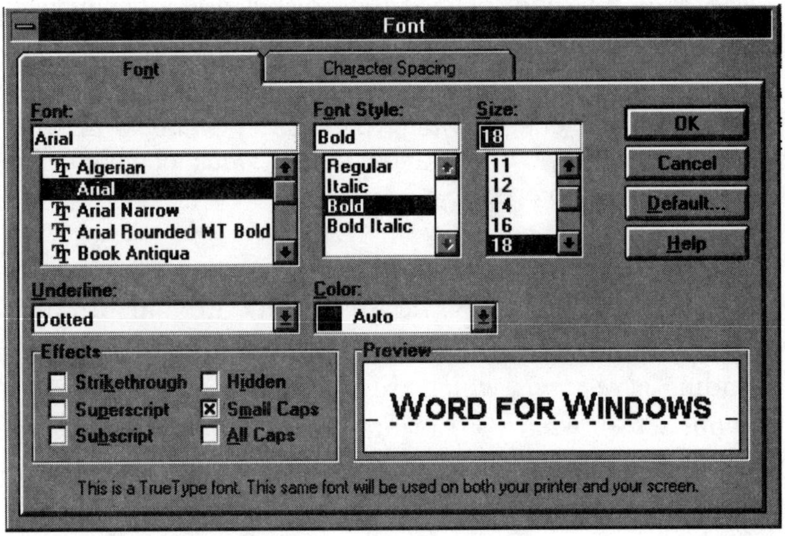

FIGURE 6–3 The sample text with formatting changes applied in the Preview window

My advice is: if you want to avoid as many font headaches as possible, use TrueType fonts.

tip You can identify a TrueType font in the font list in the Font dialog box or the Formatting toolbar by the TT symbol that appears before the name in the list.

Figure 6–3 shows the selected text in the preview portion of the Font dialog box with font and attribute changes. Notice the new font name (TrueType Arial), font style (Bold), font size (18 point), the underline style (Dotted), and the effects (Small Caps).

note In case you're wondering, Font Size refers to the point size of the font. A point is a unit of measure equal to approximately 1/72 inch, so the 18-point size assigned to the example is about ¼ inch high.

Typical sizes for body text are between 9 and 12 points. Larger point sizes are typically used for headings.

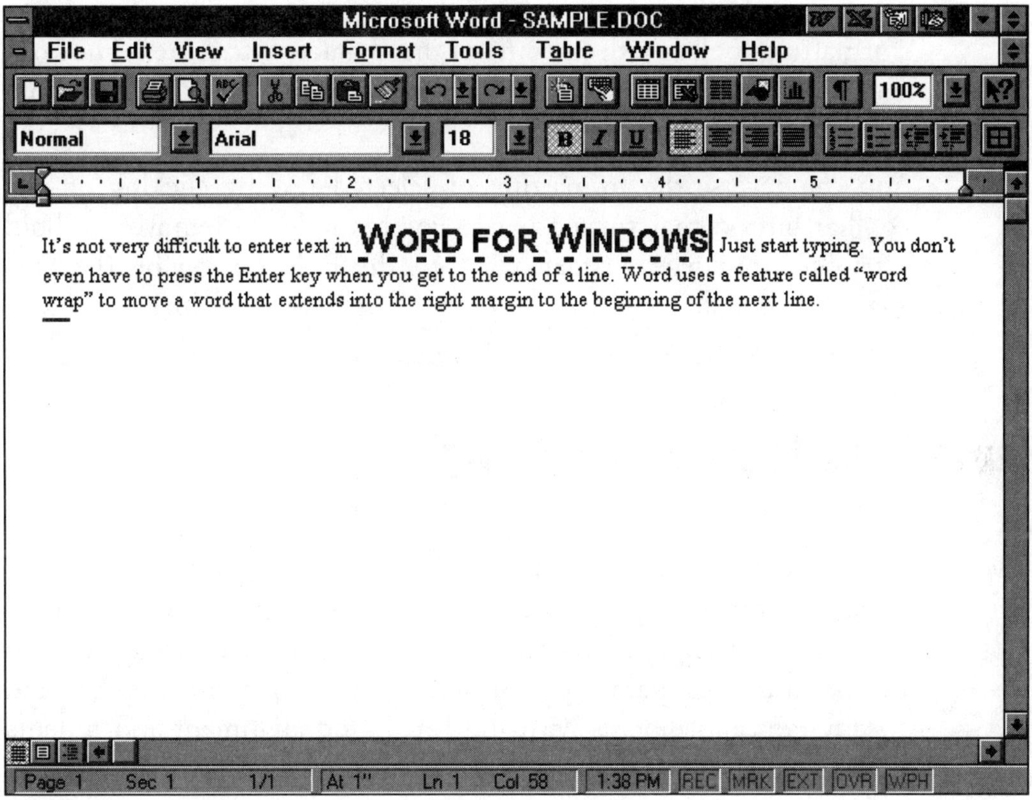

FIGURE 6–4 The formatted text in the document

tip

The default settings for almost every part of Word can be changed. To change the character formatting, make any choices that you want to be the new defaults and click on the Default button. When a dialog box appears asking if you want to make your settings new defaults, click on the OK button.

If you want to change any of the default settings later, just repeat these steps. The new default settings don't affect the active document or any saved documents. The new settings take effect only for new documents.

Figure 6–4 shows the formatted text in the document window.

With the insertion point in the text with the formatting changes, the Formatting toolbar reflects some of the character attributes. The Font and Font Size lists display the new font name and size, and the Bold button appears to be pressed.

You can reverse the formatting of selected text by clicking on the toolbar button that turned it on. For example, to remove the bold attribute from selected text, click on the Bold button on the Formatting toolbar. You can remove all character formatting from selected text by pressing Ctrl-Spacebar.

Paragraph Formatting

Paragraph formatting includes such items as indents, line and paragraph spacing, alignment, and tabs. As with character formatting, you can perform most paragraph formatting in a variety of ways. You can specify tabs and indents with the Ruler, and alignment and indents with the Formatting toolbar.

The other paragraph formatting options are set using the Paragraph and Tabs dialog boxes. You can open both of those boxes from the Format menu. Or, you can open the Paragraph dialog box from the shortcut menu with a right-click in the paragraph you want to format; you can then open the Tabs dialog box by clicking on the Tabs button in the Paragraph dialog box.

The paragraph formatting you specify is applied to all selected paragraphs or, if there is no selection, the entire paragraph containing the insertion point. Keep in mind that you don't have to select all of a paragraph to have it included in the group of paragraphs to be formatted. If only the last letter of one paragraph and the first letter of the next were selected, any paragraph formatting specified would be applied to all of both paragraphs.

Before we continue exploring paragraph formatting, we should discuss what a paragraph is. You may think you learned this back in your fourth grade English class, but Word defines a paragraph in a very specific way. A Word paragraph is any text or object followed by a paragraph mark (¶).

When you start creating a Word document, a hidden paragraph mark indicates the end of your first paragraph, even before you type it. When you press Enter, another paragraph mark is automatically inserted to indicate the end of the next paragraph. Objects, such as graphics and charts, also end with paragraph marks.

Okay, so now we know how Word defines a paragraph. What good is this information, especially since we can't see the marks? The answer is that the paragraph mark is critical if you want to be able to use paragraph formatting. And the marks can be displayed with the click of a toolbar button. To display paragraph marks, as well as all other non-printing characters, such as space and tab marks, click on the Show/Hide ¶ button on the Standard toolbar. Figure 6–5 shows a document with non-printing characters displayed.

CAUTION

The importance of paragraph marks can't be overstated. The paragraph mark actually contains the formatting information for the paragraph with which it is associated. If you accidentally delete a paragraph mark while deleting text, you'll be deleting the paragraph formatting, and the paragraph will use the formatting from the previous paragraph mark.

This might not be a problem if the preceding paragraph has the same formatting as the one whose mark you have deleted. But if the preceding paragraph had different indents or line spacing, for example, you could end up with a messed up document.

One way to avoid this situation is to work with the non-printing characters displayed. You won't be as likely to delete a paragraph mark accidentally if you can see it. If you find it too distracting to work with all those marks on your screen, keep them off while you enter text but turn them on before you make deletions.

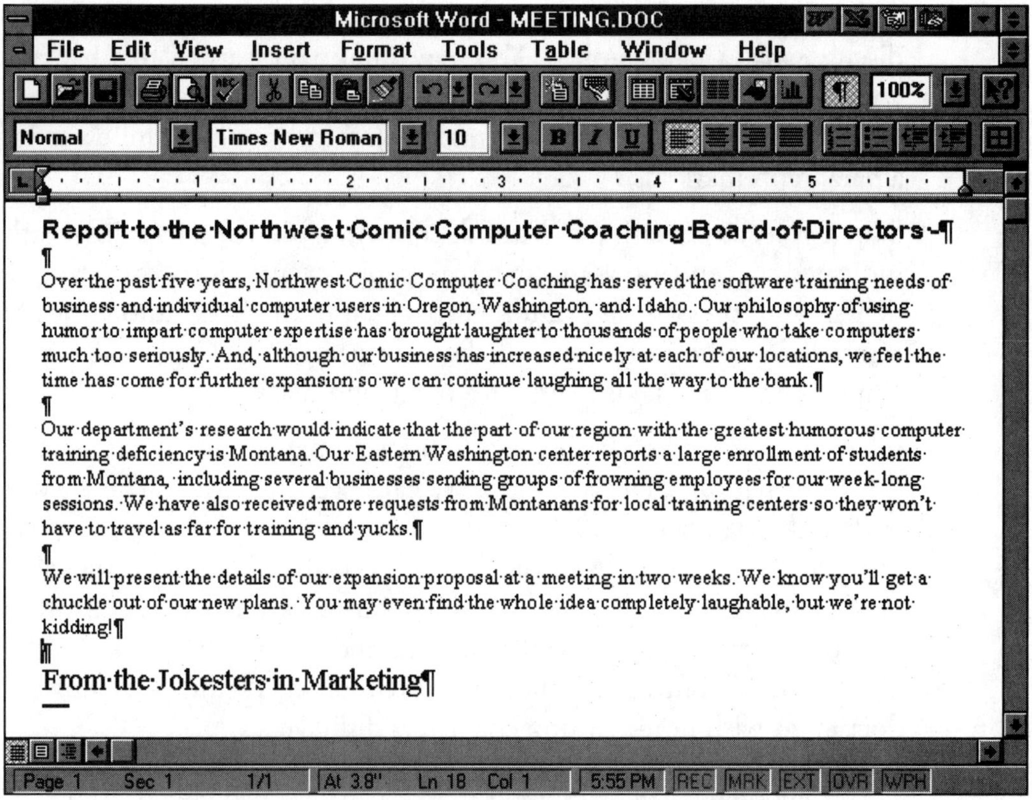

FIGURE 6–5 A document with non-printing characters displayed

> If you do manage to delete a paragraph mark that you didn't mean to, simply click on the Undo button on the Standard toolbar, and the mark will be restored.

It's best to use Word's paragraph formatting, instead of pressing Enter an extra time, to add space between paragraphs. If you press the Enter key, as was done in the document shown in Figure 6–5, you're stuck with a full blank line. If you use Word's paragraph spacing feature, you can specify a bit less than a full line, which generally looks better. It's also a good idea to use Word's indent feature, instead of pressing the [Tab] key, to indent the first line of your paragraph. Figure 6–6 shows the Indents and Spacing tab of the Paragraph dialog box.

In the Indentation portion of the dialog box you can specify an amount of offset on the left and/or right side of the entire paragraph or, using the Special list, you can choose a First Line or Hanging indent. Don't confuse indents with margins. The margin is the space between the edge of the page and the point at which the text can start. An indent is the amount of space between the margin and the point at which the text actually starts.

Figure 6–7 shows the dialog box with the First Line indent set at 0.5", the Line Spacing set at 1.5", and the Alignment set at Justified.

Figure 6–8 shows the document with the paragraph formatting changes applied.

Notice that the Justify button on the Formatting toolbar appears to be pressed and the First Line Indent marker on the Ruler has moved to the half-inch mark. You could use the other alignment buttons on the

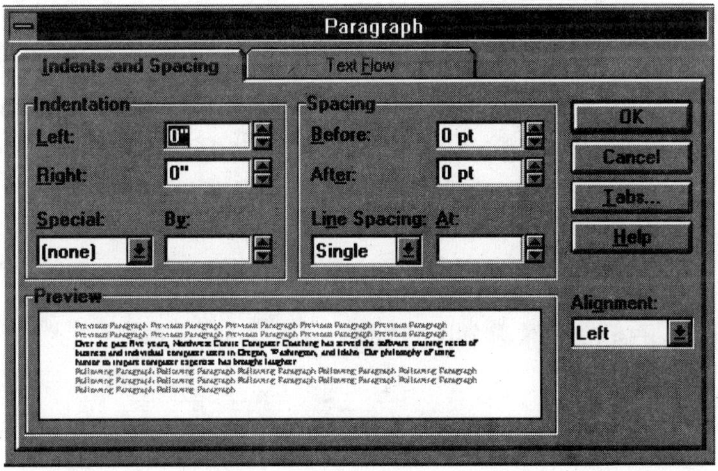

FIGURE 6–6 The Indents and Spacing tab of the Paragraph dialog box

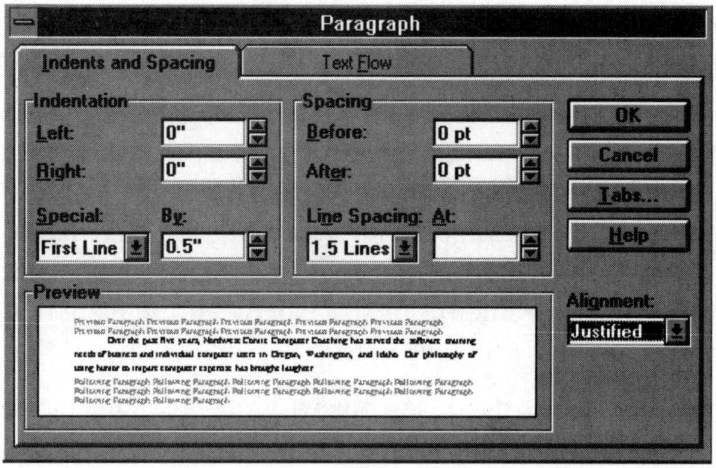

FIGURE 6–7 The Paragraph dialog box with formatting changes

toolbar to change the alignment of the selected paragraphs. You can change the indents by dragging the markers on the Ruler. For example, to change the first line indent, drag the First Line Indent marker to the new location, as shown in Figure 6–9. Don't forget to select the paragraphs first.

As the indent markers are dragged, a vertical guide is provided as a visual indicator. If you are trying to indent to a specific location, hold down the [Alt] key while dragging the indent markers to display the precise measurements on the Ruler.

Copying Formatting

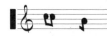

Suppose you experimented with a variety of formats before finally getting the characters or paragraphs to look just right. Now you

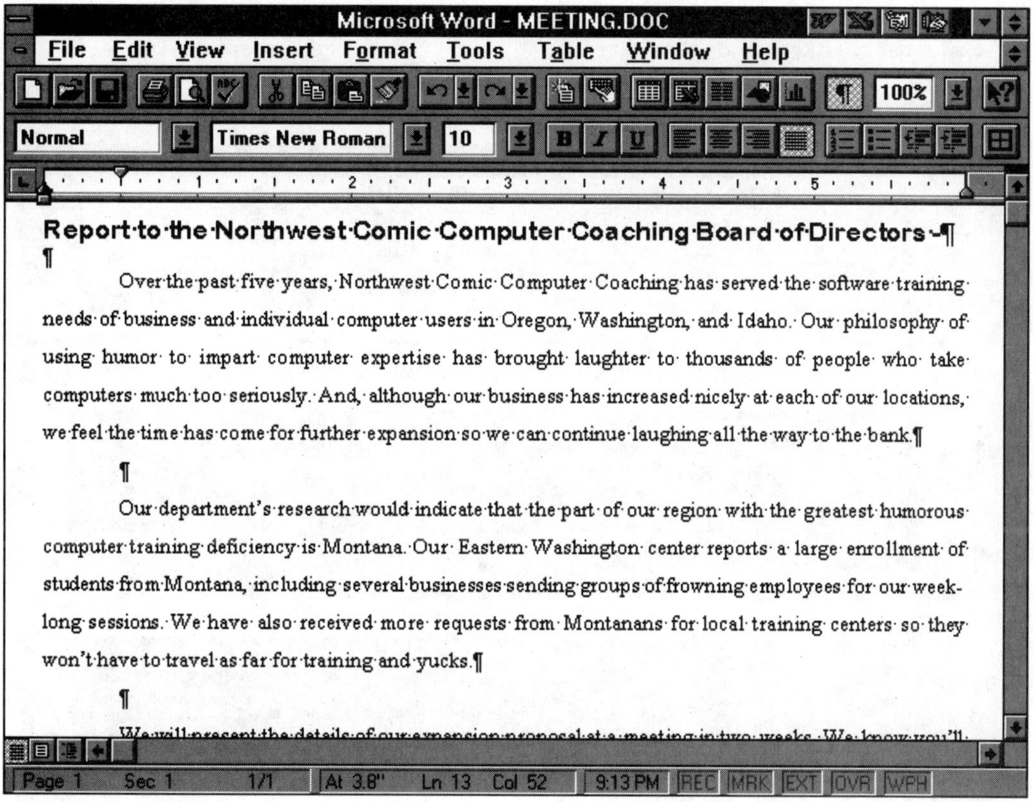

FIGURE 6–8 The document with the paragraphs formatted

realize that you want to use exactly the same formatting in another part of the document or even another document. Word's Format Painter makes this so simple you won't believe it. Don't worry, you don't need any artistic talent to use this painter.

To use the Format Painter, select the text with the formatting you want to apply elsewhere. If you want paragraph formatting to be copied, be sure to include the paragraph mark in the selection. Next, click on the Format Painter button. The mouse pointer turns into an I-beam with a

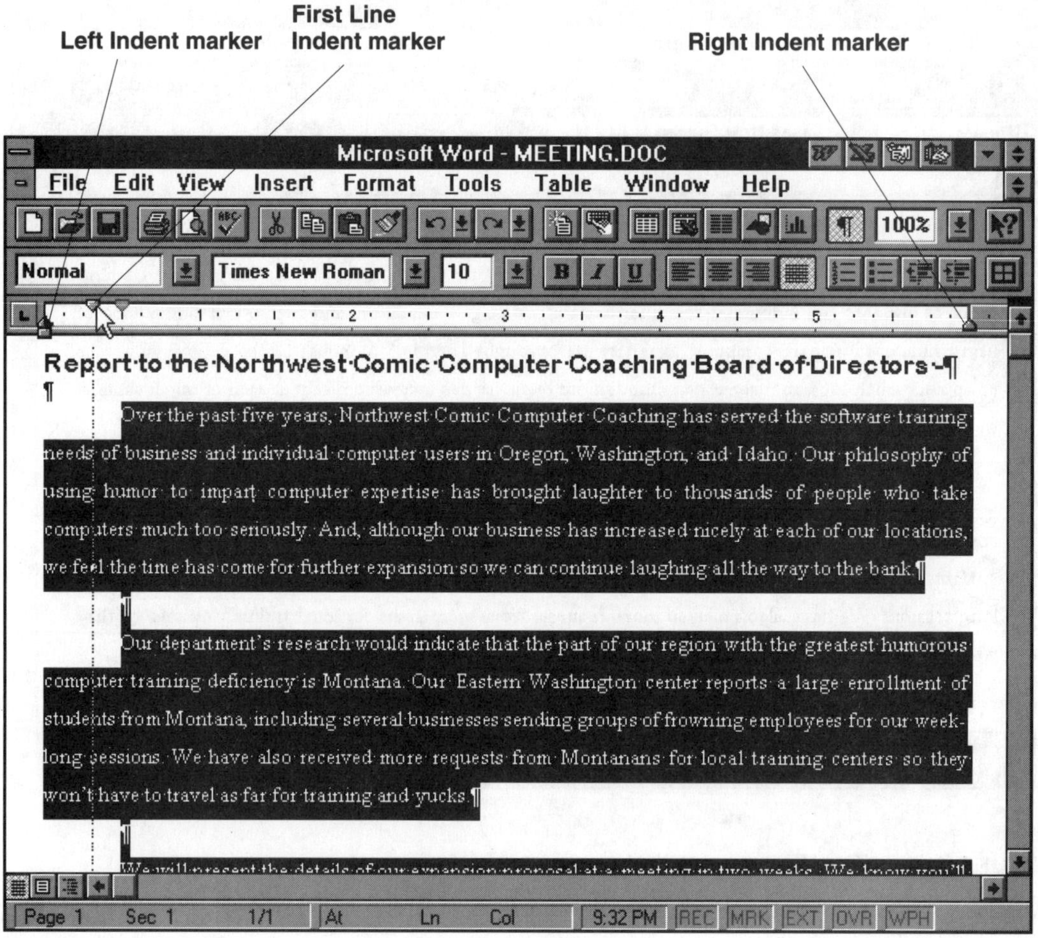

FIGURE 6–9 The First Line Indent marker being dragged

paint brush attached. To apply the formatting, simply paint (drag) over the text you want to format, as shown in Figure 6–10.

When you release the mouse button, the formatting will be applied. If you want to apply the formatting to more than one section of text, double-click on the Format Painter button before painting and then

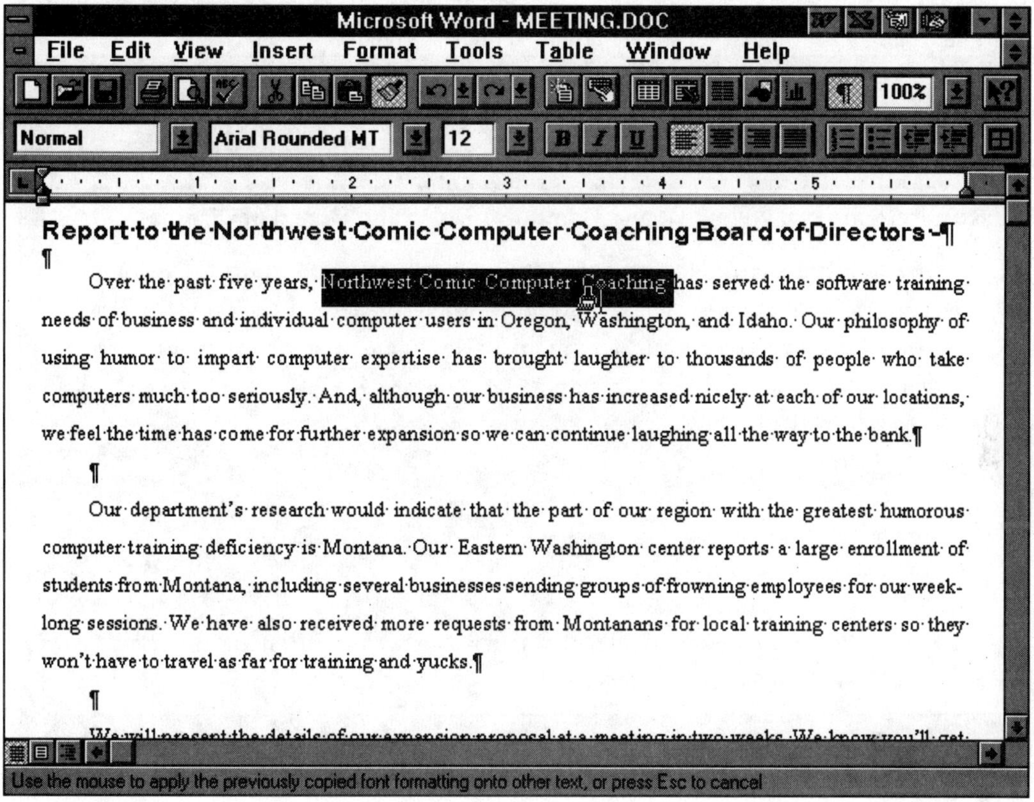

FIGURE 6–10 Format painting

press [Esc] or click on the Format Painter button again to stop format painting.

note Another way to apply and copy formatting is with styles. Using styles can greatly increase Word's power and flexibility. Chapter 7 explains what styles are and how to use them.

tip You can see the formatting for any character or object in your document by clicking on the Help button on the Standard toolbar

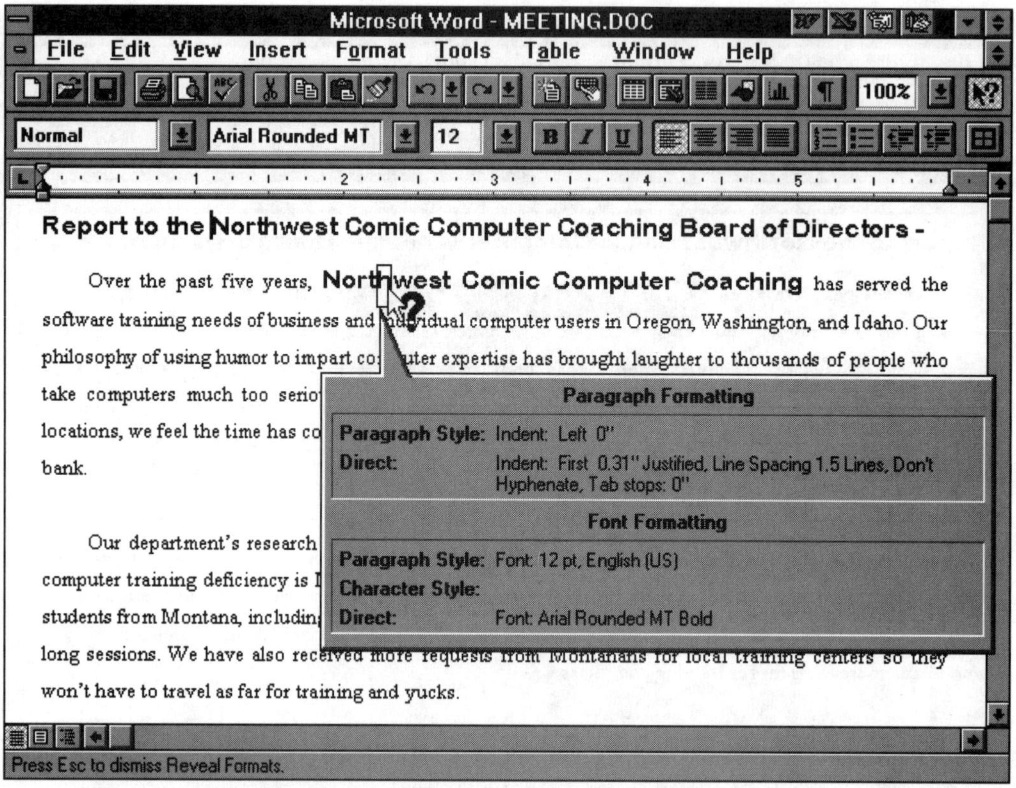

FIGURE 6–11 The formatting information box

and then clicking on the character. A message box containing the formatting information pops up, as shown in Figure 6–11.

Setting and Using Tab Stops

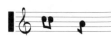

Using tab stops is one way to line up rows and columns of text. Perhaps the most common use for the Tab key in the days of typewriters was for indenting the first line of paragraphs. As discussed earlier, you're better off using the First Line Indent feature for this purpose.

Pressing the Tab key moves the insertion point to the next tab stop position. Word supplies preset tab stops every 0.5", but you can add new tab stops wherever you like by clicking on the Ruler where you want each new tab stop or by entering measurements in the Tabs dialog box. When you add tab stops, the preset tab stops to the left of the custom tab stop are cleared, but other custom tab stops are preserved.

CAUTION

Never use the Spacebar to line up columns. You may, with great difficulty, be able to make your columns appear to be lined up on the screen. But, when you print your document, the results will surprise you. Using the Spacebar also limits your ability to edit the spaces between columns. For example, if you had 20 rows and 4 columns and you wanted to add an extra 0.25" between columns, you would have to make adjustments in 60 places. If you used tab stops, you could modify just three tab stop positions.

There are four types of tab stops: left-aligned, right-aligned, centered, and decimal. A left-aligned tab stop is just like the tab on a typewriter. When you move to a left-aligned tab stop and start typing, the text flows from the tab stop position to the right. Text typed at a right-aligned tab stop flows to the left. Text typed at a centered tab stop is centered at the tab stop position. Decimal tab stops are useful when you have to enter a column of numbers and want them to line up on their decimal points.

The default tab type is left-aligned. To add a left-aligned tab stop, simply click on the Ruler where you want the new tab stop located. An L-shaped mark appears on the Ruler indicating the position of the new left-aligned tab stop. To add tab stops with one of the other alignments, click on the Tab Alignment button on the far left side of the Ruler to cycle through the various alignment marks and then click on the Ruler to locate the tab.

tip

There are two things you can do in the Tabs dialog box. First, you can use a fifth type of tab stop called a *Bar tab.* A Bar tab is a vertical line inserted at the specified position. This can be useful for separating columns. It's not really a tab stop, because it's automatically inserted and you can't press the Tab key to move to it.

An even more useful option in the Tabs dialog box is the ability to add leaders to tab stops. Leaders are dots, dashes, or lines that precede a tab stop. The leader flows from the tab stop position to the preceding tab stop or the left margin, whichever it encounters first.

And here's one more little tip at no extra charge. You can open the Tabs dialog box by double-clicking on any tab marker on the Ruler.

Figure 6–12 shows some sample tabular columns. Notice the tab-stop marks on the Ruler for the different columns.

Changing or deleting tab stops is as easy as changing the indents on the Ruler. To change a tab stop's position, just drag it left or right on the Ruler. As you drag, you'll see a vertical guide just like the guide you see when dragging indent markers. To delete a tab stop, just drag it down off the Ruler and release the mouse button.

Don't forget that tab stops are part of paragraph formatting. The new tab stops will apply only to the paragraphs that were selected when the tab stops were added or to new paragraphs added after the tab stop changes if those new paragraphs don't have their own tab stop settings.

tip

Word provides other options for setting up rows and columns. In fact, the other methods are often preferable since they provide greater flexibility. You can use the Table feature within Word, or if you need the functionality of the Excel spreadsheet, you can insert actual worksheets into your Word documents. Chapter 9 covers the Table feature.

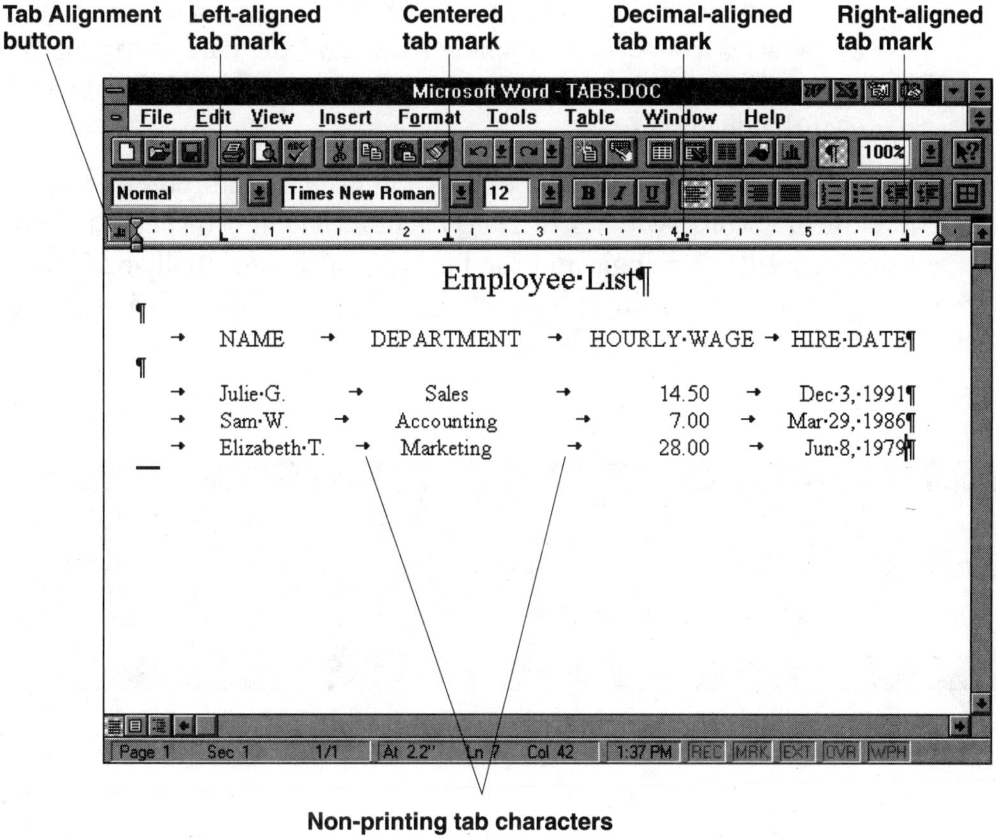

FIGURE 6–12 Tabular text with non-printing characters displayed

Adding Headers, Footers, and Page Numbers

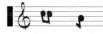

Headers and footers are the text or graphics elements you want to appear on each page of your document. You can also have headers and footers on just odd or even pages. Headers usually appear at the top of

the page, and footers appear at the bottom. For example, you might use a header to insert your company name and the date at the top of each page. You could use a footer to insert the page number or the name of the document.

Choose View➢Header and Footer to add headers and footers to your document. Word switches to Page Layout view and displays a non-printing header rectangle and the Header and Footer toolbar to facilitate creating and editing headers and footers. Figure 6–13 shows a header entered in the header area.

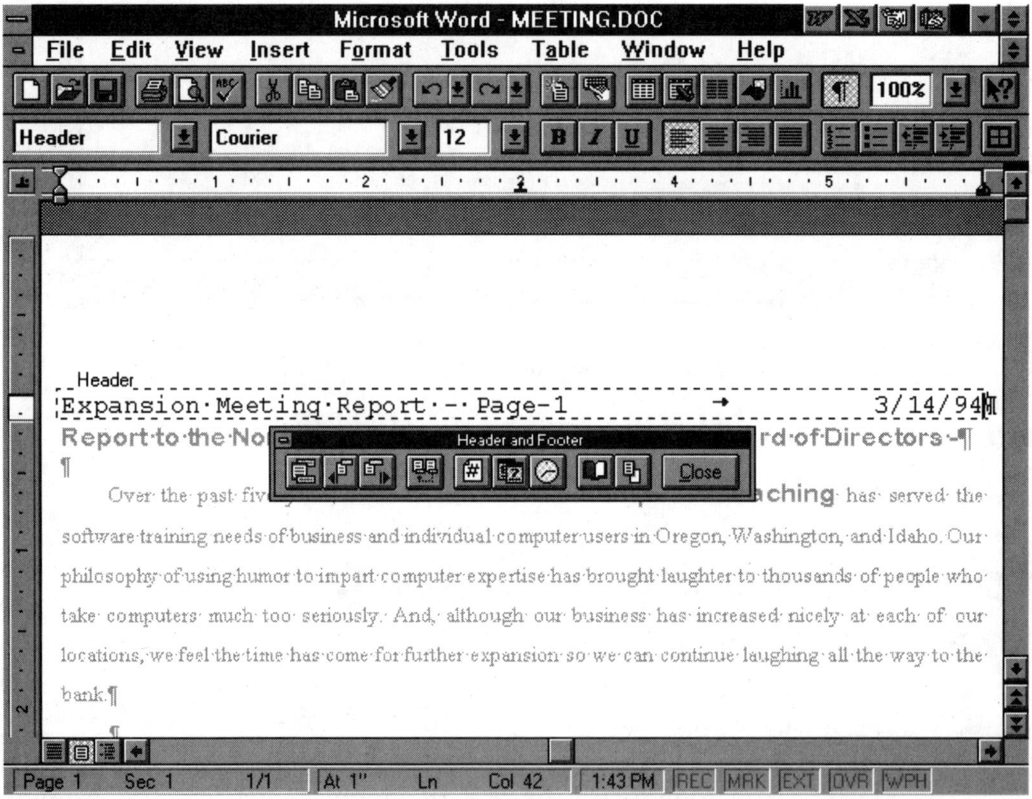

FIGURE 6–13 The header area and Header and Footer toolbar

While you are adding or editing a header or footer, the other text in the document is dimmed. If you want it hidden entirely, you can click on the Show/Hide Document Text button on the Header and Footer toolbar.

You can add any text or graphics you like to a header or footer using the same methods you would use in the body of the document. If you want to add the page number, date, or time to a header or footer so these items appear on every page that has the header or footer, click on the appropriate button on the Header and Footer toolbar.

When you click on the Close button on the Header and Footer toolbar, the header or footer will be added to the document and you will be switched back to the view you were in before you started adding the header or footer. If you were already in Page Layout view, your header or footer will be visible but dimmed. If you want to edit the dimmed header or footer, the easiest way is to double-click on it to display the header of footer rectangle.

If you were in another view, the headers and footers won't be displayed, but you can view them by switching to Page Layout view or choosing View➢Header and Footer again.

You can add page numbers to your document without using the Headers and Footers dialog box. Choose Insert➢Page Numbers to display the Page Numbers dialog box, as shown in Figure 6–14.

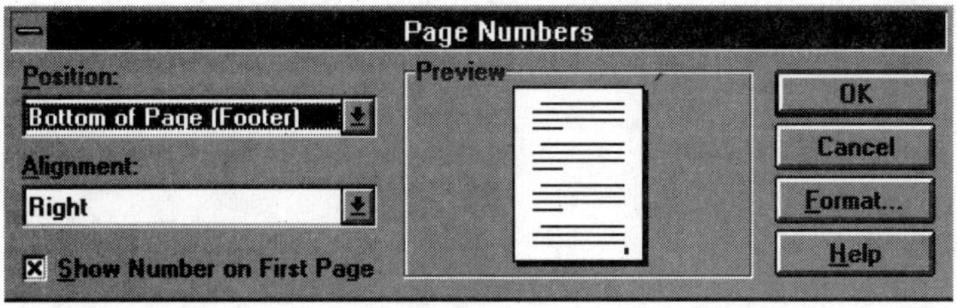

FIGURE 6–14 The Page Numbers dialog box

Page numbers inserted in a document with the Page Numbers dialog box are also placed in headers or footers. Use the Position drop-down list to specify whether you want the page number to appear at the top of the page (in a header) or at the bottom (in a footer). Use the Alignment drop-down list to specify the location of the page number within the header or footer. You can also choose the page number format by clicking on the Format button.

note Because headers and footers affect the entire document, it doesn't matter where your insertion point is when you create them, unless your document has more than one section, in which case you can specify a different header and footer for each section.

If you want different headers or footers on odd and even pages or on the first page, click on the Page Setup button on the Header and Footer toolbar to display the Page Setup dialog box and click in the Different Odd and Even or Different First Page check box.

Summary

In this chapter, you learned to apply character and paragraph formatting to transform your document into a thing of beauty.

The next chapter explains another powerful method of formatting—styles.

7

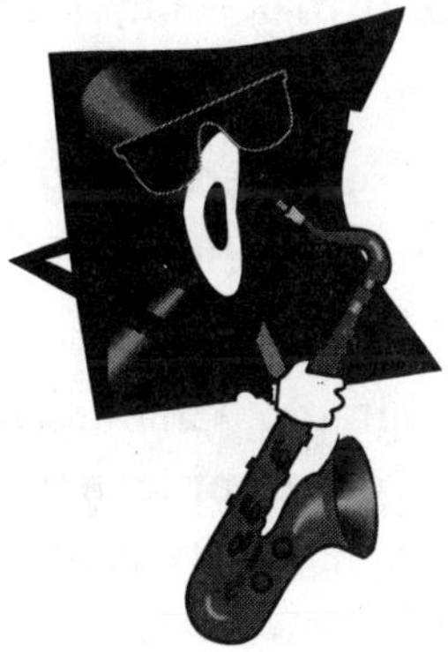

Word for Windows— Formatting with Styles

Word's Styles feature gives you the ability to format various elements of your documents easily and consistently. With styles, applying many formatting attributes to an element of your document is as easy as applying one attribute manually. But perhaps the best feature of styles is the ease with which they allow you to change the formatting of all the portions of your documents with that style applied.

Styles Overview

In Chapter 6 you learned how to apply formatting attributes directly to elements in your documents. Styles provide another way to apply and copy formatting. A style is simply a named combination of character or paragraph formats. Styles are such an integral part of Word that you've been using styles already, even if you weren't aware of it. Everything you enter in Word is based on a style. If you don't specify any other style, your document will be formatted in a style called *Normal.* That doesn't mean that other styles are abnormal. They just have different names.

You can tell which style you're using by positioning the insertion point in the text whose style name you want to determine and looking in the Style box on the Formatting toolbar.

Word has two types of styles: character and paragraph. Character styles do exactly what you would expect. You could, for example, have a character style called Cool Text that specified a font, font style, and font size. You could apply the style to selected text by choosing Cool Text from the Style list on the Formatting toolbar or by choosing Format➢Style and clicking on the style name and then on the Apply button.

Paragraph styles, on the other hand, can include character as well as paragraph formatting. So, if paragraph styles can include character formatting, why would you ever want to use character styles? Simple. The character formatting in a paragraph style is applied to the entire paragraph. In other words, suppose you create a paragraph style whose only formatting is bold character formatting. When you apply this style, all the text in the selected paragraph or paragraphs will be bold. You can apply a character style to just the amount of text you select within a paragraph.

There are tremendous advantages to using styles to apply formatting. Once you've created some text with all the formatting attributes you want, you can use the Format Painter to copy the formatting as long as the document is active. But, if you want to apply the same formatting to portions of future documents in future Word sessions, a style makes doing so a snap.

Styles also make it exceptionally easy to make global changes. Let's say you have created styles for all the elements you plan to incorporate in your company documents. The company design guru then decides that the font, indents, line spacing, and other formatting attributes should be changed—not only for future documents, but for existing documents that are reprinted on a regular basis.

If all the formatting had been applied directly to the various elements of the documents, it would be a painstaking and time-consuming process to replace all the old formatting with the new, improved formatting. You would also have to keep track of which documents had been changed as you opened them in the future.

If you had applied the formatting with styles, you could simply edit the styles to include the new formatting and—presto change-o—all existing documents would be automatically changed to reflect the new style definitions as they were opened.

Automatic Styles

Word includes a number of styles that are applied to certain elements of your document without any intervention on your part. Among the elements that are automatically formatted with styles are headers and footers, footnotes, page numbers, and headings. When you create a header, for example, you don't have to apply a style. It already has the Header style attached.

If you are creating a document with several heading levels, you don't have to apply styles to the headings as long as you let Word know which heading level you want.

tip

You can easily create an outline in Word using Outline view and the Outline toolbar. If you just want to create headings, type the heading text and press Alt-Shift-← to make it a level-1 heading or Alt-Shift-→ to make it a level-2 heading.

Pressing Alt-Shift-→ again makes a level-2 heading a level-3 heading. (The same keystrokes would make a level-3 heading a level-4 heading.) You can press Alt-Shift-← to make a level-2 heading a level-1 heading. The bottom line is that Alt-Shift-← promotes the heading one level, and Alt-Shift-→ demotes the heading one level.

The Style name box on the Formatting toolbar displays the name of the heading style that has been applied to the text.

You are never stuck with what Word gives you when it comes to styles. All styles can be modified to meet your requirements, whether they are styles that are included with Word or ones that you create yourself.

Templates Overview

When you create a style, it is, by default, stored with the document in which you created it. This is appropriate if you want to use the style only in that particular document. However, you'll probably want to use most styles you create in a variety of documents. For this reason, you'll want to store your styles in templates.

A template is a model on which you base your documents. Just as every element of every Word document has a style, every document has a template. And, just as the default style is called Normal, the default template is also called Normal. A template can be a complex pattern that includes standard text, graphics, and any other elements you would always want in documents based on that template. A template can also be just a place to store a collection of the styles you often use when creating a certain type of document based on that template.

Templates can also contain macros and AutoText entries. Macros and AutoText will be covered in Chapter 10.

The Normal template doesn't contain any standard text or graphics. Unless you modify it, it is just the place where the Normal automatic styles are stored. It is also where you will store other styles to ensure that they will be available to all your documents. Think of the Normal template as the global template. All styles, macros, and AutoText entries that you store in Normal are available everywhere.

Word provides an assortment of templates to help you assemble many types of documents. For example, you can build new documents based on templates that contain styles specifically designed to facilitate the creation of fax cover sheets, brochures, invoices, memos, and even manuscripts.

To base a document on one of these templates, choose File➢New to display the New dialog box, as shown in Figure 7 –1.

Be sure the Document option is selected in the New portion of the dialog box and then choose the template that appears to meet your needs. As you click on each template name, the Description portion of the dialog box displays a brief description of that template. When you click on the OK button, the template opens, with all its styles and any other elements it contains available to you.

Notice that many of the template names end with the word *Wizard.* A Wizard is a template to which Word has added dialog boxes to guide you through the process of creating a particular kind of document. For example, if you choose the Newslttr Wizard, you'll be stepped through a series of dialog boxes requesting the information required to format a newsletter. Figure 7–2 shows the first Newsletter Wizard dialog box.

FIGURE 7-1 The New dialog box

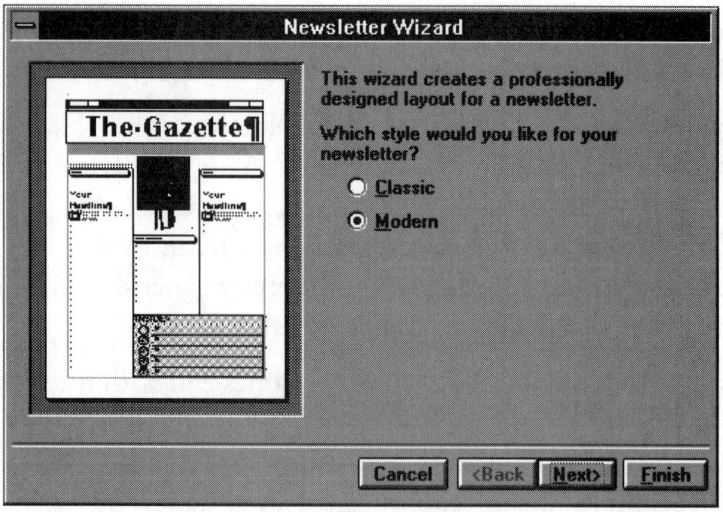

FIGURE 7-2 The first Newsletter Wizard dialog

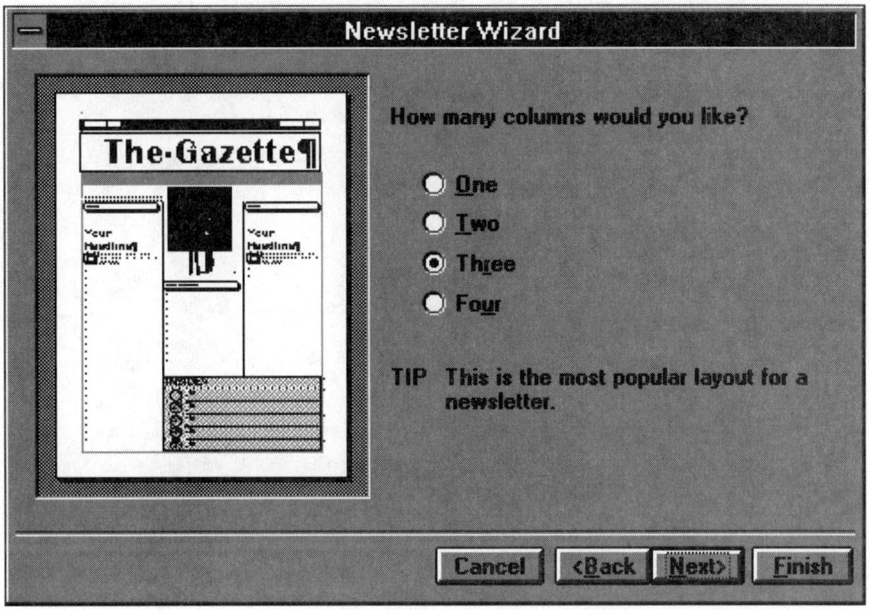

FIGURE 7–3 The second Newsletter Wizard dialog box asks for the number of columns for the newsletter.

In each dialog box (Figures 7–4 to 7–7), be sure the options are set the way you want them and then click on the Next button.

If you have to go back to a previous Wizard dialog box to change an option, you can click on the Back button. Otherwise click on the Next button.

When you reach the last dialog box, click on the Finish button to display the structure of your newsletter. You'll have to add any text and graphics you want to use, but the Wizard has given you a running start.

You can edit any of the elements of a document created with a Wizard, just as you would with any other document.

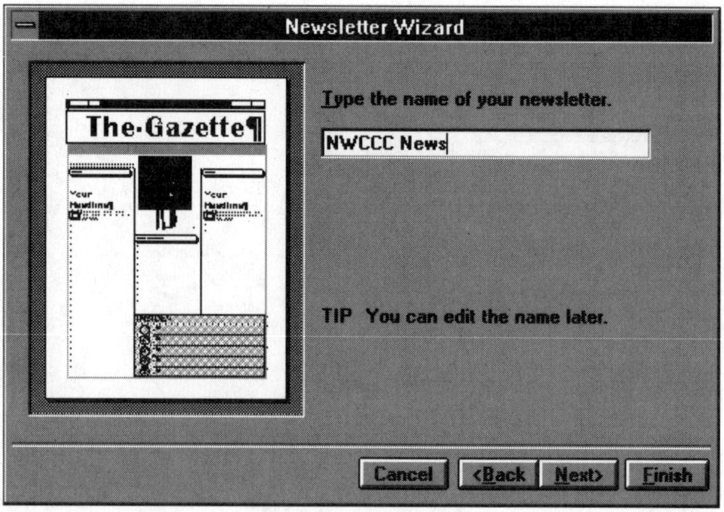

FIGURE 7–4 The third Newsletter Wizard dialog box asks for the name of the newsletter.

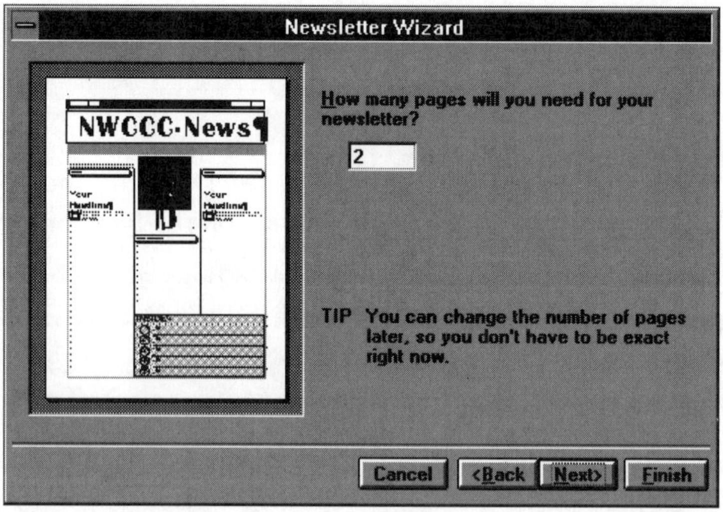

FIGURE 7–5 The fourth dialog box asks how many pages will be needed for the newsletter.

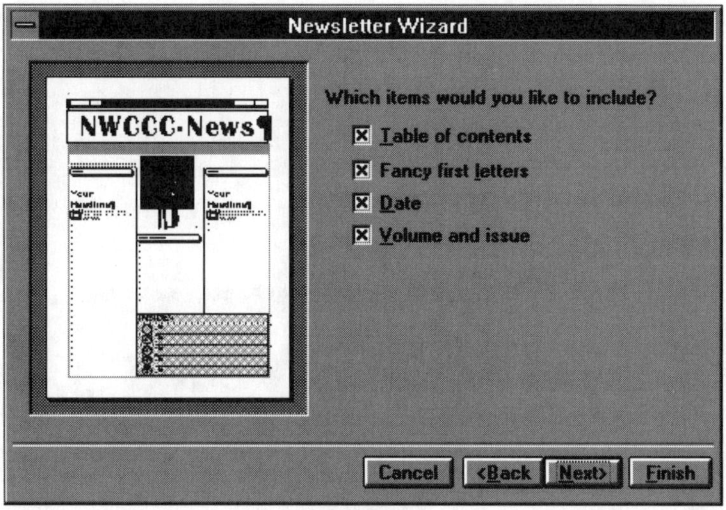

FIGURE 7–6 The fifth dialog box asks which elements to include in the newsletter.

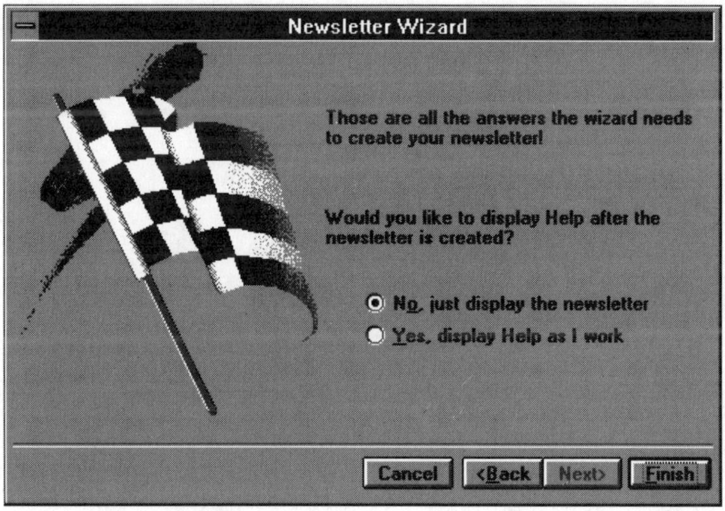

FIGURE 7–7 The final dialog box

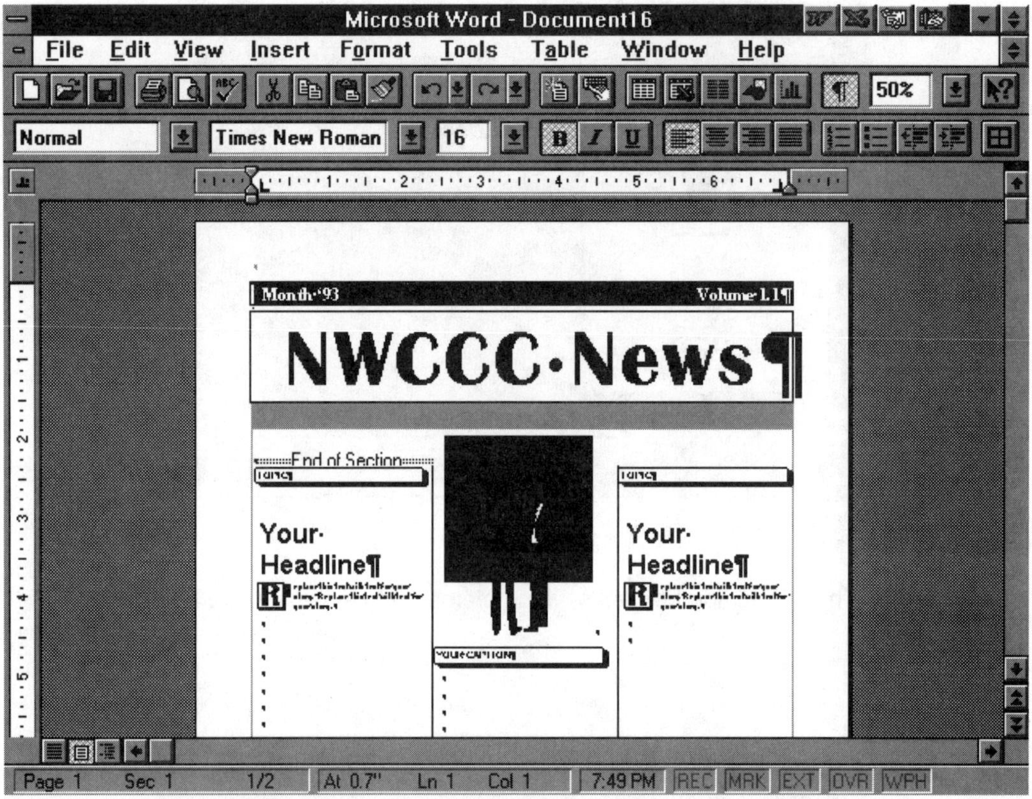

FIGURE 7–8 The structure of the newsletter

Formatting with Styles

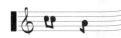

The easiest way to create a new paragraph style is to format a paragraph in your document with the attributes you want for the style, select the paragraph, click in the Style box on the Formatting toolbar (highlight the current style name), type the name of the style you want to create, and then click anywhere in the document.

The new style is now available for this document and can be applied by selecting the paragraphs to which you want to apply it and choosing its name from the Style list by clicking on the Style button on the Formatting toolbar. If, however, you want this style to be available for use in other documents, you must copy it to a template.

You can also create a paragraph style by using the Style dialog box, but to create a *character* style, you *must* use the Style dialog box. Choose Format➢Style to display the Style dialog box, as shown in Figure 7–9.

Click on the New button to display the New Style dialog box, as shown in Figure 7–10.

Enter a name for the new style in the Name box. Then choose whether you want to create a Paragraph or Character style in the Style Type drop-down list. If you already have another style that includes

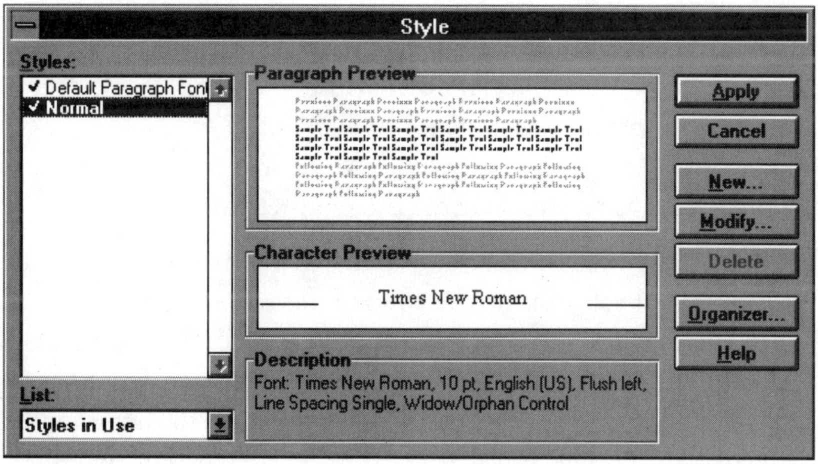

FIGURE 7–9 The Style dialog box

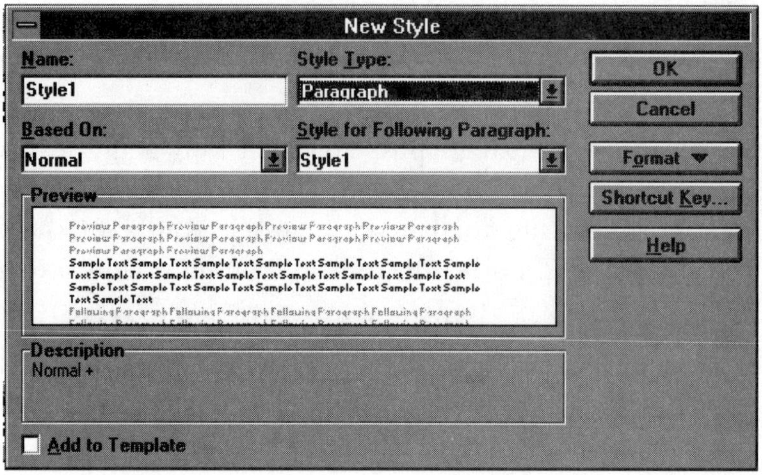

FIGURE 7–10 The New Style dialog box

most of the attributes you want to use for your new style, choose that in the Based On drop-down list.

If you are creating a paragraph style, you can specify a Style For Following Paragraph. This can be a terrific aid when you want to use a style that applies special formatting—say, for a chapter title—but want to return to the Normal style or some other body text style after you press Enter. This way, you don't have to specify a different style name after using the style for the chapter title.

One of the most important items in the dialog box is the Add To Template check box in the lower-left corner. If you leave this check box unchecked, the new style you create will be available only for the document you are currently working in. If you want the style to be available for all documents based on the current document's template, make sure this check box is checked. If the current document is based on the Normal template, the style will be available to all future documents.

If you don't add the style to the template, or if the template you add it to isn't one you regularly use, you can use the Organizer dialog box—available by clicking on the Organizer button in the Style dialog box—to copy styles to other templates.

The final step in creating a new style is to specify the formatting attributes for the style. Click on the Format button and choose the category of formatting (Font, Paragraph, Tabs, and so on) to display the dialog box for that type of formatting. Use the formatting dialog boxes the same way you would if you were directly formatting the document.

After choosing the formatting attributes for the style, the Preview portion of the dialog box displays an example of how the style will affect text, and the Description portion of the dialog box lists all the formatting you've chosen, as shown in Figure 7–11.

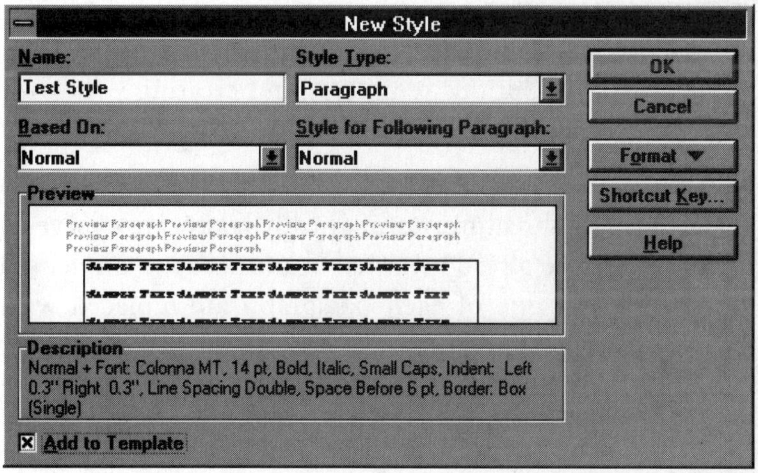

FIGURE 7–11 The New Style dialog box with the Test Style defined

Notice in the Description area, that the style description starts with the name of the style on which the new style is based. If you didn't choose a style to base the new style on, it's based on the Normal style.

CAUTION

You can assign a shortcut key to make it easier to apply styles you use often, but I suggest you avoid this feature until you are thoroughly familiar with the shortcut keys Word has already assigned to various features.

If you do want to assign a shortcut key, click on the Shortcut Key button in the New Style or Modify Style dialog box and press the shortcut key combination you want to assign. If that combination is already assigned to a feature or style, a Currently Assigned To message will appear. However, Word will let you go ahead and assign the shortcut key to the style without further warning, potentially removing a convenient shortcut you already had. So, be careful.

Automatic Formatting

In addition to formatting your documents with the styles that Word includes with its various templates and creating your own styles, you can let Word apply styles and other formatting for you with the AutoFormat feature.

The AutoFormat feature automatically takes care of several formatting *faux pas* that I've already warned against. For example, spaces used to indent the first line of each paragraph are replaced with paragraph indents, extra paragraph marks are placed between paragraphs, and symbol representations such as (C) and (TM) are replaced with the proper © and ™ symbols.

There are two ways to use the AutoFormat feature. When you click on the AutoFormat button on the Standard toolbar, Word analyzes your document and makes whatever changes it deems appropriate. If you want the opportunity to review the formatting changes Auto-Format wants to make, choose Format➢AutoFormat and click on the OK button. Word presents you with dialog boxes, allowing you to review the suggested changes and accept or reject some or all of them. You can also invoke the Style Gallery to apply the style definitions in another template to your document.

CAUTION

Although the AutoFormat feature can make formatting and applying styles to your document easy and painless, Word can only make a best guess as to what you had in mind for the formatting of your document. Since it often guesses incorrectly, you could actually save time by taking care of the formatting yourself.

If you do decide to use the AutoFormat feature, you'll find it more manageable and less confusing if you understand how to apply and change the formatting directly and with styles.

Of course, if you use AutoFormat on a document and you are horrified by the results, simply choose Edit➢Undo AutoFormat, and your document will revert to is original state.

Summary

In this chapter, you learned to multiply Word's formatting power by using styles. As your Word proficiency increases, you may wonder how you ever lived without styles.

The next chapter covers Word's robust proofing tools, which help you ensure that your documents are free of spelling and grammatical errors and help you find alternative words to make your documents more interesting and persuasive.

8

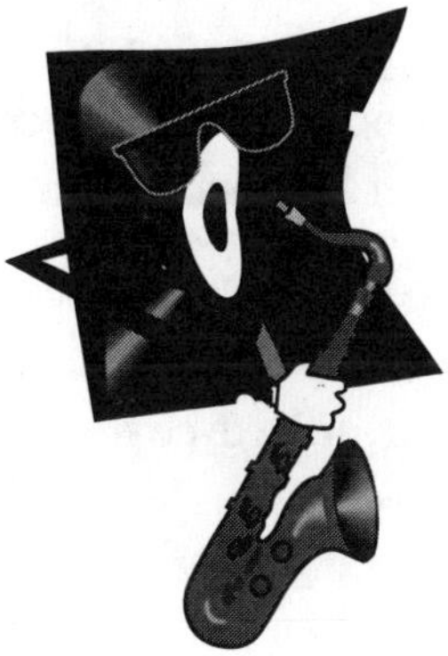

Word for Windows—Proofing Your Work

It doesn't matter how wonderful your document looks if it has spelling or grammatical errors. Your reader will usually assume that you didn't put much thought into the document, and he or she won't either. In addition to making sure the document is technically correct, it's critical that each word in the document be the best choice to convey what you have in mind.

Word proofing tools give you all the ammunition you need to ensure that your document not only looks right, but is right.

Using the Speller

Nothing attracts the wrong kind of attention to your document faster than spelling errors. With Microsoft Office, there's no excuse for most spelling errors. Each of the Office programs uses the same spell-checking system to catch misspelled words and typos.

To start the spell checker, click on the Spelling button on the Standard toolbar or choose Tools➢Spelling. If text is selected, just the selected text will be checked for spelling errors. When Word finishes checking the selected text, however, you'll be presented with a dialog box asking if you want to check the remainder of the document. If no text is selected, the entire document will be checked.

When Word checks spelling, it compares each word in your document with the list of words in its dictionary. If there is no word in the dictionary that matches a word in the document, Word correctly assumes that the word might be misspelled and presents the Spelling dialog box, as shown in Figure 8–1.

The suspect word is selected in your document to draw your attention to it, and it is entered in the Not In Dictionary text box. If Word has suggestions for correctly spelled words that might be what you had in mind, those appear in the Suggestions list; the most likely candidate appears in the Change To text box.

You have several options. If the word in question is actually spelled correctly, as might be the case with an industry-specific term or a person's name, you can click on the Ignore button to have Word leave the word alone. If, however, the same spelling of the word appears elsewhere in the document, Word will find and ask you about each occurrence. If you want Word to ignore all occurrences of this word, click on Ignore All.

If the word is one you use regularly, and you don't want to bother telling Word what to do with it in future documents, you may want

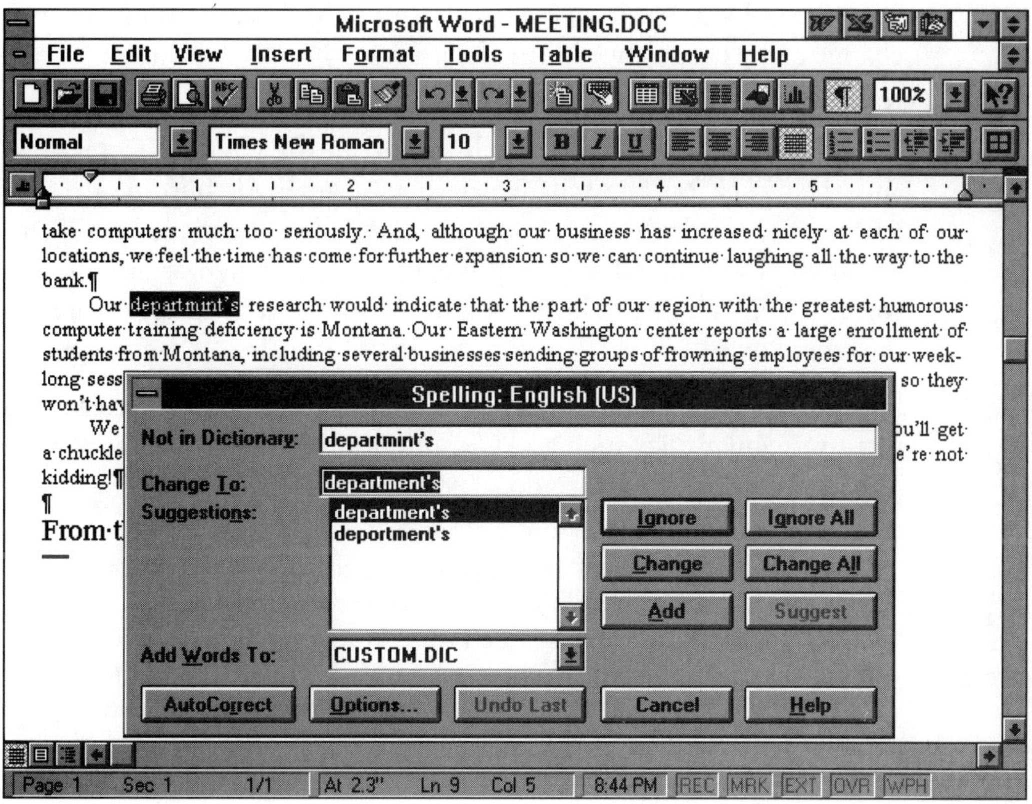

FIGURE 8–1 The Spelling dialog box

to add it to the dictionary. When you click on the Add button, the word is added to a separate custom dictionary. Although you can have more than one custom dictionary, it generally is most convenient to store all your added words in a single custom dictionary, unless you have a huge number of words to add or are using one of the third-party add-on dictionaries available for Word.

If the selected word is, in fact, incorrectly spelled and one of the suggestions is the correct alternative, click on the correct suggestion, if it isn't already in the Change To box, and then click on the Change button to change only this occurrence or the Change All button to change every occurrence in the document.

If the word is spelled incorrectly but Word offers no suggestions or no correct suggestions, simply edit the word in the Change To text box and then click on the Change or the Change All button. If, after editing, the word still doesn't match any word in the dictionary, Word lets you know with a dialog box that asks if you really want to use that word. If you choose No at that point, Word gives you suggestions for the edited word.

In addition to catching possible misspellings, the spell checker alerts you to irregular case, such as *YOu,* and double words, such as *the the,* and lets you decide what to do.

CAUTION

Don't assume that, just because you spell checked your document, it is free of spelling errors. Remember that all the spell checker does is determine if each word in your document matches a word in the dictionary. Suppose you typed *too* instead of *to* or *planing* instead of *planning.* The words you entered are real words that exist in the dictionary, so Word won't catch them as misspellings. But, because of their context, they are misspelled.

If you can't rely on Word's spell checker to entirely rid your document of spelling errors, what can you do? Unfortunately, the solution is to proofread your documents even after you spell check them. If it's any comfort, the spell checker will save you time and catch spelling errors and typos you might miss.

You should also consider using the grammar checker described later in this chapter, which will catch some of these types of spelling errors.

note

The AutoCorrect button lets you add the misspelled word and its correct spelling to the list of AutoCorrect entries so the next time you type the misspelled word it will be automatically corrected. The AutoCorrect feature is covered in Chapter 10.

Using the Thesaurus

When you know the word you used in your document isn't the best possible word, but you just can't think of a good alternative, Word's thesaurus feature comes to the rescue. Word's thesaurus works like a printed thesaurus but requires much less effort on your part. You can instantly find synonyms for a word. Then, if one of the synonyms looks like a better choice, but maybe not the best choice, you can instantly find synonyms for that word.

To use the thesaurus, place the insertion point in the word for which you want synonyms, or select the word, and choose Tools➢Thesaurus to display the Thesaurus dialog box with the list of synonyms, as shown in Figure 8–2.

The word you've looked up is selected and also entered in the Looked Up box. The word's meaning and its part of speech are displayed in the Meanings list. If the word has several meanings, they are all listed. The Meanings list may also have an Antonyms or Related Words entry so that you can look up words with opposite meanings and other related words.

If you see an alternative word in the Replace With Synonym list and you want to replace the selected word with it, click on it (if it isn't already highlighted), and then click on Replace. If you want synonyms for one of the words in the Replace With Synonyms or the Meanings list, click on the word, and then click on the Look Up button, or you can just double-click on the word.

tip A printed thesaurus doesn't have synonyms for every word in the dictionary, and neither does Word's thesaurus. If you try to find synonyms for a word and the thesaurus draws a blank, try to think of a synonym, even if it's a worse choice for your document. Then enter it and use the thesaurus to find synonyms for that word. You may get lucky and find just the right word.

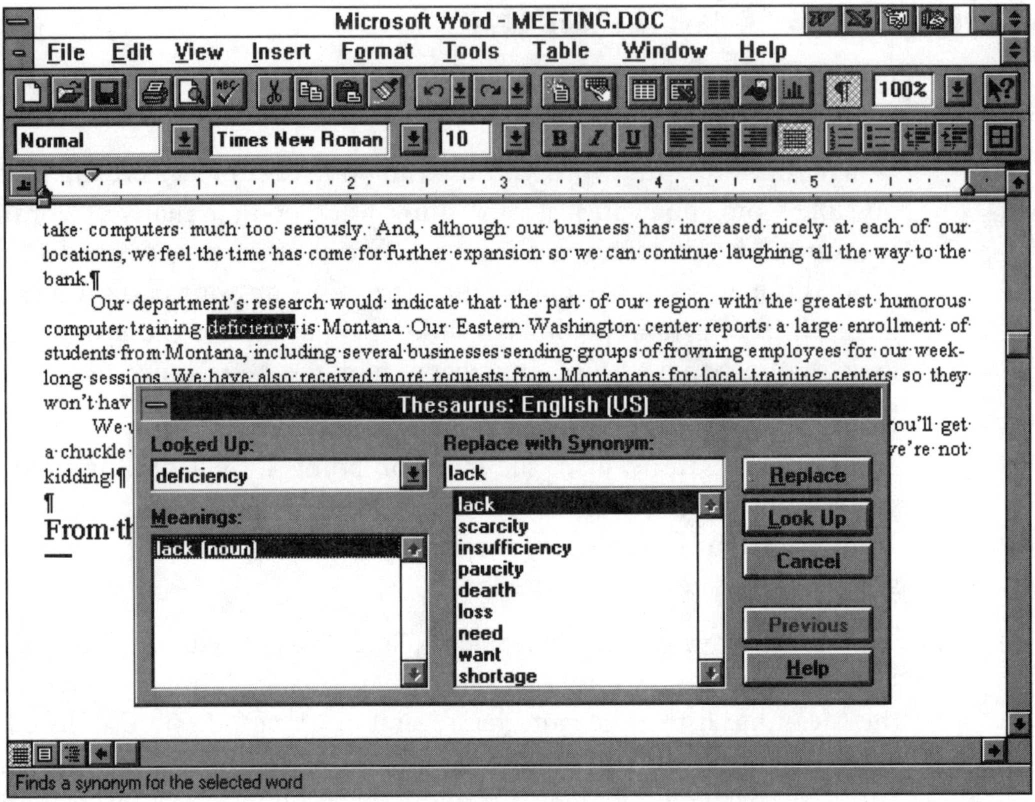

FIGURE 8–2 The Thesaurus dialog box

Using the Grammar Checker

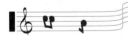

Word's grammar checker can help you catch myriad grammatical problems and even help you determine how easy the document is to read. The grammar checker can check for such problems as run-on sentences and sentence fragments, subject-verb agreement, double negatives, punctuation errors, and sexist usage.

tip If you are going to use the grammar checker, there's no need to use the spell checker first. The grammar checker can check for spelling errors while checking for grammatical errors. In fact, it uses the same dictionary and dialog boxes that the spell checker uses.

To start the grammar checker, choose Tools➢Grammar. As with the spell checker, if text is selected, just the selected text will be checked. However, when Word finishes checking the selected text, you'll be presented with a dialog box asking if you want to check the remainder of the document. If no text is selected, the entire document will be checked.

When Word starts checking the document, it first checks sentences for spelling errors, unless the spell-checking option has been disabled, and then it checks for grammatical errors. If a spelling error is found, you'll see the same Spelling dialog box you see when you spell check a document without the grammar checker. When grammatical errors are encountered (I say *when,* not *if,* because in my documents, Word always finds grammatical errors) it highlights the sentence containing the problem and displays the Grammar dialog box, as shown in Figure 8–3.

Notice that, in the example, the grammar checker spotted what amounts to a spelling error that the spell checker wouldn't catch. In this case it was smart enough to figure out that *departments* should be *department's* in the context of the sentence. Pretty amazing.

The problem sentence is shown in the Sentence portion of the dialog box with the problem word or phrase displayed in red if you have a color monitor. The Suggestions portion of the dialog box may give a suggestion for correcting the problem. If you want an explanation of the type of problem the grammar checker is attempting to fix, click

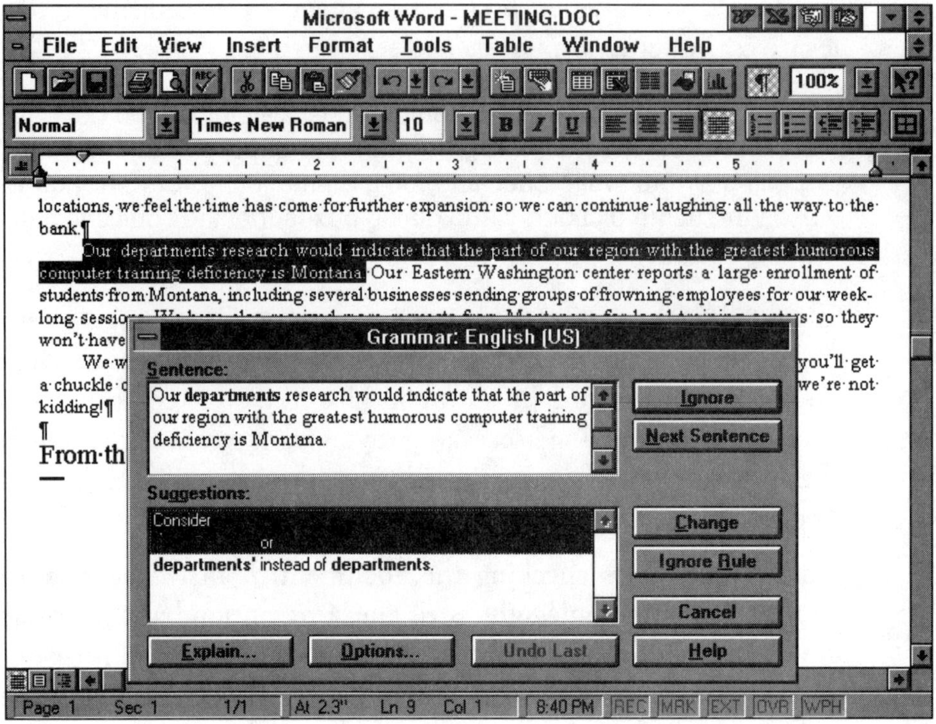

FIGURE 8–3 The Grammar dialog box

on the Explain button to display a Grammar Explanation box, as shown in Figure 8–4.

Double-click on the Grammar Explanation box's Control-menu box to remove it.

After you've examined the problem and the suggestion, you have several options. To leave the highlighted text the way it is, click on the Ignore button. The grammar checker will move on to the next problem word or phrase, even if it's in the same sentence. If you want to leave the entire sentence the way it is—even if more problems are detected—click on the Next Sentence button. To correct the sentence

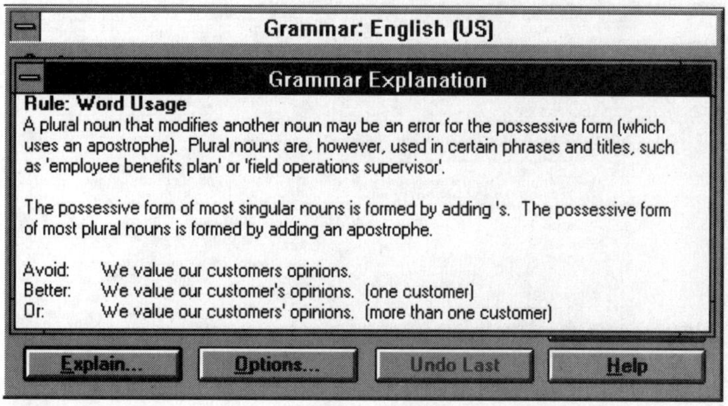

FIGURE 8–4 A Grammar Explanation box

in accordance with the suggestion, click on the Change button. If you don't want the grammar checker to stop on any other similar problems, click on the Ignore Rule button.

You may decide that a problem the grammar checker finds requires a change but you don't want to take its suggestion. You can click in the text and make the changes you want manually. When you are finished, click on the Start button (which takes the place of the Ignore button when you are editing outside the dialog box) to continue checking the document.

Grammar is not an exact science, and you may want to customize the way the grammar checker identifies potential problems in your documents. To change the grammar checking options, click on the Options button to display the Grammar portion of the Options dialog box, as shown in Figure 8–5.

It's a good idea to keep the Check Spelling and Show Readability Statistics check boxes checked. Also, you can specify that the grammar in your documents be checked based on the rules for Business Writing or for Casual Writing, or you can customize the settings even further

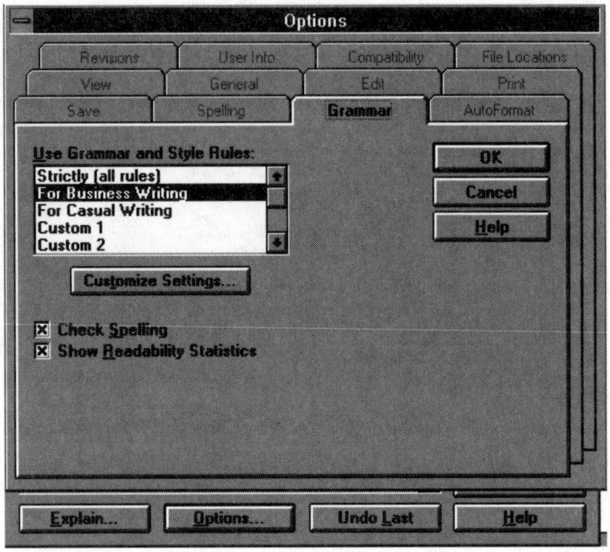

FIGURE 8–5 The Grammar portion of the Options dialog box

by selecting the Customize Setting button to display the Customize Grammar Settings dialog box, as shown in Figure 8–6.

Change the options in this dialog box to specify exactly how the grammar checker will analyze your document and which rules it will apply. Use the Explain and Help buttons to learn more about the various options. When you have finished changing the settings, click on the OK button and then on the Options dialog box OK button to accept your changes and return to the grammar checker.

When the grammar checker finishes checking your document, the Readability Statistics dialog box appears, as shown in Figure 8–7.

This dialog box gives you some potentially valuable information about your document that may lead you to do some further editing.

CAUTION

Don't rely on the grammar checker to fix all your grammatical problems. You must have a basic understanding of English before many of the grammar checker's suggestions will make

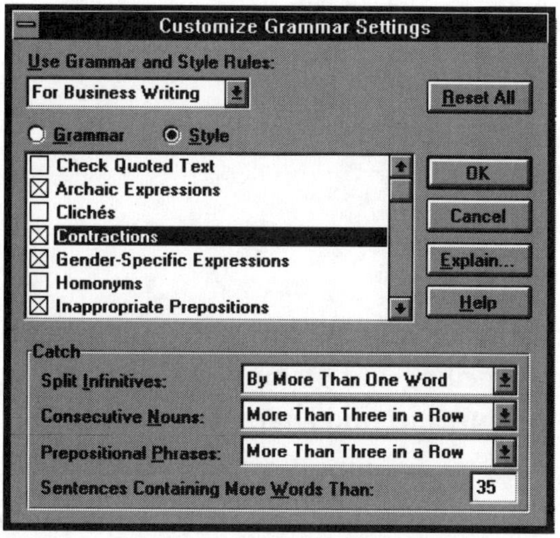

FIGURE 8–6 The Customize Grammar Settings dialog box

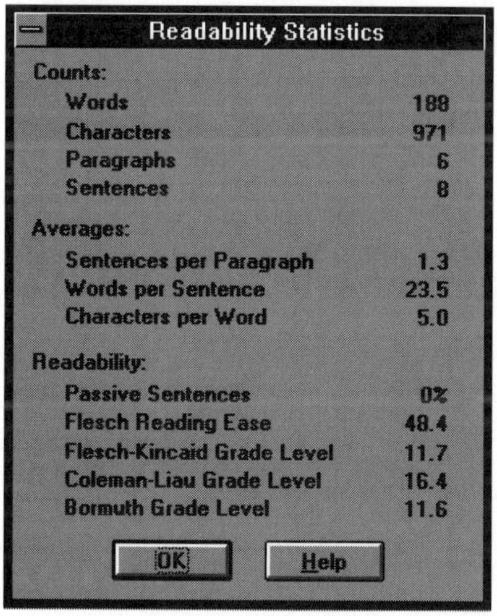

FIGURE 8–7 The Readability Statistics dialog box

sense and before you will feel confident accepting or rejecting its suggestions.

Summary

In this chapter, you learned to use Word's proofing tools to reduce the number of spelling and grammatical errors in your documents and to use the thesaurus to find alternate words.

In the next chapter I'll teach you some table manners—how to use Word's Tables feature to create rows and columns of data easily.

9

Word for Windows—Table Talk

There's no easier way to arrange text into rows and columns than by using Word's Table feature. For creating lists and parallel (side-by-side) columns, even adding graphics, the Table feature is the place to start.

Tables—An Overview

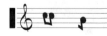

In Chapter 6, you learned to set up "tables" of data using tab stops. Certainly tab stops are useful for a variety of tasks. You'll even find occasion to set tab stops within the tables you create using Word's Table feature. You'll probably find that working with tables is much easier than working with tabular data for a variety of reasons.

Tables are much like spreadsheets, so if you are familiar with a spreadsheet program such as Microsoft Excel or Lotus 1-2-3, you won't have any trouble adjusting to working with tables. In case you aren't familiar with spreadsheet programs, I'll go over a few helpful basic concepts.

A table is made up of vertical *columns* and horizontal *rows* that create a grid of *cells*. A cell is a rectangular area that is the intersection of a column and a row. It is even possible to use formulas to perform math in a table, much as you would in a spreadsheet. You even refer to cells in a table by their column letter and row number to create formulas just as you do in a spreadsheet program. Data in a table can be formatted using the same methods you would use to format any other data in a Word document.

note If tables are so much like spreadsheets, then why, you may be wondering, wouldn't it make sense just to use Excel, the spreadsheet program that comes with Office, and forget about all this table foolishness? I'm glad you asked, and I even have some answers.

First, if you are creating rows and columns of data—whether text or numbers or both—but you don't need sophisticated math capabilities, it's easier and faster to stay within Word. Even though you can bring an Excel spreadsheet into a Word document, it does add another level of complexity to the document and it puts added strain on your computer's resources. Because your computer has to work with two programs simultaneously, everything you do in the document will probably take more time. Also, Word's word-processing capabilities actually give you greater control over the formatting of tables containing primarily text data than you would have in Excel.

One of the best reasons to use and understand tables is that they make it easy to build and manage database lists for use in mail-merge operations (combining data in a database, such as names and addresses with a form letter). When you create a database list for use in mail-merge operations, it is automatically stored as a table, so understanding tables will increase your ability to work with databases in Word.

Word displays tables with gridlines (unless you turn them off by choosing Table➢Gridlines) that let you know where the rows and columns begin and end. Like the non-printing characters, the gridlines are displayed only for visual guidance; they don't print. A bit later in the chapter, you'll learn to add borders by using the AutoFormat feature. And, speaking of non-printing characters, if you have non-printing characters displayed, (paragraph and space marks, etc.) you'll see a cell marker in each cell and an end-of-row marker at the end of each row.

Constructing Tables

There are several ways to insert a table into your document. First, position the insertion point where you want to place the table. Next choose Table➢Insert Table or use the Insert Table button on the Standard toolbar. I'll show you both methods, because there are advantages to each.

To insert a table by using the Insert Table button, click on the button to display a table grid of 4 rows by 5 columns, as shown in Figure 9–1.

If you don't need a table any larger than 4 by 5, you can click in one of the grid cells to insert a table of that size. If you need a larger table, you can drag the mouse in the grid down and to the right until you expand the grid to the size table you want. The number of rows and columns will be displayed at the bottom of the grid as you drag, as shown in Figure 9–2.

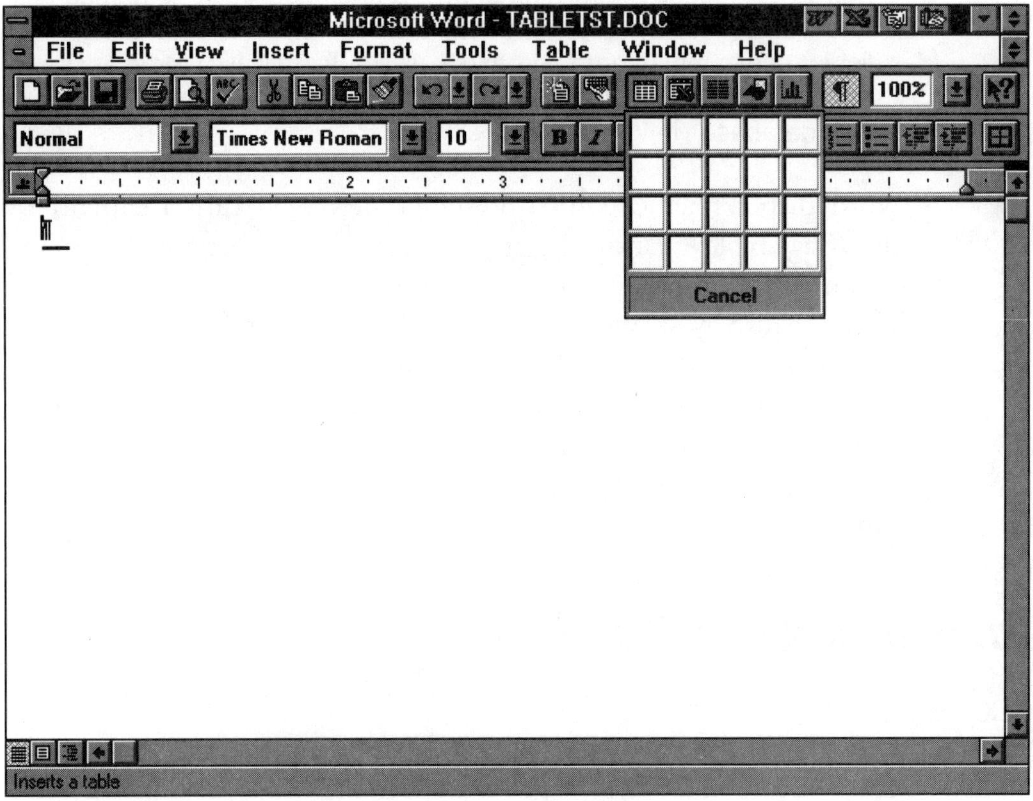

FIGURE 9–1 The initial table grid using the Insert Table button

When you release the mouse button, the table is inserted in your document, as shown in Figure 9–3.

Notice that the indent markers on the Ruler are positioned to affect only the contents of the cells in the first column (where the insertion point is), unless you have cells in multiple columns selected. If you move the insertion point to another column, the indent markers move to the new column and will affect only cells in that column.

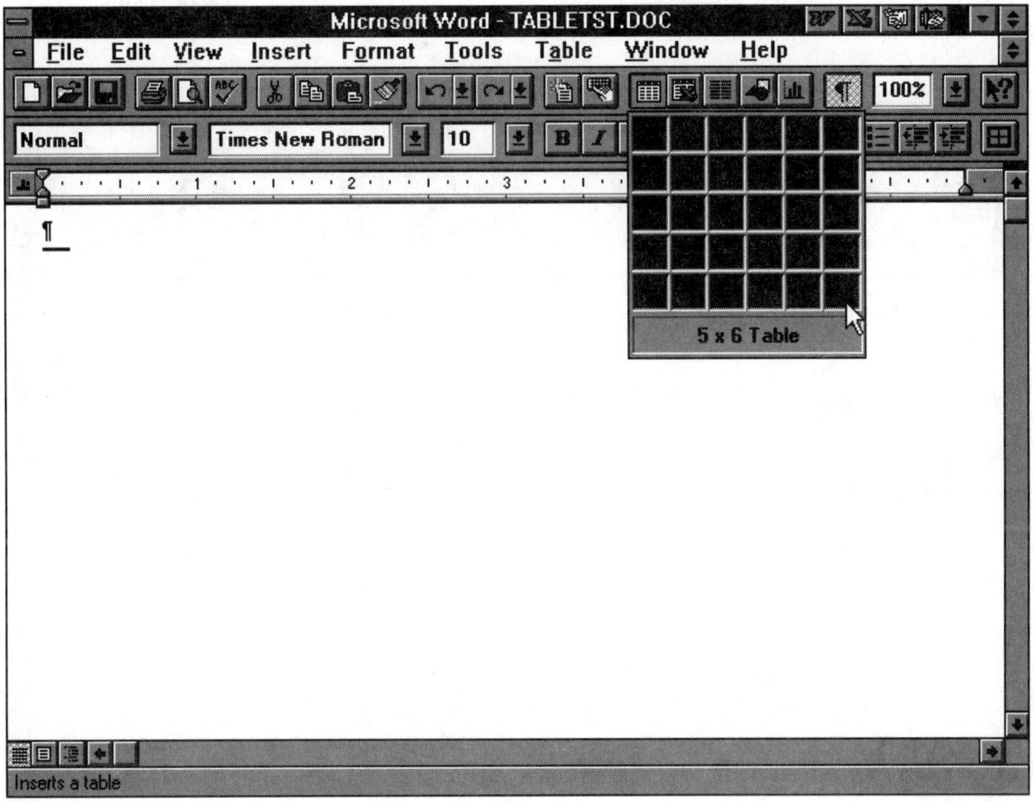

FIGURE 9–2 The expanded table grid

When you change indents for tables using the Ruler's indent markers, the indents for the cell (or selected cells) are changed. If you enter more than one paragraph of data in a cell, each paragraph can have its own indents.

note Using the Insert Table toolbar button, you can't create a table larger than the 16-row by 10-column table that will fit on your screen in standard VGA resolution. If you're using a higher screen resolution, you'll be able to create a larger table.

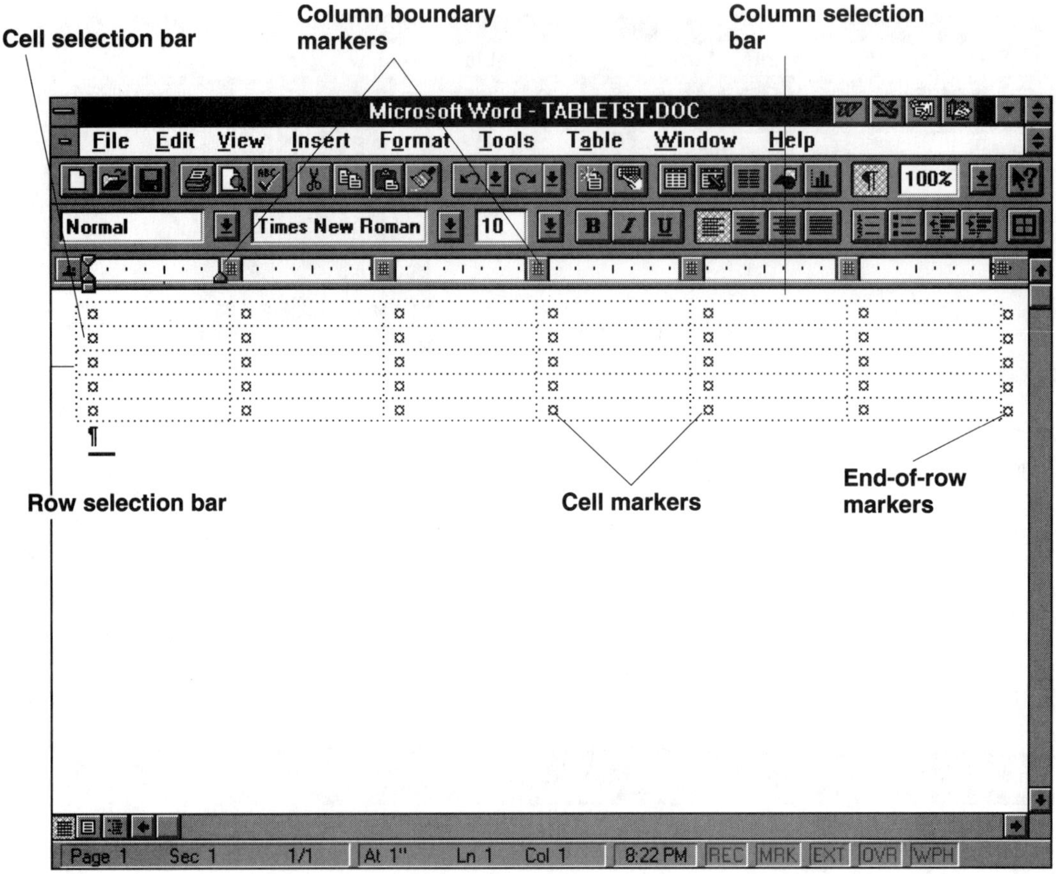

FIGURE 9–3 A 5-row by 6-column table

The way around this limitation, if you need to insert a larger table, is either to use the Table➢Insert Table command to create the size table you need or to add rows and/or columns to a smaller table inserted with the toolbar button.

To create a table using the menu commands, choose Table➢Insert Table to display the Insert Table dialog box, as shown in Figure 9–4.

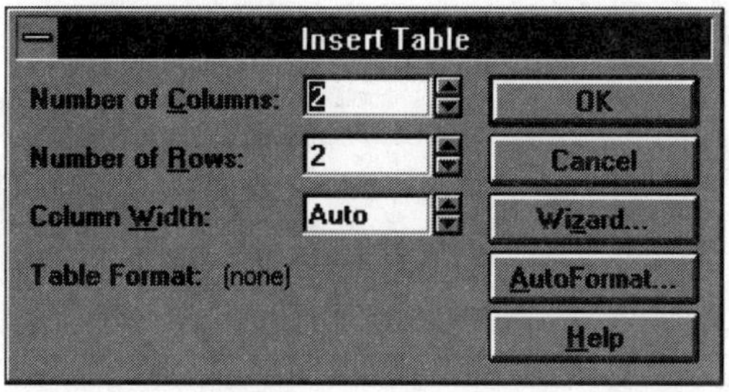

FIGURE 9–4 The Insert Table dialog box

The dialog box has a default value of 2 entered in both the Number of Columns box and Number or Rows box, but you can enter your own values for the table size you want. You can also change the column width in this dialog box. Leaving the column width set to Auto will produce columns whose width is adjusted to fit all of them on the screen.

If you change only the number of columns and rows in this dialog box, the table that appears on the screen will look just like one inserted using the toolbar button. However, you have a couple of interesting alternatives to consider before inserting the table.

If you want to be stepped through the process of creating and formatting a table, you can click on the Wizard button to invoke the Table Wizard. The Table Wizard lets you choose options for the table's style, headings, type of contents, and format. Use the Table Wizard dialog boxes just as you did with the Newslttr Wizard, covered in Chapter 7.

If you don't care to go through the Wizard's step-by-step table creation process but you do want to take advantage of some automatic formatting, you can click on the AutoFormat button to apply one of the predefined table formats. The Table AutoFormat dialog box appears, as shown in Figure 9–5.

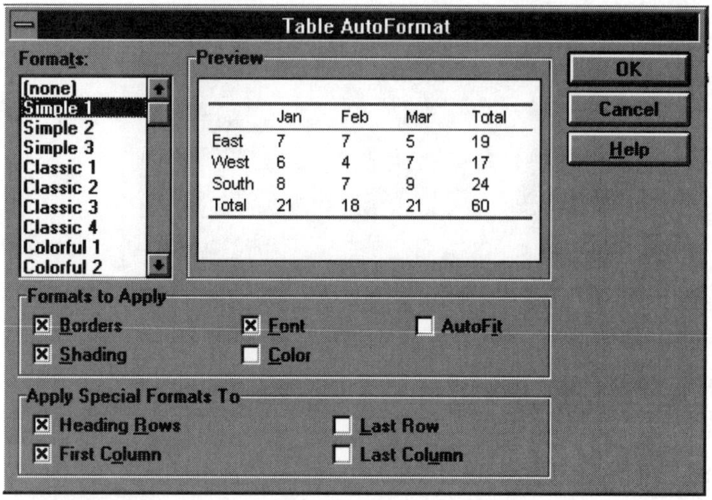

FIGURE 9–5 The Table AutoFormat dialog box

Click on any of the formats in the Formats list and choose any of the options in the Formats to Apply and Apply Special Formats To portions of the dialog box. The Preview portion of the dialog box displays an example of a table with the specified formatting applied, as shown in Figure 9–6.

Click on the OK button in the Table AutoFormat dialog box to accept the formatting and apply it to the table.

note If you aren't sure how you want your table formatted before you create it or if you change your mind about any of the attributes AutoFormat has applied, you can use the AutoFormat feature after the table is on your screen. To apply or change the AutoFormat attributes of an existing table, choose Table AutoFormat from either the Table menu or the shortcut menu by right-clicking on the table. If you don't want Table AutoFormat to override all of your formatting, click in the check boxes at the bottom of the dialog box so that only the desired attributes are applied.

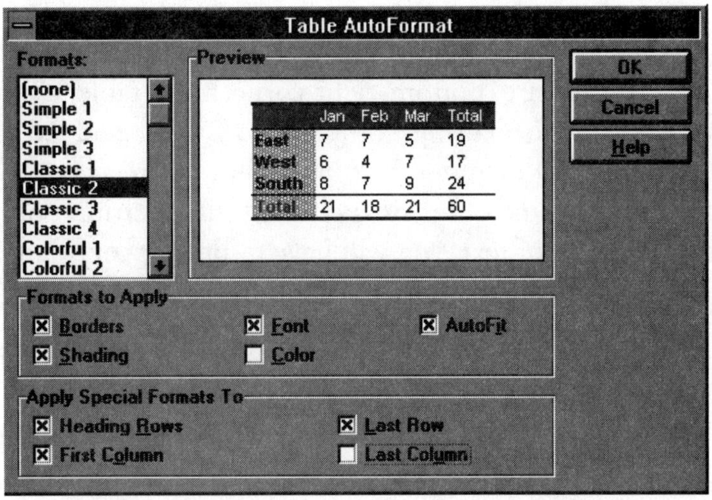

FIGURE 9–6 The Table AutoFormat dialog box with formatting options chosen and a sample in the Preview box

Entering, Editing, and Selecting Text in Tables

Once the table structure is on the screen, you can enter and format table data just as you would any other data in a Word document. To enter text in a table, move the insertion point to the cell in which you want to enter the text and start typing. You can move the insertion point by clicking in a cell or using one of several keyboard shortcuts. If your table doesn't fit on the screen, you can use the scroll bars to reposition your view of the table.

To move the insertion point a cell to the right, press Tab. To move a cell to the left, press Shift-Tab. If you press Tab while the insertion point is in the last (bottom-right corner) of a table, a new blank row with the same formatting as the last row will be added to the table. . To move up or down one row in a column, press ↑ or ↓. If there is more than one line of text in a cell and the insertion point isn't on the first or last line of text, you will have to press ↑ or ↓ more than once to move up or down a row.

To select a portion of the text in a cell, use the same method you use for selecting text outside a table. Once text is selected, you can edit or format the text using all of Word's familiar editing and formatting tools.

To format an entire cell, column, or row, you must select it. Selecting any portion of the contents of two or more cells will automatically select the entire contents of those cells. To select a single cell, click on the cell's selection bar, which appears between the cell marker and the left cell gridline.

To select a row, click on the row's selection bar. To select a column, click on the column's selection bar. You can tell when the mouse pointer is in a cell or a row selection bar because the pointer becomes an arrow angled to the right. When the pointer is in a column's selection bar, the mouse pointer becomes an arrow pointing down. You can also use commands from the Table menu to select rows, columns, or the entire table.

You can apply standard formatting to the selected portions of the table, but the easiest way to determine which specific formatting options are available is to take a look at the shortcut menu options by right-clicking on the selection.

As the text you enter in a cell reaches the margin, the words wrap to the next line just as text does outside a table. If you want to adjust a column's width to accommodate the contents of cell, the easiest way is to use the mouse to drag the column boundary markers. You don't have to point to the boundary marker to move it; you can also move it by positioning the mouse pointer over the gridline below the boundary marker so the pointer changes to a double arrow separated by two vertical lines. This is another good reason to keep the gridlines turned on.

If no cells in the column are selected, moving the column boundary markers adjusts the width of the entire column, but if one or more cells are selected, moving the column boundary marker adjusts the column width of just the selected cells.

tip If you want the column width to adjust to accommodate the longest entry in the column, you can use a feature called AutoFit. To use the AutoFit feature, select the entire table by triple-clicking in the selection bar (on the left side of the table), choose Cell Height and Width from the Table or shortcut menu, and click on the Column tab of the Cell Height and Width dialog box. Finally, click on the AutoFit button. You can also apply AutoFit to the table by using the Table AutoFormat feature discussed earlier in the chapter.

The column widths will be adjusted so the text doesn't wrap unless the width will not fit on the page.

To adjust the row height, you can use the Cell Height and Width dialog box, which is accessible from either the Table menu or the shortcut menu. You might, however, want to consider switching to Page Layout view, which displays the vertical ruler with row boundary markers. Then you can simply drag the markers with the mouse to adjust the row height.

Using Math in Tables

I won't spend much time discussing the various math functions available in tables. If you want to do any serious work with numbers, it usually makes more sense to do it with Excel. You'll learn how to bring Excel worksheets with all their functionality into Word later in the book. You'll even learn how to create Excel worksheets completely within Word.

There are times when it does make sense to use simple math operations in tables. If your table is primarily text-oriented and you just want to add a few rows or columns of numbers, this is quite easy to accomplish using table math.

To add the numbers above or to the left of a cell, position the insertion point in that cell and choose Table➢Formula to display the Formula dialog box, as shown in Figure 9–7.

Word can tell if there are numbers above or to the left of the cell and assumes that you want to add those numbers. If you don't want any special formatting for the result, just click on the OK button. You may, however, want to format the result with one of the number patterns in the Number Format list. Click on the arrow next to the Number Format list to display the available number formats, as shown in Figure 9–8.

Choose the pattern for the number format you want for your result and then click on the OK button. The result will look just like an ordinary number that you entered, as shown in the example table in Figure 9–9.

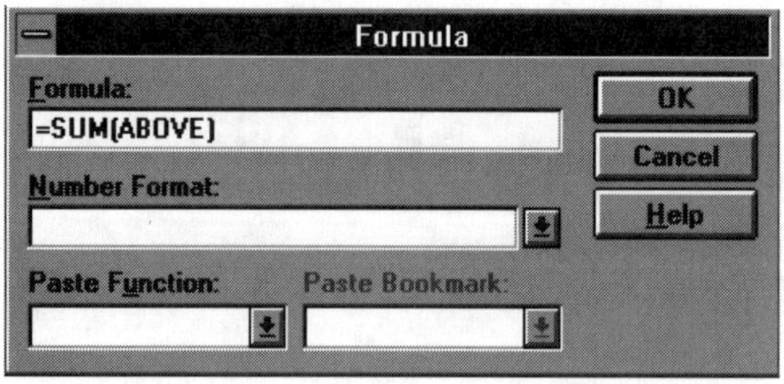

FIGURE 9–7 The Formula dialog box

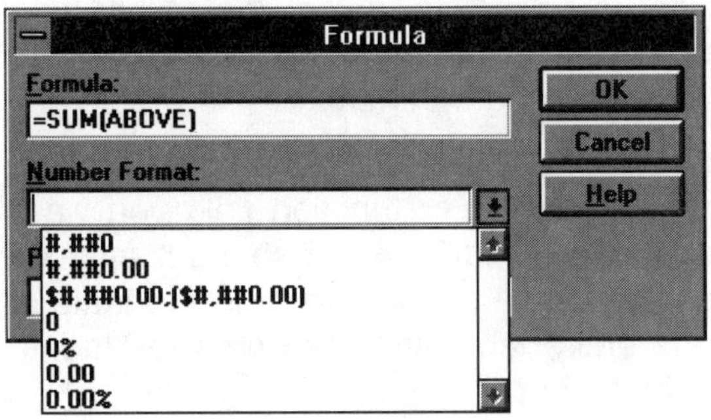

FIGURE 9–8 The Number Formats list

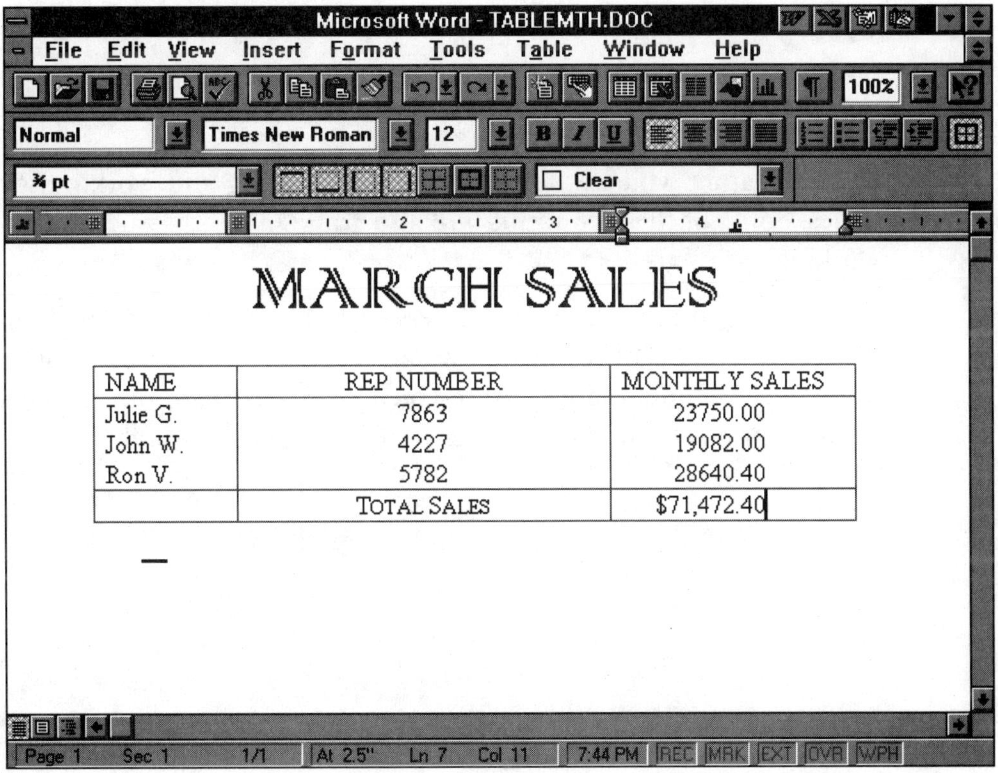

FIGURE 9–9 A table with a field that adds the total sales in the last column

CAUTION

When you use math in tables, the results don't automatically update when your numbers change. This is one reason to use Excel when working with math.

To update the results, position the insertion point in the cell that contains the formula or function field you want to update and choose Update Field from the shortcut menu or press F9. If you want to update several fields in the table at once, you can select the entire table and then choose Update Field from the shortcut menu or press F9.

You can ensure that the results of your formulas and functions are updated when you print by choosing Update Fields on the Print tab of the Options dialog box.

Summary

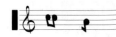

In this chapter, you learned the basics of creating and working with tables. Some of these concepts will also come in handy when we start working with Excel.

You'll find some more table pointers in the next chapter. You'll also learn to take some of the drudgery and repetition out of your work by using macros and merges. And you'll learn to customize some of Word's options to make it a better fit for your working style.

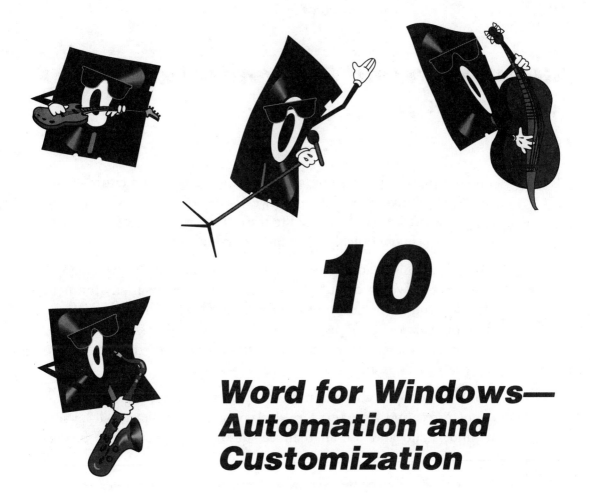

10

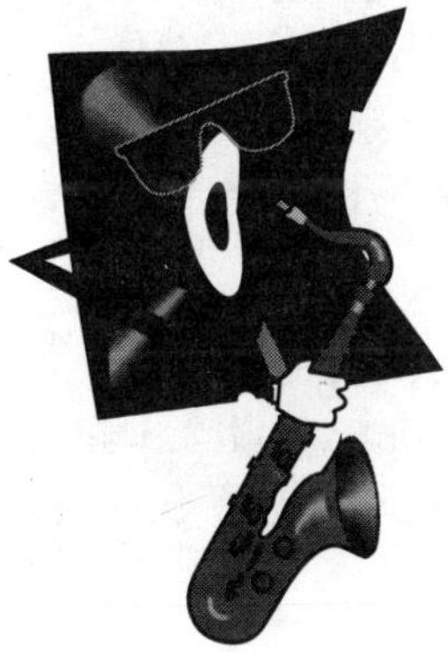

Word for Windows—Automation and Customization

If the point of using a word-processing program is to save time and allow for easier editing and formatting of the document than is possible with a typewriter, Word's abundance of automation and customization features for speeding word processing tasks is more than mere icing on the cake.

Automation and Customization—An Overview

This chapter looks at some of the many methods for cutting your word-processing work down to size. Some of the sections in this chapter won't seem to be related to the others, except that they all help you to work more quickly, efficiently, or comfortably.

My goal in this chapter is to convince you that you can change virtually any of Word's default settings and customize your environment and that you don't have to settle for doing things "their way." If you find any part of Word awkward or inefficient, rest assured that you can probably use one of the methods discussed in this chapter to correct the situation.

Some of the topics covered in this chapter, such as setting options and AutoCorrect and AutoText, are so straightforward that you'll be able to understand and use all their capabilities with very little further exploration.

Other topics, especially macros and merges, are so complex that I'll only be able to scratch the surface. Further study—and even some knowledge of programming—is necessary if you want to take full advantage of these more complex subjects. Don't let that last caveat deter you from exploring these features, even if you don't know a thing about programming and don't care to spend the time studying. Using these features with just the knowledge you'll pick up here will greatly enhance your productivity.

Customizing Word

Microsoft Word can be so thoroughly customized that I can't cover every possible option here. I have to start somewhere, however, so let's look at the customization options available through the Options dialog box. You saw the Options dialog box in Chapter 8. Now you'll have a chance to look at some of the other options available.

Changing the Location of Files

Choose Tools➢Options to display the Options dialog box, as shown in Figure 10–1.

The Options dialog box tab that is selected when you choose Tools➢Options depends on which tab was selected the last time the

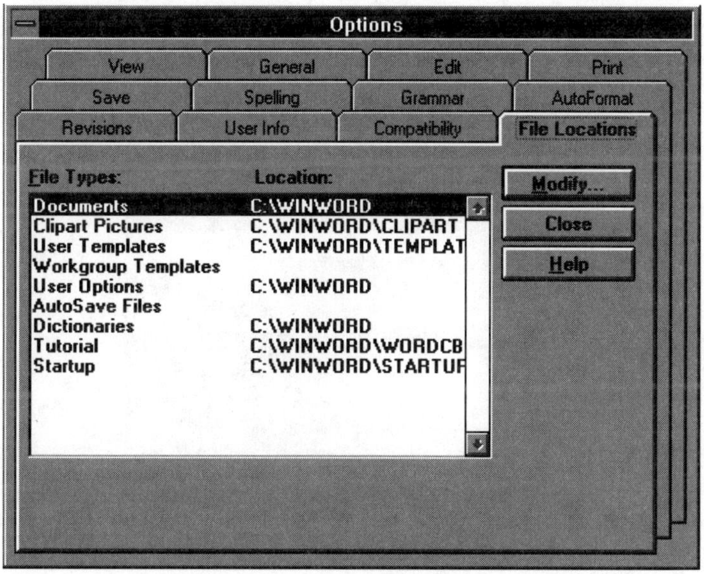

FIGURE 10–1 The File Locations tab of the Options dialog box

dialog box was closed. If the File Locations tab isn't selected, you can click on it now so you can follow along.

Changing the directories in which Word looks for various files is one of the first places you'll want to start customizing. You'll probably want to choose a directory for documents other than the default C:\WINWORD (or whatever directory you use to store your Word program files). To change a default directory, click on the file type for which you want to change the directory in the File Types list, and then click on the Modify button to display the Modify Location dialog box, as shown in Figure 10–2.

Choose the desired directory and drive, and then click on the OK button. If the directory doesn't exist, you can click on the New button and enter a name for your new directory in the Create Directory dialog box.

CAUTION

If you've saved files in the default directories and then change the default location of those files, the files will no longer show up when you try to open them. For example, if your first documents were saved in the C:\WINWORD directory and you change your

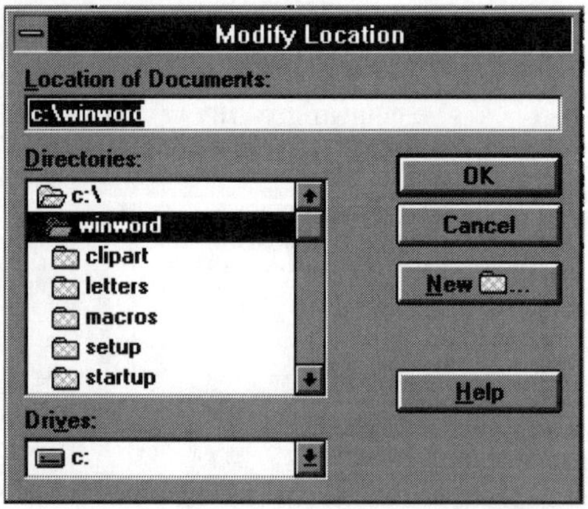

FIGURE 10–2 The Modify Location dialog box

document directory to C:\MYFILES, the saved files won't show up in the Open dialog box unless you change the directory in the dialog box.

After changing default directories, you'll probably want to move or copy files to the new directory. The most common way to move files from one directory to another is to use the File Manager program included with Windows. If you are unfamiliar with File Manager, consult the Windows documentation or one of the other Prima books on Windows.

Changing Edit Options

Click on the Edit tab to display the Edit portion of the Options dialog box, as shown in Figure 10–3.

The Edit tab of the Options dialog box provides a variety of options for changing the way you edit documents. For example, if you find it

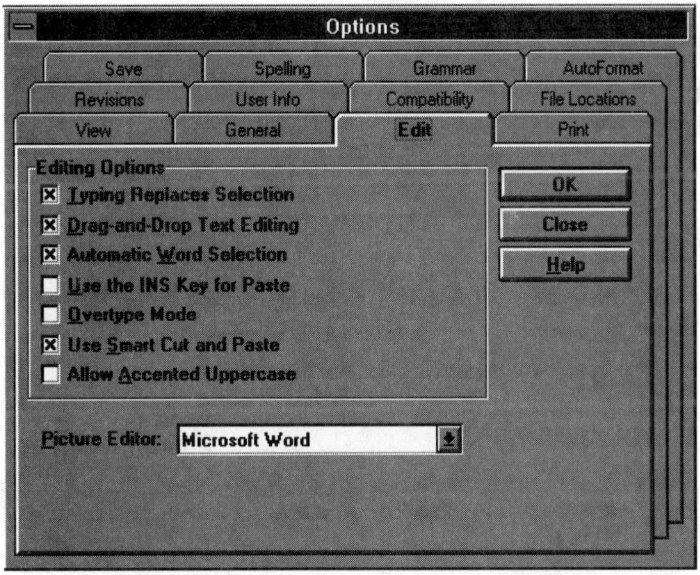

FIGURE 10–3 The Edit tab of the Options dialog box

irritating that Word selects two words as a block when you want to select just a portion of that block, you can click in the Automatic Word Selection check box to turn off that feature—although I can't think of a good reason to do so.

Another option is the default picture editor. When you edit a picture in a Word document, the original default editor is the one that comes with Word. You may, however, want to use the more powerful editor that comes with PowerPoint. By choosing the PowerPoint editor from the list, you make its tools available to you for picture editing.

Most of the other options here are self explanatory, but if you need further explanation, click on the Help button to display the help screen for a particular tab.

Changing General Options

Click on the General tab to display the General portion of the dialog box, as shown in Figure 10–4.

A couple of the options on the General tab of the dialog box are worth considering. Notice that the Recently Used Files List check box is checked by default. This is the option that causes the four most recently used files to appear on the File menu so you can open one by just clicking on its name. This is a terrific feature—so terrific, in fact, that you may want to have even more files displayed. You can change the value in the Entries box by clicking on the up or down arrow button next to the box. You can have a maximum of nine recently used files displayed.

Another option to consider is the Measurement Units. The default setting is inches. If you are more comfortable working in centimeters, points, or picas, you can change to one of those measurements.

Changing Save Options

Click on the Save tab to display the Save portion of the dialog box, as shown in Figure 10–5.

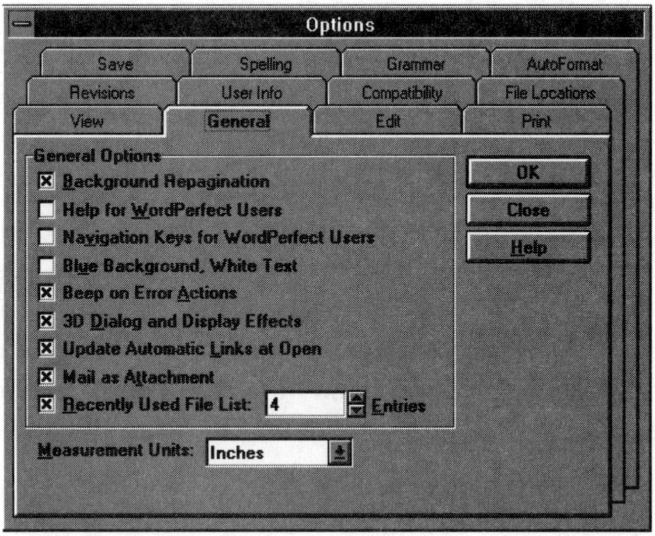

FIGURE 10–4 The General tab of the Options dialog box

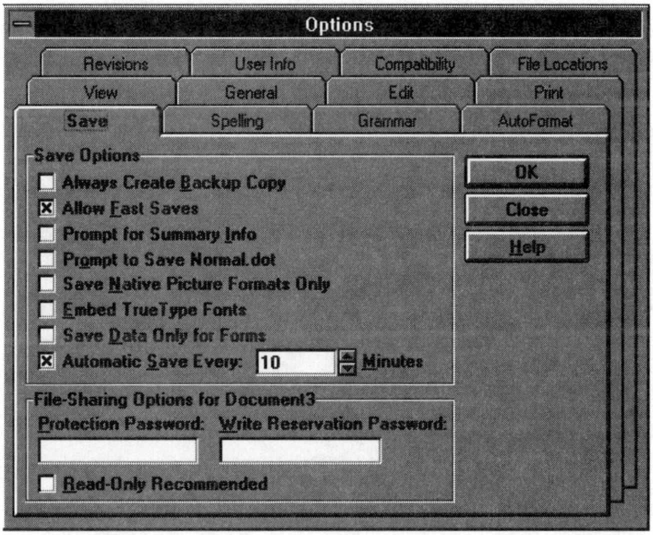

FIGURE 10–5 The Save tab of the Options dialog box

The final group of options we'll examine are the options that govern the way you save your documents. As I discussed earlier, nothing is more important than making sure that your documents are safe and secure. The Save tab of the Options dialog box lets you be extra safe and secure by choosing automatic save options.

The Automatic Save Every option causes Word to save your active document automatically at the interval specified in the Minutes box. The default value is 10 minutes, but you can change the value using the up and down arrow buttons. You'll want to set the value to a short enough interval that you won't lose too much of your work if the power goes out. Usually something between 10 and 20 minutes is about right.

One other option you might want to consider, especially if you are sharing documents with others who don't have the same fonts installed on their computers that you have, is to embed TrueType fonts. With this option, the recipient of the document will be able to edit and print the document. The disadvantage of this option is that it increases the size of your document files, so you should use this option only when necessary. Click on the OK button to accept your option changes.

Customizing Toolbars

In addition to the changes you can make in the Options dialog box, you can also use the Customize menu to add, delete, and move menu items and keyboard shortcut keys. This dialog box also lets you customize toolbars to display the buttons you use most often. You can open the Customize dialog box by choosing Customize from the Tools menu or from the Toolbar shortcut menu that appears when you right-click on any toolbar. It can also be reached by clicking on the Customize button in the Toolbars dialog box, which we'll look at a little later.

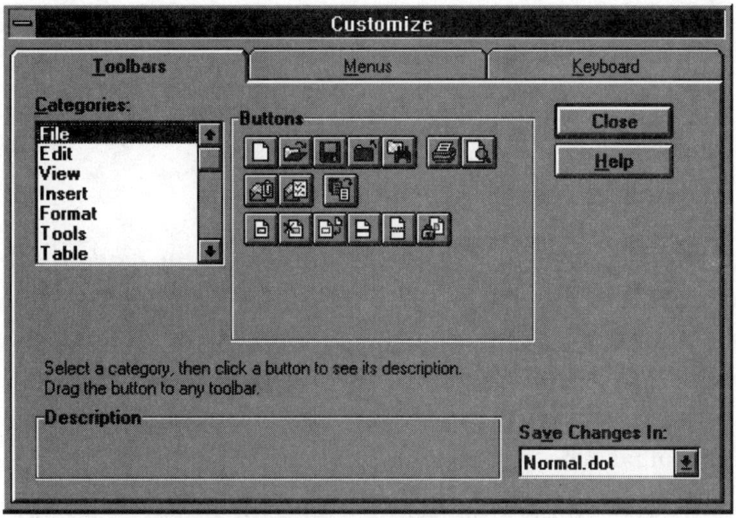

FIGURE 10–6 The Toolbars tab of the Customize dialog box

Right-click on a toolbar and choose Customize from its shortcut menu to display the Toolbars tab of the Customize dialog box, as shown in Figure 10–6.

With the Toolbars tab of the Customize dialog box on screen, you can remove a button from any toolbar that's displayed by dragging the button from its toolbar onto the document area and then releasing the mouse button. If you want to reposition a button on the toolbar to make it more convenient, just drag it to its new position.

If you have too many buttons in a toolbar, some of the buttons on the right side of the toolbar may not be visible unless you undock it and use it as a floating toolbar, as discussed in Chapter 5. It's usually more convenient to use docked toolbars, so it's a good idea to delete a few unneeded buttons from a crowded toolbar to make room for new ones.

FIGURE 10–7 The Formatting toolbar with a new button in place

To add a new button to a toolbar, click on the category that you want to use in the Categories list; then click on the button you want to use in the Buttons portion of the dialog box. Its description is displayed in the Description portion of the dialog box. If the button you clicked on is, in fact, the button you want to use, drag it to the position on the toolbar where you want it.

Figure 10–7 shows the Formatting toolbar with the Underline button removed and the 1.5 Space button from the Format category in its place.

note You can add buttons from any category to any toolbar. You could, for example, add buttons from the Format category to the Standard toolbar.

After you've made whatever toolbar changes you want to make, click on the Close button.

If you've really made a mess of one of your toolbars, you can reset it to its original state using the Toolbars dialog box. To open the Toolbars dialog box, choose View➢Toolbars or choose Toolbars from the toolbar shortcut menu.

To reset a toolbar to the way it was before, click on it in the Toolbars list, and click on the Reset button. Then click on the OK button in the Reset Toolbar dialog box to confirm that you want to reset the toolbar.

tip The Large Buttons check box at the bottom of the Toolbars dialog box lets you enlarge the size of the toolbar buttons. If you are using a higher resolution screen than standard VGA, the standard-sized buttons may be so small that you will have difficulty seeing the images.

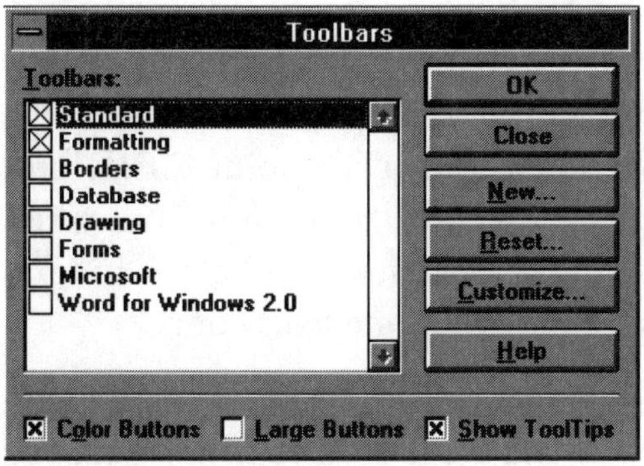

FIGURE 10–8 The Toolbars dialog box

This could also be a useful option for visually impaired users operating at standard VGA resolution. The downside to using large buttons in standard resolution is that fewer buttons will fit on the screen, so you may have to remove some buttons from docked toolbars or move the toolbars to other parts of the screen.

Recording and Playing Macros

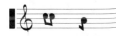

If you really want to save yourself time, macros are for you. A macro is simply a named series of tasks that you can "play back" when you want to repeat those tasks.

There are two ways to create a macro. For a simple set of tasks, the easiest way to create a macro is to turn on the macro and then perform the tasks. If you want to create a complex macro, you may have to write a macro using Word's WordBasic programming language. I won't cover macro programming here, but the help facility has reference information about the macro language. If you want to learn to program using the macro language, you can order the Word Developer's Kit from Microsoft using the form provided with the software.

You can use macros to automate almost any task. Perhaps the most common use of recorded macros is to apply formatting changes to your documents. For example, suppose you regularly change portions of your documents to a 12-point Arial font, double-spaced, and center-aligned. It would require four individual actions on your part to apply all those attributes manually. Using a macro, however, you can apply all of them in one fell swoop.

tip Word comes with several useful macros that you may want to install. You'll find these macros in a file named MACRO60.DOT and information about it and the macros in it is available in a README file. To open the macro README file, double-click on the Help button on the Standard toolbar, type **readme**, and press Enter twice. Then scroll down until Supplied Macros is visible and click on it.

To start recording a macro, choose Tools➢Macro to display the Macro dialog box, as shown in Figure 10–9.

If there are any macros available, they appear in the Macro Name list. Enter a name for your new macro in the Macro Name text box and then, if you want to, type a description of the macro's function in the Description box. Now click on the Record button to display the Record Macro dialog box, as shown in Figure 10–10.

You can proceed with your macro recording by just clicking on the OK button, but you'll probably want to take advantage of one or more of the three options in the Assign Macro To portion of the dialog box. You can assign the macro to a toolbar button, a menu item, or a shortcut key.

Why would you want to assign the macro to a toolbar, menu item, or shortcut key? Well, the macro we used as an example, which applies four formatting attributes, would require only four actions to apply manually. If you had to open the Macro dialog box, choose the macro, and click on the OK button to run the macro, it wouldn't be worth the trouble to use it. But, if you could run the macro by

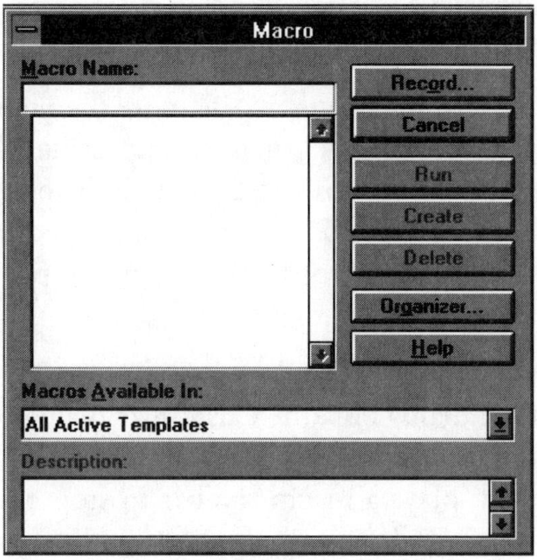

FIGURE 10–9 The Macro dialog box

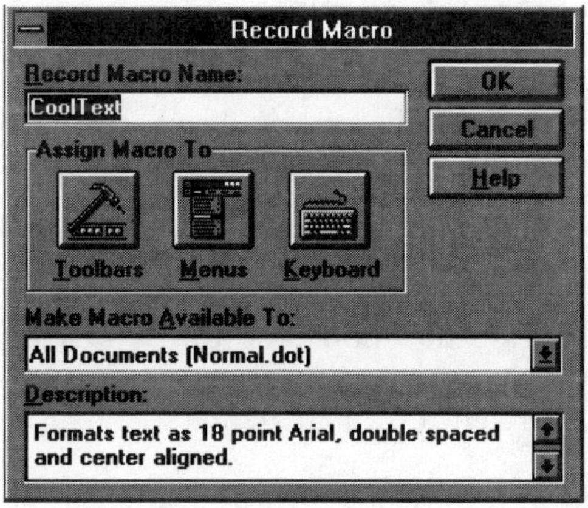

FIGURE 10–10 The Record Macro dialog box

pressing a shortcut key combination or clicking on a toolbar button, it would clearly save enough time to make it worthwhile.

It usually doesn't make sense to use more than one of these options for a particular macro, but you may end up using all three approaches as your collection of macros expands. The dialog boxes for the various Assign Macro To options step you through the process, but as we create the example macro, we'll look at the process of assigning the macro to a toolbar.

When you click on the Toolbar icon button in the Assign Macro To portion of the dialog box, the Customize dialog box appears. Clicking on the Close button in the Customize dialog box starts the recording process and displays a macro toolbar to stop or pause the recording. The mouse pointer has the image of an audio cassette tape attached to indicate that you are recording.

At this point, you can simply carry out the steps you want included in your macro and, when you are finished, click on the Stop button on the Macro Record toolbar. The macro is now available by choosing it from the Macro dialog box. You must still perform a few more steps to get this macro onto a toolbar.

Right-click on a toolbar and then on Customize to display the Toolbars tab of the Customize dialog box. Next, scroll down the Categories list and click on Macros. The available macros are displayed in the Macros list. Drag the macro to the desired position on a toolbar. As you drag, the mouse pointer will have the outline of a button attached.

When you release the mouse button, you'll have a blank button on the toolbar, and the Custom Button dialog box will be displayed, as shown in Figure 10–11.

The Custom Button dialog box displays a variety of button designs you can assign to your new button. You can even create your own design or edit one of the existing designs, but we won't cover that here.

To use one of the available button designs, click on it; then click on the Assign button and the Close button in the Customize dialog box.

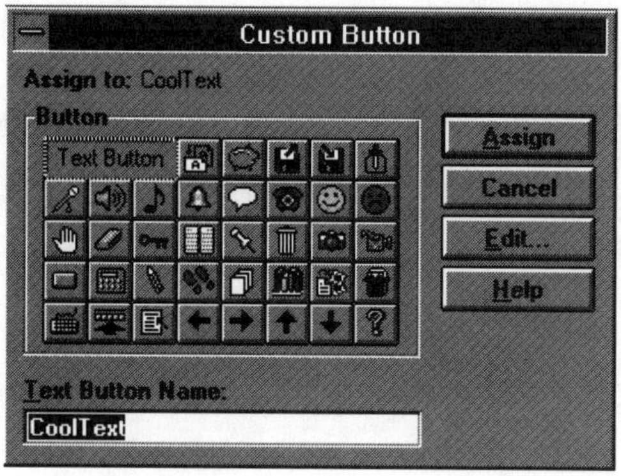

FIGURE 10–11 The Custom Button dialog box

Your button with its new design—along with its own ToolTip, which displays the name of the macro when you point to the button—appears on the toolbar, as shown in Figure 10–12. You can now run this macro by simply clicking on the toolbar button.

Macros offer incredible power with unlimited possibilities for enhancing Word's utility and saving you time. Whatever time you spend learning the ins and outs of recording macros, and perhaps even learning some programming to extend your macros even further, will be one of the best investments you can make.

Using Mail Merge

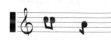

Have you ever sent the same letter to 30 different people and actually retyped each one using a different name and address? Of course, in Word, you can just change the name and address on the same document before you print each one. Hey, how could you save more time than that?

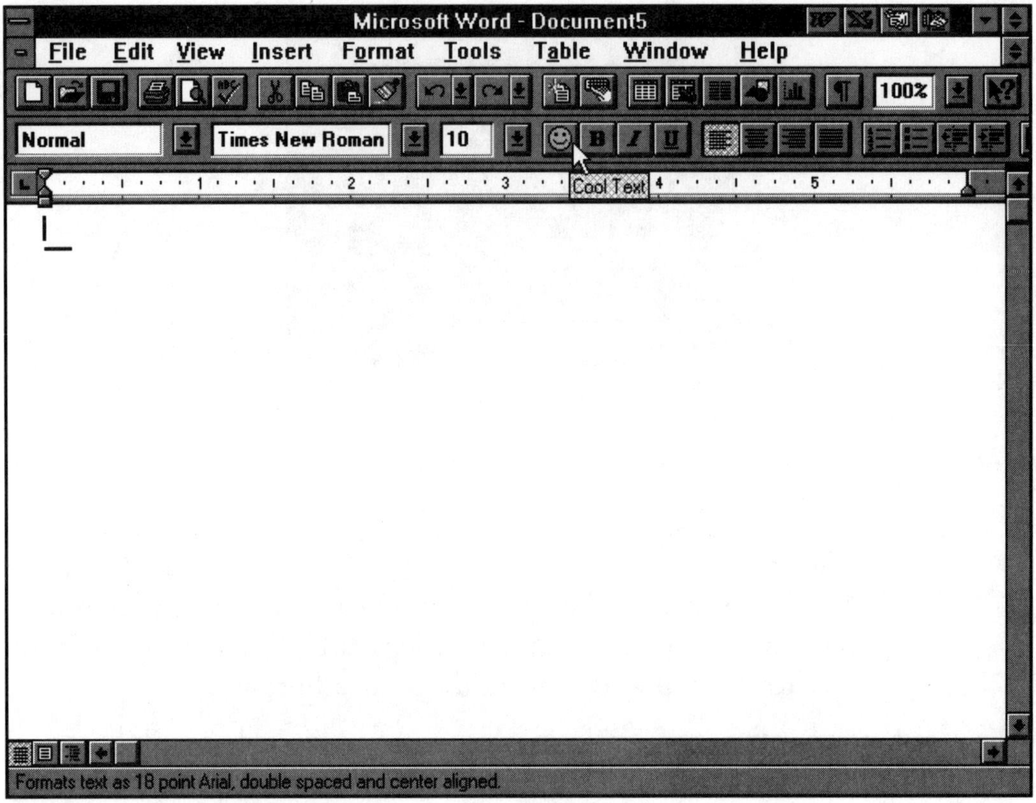

FIGURE 10–12 The Formatting toolbar with the button for the macro and its associated ToolTip

Wait a minute. What about the envelopes? And what about next month's mailing to the same group? Relax. Word's Mail Merge feature lets you create a list of names and addresses (or whatever you want to make a list of, store it as a data source file, and then merge the list with a main document.

Word makes creating the main document and the data source file easy with the Mail Merge Helper. The Mail Merge Helper works much like a Wizard in the sense that it steps you through the process of creating the required files.

note You can use existing data source files created with external database programs such as Access or dBASE. I won't cover the steps for doing this, but the process is essentially the same as the process for using a data source document within Word.

To start the process of creating a mail merge, choose Tools➢Mail Merge to display the Mail Merge Helper dialog box, as shown in Figure 10–13.

Click on the Create button in the Main Document portion of the dialog box and choose the type of main document you want to create. The first three choices—Form Letters, Mailing Labels, and Envelopes—are the most common. For this example, we'll create a form letter, so click on Form Letters in the drop-down list and then click on the Active Window button in the next dialog box, or click on the

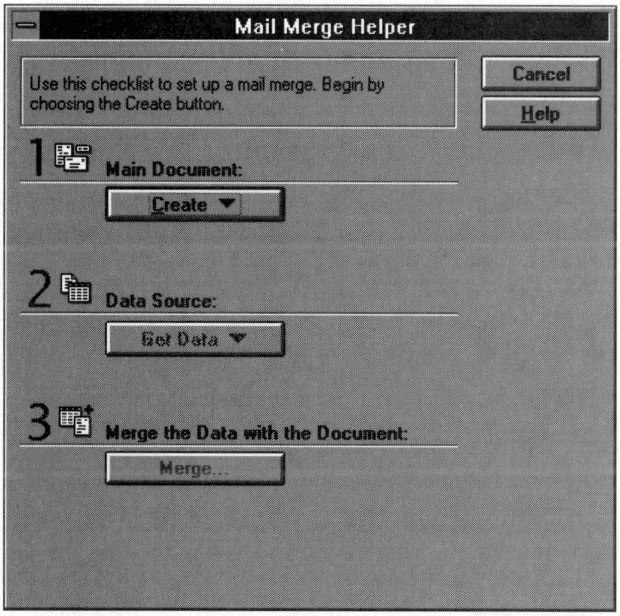

FIGURE 10–13 The Mail Merge Helper dialog box

New Main Document button if you already have a document on your screen.

tip If you want to use an existing document as your main document, open it before starting the Mail Merge creation process. Then, when you choose Active Document Window, you'll be using the existing document.

An Edit button appears in the Main Document portion of the Mail Merge Helper dialog box, but you must create your data source document before editing your main document.

Click on the Get Data button and then on Create Data Source to display the Create Data Source dialog box, as shown in Figure 10–14.

When you create a data source document, you are actually creating a database file. Two terms that are important to understand when working with databases are *record* and *field.*

A field is a category of information in a database. A record is a collection of fields pertaining to one entry in the database. For example,

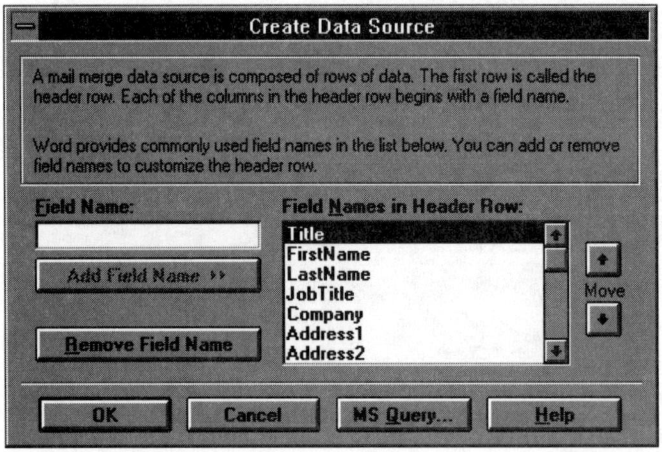

FIGURE 10–14 The Create Data Source dialog box

if you were creating a customer database, you might have a field for each customer's name, one for the address, and another for the phone number. Other fields might be included for such information as the last contact date, amount of the last sale, and so on. All the fields for one customer are called a record.

In the Create Data Source dialog box, Word provides a list of the fields most commonly used for keeping track of names and addresses. You can delete any of the supplied fields you don't plan to use by clicking on the field names in the Field Names In Header Row list and then on the Remove Field Name button. You might, for example, want to remove the Country field name if all the people in your database live in the United States.

You can also add any fields you need. If you want to keep track of the last contact date, you could add a LastContact field by entering **LastContact** in the Field Name text box and then clicking on the Add Field Name button.

You can change the position of the fields in the database by clicking on a field name and then using the up and down arrow buttons to the right of the scroll bar for the Field Names In Header Row list.

Once you have all the fields you want, click on the OK button to display the Save Data Source dialog box, as shown in Figure 10–15.

Enter a name for your data source document and click on the OK button. You can give the data source any name you wish, but it will be helpful if you use a name that reflects its contents, at least to you.

Click on the Edit Data Source button in the next message dialog box to display the Data Form dialog box, as shown in Figure 10–16.

Enter the appropriate information in each field text box for each record; then click on the Add New button to accept the record and clear the form so you can start entering a new record. Figure 10–17 shows a filled-in data form for one record.

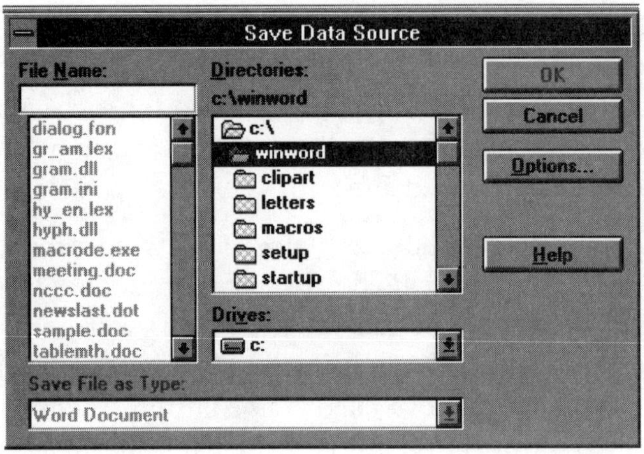

FIGURE 10–15 The Save Data Source dialog box

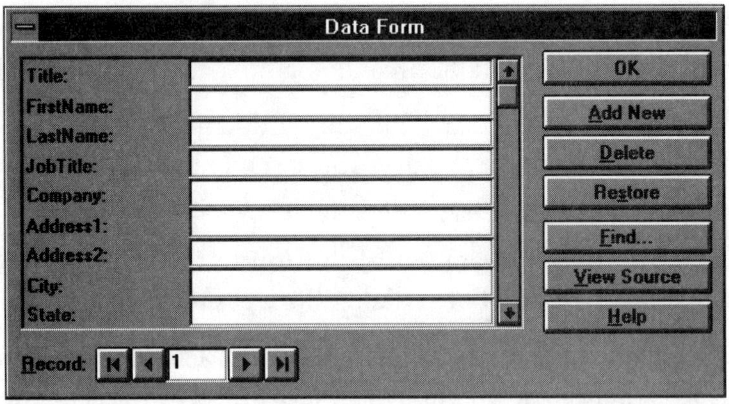

FIGURE 10–16 The Data Form dialog box

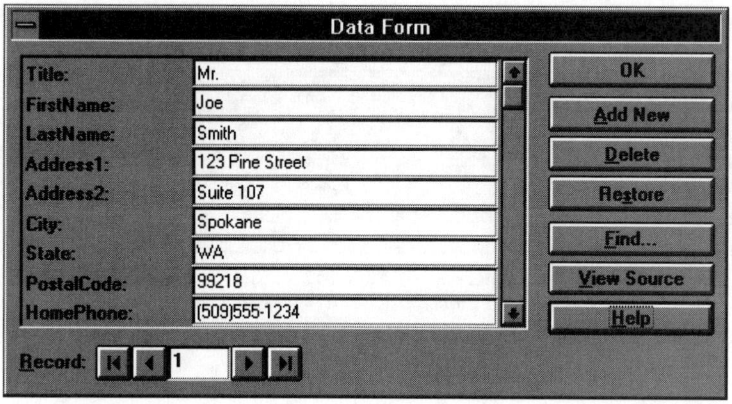

FIGURE 10–17 A filled-in data form in the Data Form dialog box

CAUTION

It's crucial that you use the same type of field information in each record. For example, if you enter **Ms.** in the Title field, **Jane** in the FirstName field, and **Smith** in the LastName field for one record, don't enter **Mr. Joe Doakes** in the LastName field of the next record. If you aren't consistent in the way you enter the data in your records, they won't be merged into your main document properly.

If you want to review or edit any of the records, you can move backward or forward by clicking on the left and right arrows on either side of the Record number text box. If you want to view the underlying data source document, click on the View Source button to display the source as it is laid out in its table form with the field names in the header row, as shown in Figure 10–18.

Notice the Database toolbar that has been added under the Formatting toolbar. This toolbar provides buttons for working with Word databases. For example, if you want to sort the data in the table, you can click on the Sort Ascending or Sort Descending button, and the data will be sorted accordingly. If you want to sort the records by

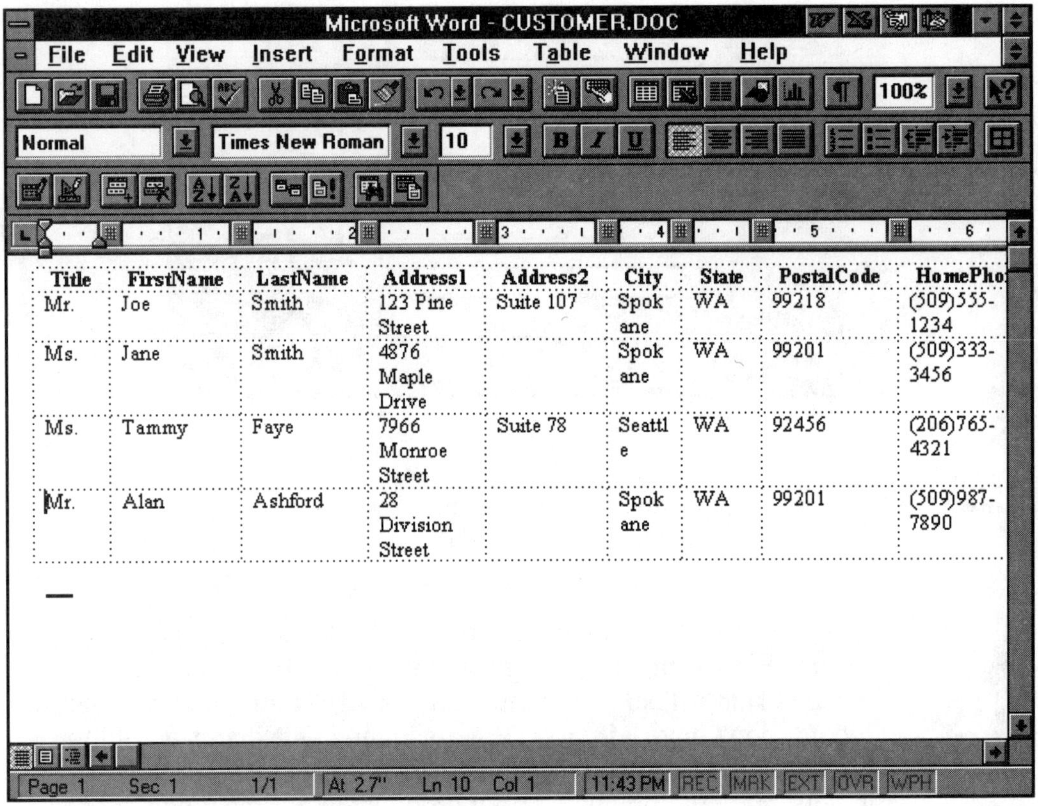

FIGURE 10–18 The data source table

in the LastName column and then click on the Sort Ascending button on the Database toolbar. Instantly, the database is sorted, as shown in Figure 10–19.

When you have finished looking at the data source table, save the document by clicking on the Save button on the Standard toolbar and then click on the Mail Merge Main Document button on the right side of the Database toolbar. The main document with the Mail Merge toolbar is displayed, as shown in Figure 10–20.

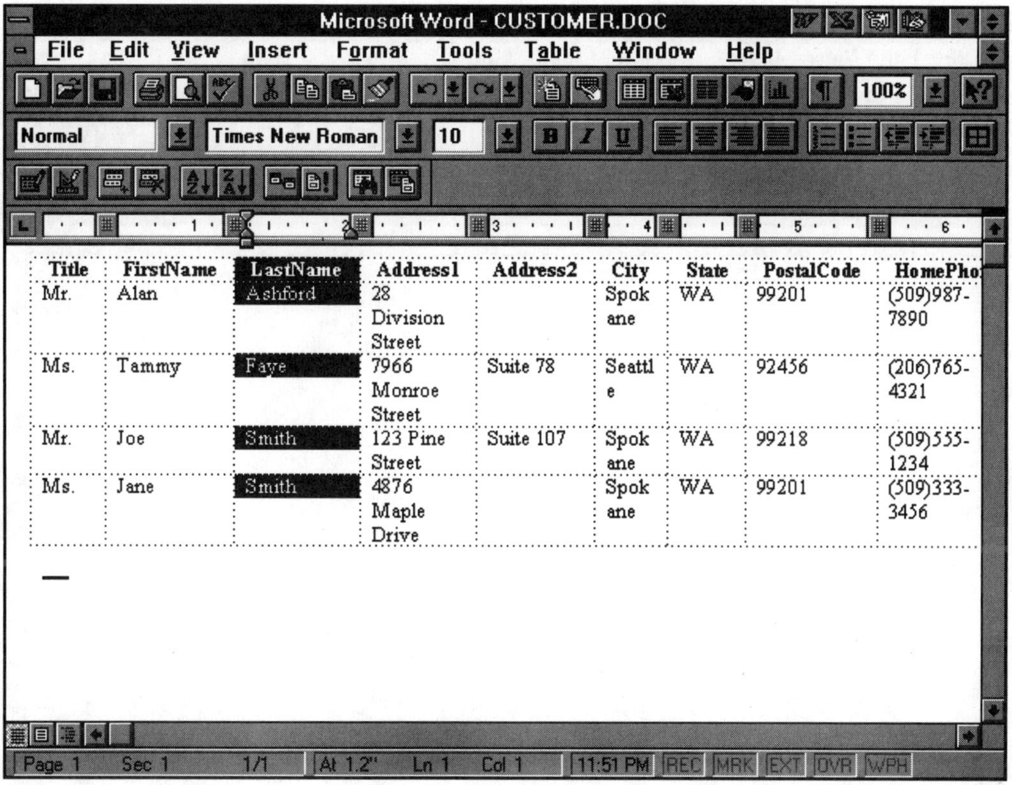

FIGURE 10–19 The database sorted in ascending alphabetical order

note You can just click on the OK button in the Data Form dialog box to go directly to the main document without first displaying the data source table.

You can now create your main document just as you would any other document. However, where you would normally type the information pertaining to the specific recipient, use the Insert Merge Field button on the Mail Merge toolbar to draw the appropriate information from the data source document into the mail-merge document when you perform the merge.

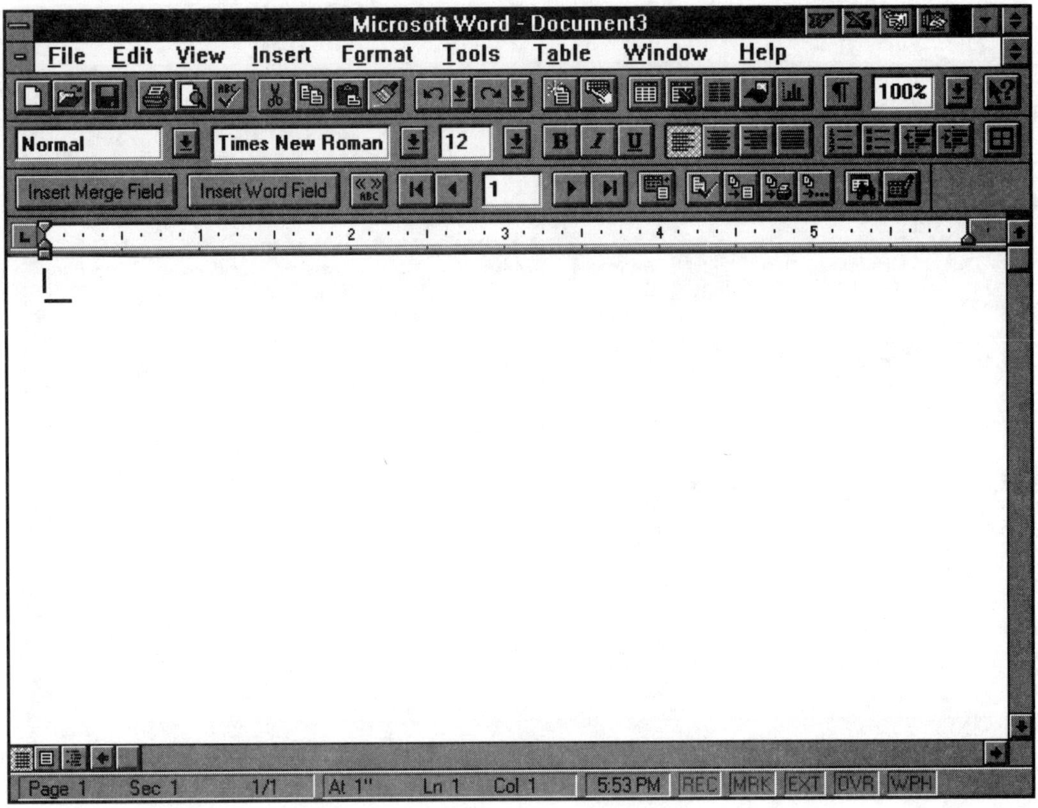

FIGURE 10–20 The main document with the Mail Merge toolbar

To insert a field, position the insertion point where you want the data source data brought into your document and click on the Insert Merge Field button to display a drop-down list of the available field names from the data source document, as shown in Figure 10–21. Then click on the name of the field you want to insert.

More than one field can be placed on a line. You would, for example, want to place the Title, FirstName, and LastName fields on the same line so the person's entire name would appear on the same line. The idea is to place the fields in your main document so the data will end

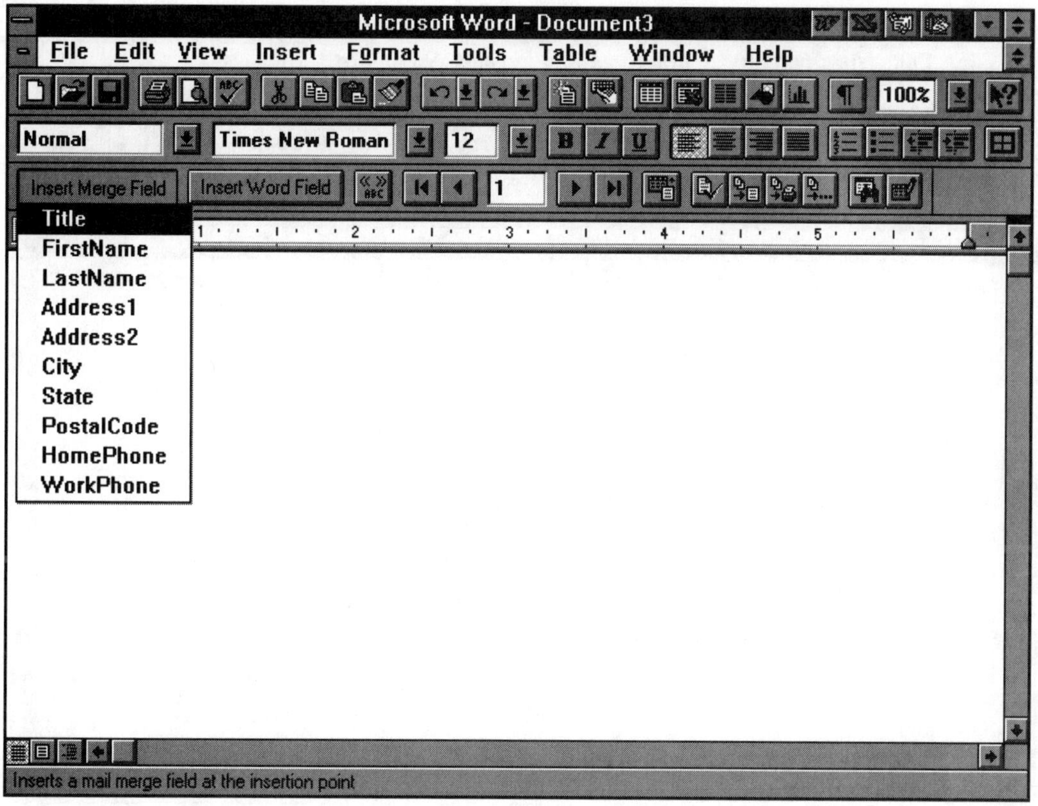

FIGURE 10–21 The drop-down list of field names

up where you want it after the data is merged. Don't forget to save your main document, just as you would any other Word document.

Figure 10–22 shows a typical main document with all the necessary merge fields inserted.

Notice the double-angle brackets surrounding each of the field names in the main document. Also, notice the spaces and punctuation between fields. Punctuation and spaces must be placed outside the brackets. For example, on the line containing the City, State, and PostalCode fields, the City field is followed by a comma and a space,

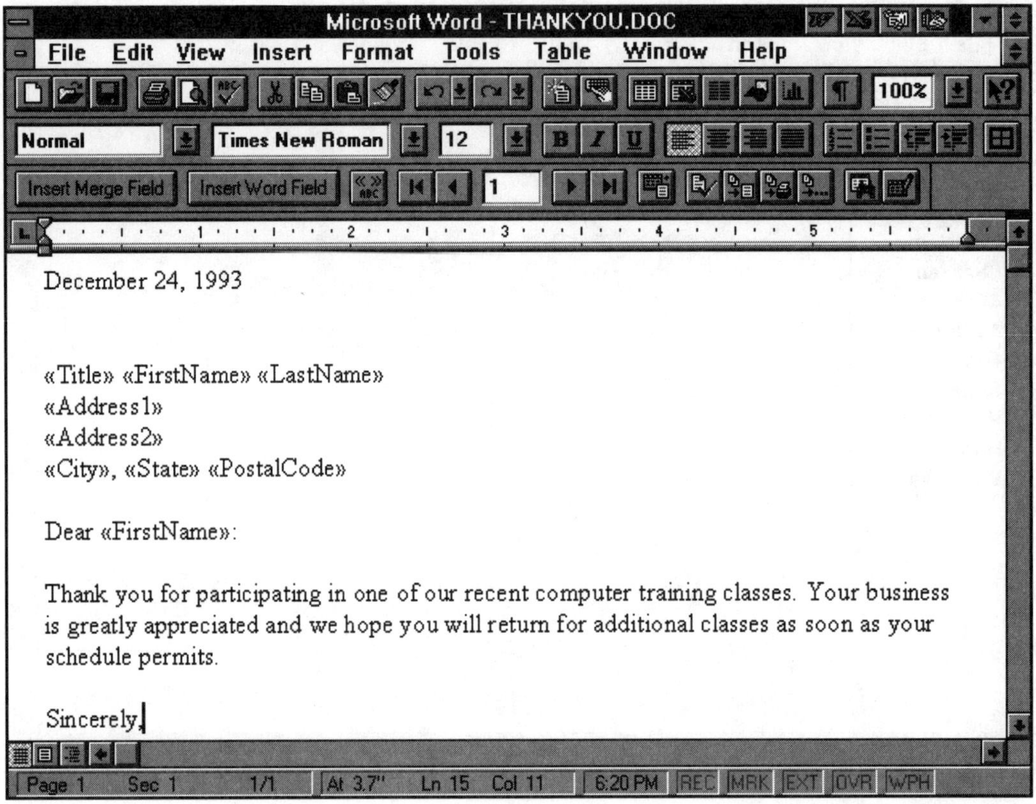

FIGURE 10–22 The main document with the merge fields inserted in the proper places

and the State field is followed by just a space. This is the same spacing and punctuation you would use if you were entering the city, state, and postal code directly.

tip

In the example, the FirstName field is used twice: once as part of the inside address and again for the salutation. Although this will work, you may not want to address all customers by their first names. And it would be tacky to address them by their complete names as in Dear Mr. Alan Ashford.

There is a simple solution to this dilemma. Add a Salutation field to the data source document (most easily done while creating the data source document) so you can enter the appropriate salutation for each customer. If you know the customer well, perhaps using the first name is appropriate. If you don't know him or her well, an appropriate salutation would probably be Mr. Ashford or Ms. Smith.

After you enter the text and insert the fields for the main document, click on the Merge To New Document button on the Mail Merge toolbar to merge the data source data with the main document. The field names are replaced with the data from the data source, as shown in Figure 10–23.

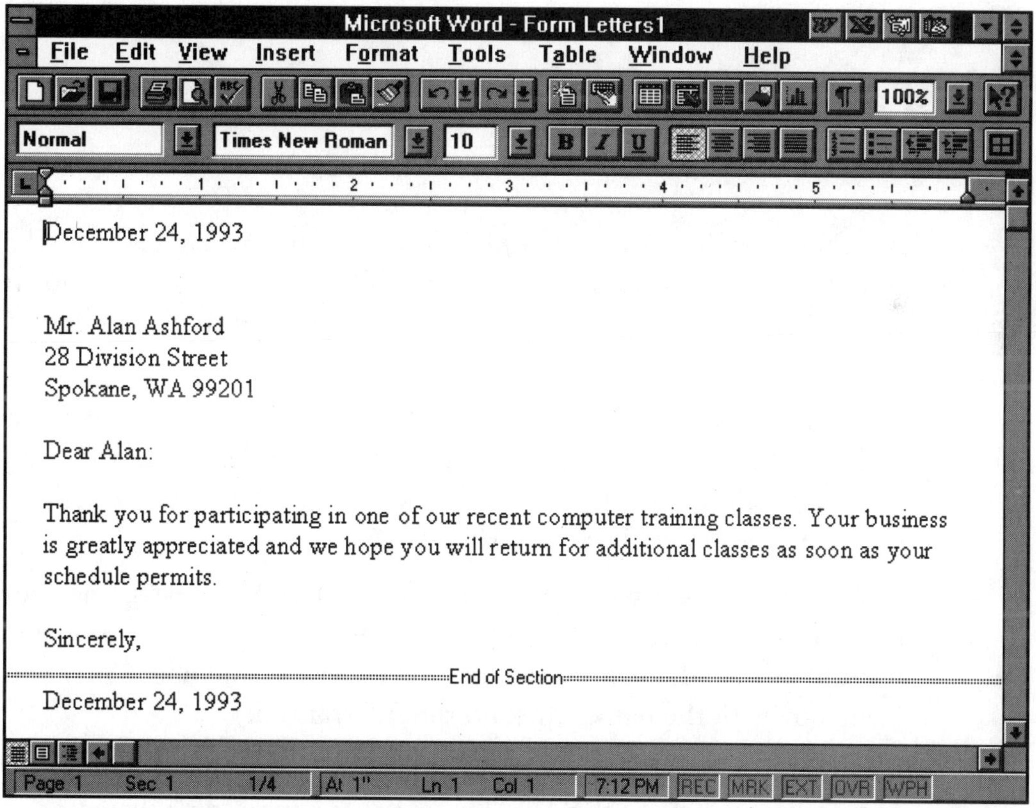

FIGURE 10–23 The new form letter document

Scroll through the pages to be sure all the records from your data source were used. Also, notice that blank lines have been removed for fields that don't contain data. For example, the Address2 field (used for four-line addresses) occupies a separate line in the example main document, but the first letter, which has only a three-line address, doesn't have a blank line between the address line and the line with the city, state, and zip.

You can print the document now, and each form letter will print on its own page. If you aren't ready to print the document, you can save it, but there usually isn't a need to save a form letter document, because you can always re-merge the source data with the main document.

Using AutoText

Another feature used for automating document creation is the AutoText feature. AutoText (called the Glossary in previous versions) lets you store text or graphics and insert them in future documents as needed.

To add an AutoText entry, select the text or graphics you want included and then choose Edit➢AutoText or click on the Edit AutoText button on the Standard toolbar to display the AutoText dialog box, as shown in Figure 10–24.

Word uses the first part of the selection as the AutoText name, but because you want to be able to identify the text easily, you'll probably want to change the name to something easier to remember. After you are happy with the name, click on the Add button.

To insert the AutoText into your document, position the insertion point where you want the AutoText entry to appear, type the name of the AutoText entry, and then press F3 or click on the Insert AutoText button on the Standard toolbar.

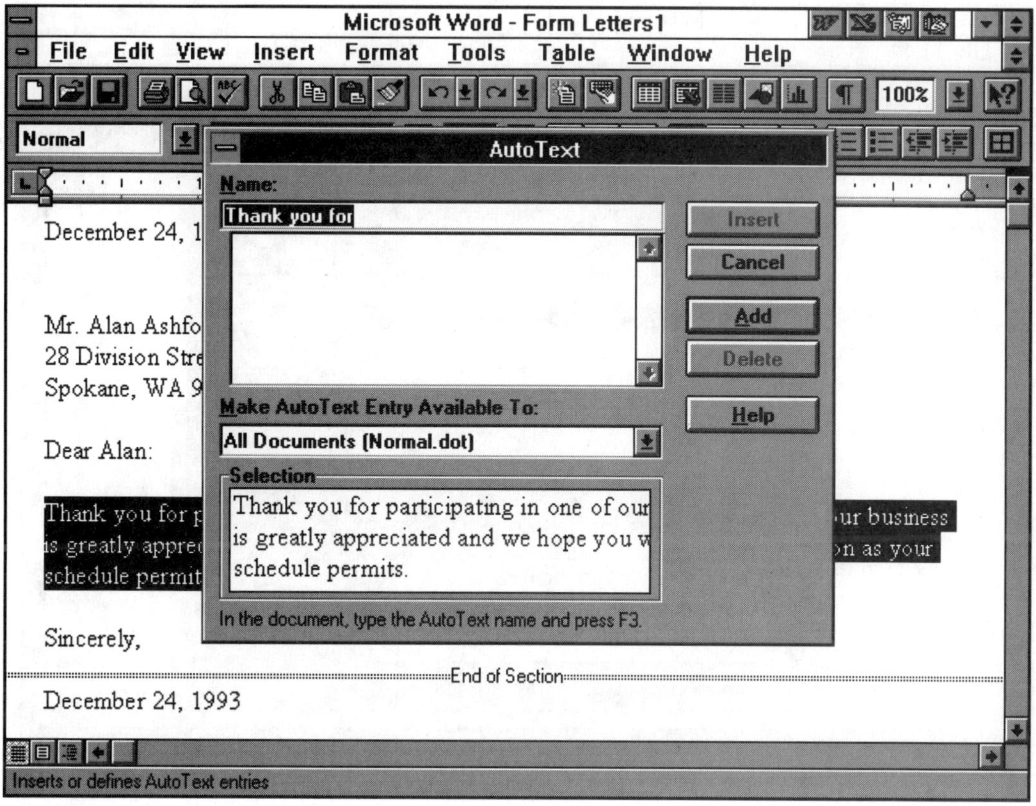

FIGURE 10–24 The AutoText dialog box

If you want to insert an AutoText entry without the formatting that was included when you assigned the entry, position the insertion point where you want the entry, but don't type the AutoText name; then choose Edit➢AutoText to display the AutoText dialog box with the Insert As options, as shown in Figure 10–25.

Click on the AutoText entry in the Name list. Then click on Plain Text option button and the Insert button. The AutoText will be entered into your document using the formatting of the surrounding text.

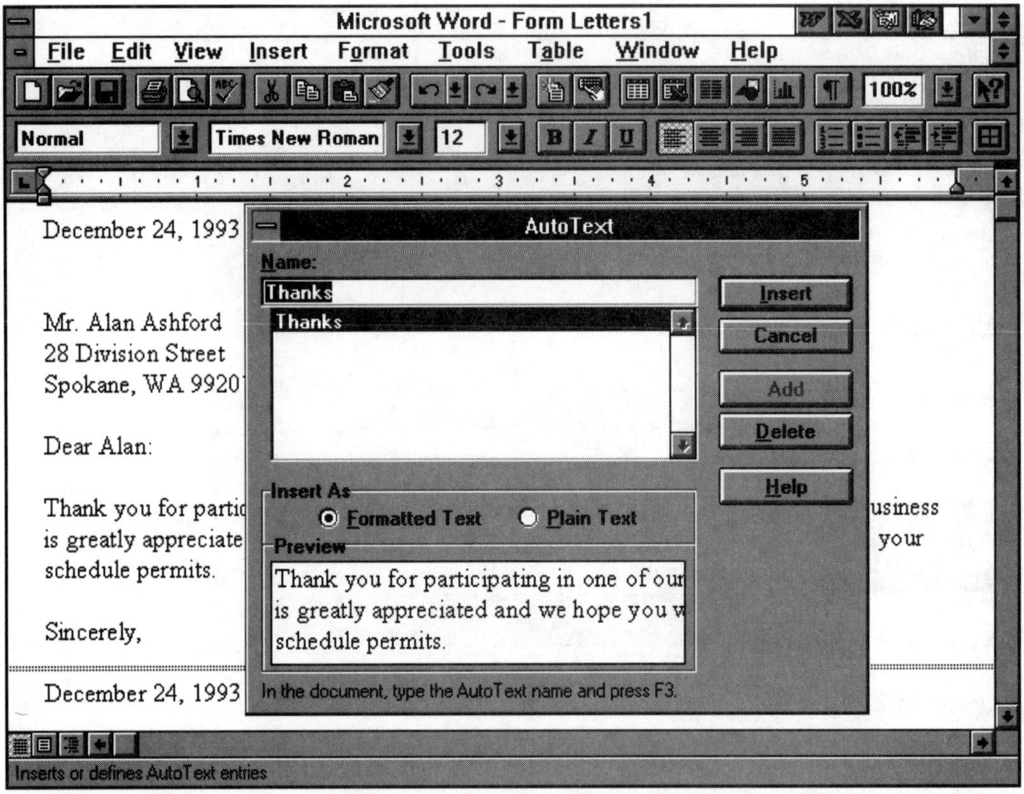

FIGURE 10–25 The AutoText dialog box with the Insert As options

Using AutoCorrect

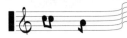

AutoCorrect is similar to AutoText. It replaces a short AutoCorrect name with another text or graphic. Unlike AutoText, AutoCorrect can make the change automatically. In fact, AutoCorrect has been working behind the scenes, perhaps without your even realizing it.

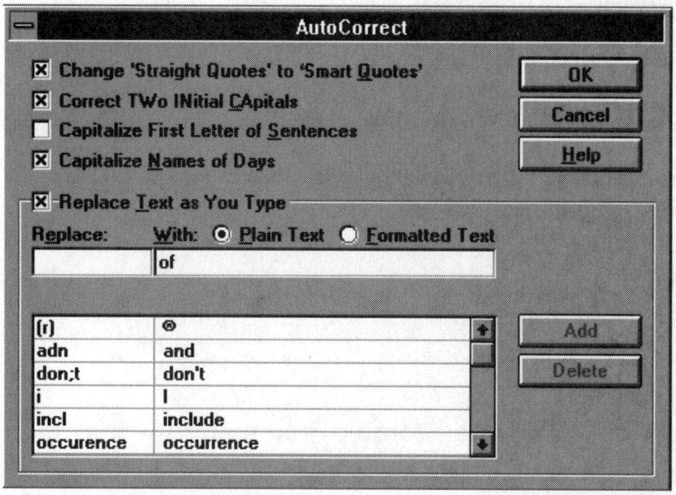

FIGURE 10–26 The AutoCorrect dialog box

We touched on the AutoCorrect feature briefly in Chapter 8. While spell checking, you can add a misspelled word and its correct replacement to the list of AutoCorrect entries so that the next time you make the same mistake, it will be corrected automatically.

AutoCorrect includes a number of common errors and their correct forms and takes care of those for you. You can add other entries to the list as well.

Suppose you have the nasty habit of typing *fo* instead of *of.* To make this an AutoCorrect item, select *of* in your document, and then choose Tools➢AutoCorrect to display the AutoCorrect dialog box, as shown in Figure 10–26.

Type the incorrect version, **fo**, in the Replace text box, choose the Plain Text or Formatted Text option, and then click on the Add button.

Notice the list of common errors and their replacements at the bottom of the dialog box. AutoCorrect has already been taking care of these for you. Also notice the AutoCorrect options in the top portion of the dialog box. You can turn any of these on or off by clicking in its check box.

Summary

This chapter explored some of the many ways to increase your document creation efficiency. You should now have a good understanding of Word's capabilities and feel comfortable using them.

In the next chapters, we'll start exploring the Excel spreadsheet program. Having worked with Windows and Word, you'll be surprised at how familiar many of Excel's features and procedures seem. You'll be creating Excel worksheets in no time at all.

Section IV

A Short Course in Excel for Windows

11

Excel—The Basics

Spreadsheet programs really got the personal computer industry off the ground. By allowing people to use mathematical formulas and functions to manipulate numbers, spreadsheets make it easy to play what-if. Suppose you need to put together a budget for your business. You could use a spreadsheet to answer such questions as, "What if we reduce inventory by 7% and sales drop 2%?" or "What if the cost of health insurance increases 18%?"

The Excel spreadsheet program is a paradox. It is at once an incredibly powerful, flexible, and sophisticated spreadsheet program; at the same time, it's easier to use than most of the smaller programs that can't do half of what Excel does.

You'll be amazed at how quickly you'll feel at home with Excel. Its menus, toolbars, and dialog boxes are virtually identical to those in Word, so you already know how to perform many tasks in Excel.

Overview of New Features in Excel for Windows 5.0

You've already learned about many of the new features in Excel 5.0, because many of them have also been incorporated into Word 6.0. The way toolbars can be moved and customized is essentially the same in both products, as is the help facility. As in Word, a ToolTip appears when you move the mouse pointer over a toolbar button.

You can produce a shortcut menu for almost any object on the screen by right-clicking, and you can complete many tasks with the help of Wizards.

However, the folks at Microsoft have provided Excel with several new goodies of its own, and we'll examine some of them here.

The TipWizard

I said the help facility works the same way as Word's. However, Excel has added a piece of help wizardry that may make you think the program is smarter than you are. The TipWizard "watches" you perform an action and suggests a better way to do it.

Workbooks

All sheets—whether worksheets, chart sheets, or macro sheets—are stored in workbooks. When you save your work, all the sheets in the active workbook are saved. This makes organizing related sheets easier and more logical. You can even name the individual sheets and have their names appear on Sheet Tabs at the bottom of the workbook window.

In-Cell Editing

You don't have to edit a cell's contents on the formula bar anymore. By double-clicking on a cell (or pressing F2), you can edit the cell's contents right in the cell. This can make editing much more efficient.

Function Wizard

Like Word, Excel provides many Wizards to help you perform a variety of tasks. One Wizard that deserves special mention is the Function Wizard.

Using functions, especially the more complex ones, has always been one of the more confusing spreadsheet tasks. The Function Wizard guides you through the process of filling in the required information for the function you are using. This is one of Excel's greatest contributions to spreadsheet usability.

Drag and Plot

Adding a new data series to a chart used to require some thought and several mouse actions or keystrokes. To add a new data series in Excel 5, just drag it onto the chart. It's that simple.

Improved List Management

Working with database lists in Excel is vastly improved in this version. The AutoFilter feature lets you display records in your list that meet certain criteria by clicking on a drop-down arrow on each column in the list.

Sorting the list is easier now that Excel automatically recognizes the parts of the list to sort. There's even a feature to subtotal groups within the list.

Starting Excel and Touring the Screen

If the Microsoft Office Manager toolbar is available, click on the Microsoft Excel button to start Excel. If the Office Manager isn't running, open the Microsoft Office group icon in Program Manager and then double-click on the Microsoft Excel icon. Figure 11–1 shows the opening Excel screen.

note

You don't have to exit Word before starting Excel. In fact, after you learn more about sharing data among the Office programs, you may find it useful to have two or more of the programs running simultaneously.

The one possible disadvantage to having both programs running at once is that speed can suffer. If your computer is fast enough and has enough memory, you may not notice any difference, but if you are using a slower machine, you don't want to burden it unnecessarily.

Worksheets, like the tables in Word, are made up of rows and columns. A rectangular intersection of a row and a column is a cell. In contrast to Word tables, Excel worksheets display column-heading letters and row-heading numbers. The active cell or range is surrounded by a selection border. Above the row headings and to the left of the column headings is the Select All button for selecting all the cells in a worksheet. The *sheet tabs* at the bottom of the worksheet display the names of the worksheets in the active workbook.

Below the Standard and Formatting toolbars, where the ruler would be in Word, are the *name box* and the *formula bar.* The name box displays the address of the active cell and provides a quick way to name a cell or range of cells or to move to a cell or range. The formula bar displays the value or formula in the active cell.

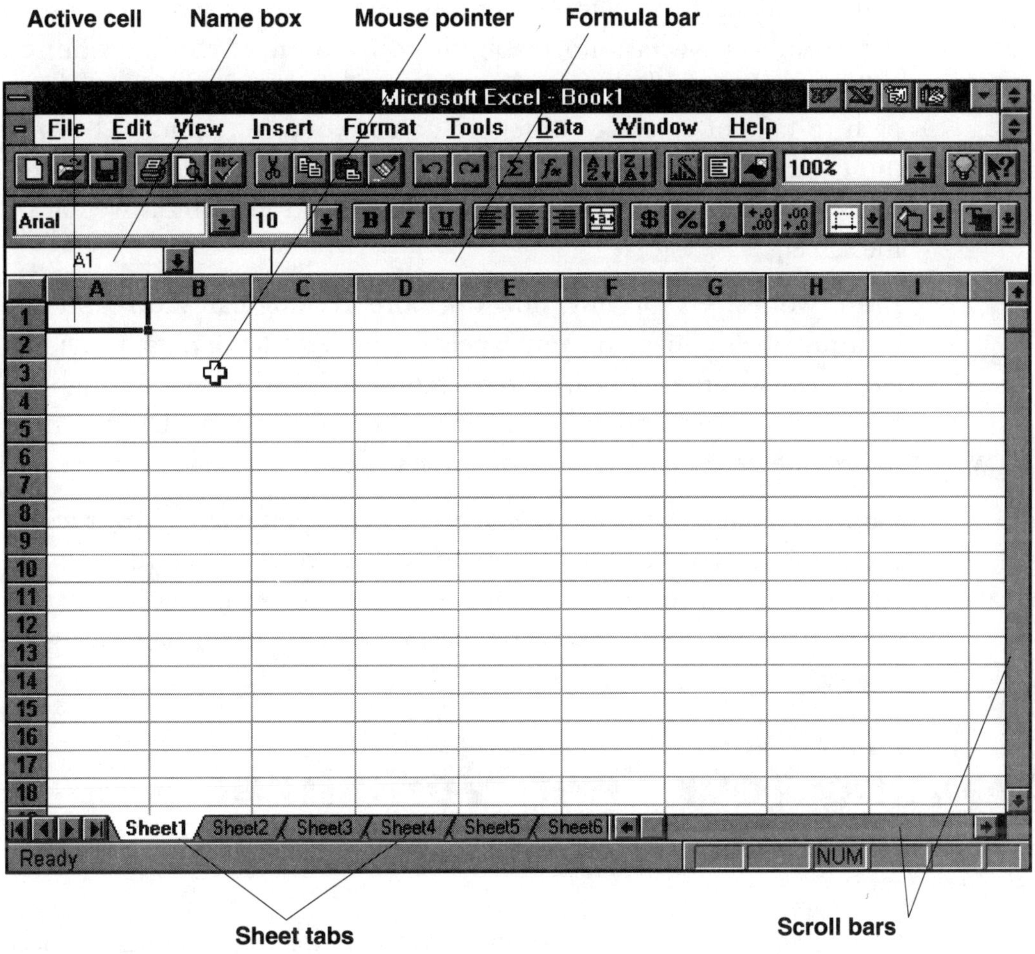

FIGURE 11-1 The opening Excel screen

Planning a Worksheet

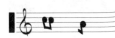

You could just dive right in and start entering the data you think you'll need for your worksheet, but like most things in life, your worksheets can benefit greatly from a little planning.

You should start the planning process by determining the purpose of the worksheet—what information it needs to present and to whom it will be presented. Are you trying to analyze data to determine the best path to take or convince others to accept your conclusions? Keep in mind that the ultimate product of most worksheets is the printed page, so structure your worksheet to look good in print as well as on the screen.

Most worksheets occupy one or more rectangular areas and use column labels above and row labels to the left of the data, providing clues to what the worksheet data represents. Give some thought to how well the row and column labels describe the data. Do you need to provide better labels, more detail, less detail?

Don't feel that you must think of every detail you want in your worksheet ahead of time. Like documents you create in Word, you can edit, revise, and restructure as much as needed. Planning the spreadsheet will generally yield the desired results with less struggle, however.

Creating Your First Worksheet

Once you've done your planning, you can start entering the labels, values, and formulas. Usually, you'll start in the upper-left corner of the worksheet. If you find that you need to add more rows or columns within or around your worksheet, you can do so.

To enter data in an Excel worksheet, just move to the cell in which you want to enter data and start typing. You can move to a cell (make it the active cell) by clicking on it or by using one of the arrow keys or one of the keyboard shortcut key combinations. An easy way to move to a far-off cell is to click in the name box (just to the left of the formula bar), type the desired cell address, and press Enter.

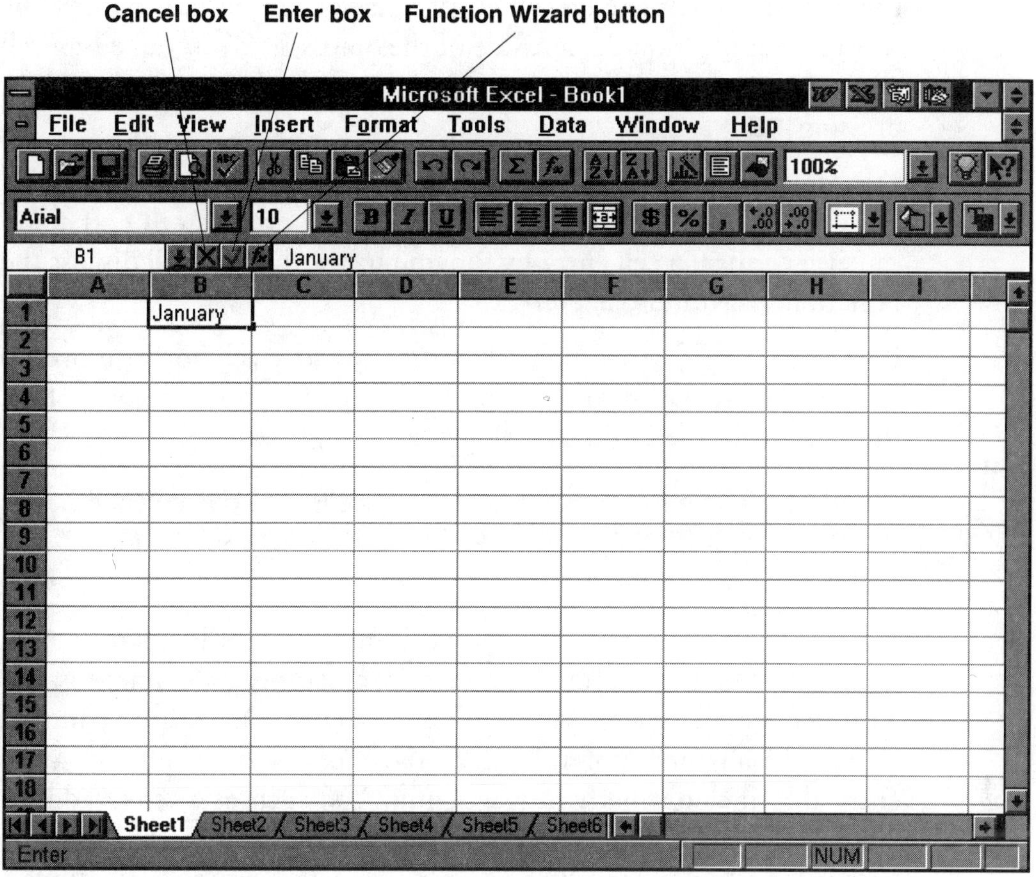

FIGURE 11–2 The formula bar with the cancel and enter boxes and the Function Wizard button

As you start entering data in a cell, the data appears on the formula bar. In addition, a *cancel box*, an *enter box*, and a *Function Wizard* button appear on the left side of the formula bar, as shown in Figure 11–2.

If you have to correct a cell entry before you finish entering it, you can press the Backspace key or move the mouse pointer into the cell, where it turns into an I-beam pointer, and click. Clicking in the cell before you've completed a cell entry puts you in the Edit mode. The word *Edit* appears on the left side of the Status Bar. You can edit a cell entry that has already been accepted by double-clicking in the cell or pressing F2.

You can click on the cancel box or press Esc to cancel a cell entry. You can click on the enter box or press Enter to confirm a cell entry. You can also confirm a cell entry by moving to another cell. I'll discuss the Function Wizard in Chapter 12.

If you press Enter to accept a cell entry, the active cell border moves to the next cell down in the column, unless you turn this option off in the Edit tab of the Options dialog box.

tip If you have to enter data into a range of cells, you can select the range and just press Enter to move to the next cell in the selection.

You can enter either text or numbers in a cell; Excel is smart enough to know which it is. If you enter text, its default cell alignment is left. The default alignment for numbers is right. Of course, you can change the alignment of any cell or range of cells. If you make a cell entry that includes both text and numbers, such as a street address like 1224 Pine Street, Excel treats the entry as text. This makes sense, because you couldn't use such an entry in mathematical calculations.

note If you enter more text than the column width can accommodate, it will spill over into the next column, unless the cell in the next column contains data, in which case the text in the first column will be truncated.

Numbers that are too wide for the column are displayed in scientific notation. For example, 1000000000 is displayed as 1E+09 in the cell. But the actual number you entered is displayed on the formula bar when the cell containing that number is the active cell.

In Chapter 13 you'll learn to format numbers. If a number that is too wide for the current column width is formatted as something

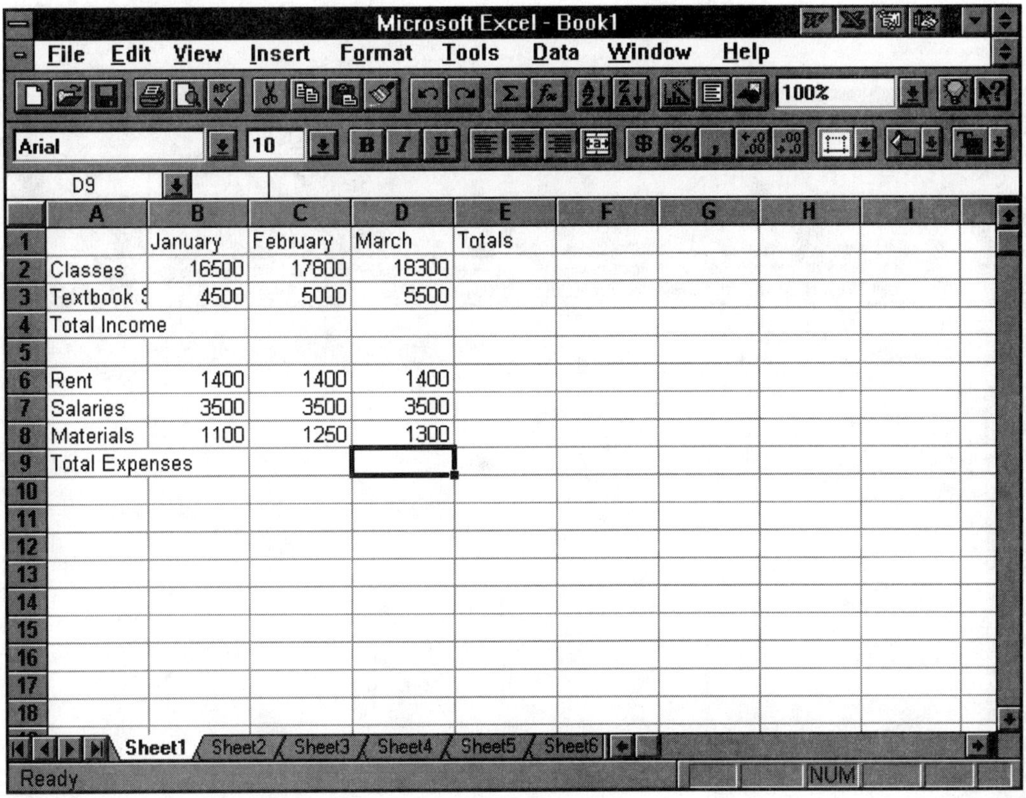

FIGURE 11-3 A simple worksheet without any formatting

other than the default General format, it will be displayed as a series of number signs—#######.

You'll also learn in Chapter 13 to adjust column widths to accommodate your cell entries.

Using the TipWizard

Often, what seems like a good way to perform a task in Excel isn't the most efficient way. For example, suppose I entered **January** in cell B1,

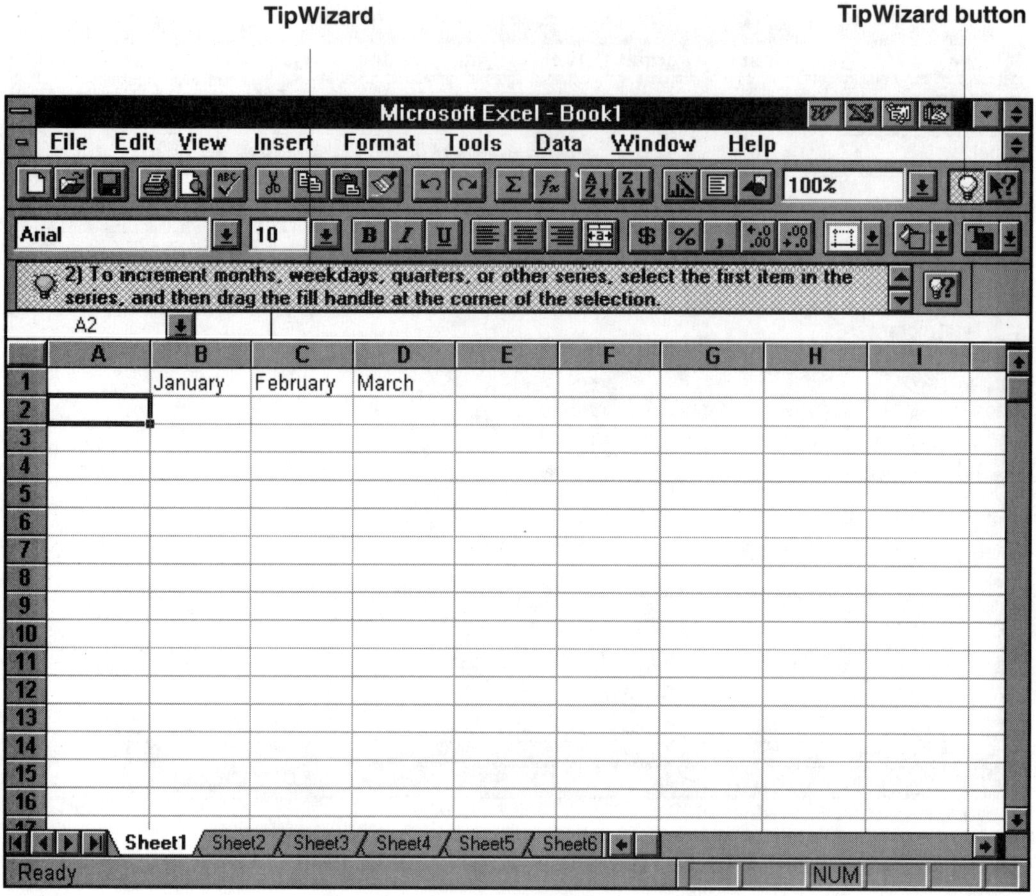

FIGURE 11–4 The TipWizard toolbar offers a suggestion.

February in cell C1, and **March** in cell D1. There is an easier way to accomplish this, and Excel's TipWizard knows what it is.

When the light bulb in the TipWizard button lights up, you can click on the button to display the TipWizard toolbar between the Formatting toolbar and the formula bar, as shown in Figure 11–4.

In this example, the TipWizard suggests using the *fill handle* in the lower-right corner of the border surrounding the active cell and dragging it to increment months, weekdays, quarters, etc. I'll cover other uses for the fill handle later.

If you want to see more detailed help relating to the tip, click on the Tip Help button on the right side of the TipWizard toolbar. After you are finished with the TipWizard, you can close it by clicking on the TipWizard button on the Standard toolbar. If you like, you can keep the TipWizard displayed so you can see new tips immediately. When there is more than one tip in an Excel session, you can use the up and down arrows on the right side of the TipWizard toolbar to see the other tips.

Saving Your Work and Closing the Workbook

Saving an Excel workbook is just like saving a document in Word except that the default workbook extension is .xls instead of .doc. Just choose File➢Save (or Save As) or click on the Save button on the Standard toolbar and enter a name in the Save As dialog box's File Name text box; then check to be sure the workbook will be saved in the proper directory. A Summary Info dialog box, in which you can enter additional descriptive information about the workbook, will appear. If you don't want to be bothered with this dialog box in the future, you can turn it off in the General tab of the Options dialog box.

The next time you want to save your workbook, choose File➢Save or click on the Save button, and the old version will be replaced with the edited version.

Like Word, Excel has an AutoSave feature, but instead of using the Options dialog box to specify AutoSave settings, Excel's AutoSave is a menu item of the Tools Menu. If AutoSave is operating, you will see a check mark in front of the AutoSave menu command. If you want to adjust the interval between saves, choose Tools➢AutoSave and make the adjustment in the AutoSave dialog box. This dialog box also lets you choose whether to save just the active workbook or all open workbooks and whether the system prompts you before saving—which is a good idea.

If you don't have an AutoSave item on the Tools menu, choose Tools➢Add-Ins to display the Add-Ins dialog box; then click on the AutoSave check box and on the OK button.

To close the workbook, choose File➢Close or double-click on the document's Control-menu box. If the workbook hasn't been saved, you'll be prompted to save it before closing.

Opening a workbook is just like opening a Word document. The bottom of the File menu displays the four most recently opened files, just as Word does. Unlike Word, Excel does not allow you to change the number of recently opened files that are displayed. It's four or nothing. You can turn off the display of recently opened files in the General tab of the Options dialog box.

Summary

This chapter covered the basic elements of an Excel workbook and how to create a simple worksheet.

The next chapter provides the tools for making the worksheet useful by adding formulas and functions, by naming ranges and inserting rows and columns, and by moving and copying data.

12

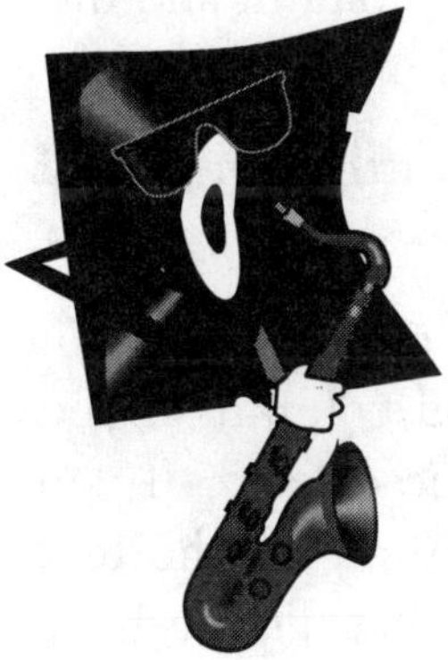

Excel—Building Blocks

Building a successful worksheet, like creating an effective word-processing document, involves edits and additions. In this chapter, you'll learn to use the basic building blocks of a worksheet.

Inserting and Deleting Rows and Columns

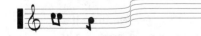

Unlike a word processing document, a worksheet does not allow you to just move to where you want to add new data and start typing. You must usually insert a new row or column. You'll also find that just deleting the data in a row or column leaves you with an empty row or column.

Of course, if the planning you did was perfect and allowed for exactly the correct number of rows and columns, you'll never have to add or delete any. However, most people's planning (especially mine) is less than flawless. For example, the worksheet created in the last chapter didn't leave a row at the top for a title. It's a good thing that inserting and deleting rows and columns in Excel is a simple procedure.

The easiest way to insert or delete a row or column is to right-click on a gray row or column heading. This selects the row or column and displays its shortcut menu. Figure 12–1 shows the row shortcut menu.

The column shortcut menu is exactly the same except that, instead of a Row Height option, it has a Column Width option.

If you click on Insert, a row will be inserted above the selected row or a column will be inserted to the left of the selected column. If you click on Delete, the selected row or column will be deleted. If you want to remove only the contents of the row or column, the shortcut menu has a Clear Contents option that lets you do that. Figure 12–2 displays the example worksheet with a row inserted above the first row of data.

CAUTION

Inserting and deleting rows and columns can wreak havoc with your worksheet if you don't do it with the greatest of care. As you build your worksheet and add formulas, it's easy to disrupt references between cells without realizing what you've done. It's especially easy if you have data in a larger worksheet that isn't currently visible.

Take a look around your worksheet before inserting or deleting. It's also a good idea to save your work before performing a potentially dangerous task. Of course, you can use the Undo feature to reverse an insertion or deletion, but unlike Word, Excel can undo only the very last thing you did. If you don't realize that you need to undo before you do something else, it will be too late.

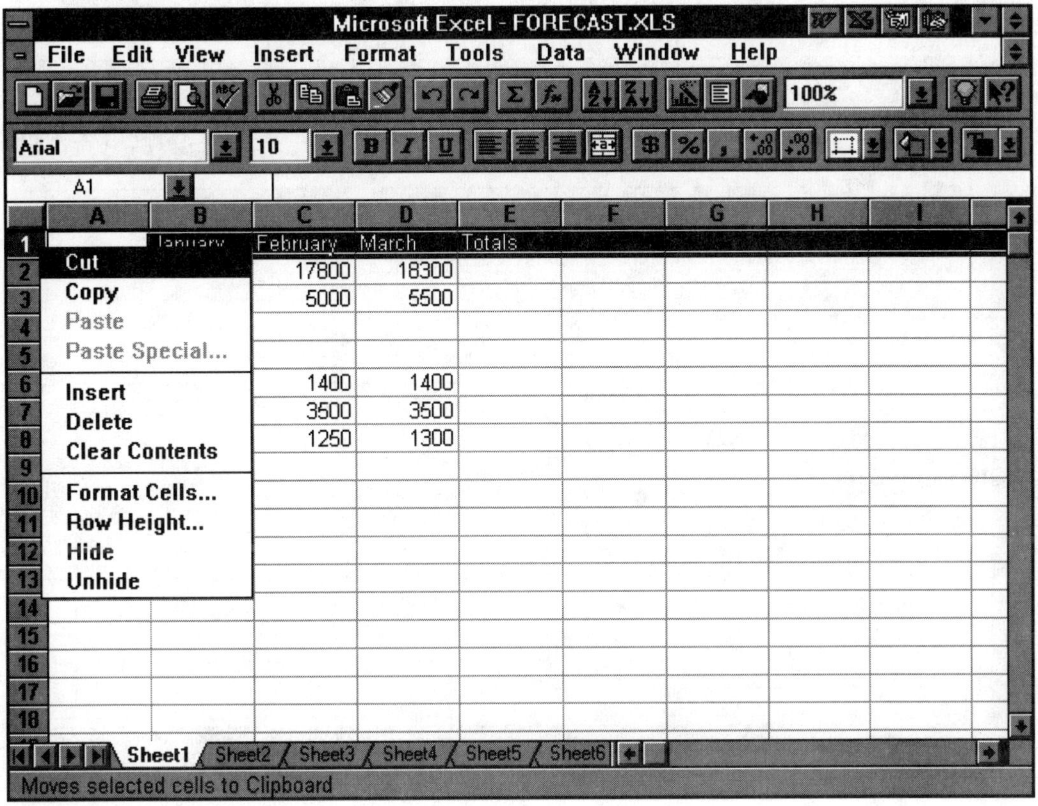

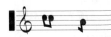

FIGURE 12–1 The row shortcut menu

Adding Formulas and Functions

Without the ability to add mathematical formulas and functions, spreadsheet programs wouldn't serve a very useful purpose. It's this ability that makes it possible to play what-if, by changing some of the

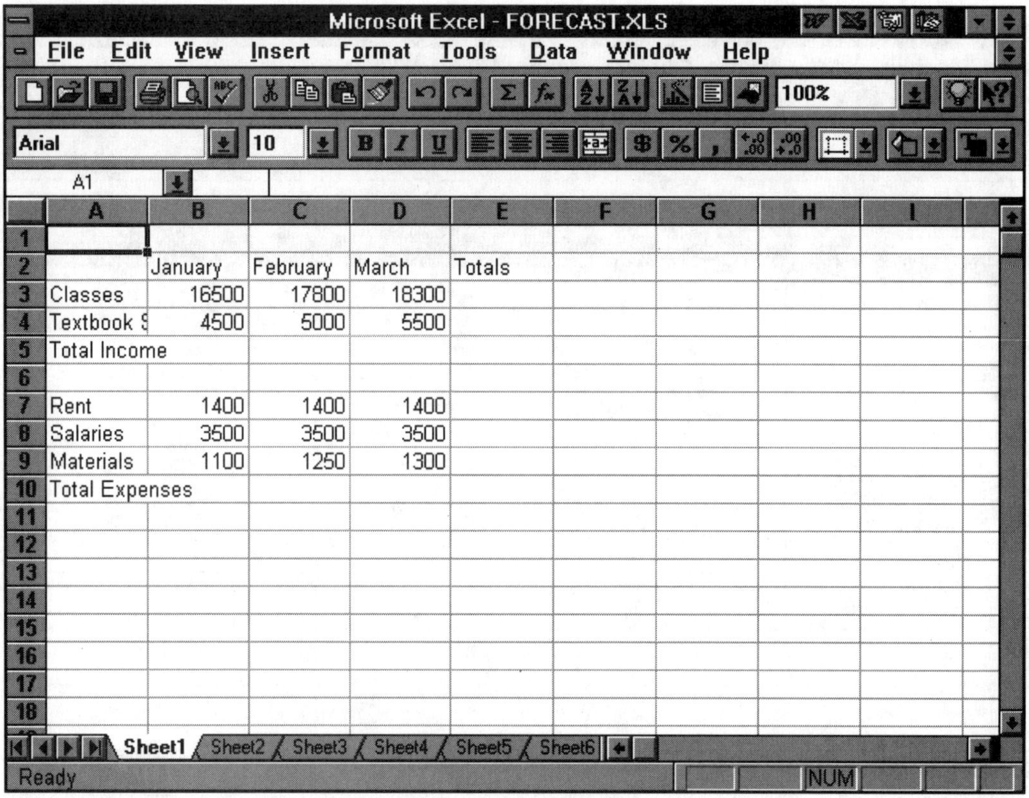

FIGURE 12–2 A row has been inserted in a worksheet and the other rows have been renumbered.

values in the worksheet and watching the results in the cells containing the formulas and functions.

Before you start using Excel's math capabilities, you must understand the difference between formulas and functions. A *formula* is a mathematical statement using *operators*—such as + for addition, - for subtraction, ∗ for multiplication, and / for division—that perform calculations using values in other cells. A *function* is simply a predefined formula. Formulas can be extremely complex and require a lot of time and effort to create and later recreate, especially if the values of many different cells are referenced. Functions just make the process easier.

For example, to add up the total income for January in the sample worksheet, you would create a formula in cell B5 to add the values in cells B3 and B4. An Excel formula always starts with an equal sign, so the actual formula would be =B3+B4.

When you enter this formula in B5, the cell will display the result of the formula, but the formula bar will display the formula if B5 is the active cell, as shown in Figure 12–3.

This simple formula was easy to create, because it referred to only two cells. But suppose you had to reference 10 or 20 cells? A formula like =B3+B4+B5+B6+B7+B8+B9+B10+B11+B12 can be pretty unwieldy. Using the Sum function would make this easier by allowing you to refer to the range of cells you wanted to sum (add up) rather than naming each individual cell.

Most functions, including the Sum function, require arguments to tell the function where and/or how much to use its operators. The arguments are enclosed in parentheses. Using the Sum function, the only required argument is the range of cells to sum. So using the Sum function to add cells B3 through B12 would look like =SUM(B3:B12). You don't even have to add the closing parenthesis. Excel is smart enough to know that it is needed and adds it automatically. Figure 12–4 shows the Sum function used in cell C5 to sum the values in C3 through C4.

As if these formulas and functions didn't make adding numbers easy enough, Excel includes a smart AutoSum feature that will figure out what you want to sum, given the location of the active cell, and do it for you.

For example, to place the Sum function in cell D5 to add up the contents of cells D3 through D4, click on cell D5 to make it the active

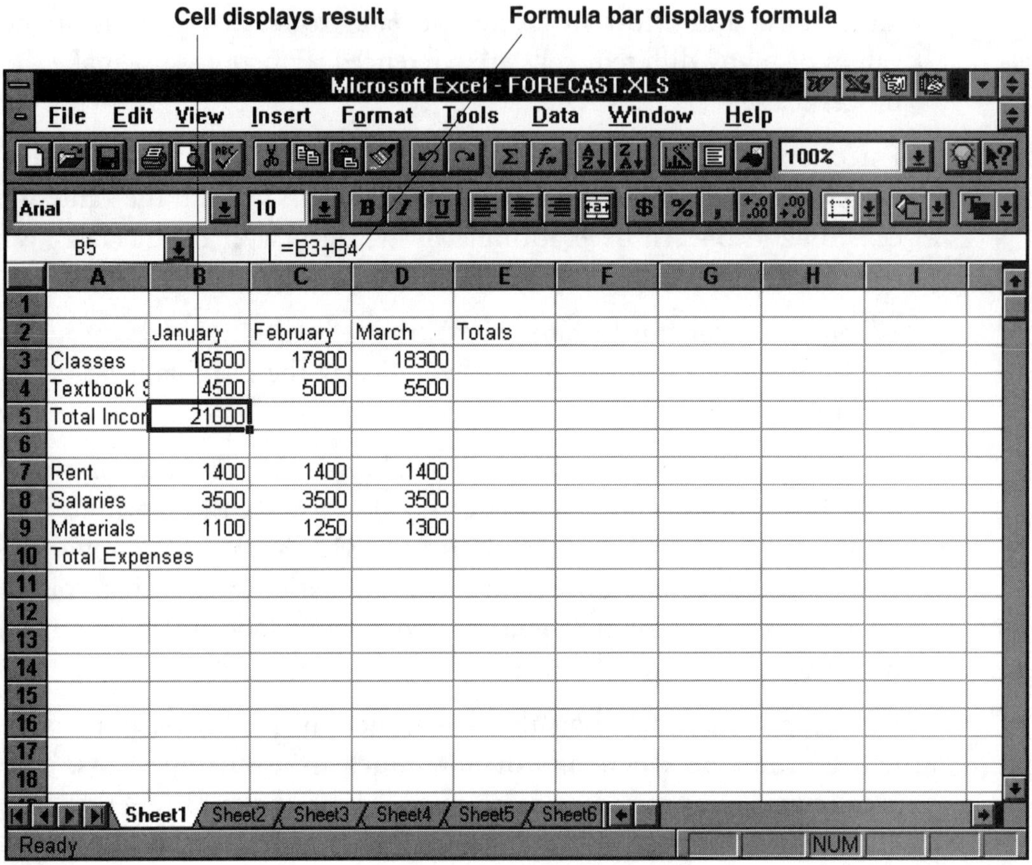

FIGURE 12–3 The result of a formula in cell B5 with the formula displayed in the formula bar

cell, then just click on the AutoSum button on the Standard toolbar. Excel displays the proposed argument (range of cells) and places a moving border around those cells. If what Excel is proposing is correct, click on the enter box or press the Enter key. If you are sure that Excel will know which cells you want to sum, you can double-click on the AutoSum button to have Excel complete the entry without requiring confirmation.

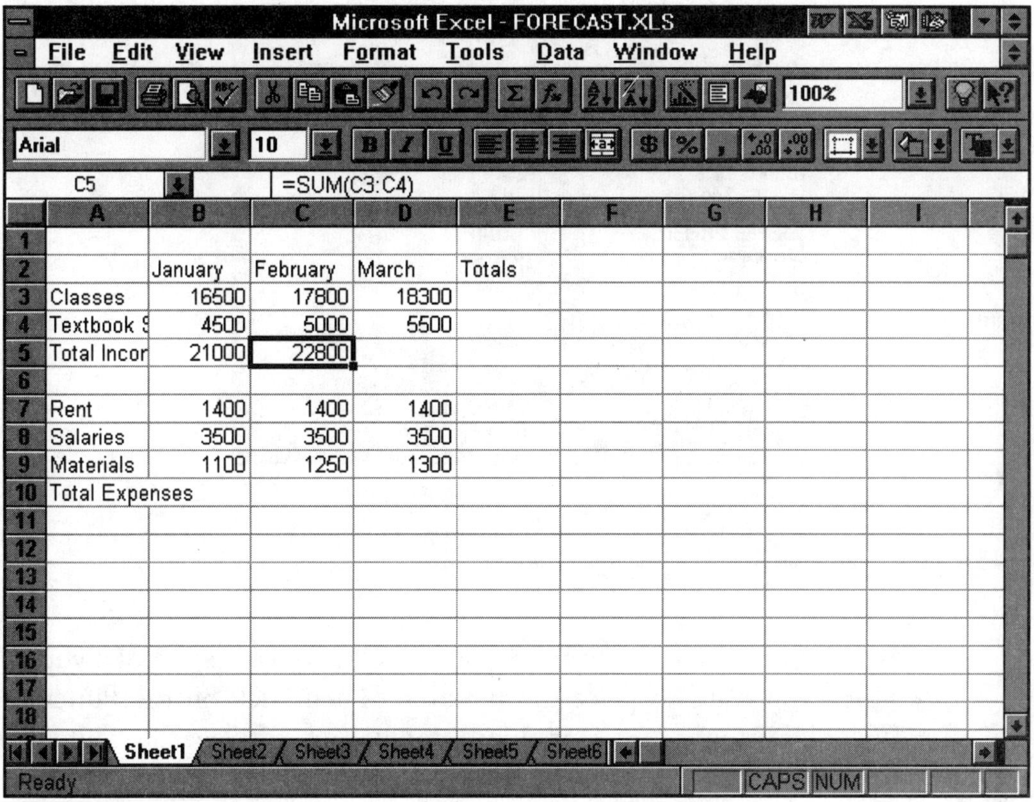

FIGURE 12–4 The Sum function has been used to sum the values in C3 through C4.

Using the Function Wizard

Excel includes a broad range of functions for performing almost every sort of calculation you can imagine. Using the Function Wizard, you can choose the function you want from several categories, including Financial, Math and Trig, and Statistical.

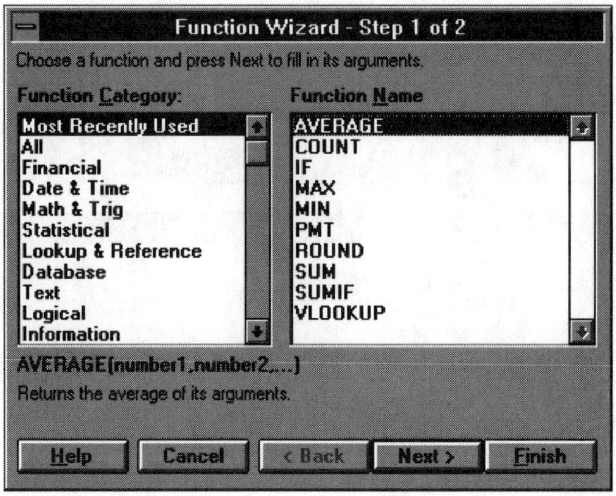

FIGURE 12–5 The Function Wizard dialog box

To use the Function Wizard, be sure the active cell is the one you in which you want to place the function. Then click on the Function Wizard button on the Standard toolbar to display the Function Wizard dialog box, as shown in Figure 12–5.

Another way to invoke the Function Wizard is to type an equal sign in the cell that is to contain the function and then click on the Function Wizard button on the formula bar.

Click on the appropriate category in the Function Category list and then click on the function you want to use in the Function Name list. If you're not sure which category the function you want to use is in, choose All to display all the functions in the Function Name list. Using the All category does have the disadvantage of displaying so many functions that it can take a lot longer to find the one you want.

tip When you click on a Function name, the proper syntax for the function and a brief description of its purpose are displayed at the bottom of the Function Wizard dialog box. If that doesn't tell you everything you want to know about that function, click on the

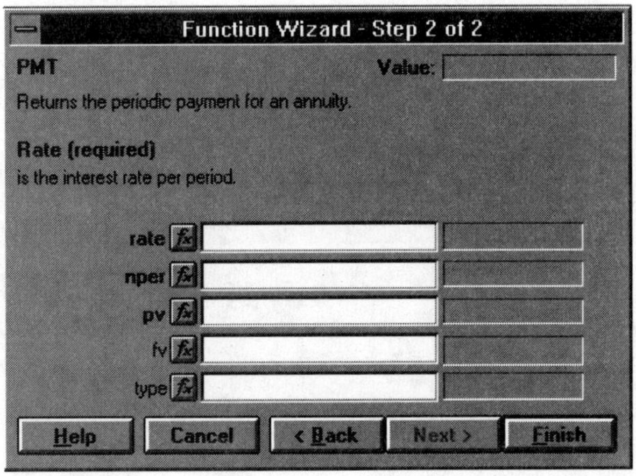

FIGURE 12–6 The second Function Wizard dialog box

Help button in the dialog box to see a complete help screen for that function.

For this example, I'll use the PMT function, located in the Financial category, to calculate the monthly payment for the Montana Training Center's new computer equipment.

After clicking on the function you want to use, click on the Next button to display the second Function Wizard dialog box, as shown in Figure 12–6.

The easiest way to enter the function's arguments is to click on them. If the Function Wizard dialog box is obscuring the cells containing the values for the arguments, move the dialog box out of the way by dragging it by its title bar.

In the example, the rate is in cell B3. Clicking on B3 enters B3 in the Rate text box and the current value in B3, 0.0925 (the decimal equivalent of 9.25%), in the box to the right. Since we want the monthly payment and 9.25 is an annual percentage rate, I'll type **/12** after the B3 in the text box to divide the value in B3 by 12 months.

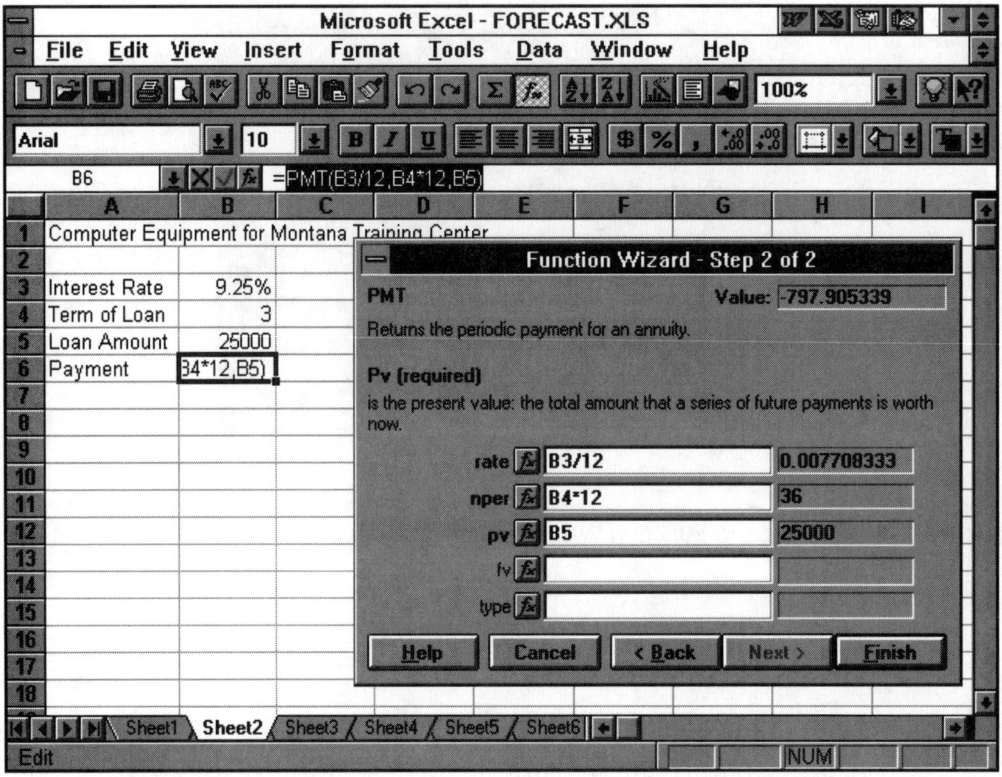

FIGURE 12–7 The filled-in dialog box

Press the [Tab] key to move to the next argument text box. In this case it's nper (number of payment periods). The cell containing the number of payment periods is B4. After clicking on B3 I'll type ***12** to multiply 3 years by 12 to keep things in the monthly format. The value for the pv (present value) text box is in B5. Figure 12–7 shows the filled-in Function Wizard arguments.

Notice that the Value in the upper-right corner of the dialog box displays the result of the calculation. After entering all the arguments, click on the Finish button to complete the function. The payment amount in cell B6 is in parentheses (and in red if you have a color monitor) because it is a negative number. It's negative because the payment represents money being paid rather than money being received, which would be a positive number.

Moving and Copying Ranges

When you move or copy in a Word document, you move or copy the text, the formatting, or both. In Excel, you have one more element to consider—formulas and the cells they reference.

To move the active cell or range, move the mouse pointer to the border, outlining the cell or range so the pointer turns into an arrow, and drag to the new location. If formulas were included in the moved range, they remain intact. For example, if you move cell B5 (containing the formula =B3+B4) to G73, the contents of G73 will be =B3+B4. You can also move ranges by choosing Edit➢Cut and Edit➢Paste.

If you want to copy a cell or range, things can work a bit differently. For example, if you copy cell B5 (containing the formula =B3+B4) to G73, the formula in G73 will be =G71+G72. What the heck is going on here? What's happening is called *relative reference.* When you copy a formula, by default, the logic of the formula, rather than the actual formula, is copied. The logic of =B3+B4 is "add the contents of the cell two rows up to the contents of the cell one row up."

You can copy a cell to an adjacent range by pointing to the fill handle so the pointer turns from a thick cross to a thin cross. Drag the fill handle so the range is selected and release the mouse button.

tip Dragging the fill handle with the right mouse button displays a shortcut menu with the available options. For example, if you used the right mouse button to drag the fill handle of a cell containing a formula, when you released the button, a shortcut menu would allow you to copy the cell (the same as dragging the fill handle with the left mouse button), as well as filling formats, filling values, and other options.

If the active cell contains an entry Excel recognizes as part of a series, such as December, Tuesday, or 1994, the shortcut menu will include options for filling the range with the series.

note There will be times when you will want to copy a cell's contents, not its logic. For example, suppose you want to copy a cell with the formula for the total expenses for the quarter to another portion of the worksheet but still reflect the result that was in the original cell. To do this you must use *absolute referencing.*

To make a reference in the active cell absolute, select the reference on the formula bar and press F4. Dollar signs will appear in front of the column letter and row number, indicating that this is now an absolute reference. Pressing F4 again makes the row, but not the column, absolute. Press F4 once more, and the column, but not the row, becomes an absolute reference.

Working with Range Names

You can work effectively in Excel without ever delving into the area of named ranges. But naming ranges can make it easier to move to far-off portions of a worksheet and even construct certain formulas.

For example, suppose you have a large budget worksheet spread out over dozens of columns and hundreds of rows. The portion dealing with projected expenses for 1998 is way off the screen, starting somewhere around cell BC129.

If you remembered that BC129 was where you wanted to go, getting there wouldn't be a problem. You would just click in the name box, type the cell reference, and press Enter. However, there's no way most people would be able to equate BC129 with 1998 expenses. Wouldn't it be easier if you could assign the name Expenses_98 to cell BC129? You can!

To name a cell or a range, make the cell active or select the range and then click on the name box. Type the name you want to assign and press Enter.

Once you have names assigned, you can move to them by clicking on the drop-down arrow to the right of the name box to display the list of names, as shown in Figure 12–8.

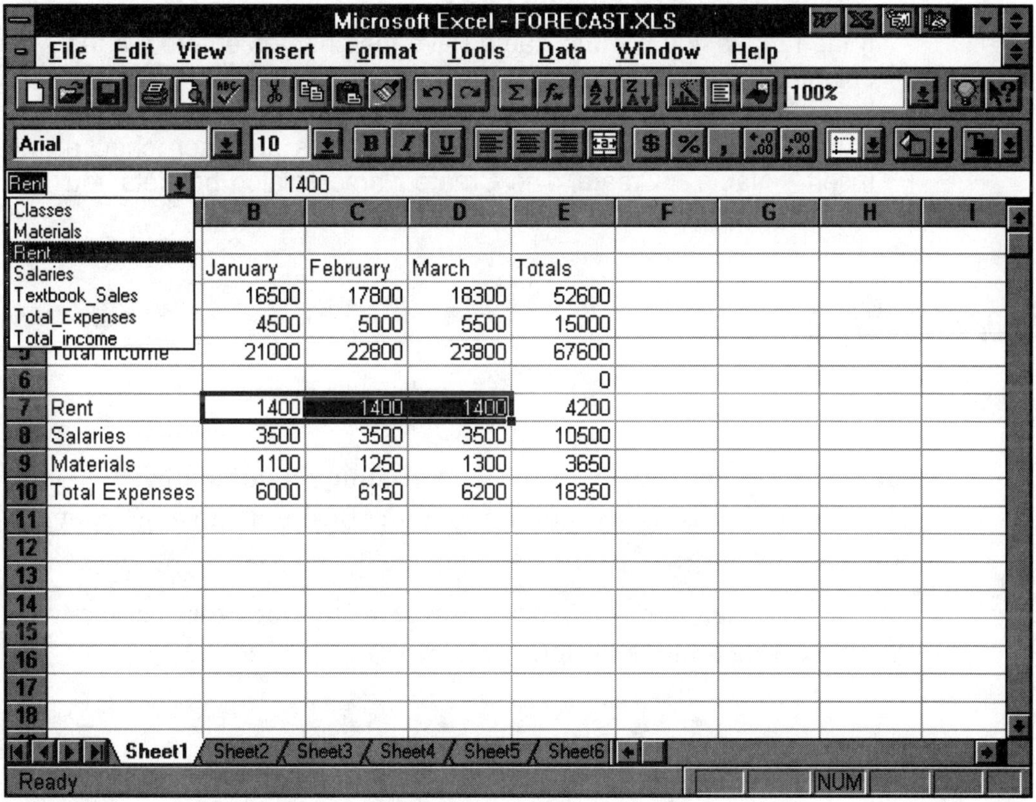

FIGURE 12–8 The Name list

If the active cell or selected range has been named, the name box displays its name. If only a portion of the range has been named, the name box displays the cell reference of the active cell.

In addition to using names to move to portions of the worksheet, you can use names in calculations. For example, if you've used the name Rent for the cells containing the rent values, you could use the Sum function to add up the rent values. The function and its argument would look like this: =SUM(Rent).

tip You can use the Apply Names dialog box, available by choosing Insert➢Name➢Apply, to convert cell references in formula arguments to name references.

If the ranges you want to name have their names entered in the column to the left or right of the range or in the row above or below, you may find it easier to create the names by doing the following. Select the range including the names and then choose Insert➢Name➢Create. The Create Names dialog box lets you use the names next to the ranges you want to name.

Summary

In this chapter, you learned some techniques for enhancing your worksheets by using formulas and functions and moving, copying, and naming ranges.

In the next chapter, you'll learn some techniques for making your Excel worksheets look better.

13

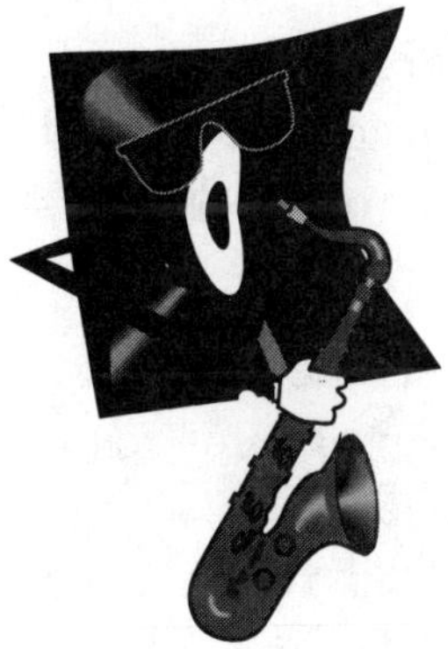

Excel—Enhancements

Now that you know how to create a functional worksheet, you'll want to make it as attractive as possible. Like well-formatted word-processing documents, great-looking worksheets go a long way toward convincing the reader that your conclusions merit consideration.

Adjusting Column Width and Row Height

You can tell when you need to make adjustments in your column widths. If the text is truncated or numbers appear as pound signs (####), widening the columns will alleviate the problem. Row height, on the other hand, doesn't usually require any intervention on your part, because it is set to AutoFit by default and automatically adjusts to font size changes.

To change the width of a column, just drag the border at the right of the column heading to the left or right until you reach the desired width. If several columns are selected, dragging one of the borders changes the width of all the selected columns.

Excel has an AutoFit feature that automatically adjusts the width of a column to accommodate its longest entry. Unlike AutoFit for rows, however, this feature must be invoked manually. The easiest way to have Excel use AutoFit for an entire column (or all the selected columns) is to double-click on the border to the right of the column heading.

CAUTION

Using AutoFit for an entire column can cause the column to be wider than you really want it to be. Suppose you have a long worksheet title that spans four or five columns entered in cell A1. Double-clicking on column A's border would widen the column to accommodate the title, which would likely be much too wide for the remainder of the entries in the column.

Fortunately, there is an easy way around this problem. Select just the cells in the column you want to AutoFit and then choose Format➢Column➢AutoFit Selection. If you want to AutoFit the entire column except for one or two cells, select the entire column by clicking on the column heading and then hold down the Ctrl

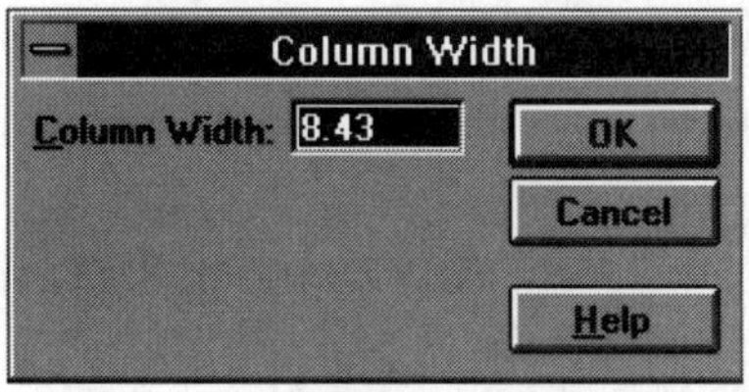

FIGURE 13–1 The Column Width dialog box

key while you click on the cell(s) you want to exclude from the selection.

Perhaps dragging to adjust the column width or using AutoFit isn't precise enough for you. If you want to adjust the column width to accommodate a specific number of characters, then choose Format➢Column➢Width or choose Column Width from the column's shortcut menu to display the Column Width dialog box, as shown in Figure 13–1.

Because you usually use proportionally spaced fonts in Excel, the number of characters is approximate. It's also based on using the default font and font size.

Another way to accommodate large amounts of text in a cell without adjusting the column width is to format the cell so the text wraps according to the current column width. This is done by choosing Format Cells from the cell shortcut menu and then clicking on the Alignment tab of the Format Cells dialog box to display the Alignment tab of the Format Cells dialog box, as shown in Figure 13–2.

Click on the Wrap Text check box and then on the OK button. The text in the cell, or selected cells, will wrap. However, the row height will also increase to accommodate the text, which may not be what you had in mind.

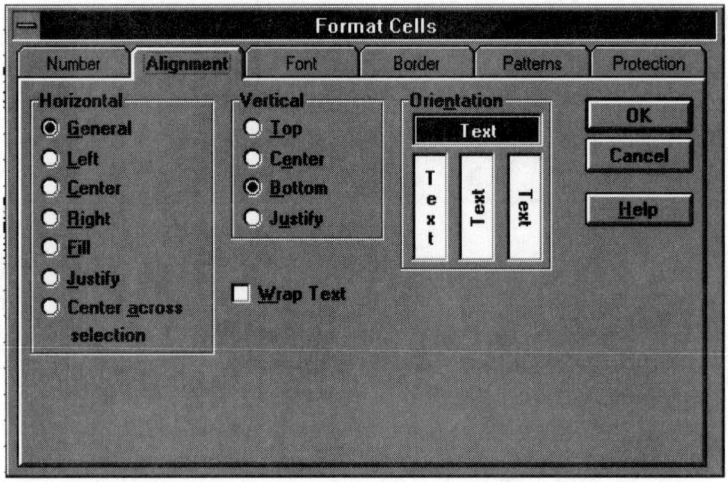

FIGURE 13–2 The Alignment tab of the Format Cells dialog box

note The Alignment tab is the portion of the Format Cells dialog box that is used for specifying how the contents of selected cells are aligned within their cells—both horizontally and vertically. You can even specify the text orientation (the direction of the text) within the cell.

Notice the Center Across Selection option, which you can use to center a cell entry across several cells.

You can adjust row height by dragging the border below its row heading number. You can also adjust row height with the Row Height dialog box, by choosing Row Height from the row shortcut menu.

note If you specify a row height, the row no longer automatically AutoFits to accommodate changes in font size. If you want to go back to AutoFit, choose Format➢Row➢AutoFit.

Formatting Values

The default value (number) format in Excel is called General. Using General formatting, numbers that are too long to fit in the current column width are displayed in scientific notation. Numbers with a zero value after the decimal point are displayed without the decimal point or the trailing zeros. Numbers with more than four decimal places are displayed with only four decimal places and rounded based on the remaining decimal places.

Regardless of how the number is displayed, Excel stores the actual number you entered in the cell. However, you will often want to display values in a certain format. Perhaps you want values that represent percentages to be displayed with percent signs and dollar amounts to be displayed with dollar signs, commas, and two decimal places. No problem. These and many other number formats are available.

You can specify certain number formats when you enter numbers into cells. For example, if you type **28%**, the number will be formatted with the percent sign. If you enter **$1,234**, the number will be formatted with the dollar sign and the comma.

In both of these examples, the actual number is stored without the formatting. In the case of the number with the percent sign, the number is actually stored as its decimal equivalent. The dollar amount is stored without the dollar sign or comma. You can tell how Excel stores the number by looking at the formula bar when the cell is active.

You can also format vales in selected cells by clicking on the Currency Style, Percent Style, or Comma Style button on the Formatting toolbar. If you want to display more or fewer decimal places, click on the Increase Decimal or Decrease Decimal button on the Formatting toolbar.

CAUTION

If you plan to create Excel charts from your numbers, as you'll learn to do in Chapter 16, don't use the toolbar buttons to format them. When you format numbers using the Currency or Comma Style toolbar button, Excel formats them as part of the Accounting category, which causes problems when you try to add them to a chart. Use the Number, Percentage, or Currency category in the Number tab of the Format Cells dialog box to format numbers you plan to include in charts.

If you want to use a number format other than one of these, select the cells you want to format and then choose Format Cells from the shortcut menu and click on the Number tab to display the Number tab of the Format Cells dialog box, as shown in Figure 13–3.

Click on a category in the Category list (the All category displays all the available formats) and then click on one of the number patterns in

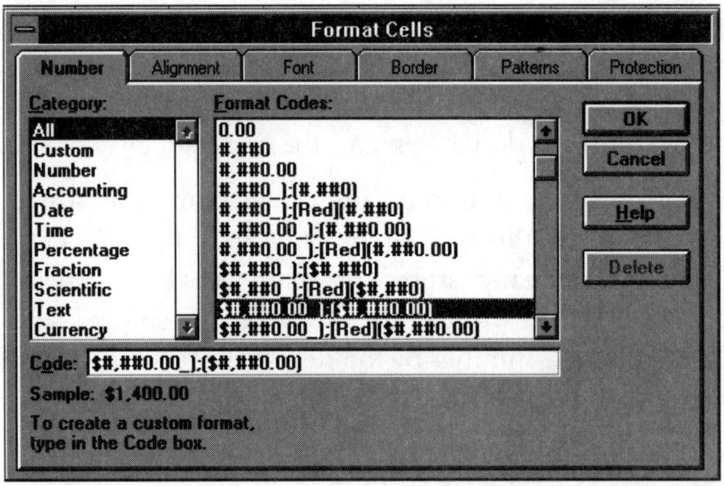

FIGURE 13–3 The Number tab of the Format Cells dialog box

the Format Codes list. Notice that the Sample portion of the dialog box displays a sample of what the value in the active cell will look like, so you can try several formats before clicking on the OK button to close the dialog box and accept the format.

Using Fonts

You can change fonts and font sizes in Excel cells just as you would in Word. Just use the Font and Font Size buttons on the Formatting toolbar or use the Font tab of the Format Cells dialog box.

note In Excel, you must change the default font and font size in the Options dialog box. It can't be changed from the Font tab of the Format Cells dialog box, as it can in Word.

Using AutoFormat

Excel has an AutoFormat feature similar to Word's that applies formatting automatically to a portion of a worksheet. Unlike Word's AutoFormat feature, Excel's AutoFormat applies direct formatting rather than using the styles feature.

Before you use the AutoFormat feature, it's usually best to select the portion of your worksheet you want Excel to format, rather than making it guess. Then choose Format➢AutoFormat to display the AutoFormat dialog box, as shown in Figure 13–4.

Click on any of the formats in the Table Format list. The Sample portion of the dialog box displays an example of a table with that format applied.

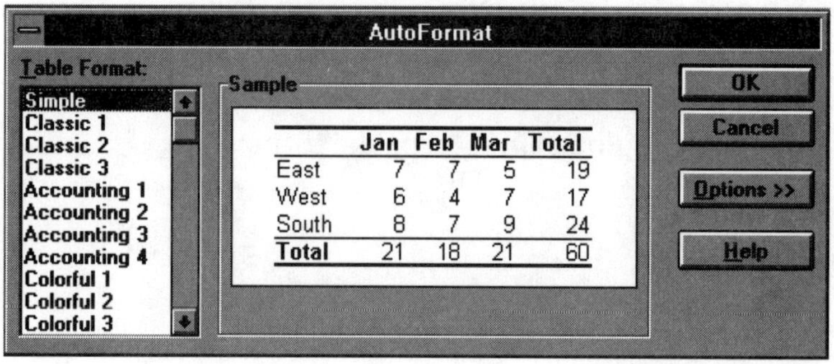

FIGURE 13–4 The AutoFormat dialog box

If you want to preserve any formatting you've already applied to the worksheet, click on the Options button to display the expanded AutoFormat dialog box with the Formats To Apply section, as shown in Figure 13–5.

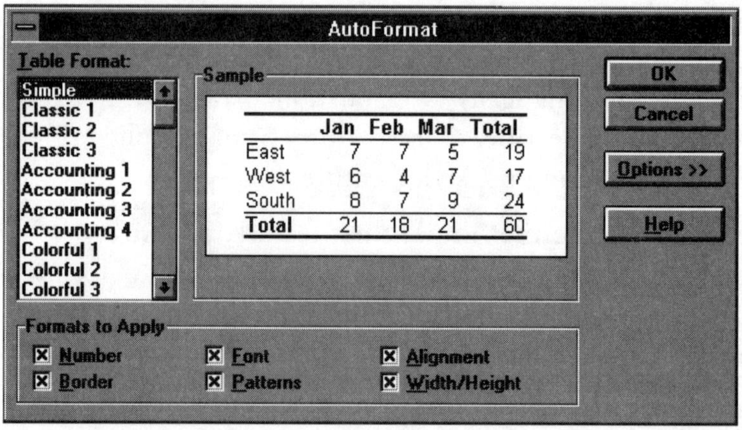

FIGURE 13–5 The Expanded AutoFormat dialog box

Click on any of the check boxes to uncheck them and keep Auto-Format from applying that type of formatting. For example, if you've already specified the fonts you want to use, click on the Font check box and your fonts will be retained.

Figure 13–6 shows our FORECAST worksheet formatted with Auto-Format's Classic 2 format.

If you decide that you don't like the results of the AutoFormatting, you can click on the Undo button on the Standard toolbar before performing any other actions.

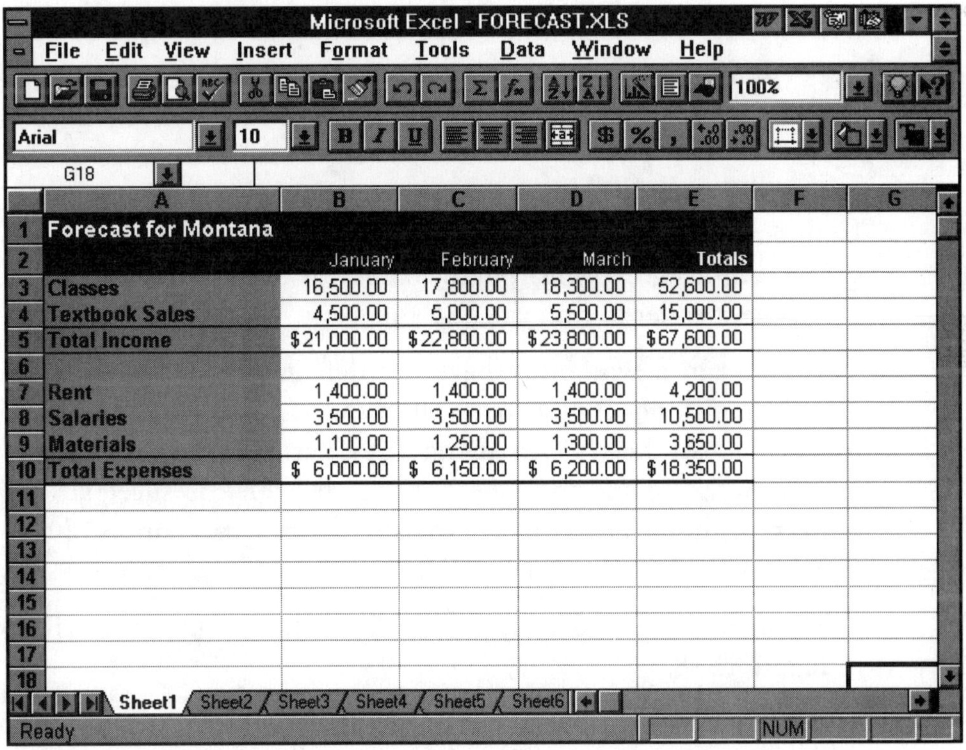

FIGURE 13–6 An AutoFormatted worksheet

Of course, you can apply formatting attributes to cells directly instead of using AutoFormat. For example, you can use buttons on the Formatting toolbar to apply borders, background colors, text colors, and alignment, as well as bold, italics, and underline. You can also use the direct formatting methods for overriding formatting after using AutoFormat.

tip If you apply borders to portions of a worksheet, you probably won't want to print the gridlines. To avoid printing the gridlines, you must turn them off in the Sheet tab of the Page Setup dialog box, which is opened from the File menu. Turning the gridlines off in the View tab of the Options dialog box affects only what appears on the screen not what appears on the printed page.

Naming Sheets

Naming your sheets doesn't change the way they appear in print or on screen, but assigning meaningful names to the sheets in a workbook can make it easier to find the one you want.

The sheets in a workbook have the default names Sheet1, Sheet2, Sheet3, and so on. If you create chart sheets (which you'll learn to do in Chapter 16) those sheets are named Chart1, Chart2, and so on. To assign another name to a sheet, right click on the sheet tab at the bottom of the sheet to display the sheet shortcut menu, as shown in Figure 13–7.

Click on Rename to display the Rename Sheet dialog box, as shown in Figure 13–8.

Type the name you want to use for the sheet in the name text box and click on the OK button. The sheet tab will display the name you've entered.

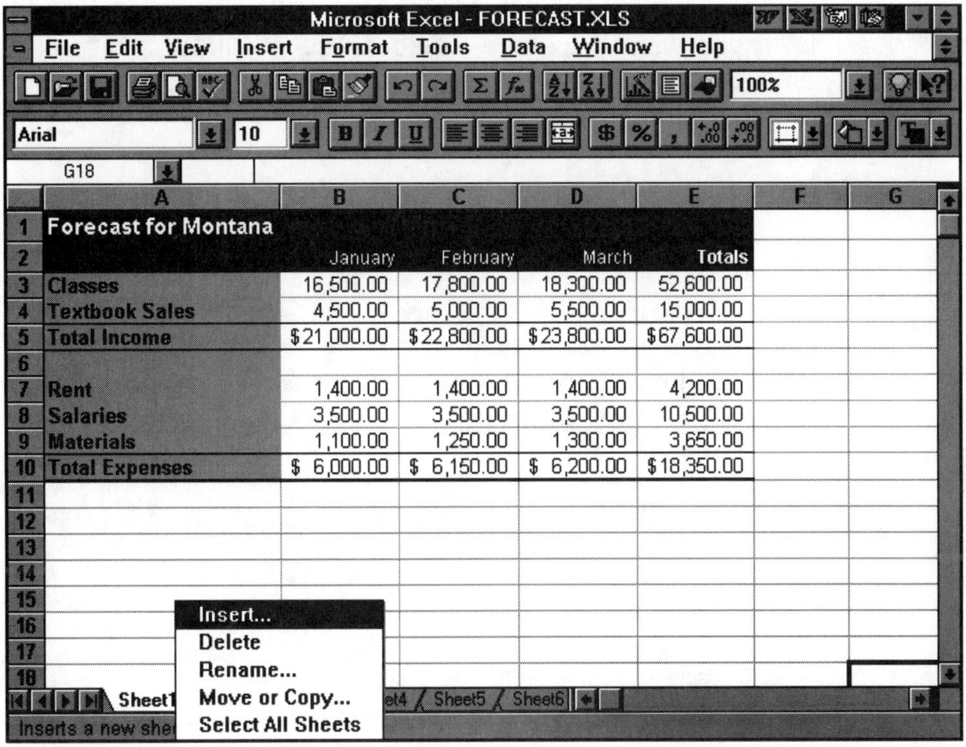

FIGURE 13–7 The sheet shortcut menu

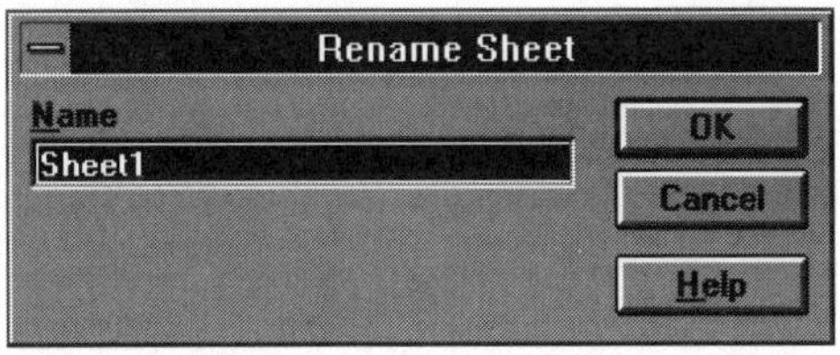

FIGURE 13–8 The Rename Sheet dialog box

note Renaming a sheet doesn't change the name you use to save the file. If you want the entire workbook saved under a different name, choose File➢Save As and enter a different name.

Summary

In this chapter, you learned to use some of Excel's formatting techniques, including the AutoFormat feature. In the next chapter, you'll learn to print your worksheets.

14

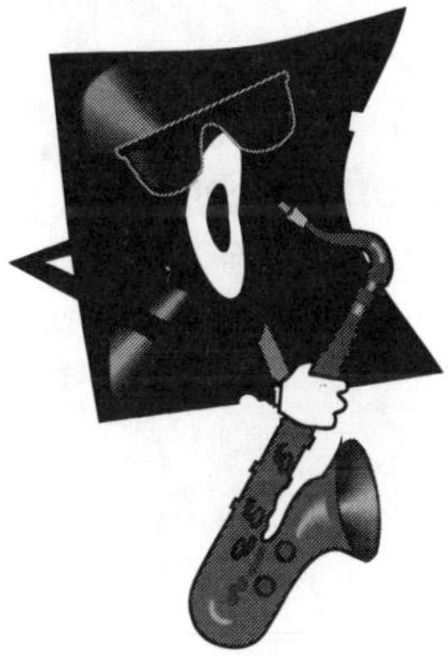

Excel—All About Printing

After you have created and formatted a worksheet, the next logical step is printing it. If you use the default settings, printing a sheet can be very simple and straightforward. Excel does, however, provide a wealth of options for making your pages look just the way you want them to.

Printing the Entire Sheet with Default Settings

If you just want to send the entire sheet to your printer with as little muss and fuss as possible, simply click on the Print button on the Standard toolbar. Be sure your printer is turned on, is on-line, and has plenty of paper loaded.

A message box will appear to let you know that Excel is printing the document, and the printed page or pages will start to emerge from your printer.

note When you click on the Print button, the worksheet prints using the original default settings or whatever settings you specified in the Page Setup dialog box for the open workbook. The Page Setup dialog box will be covered in the next section.

Specifying Pages

Before you print a worksheet for the first time, you'll probably want to specify the printing options to use. For example, you may print with or without gridlines, in portrait or landscape orientation, and you may want to add a header or a footer.

All the options that affect what comes out of your printer are specified in the Page Setup dialog box. Choose File➢Page Setup to display the Page Setup dialog box, as shown in Figure 14–1.

Among the options in the Page tab of the Page Setup dialog box are whether to print in a portrait (vertical) or landscape (horizontal)

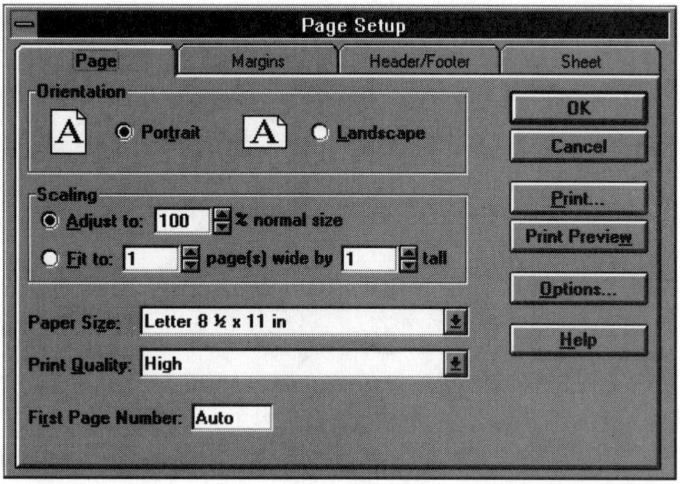

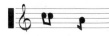

FIGURE 14–1 The Page Setup dialog box

orientation. In general, if you have to print more columns than rows, landscape is the preferred orientation.

Another option is the way the pages are scaled. You can enlarge or reduce the proportional size of the printed document by choosing a percentage in the Adjust To % Normal Size box, or you can have Excel fit the worksheet onto a specified number of pages. This can be a terrific option if you find that printing the worksheet at normal size is just a little bit too large to fit on, say, three pages. If you tell Excel to fit it on three pages, the whole document will be reduced just enough to fit.

Changing Margins

On the Margins tab of the Page Setup dialog box, you can specify top, bottom, left, and right margins for your sheets, as well as whether you

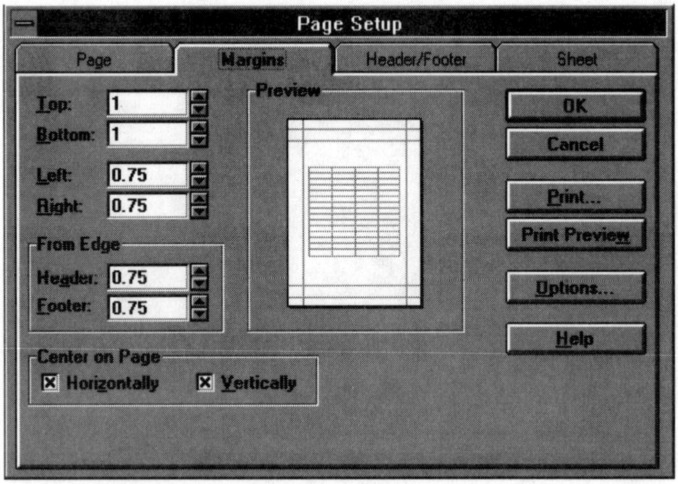

FIGURE 14–2 The Margins tab of the Page Setup dialog box

want the data centered horizontally or vertically (or both) on the page. You can also specify separate left margins for headers and footers.

The Preview area displays an example of how the settings will affect the position of the data on the page.

note Margins can also be set in Print Preview. You may even find this a preferable approach, because you can adjust them visually by dragging markers. Print Preview will be covered later in this chapter.

Specifying What Will Print

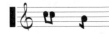

The Sheet tab of the Page Setup dialog box lets you specify which data will appear on your printed pages. This is where you choose whether to print items such as gridlines, row and column headings, and notes you've added to cells using Insert➢Note.

You can also choose to have one or more rows or columns repeat on each page. This can be a useful option if rows or columns contain labels that explain data that would be difficult to decipher without these labels.

If you always print the same region of a worksheet, you can enter the range of cells to print in the Print Area box. For example, if you always want to print cells A3 through W26, type **A3:W26** or drag over that range on the worksheet while the insertion point is in the Print Area text box. If you choose the dragging method, you can move the dialog box out of the way as much out as possible, but you can even drag over portions of the worksheet that are obscured by the dialog box.

If you drag to choose a print area, or enter it manually and later return to the Sheet tab, the entry in the Print Area box will appear as

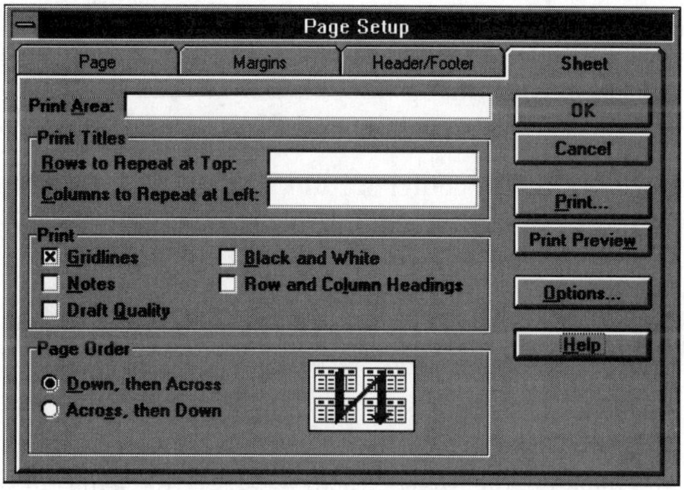

FIGURE 14–3 The Sheet tab of the Page Setup dialog box

an absolute reference with dollar signs in front of each column letter and row number.

tip If you don't want to specify a range to print every time, you can select the portion of the sheet you want to print just before printing and then choose to print the selection in the Print dialog box.

Adding Headers and Footers

The Header/Footer tab of the Page Setup dialog box lets you add headers and/or footers to your printed pages. This is how you add page numbers to the printed pages.

The default header is the sheet name. The default footer is the word *Page* followed by the page number. You can, however, choose from several predefined headers and footers or create your own custom header or footer.

Custom headers and footers are created with the same buttons you use in Word's Header and Footer toolbar, but the buttons appear in a Header or Footer dialog box when you click on the Custom Header or Custom Footer button, as shown in Figure 14–5.

The &[Tab] in the center section is the code for the sheet name. You can add other codes by clicking on one of the other buttons

Previewing and Printing the Sheet

If you haven't specified a print area in the Page Setup dialog box, select the portion of the sheet you want to print or select the sheets you want to print by holding down the Ctrl key and clicking on each

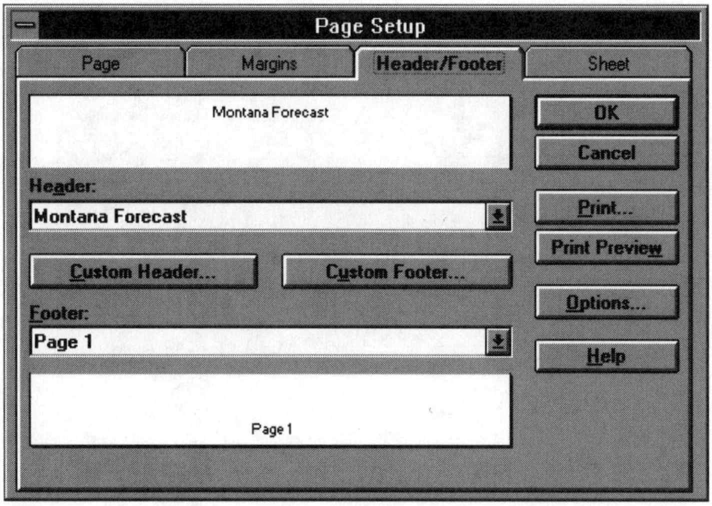

FIGURE 14–4 The Header/Footer tab of the Page Setup dialog box

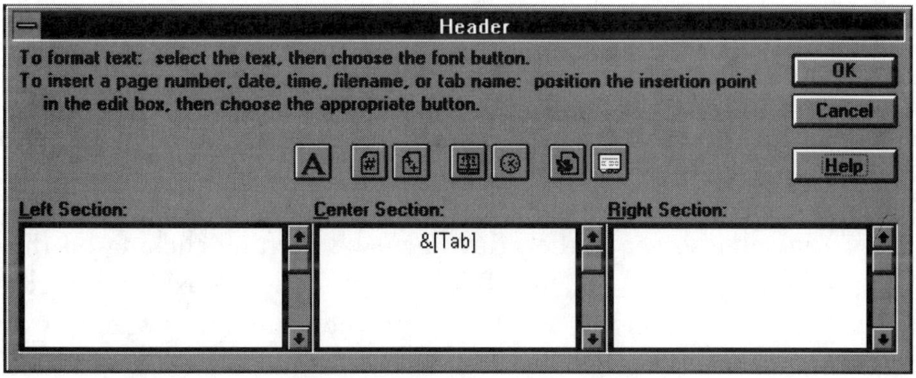

FIGURE 14–5 The custom header dialog box

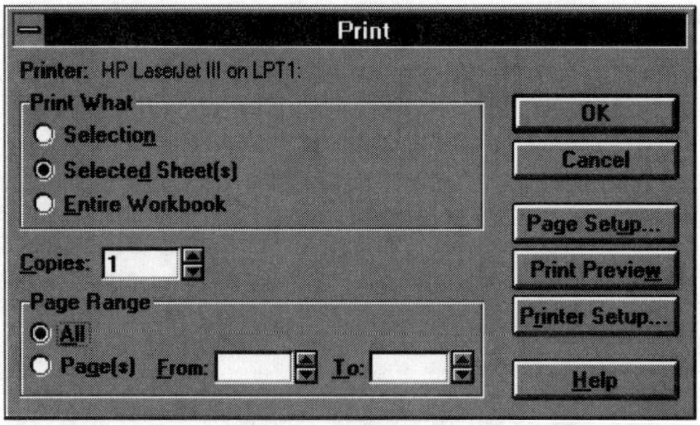

FIGURE 14–6 The Print dialog box

sheet tab you want to include. Then choose File➢Print to display the Print dialog box, as shown in Figure 14–6.

In the Print dialog box, you can specify whether you want to print the selection, selected sheets, or the entire workbook. You can also specify how many copies to print and whether to print all the pages or just certain pages.

After making your choices in the Print dialog box, it's always a good idea to preview your work before sending the pages to your printer. This can save time and trees. To preview your work, click on the Print Preview button to display the Print Preview screen, as shown in Figure 14–7.

You can also get to the Print Preview screen by clicking on the Print Preview button in the Page Setup dialog box or by choosing File➢Print Preview or clicking on the Print Preview button on the Standard toolbar.

If you want a close-up view of the page, click on the Zoom button or move the mouse pointer over the portion of the page you want to zoom in on and click. Zoom back out by clicking the mouse button again.

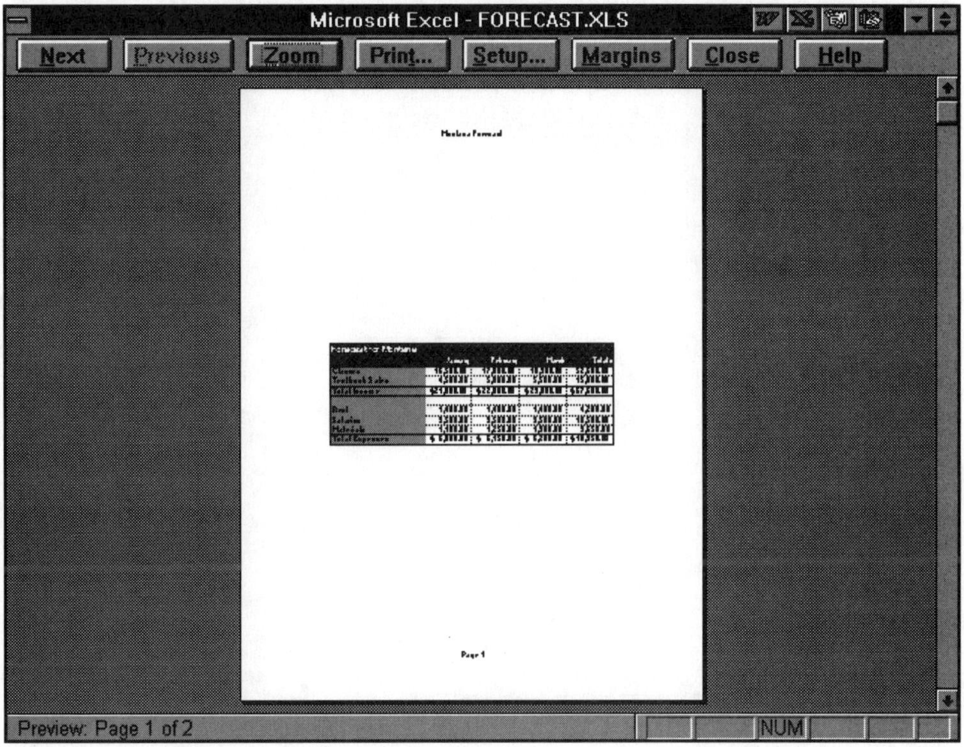

FIGURE 14–7 The Print Preview screen

If you have more pages to be printed, you can click on the Next or Previous button. If you are previewing the first page, the Previous button is dimmed. If you are previewing the last page, the Next button is dimmed.

To change margins by dragging markers, click on the Margins button to display the margin and column markers, as shown in Figure 14–8.

To change a margin or column width, position the mouse pointer over one of the markers or marker guides and drag.

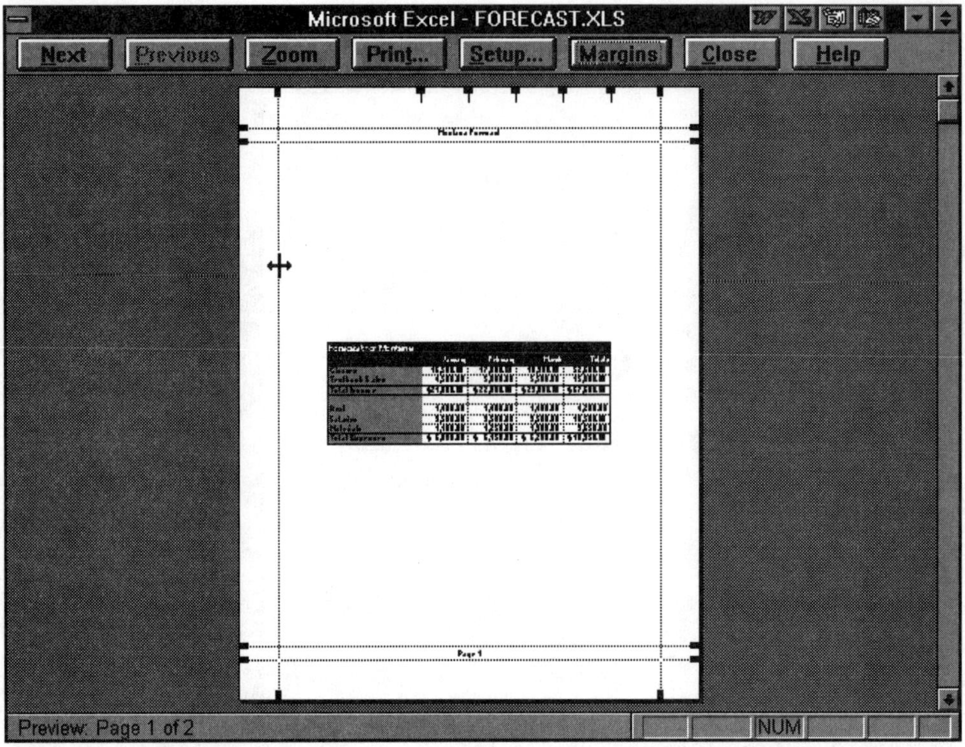

FIGURE 14–8 The Print Preview screen with the margin and column markers

When you have everything adjusted just the way you want it, click on the Print button to return to the Print dialog box and click on the OK button.

Summary

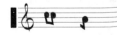

In this chapter, you learned to preview and print your worksheets and take advantage of print options and enhancements, including

changing orientation and adding headers and footers. In the next chapter, Excel's database capabilities will be explained.

15

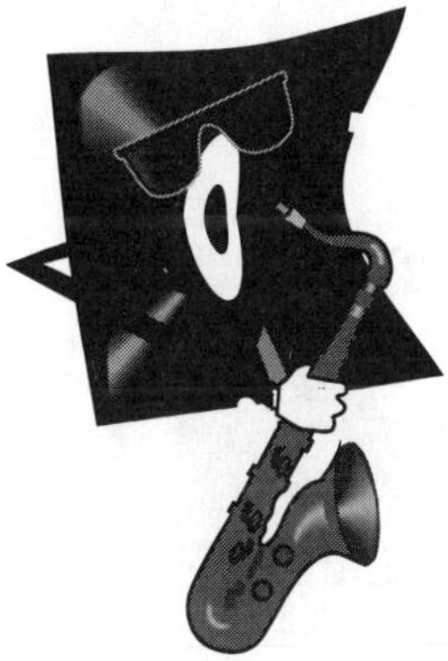

Excel—Creating Excel Databases

Like most spreadsheet programs, Excel lets you create and work with database lists. Excel 5.0 greatly expands the database capabilities and makes working with databases much easier than previous versions.

Overview of Excel Databases

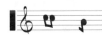

An Excel database is nothing more than a collection of related information organized in rows (records) and columns (fields). You can have any sort of data in a database. Common examples of databases are name-and-address lists and price lists.

After organizing data in a list, you can use Excel's database facilities to search for records or sort the list based on criteria you specify.

Creating a Database

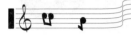

There's nothing special you need to do to create a database list in Excel. Just enter column labels (headers) for each category of data and then enter the data directly below the column labels. Figure 15–1 shows an example of the beginning of a list with column labels and one record entered.

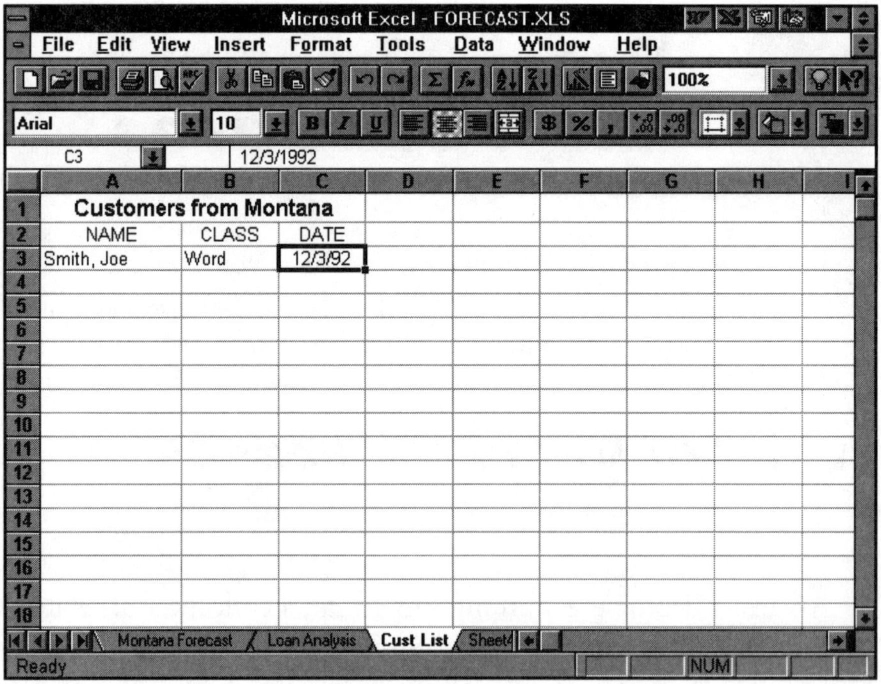

FIGURE 15–1 The start of an Excel database list

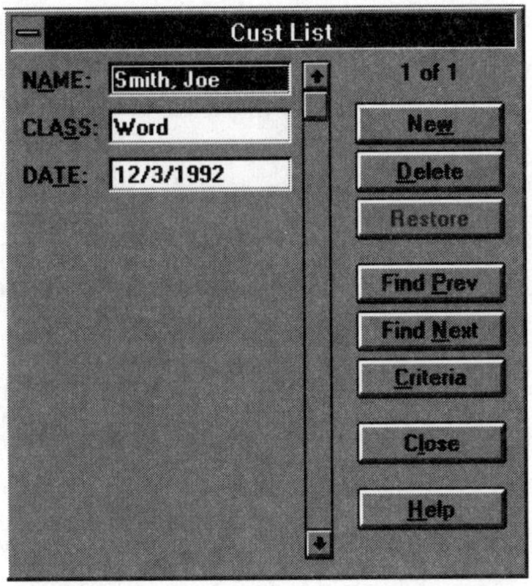

FIGURE 15–2 The data form dialog box

The list title in row one of our example is not part of the list. Nor is it important to enter the column labels in uppercase. However, if you enter the column labels in uppercase and the data in lowercase or mixed case, Excel will immediately be able to recognize which part of the list is the data and which part is the column labels.

You could continue entering records directly into the appropriate cells, but Excel provides an even slicker way to add records—the *data form.* Be sure the active cell is one of the cells in the list and then choose Data➢Form to display the data form dialog box, as shown in Figure 15–2.

The title bar of the dialog box displays the sheet name, so it's a particularly good idea to assign meaningful names to sheets containing database lists.

note In Figure 15–2, Excel has figured out that the first row of the list contained the headers and that the data below is part of the list. If Excel hadn't been able to figure it out, you would have been presented with a dialog box asking if Excel should assume the top row was the header row. If you see one of these dialog boxes, just click on the OK button.

To add new records, click on the New button and enter the data for the next record in the appropriate text boxes. After entering the data in the first text box, you can move to the next one by pressing the Tab key or by clicking in it. After entering all the data for a new record, click on the New button again if you want to add more records. If you are finished adding records for now, click on the Close button.

Notice that, as you add new records, the data is placed in the appropriate cells. Excel even retains any formatting you specified in the first record. For example, the date in the first record was center-aligned, so the dates in the succeeding records are center-aligned.

Searching for Data

In addition to aiding you in building a database, the data form dialog box is also useful for performing some database management tasks. You can use the data form dialog box to find records that meet certain criteria and delete records that are no longer needed.

If you've closed the data form dialog box, choose Data➢Form to display it again. Suppose you wanted to find all the records in our example database for students who have attended Excel classes. Click on the Criteria button, enter **Excel** in the CLASS text box, and then click on the Find Next button. The next record that meets the comparison criterion appears in the data form dialog box, as shown in Figure 15–3.

You can move through all the records that meet the search criterion by clicking on the Find Next and Find Previous buttons.

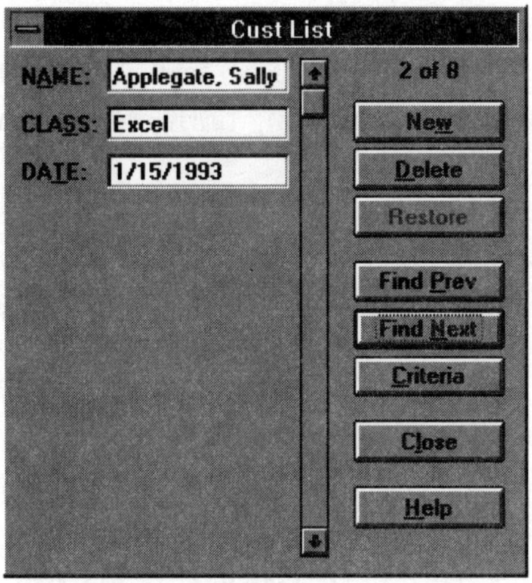

FIGURE 15–3 The first of eight records that meet the search criterion

In addition to entering exact comparison criterion, you can use comparison operators to find records in which the value in a field meets a specified condition. For example, suppose you want to find all the customers who attended classes more recently than 1/1/93. You could use the greater than (>) comparison operator in the DATE field. The entry would look like this: >1/1/92. The following is a list of comparison operators.

=	Equal to
>	Greater than
<	Less than
>=	Greater than or equal to
<=	Less than or equal to
<>	Not equal to

You can also enter comparison criteria in more than one text box to find records that match multiple specifications. For example, if you want to find all the customers who took Word classes prior to 12/31/93, you would enter **Word** in the CLASS text box and **<12/31/93** in the DATE text box. Only records meeting both criteria would be found.

Filtering Data

Using the data form to find records only lets you find one record at a time, and it limits you to finding records that meet only one criterion per column. The AutoFilter feature lets you display all the records that meet your search criteria. It also lets you specify up to two comparison criteria per column and specify whether the records must match both or only one of the criteria.

To use AutoFilter, be sure one of the cells in your list is the active cell and then choose Data➢Filter➢ AutoFilter. AutoFilter places a drop-down arrow next to each column heading in the list, as shown in Figure 15–4.

tip If the columns aren't wide enough for both the column-header labels and the drop-down arrows, you might want to widen the columns that are too narrow so the labels aren't obscured.

To filter the list so that only the records that meet your specifications are displayed, click on the drop-down arrow for one of the columns to display a drop-down list of comparison criteria, as shown in Figure 15–5.

The drop-down list includes all the unique entries for that column. If there are more unique entries than can be displayed in the drop-down list, the list will have a vertical scroll bar. You can also navigate the drop-down list by pressing the first letter of the entry you're looking for to highlight the first entry that starts with that letter.

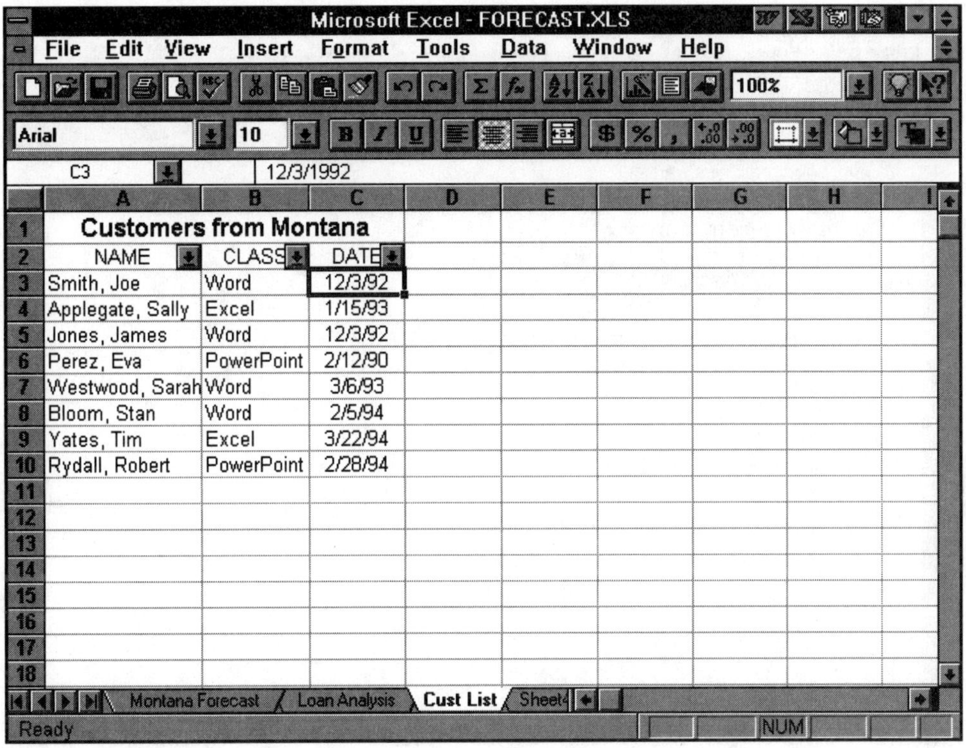

FIGURE 15–4 The AutoFilter places a drop-down arrow next to each column heading in the list.

Clicking on one of the entries causes Excel to hide all records that don't match it. If you want to display only records that contain data in that field, click on (NonBlanks). Click on (Blanks) to display records that have no data in that field. If you've chosen a comparison criterion and want to display all the records again, click on (All).

note You can tell if a criterion for a column has been specified because the drop-down arrow for that column turns blue.

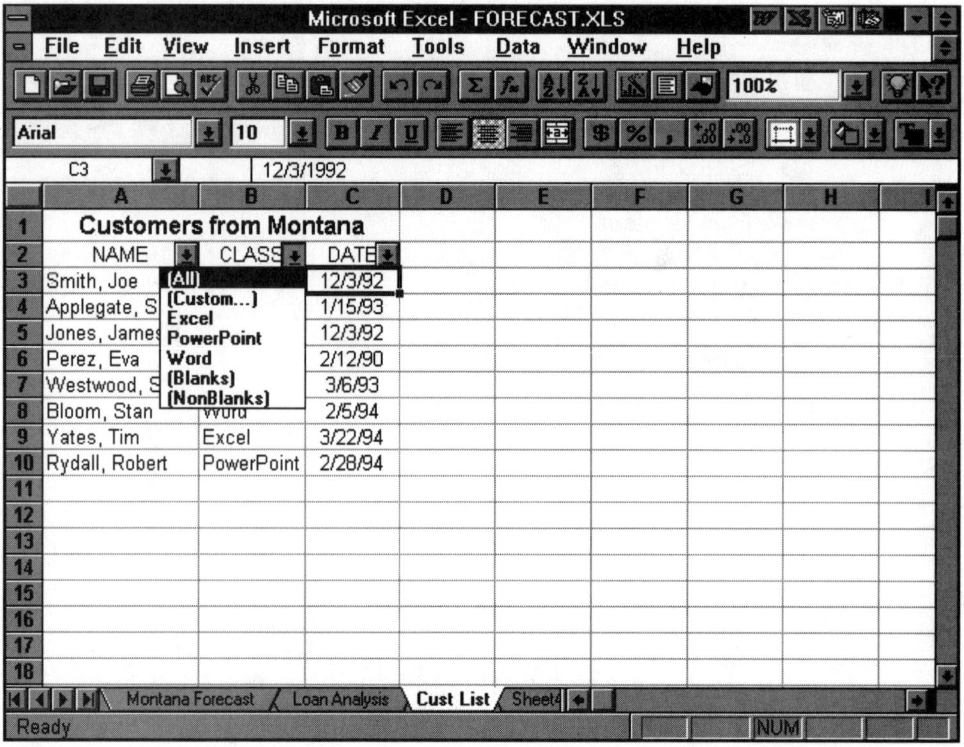

FIGURE 15–5 The drop-down list of comparison criteria for the CLASS field

You can enter comparison criteria for multiple columns. You just have to do it one column at a time. For example, suppose you want to display records for customers who attended a Word class on 12/3/92. You would first click on Word in the drop-down list for the CLASS column, so only the records with Word entered in that field were displayed. Then, to narrow the filter, you would click on 12/3/92 in the DATE drop-down list.

If you have to create custom criteria for a column, click on (Custom...) to display the Custom AutoFilter dialog box, as shown in Figure 15–6.

In the Custom AutoFilter dialog box, you first specify the comparison operator and then enter the comparison criterion in the text box. You can use the asterisk (*) and question mark (?) wildcard characters within your comparison criteria entry if you aren't sure of some of the characters. For example, if you were looking for a customer with the last name of Smith, but you couldn't remember the first name, you could enter the comparison criterion as **Smith*** (which means Smith followed by any characters).

If you want to use two criteria, enter the first one in the top text box and the other in the bottom text box; then choose the And or Or option button. If you choose And, the matching records must match both comparison criteria. If you choose Or, the records must match only one of the criteria.

When you are finished working with the filtered list, you can leave the list filtered or restore it to its original state by choosing Data➢Filter➢AutoFilter to turn the AutoFilter feature off.

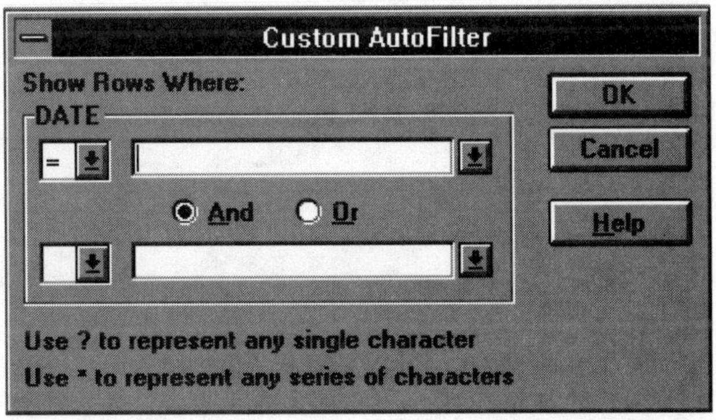

FIGURE 15-6 The Custom AutoFilter dialog box

Sorting Data

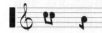

There are many reasons for sorting your lists. Often you'll have to print your list, but you can't use Excel search and filter capabilities on the printed page. Fortunately, sorting an Excel list is a snap.

To sort a list, be sure one of the cells in the list is the active cell and then choose Data➢Sort to display the Sort dialog box, as shown in Figure 15–7.

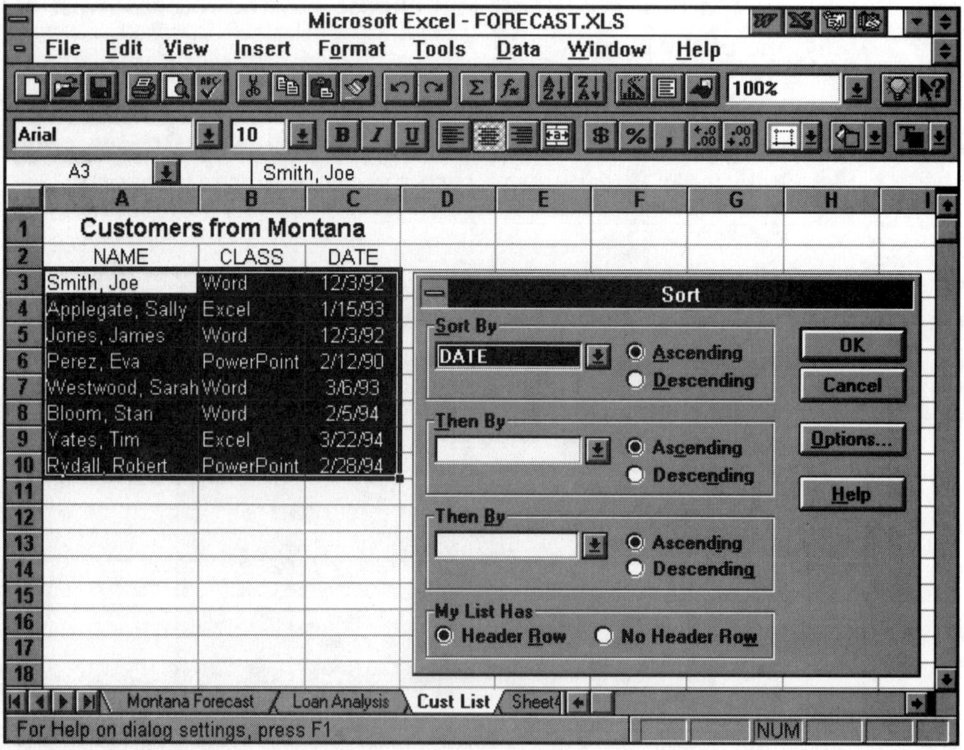

FIGURE 15–7 The Sort dialog box

The entire list is selected, which tells you that the entire list will be sorted. If the header row containing the column labels is selected, click on the Header Row option button at the bottom of the dialog box so the header row won't be sorted with the list.

Click on the Sort By drop-down arrow and click on the name of the column you want to use as the basis of your sort. Then choose the Ascending or Descending option. Ascending sorts from A through Z or 1 through 99. Descending sorts from Z through A or 99 through 1.

You might want to sort our example customer list based on the customers' last names. In a complete list of customers who have attended classes, many would have attended more than one class, so you might want to use a second sort specification in the Then By portion of the dialog box. For example, you could sort by NAME and then by DATE so that the dates of the classes would be sorted for each customer. Figure 15–8 shows the list sorted by the NAME column.

If you want to restore the list to its original order, you can click on the Undo button on the Standard toolbar immediately after performing a sort.

tip If you want to be able to return easily to the original order of a list at any time, it's a good idea to add a column for record numbers. After inserting the column, type **1** in the first cell of the new column. Then use the right mouse button to drag down to the bottom of the list and click on Fill Series. The numbers will be filled in automatically.

The database capabilities covered in this chapter are only the tip of the iceberg. Excel includes many functions specifically designed to help you manipulate data. You can also create PivotTables to cross-tabulate the data so you can view it from a different perspective.

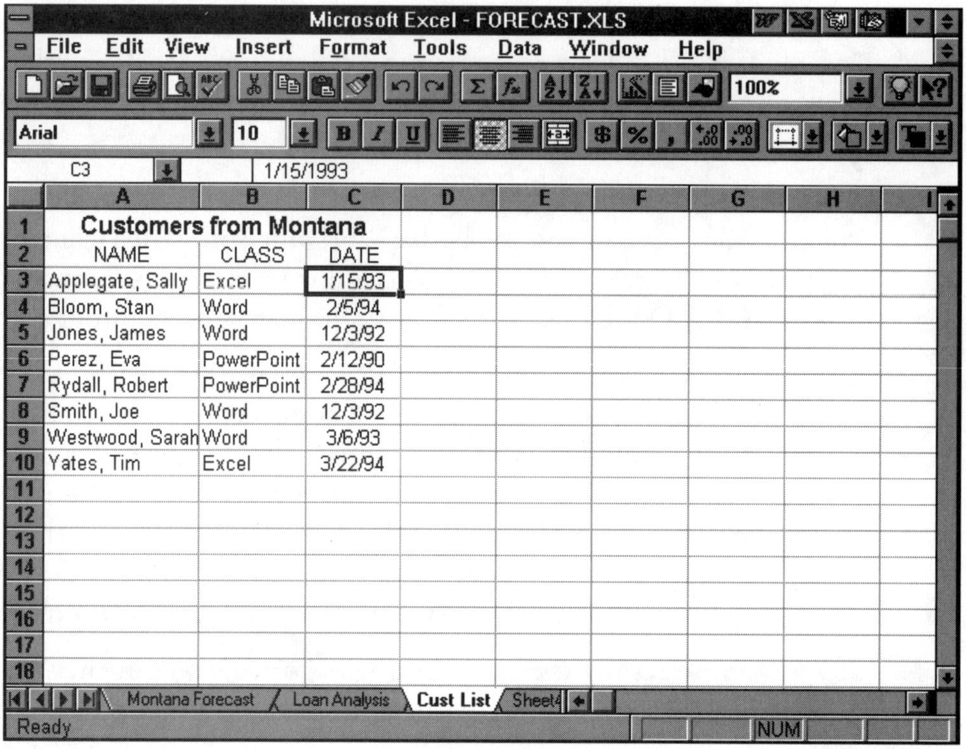

FIGURE 15–8 The sorted list

Summary

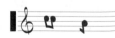

In this chapter you learned the basics of creating and working with databases. In the next chapter, you'll learn to turn dull worksheet data into dazzling charts.

16

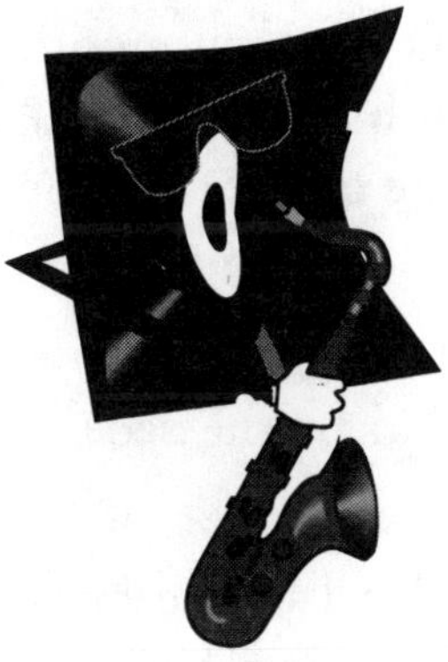

Excel—Charting Your Course

If the purpose of your worksheets is to persuade and inform, turning your numbers into charts is often the surest way to accomplish your goal. Excel lets you create an incredible variety of charts to meet virtually any charting requirement you could imagine.

Overview of Excel Charting Capabilities

A chart is simply a graphical representation of values from a worksheet. Each value that you include in a chart is called a *data point.* Data points are graphically represented on a chart by such items as slices of a pie, bars, and lines. A group of data points is called a *data series.* You can include an almost unlimited number of data series in a chart (except a pie chart, which can include only one data series). For example, suppose you want to chart the total income for each month for the new Montana Training Center. Each month's total income value is a data point and the data points for the entire quarter are one data series.

You might want to add the total expenses in a chart to make it easy to compare visually. The values of total expenses would be the second data series.

In addition to data points, you can add a title, a label to the horizontal x-axis (called the *category axis),* a legend to explain what each data series represents, and a wealth of other enhancements.

An Excel chart can be embedded in the same worksheet as the data it represents, or it may reside in its own chart sheet. In either case, the chart is linked to the data and automatically updated when the values change.

Creating an Embedded Chart

The ChartWizard steps you through the entire chart creation process, and you can make all your chart option choices in the ChartWizard.

The chart creation task is easier, however, if you select the data series for the chart and the category labels before starting the ChartWizard. Remember, to select non-contiguous ranges, select the first range and then hold down the Ctrl key while selecting the next range or ranges. In Figure 16–1 the total income data series and the category labels have been selected.

Notice that the same number of cells is selected in the row containing the data series and the row containing the category labels, even

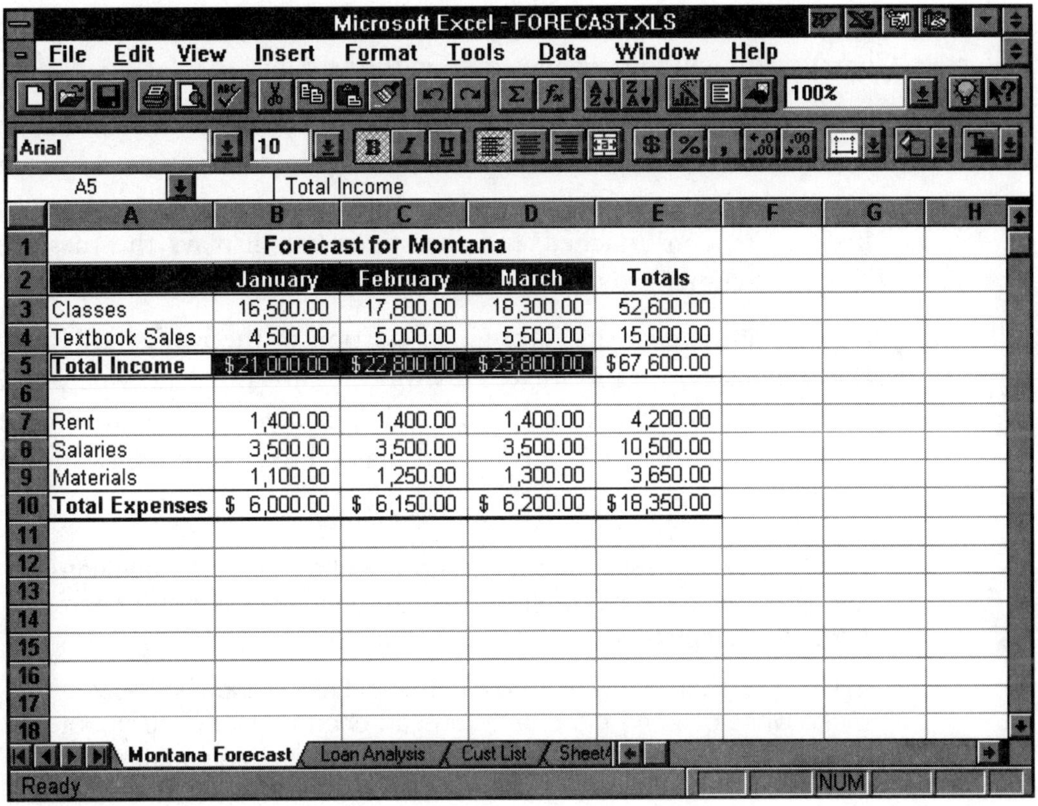

FIGURE 16–1 The selected data for the chart

FIGURE 16–2 The first ChartWizard dialog box

though the first cell in the label row is blank. This ensures that the ChartWizard will know what to do with the data.

To start the Chart Wizard to create an embedded chart, choose Insert➢Chart➢On This Sheet or click on the ChartWizard button on the Standard toolbar. The mouse pointer turns into crosshairs with a little chart icon attached and the status bar displays the message "Drag in document to create a chart."

Drag the mouse over the rectangular portion of the worksheet (preferably a blank portion so the chart won't obscure any data) where you want the finished chart to be positioned. When you release the mouse button, the first of five ChartWizard dialog boxes appears, as shown in Figure 16–2.

note

Don't worry too much about getting the chart size and position just right. It's a simple matter to resize and reposition the chart after you complete it.

In fact, you shouldn't worry too much about any of the choices you make while creating the chart. You can change your mind about any of them at any time, even after the chart has been created.

If the cells in the Range box are correct, click on the Next button to proceed to the next step in the chart creation process, as shown in Figure 16–3.

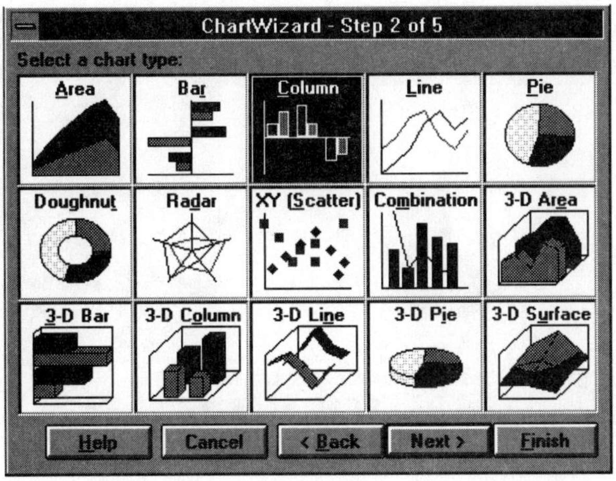

FIGURE 16–3 The second ChartWizard dialog box

The default chart type is a column chart. If you want to use a different chart type, simply click on it and then click on the Next button. There is only one data series for this chart so far, so I'll choose a Pie chart, which is good for comparing values in a single data series. Figure 16–4 shows the third ChartWizard dialog box, where you can choose from a variety of formats for the chart type.

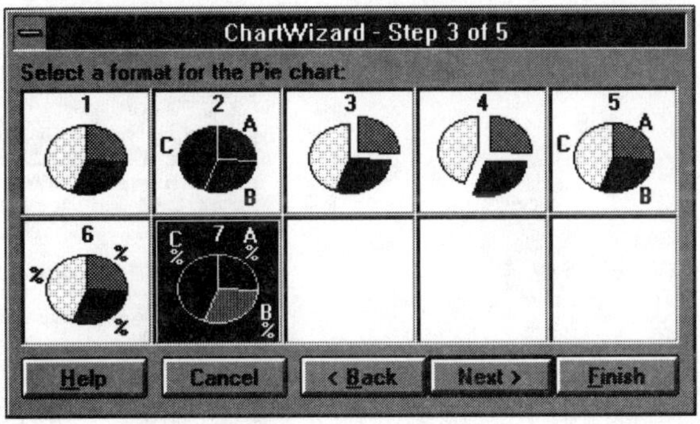

FIGURE 16–4 The third ChartWizard dialog box

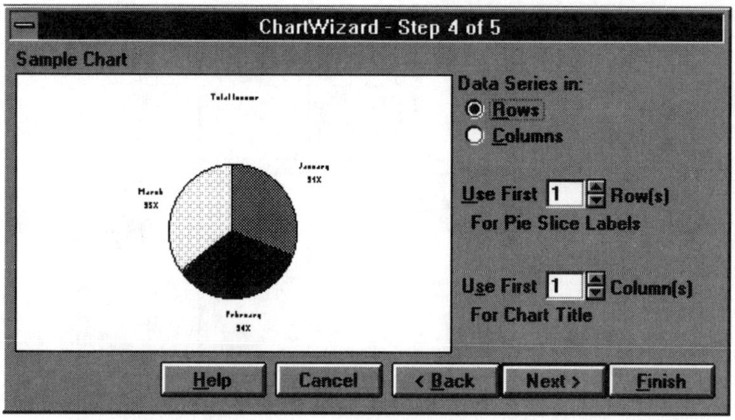

FIGURE 16–5 The fourth ChartWizard dialog box

After choosing a format, click on the Next button to display the fourth ChartWizard dialog box (shown in Figure 16–5), which shows you a preview of the chart with the options you've chosen so far.

If the settings are correct, click on the Next button to display the fifth and final ChartWizard dialog box, as shown in Figure 16–6.

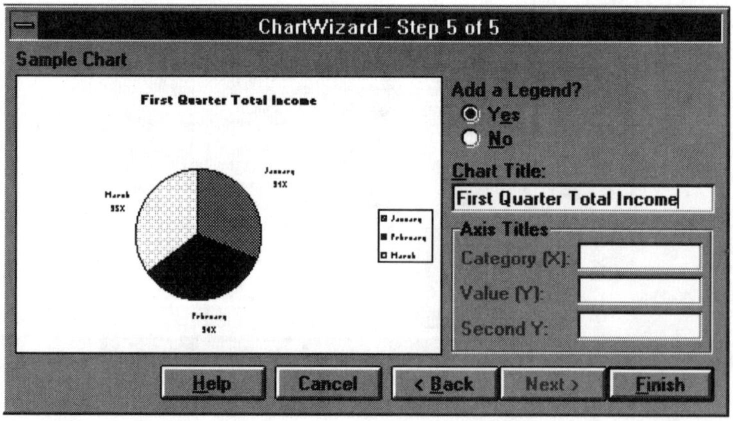

FIGURE 16–6 The final ChartWizard dialog box

Notice that I've chosen to add a legend by clicking on the Add a Legend option button. I've also added a chart title. A chart title entered in this dialog box overrides the assumed title from the last dialog box.

If you're satisfied with what you see in the sample chart portion of the dialog box, click on the Finish button to complete the chart and place it in the worksheet, as shown in Figure 16–7.

The handles on the border of the chart indicate that it is the active portion of the worksheet. You can move the entire chart by placing the mouse pointer inside the chart and dragging it to a new location.

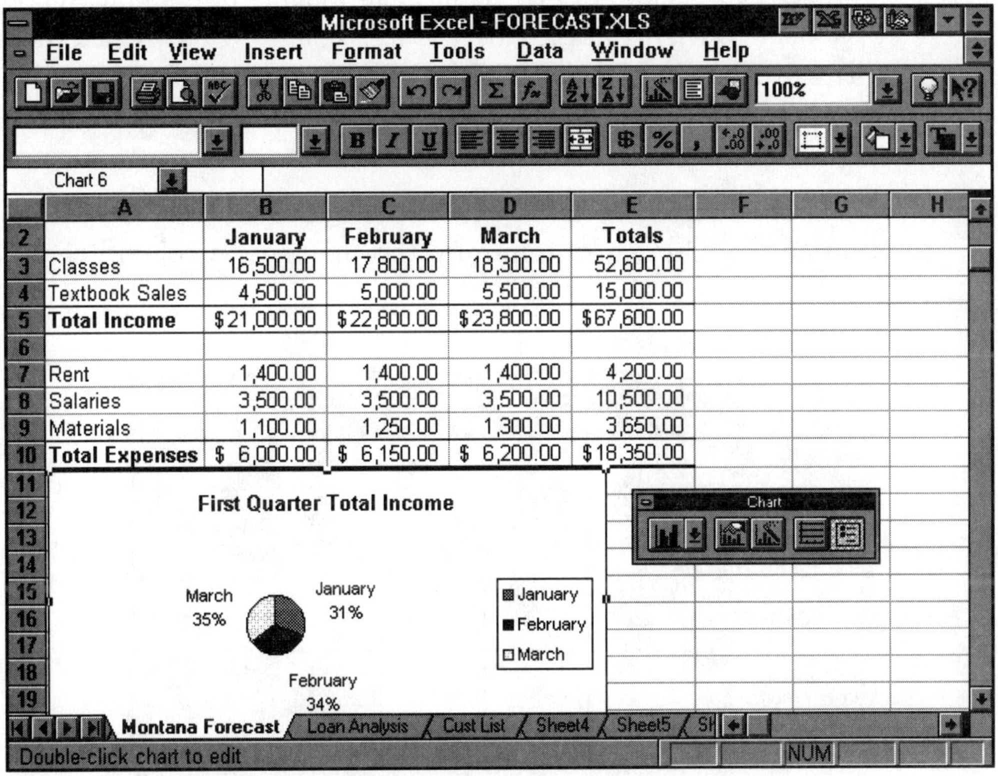

FIGURE 16–7 The chart embedded in the worksheet

You can resize the chart by positioning the mouse pointer on one of the handles and dragging, just as you would in resizing a window.

Editing an Embedded Chart

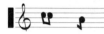

You can change any of the chart options by first double-clicking on the chart to put it in edit mode. The dashed border surrounding the chart tells you it is in edit mode.

Select the object in the chart that you want to change by clicking on it; then right-click to display its shortcut menu. For example, suppose you want to change the chart type to a column chart. Click on the chart to select it, and then right-click and choose AutoFormat from the shortcut menu to display the AutoFormat dialog box, as shown in Figure 16–8.

Click on Column in the Galleries list and then double-click on a column chart format to transform the chart into a column chart, as

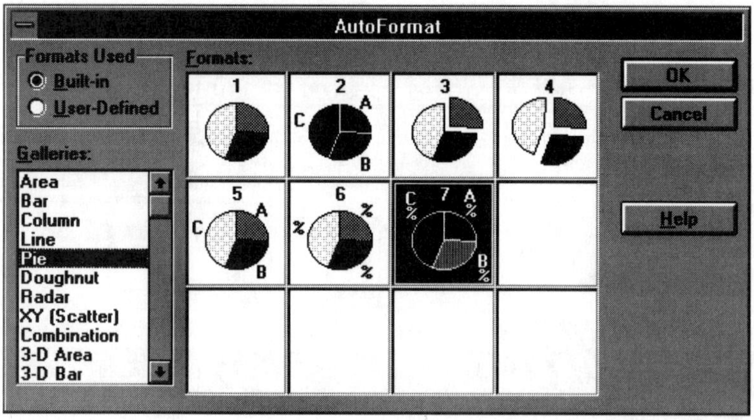

FIGURE 16–8 The AutoFormat dialog box

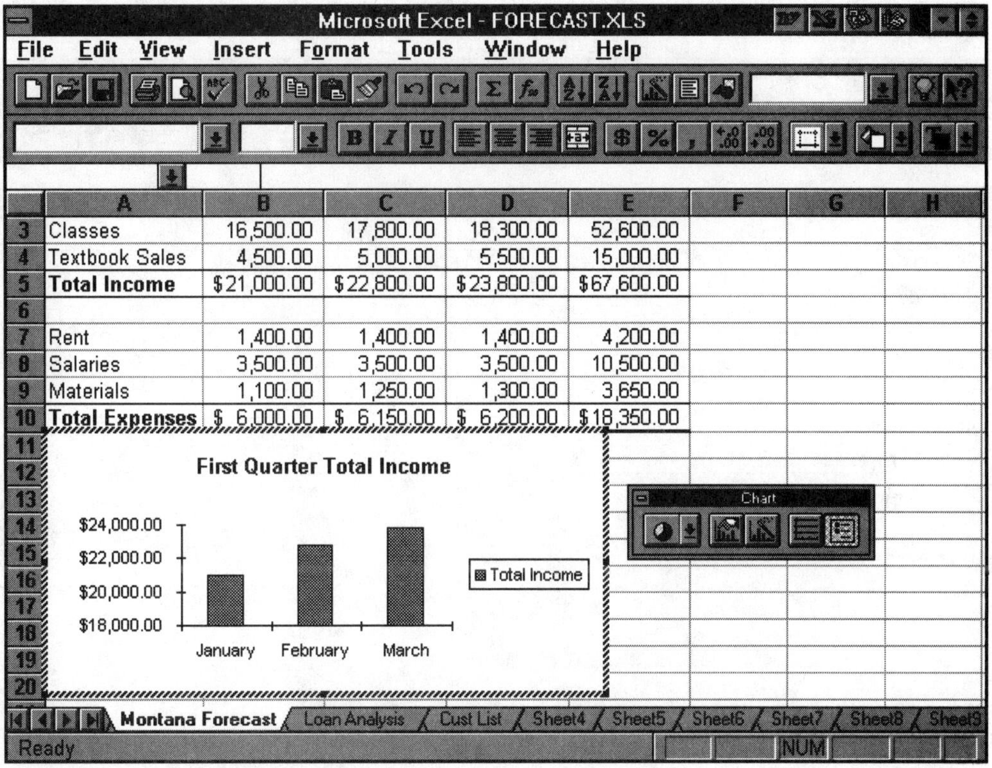

FIGURE 16–9 The same data displayed in a column chart

shown in Figure 16–9. You may have to click on the x-axis labels and change their format to achieve the results shown in the figure.

Adding a Second Data Series

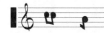

One of the niftiest new features in Excel is the ability to add a new data series by simply dragging it onto the chart. If you want to add the total expenses series to the example chart, just select the series and

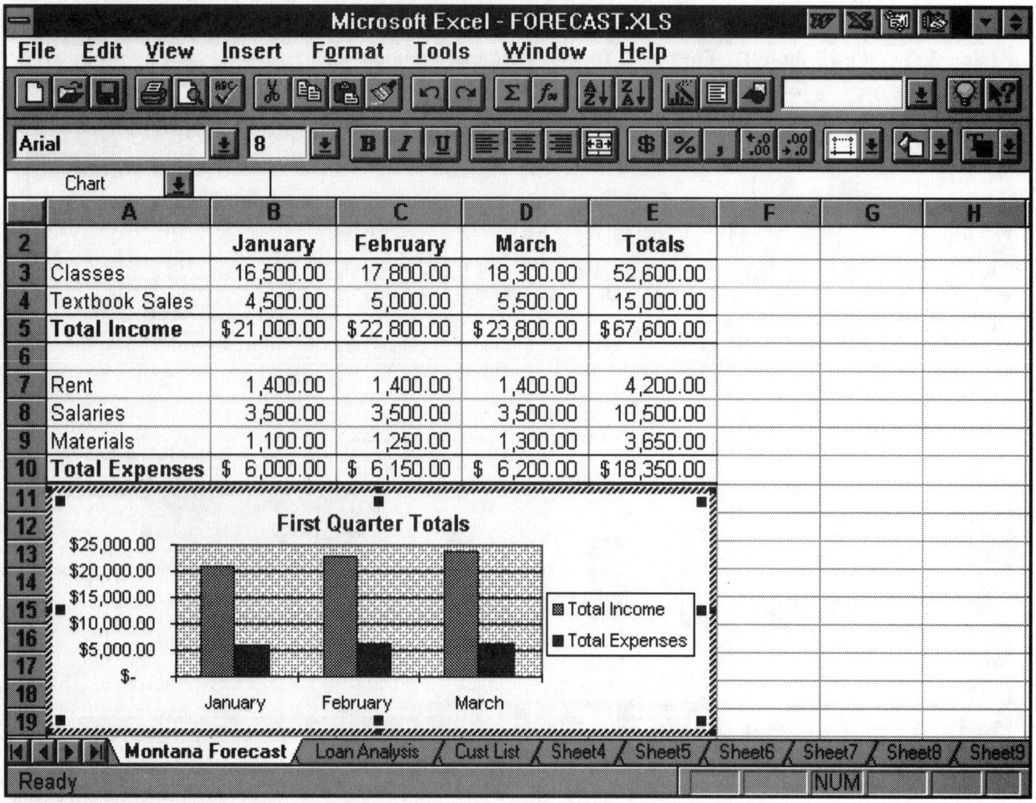

FIGURE 16–10 The chart with a second data series displayed

release the mouse button. Then drag the selection onto the chart and release the mouse button.

I know it seems as if it should be more complicated than that, but that's all there is to it. Figure 16–10 shows the chart with the second data series dropped in.

CAUTION

As mentioned in Chapter 13, numbers formatted using the toolbar buttons or the Accounting category in the Format Cells dialog box may not be usable as a data series. If you run into a problem, reformat the numbers in the Number, Percentage, or

Currency category in the Number tab of the Format Cells dialog box.

note If you are adding data that doesn't correspond to the other data series, Excel may not know what to do with it after you drag it onto the chart. If this happens, Excel will present you with a Paste Special dialog box that will let you tell Excel how you want the new data handled.

Creating a Chart Sheet

You may decide to create your chart in a chart sheet instead of embedding it in your worksheet. Doing a chart sheet eliminates the problem of sizing and placing it on the worksheet so it doesn't interfere with the worksheet data. With the chart in a chart sheet, you have the entire screen to work with, and it is ready to edit whenever the chart sheet is visible.

To create a chart sheet, choose Insert➢Chart➢As New Sheet and proceed to create the chart just as if it were an embedded chart. When the chart is finished, it will appear on its own sheet, as shown in Figure 16–11.

Printing Charts

There are no special tricks to printing charts. Just follow the same procedure you use for printing worksheets without charts. You may find that your charts print better on a black-and-white printer if you choose the Black and White option in the Sheet tab of the Page Setup dialog box.

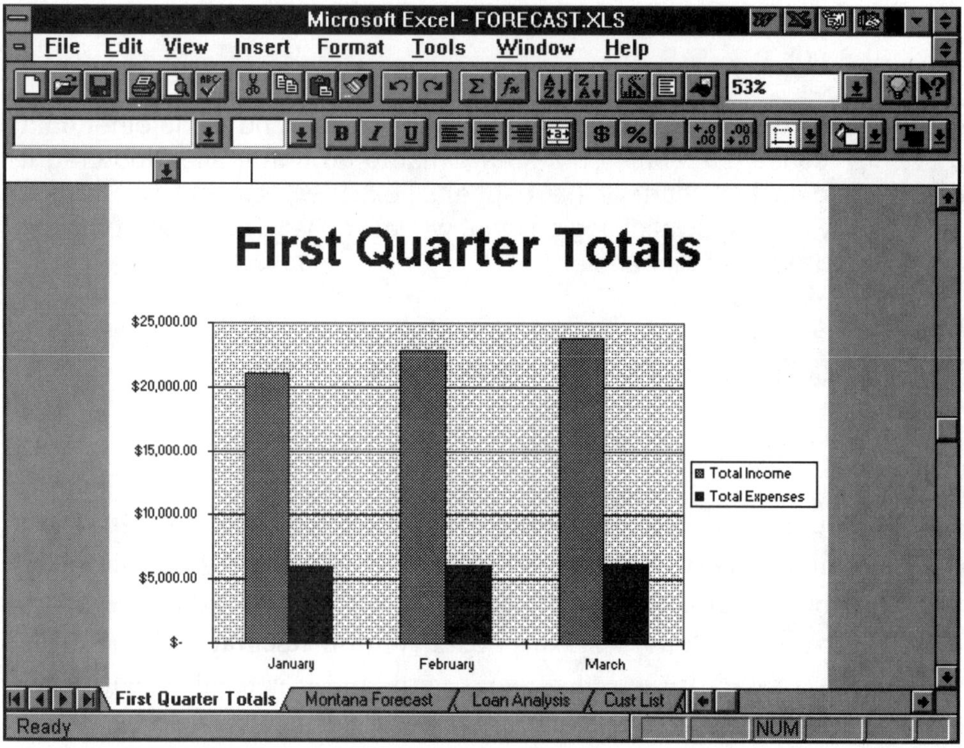

FIGURE 16–11 A example of a chart in a chart sheet

CAUTION

If your charts aren't printing, be sure that the Draft Quality option in the Sheet tab of the Page Setup dialog box isn't chosen. This option prints worksheets without charts or other graphic elements.

If your charts still aren't printing, or aren't printing properly, your printer may not have enough memory to handle the amount of graphic information you're trying to send to it. This is often the case with laser printers which require enough memory to store the image of an entire page.

You can probably purchase a memory upgrade to solve the problem. In the meantime, you can lower the graphics resolution so that you aren't sending as much data to the printer. To lower the resolution, click on the Options button in the Page Setup dialog box to display Windows printer setup dialog box and change the graphics resolution from 300 dots per inch to 150 dots per inch. That ought to do the trick. If not, you can try 75 dots per inch, but be prepared for relatively crude graphic quality.

Summary

In this chapter, you learned to create embedded charts and chart sheets from your worksheet data by using the ChartWizard. In the next chapter, you'll learn to use PowerPoint to pull your Word and Excel documents together into powerful presentations.

Section V

Getting Your Point Across with PowerPoint

17

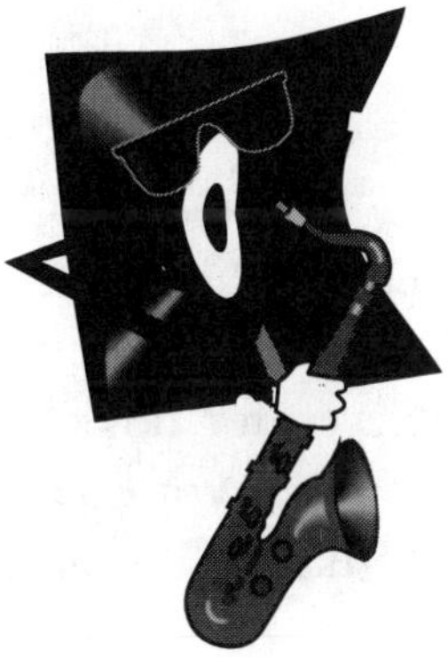

PowerPoint—Powerful Presentations

If you make presentations, whether to small or large groups, you'll wonder how you ever got along without PowerPoint. This program provides all the tools necessary to create dazzling presentations using overhead transparencies, 35mm slides, or your computer screen.

Your presentations can incorporate text, charts, graphics, and even sound and video, if your computer has the equipment to add these niceties. You can even print your presentation to hand out to your audience and create speaker's notes to help the presenter remember what to say as the presentation progresses.

Of course, you can also easily incorporate documents and pieces of documents created in your other Office programs into your presentations.

One of PowerPoint's best features is the way it can lead you by the hand through the entire process of creating a presentation. All you need to worry about is what you want to present; PowerPoint does the rest.

Overview of New Features in PowerPoint 4.0

Even if you've never used the previous version of PowerPoint and have no idea where to begin creating presentations, there's no need to panic. PowerPoint makes creating presentations easy, even for novice users. And, as Microsoft points out, if you know how to use Word 6.0 or Excel 5.0, you already know how to perform more than 100 tasks in PowerPoint.

In addition to the new features that have been added to Word and Excel—including shortcut menus for objects on the screen, ToolTips, and Wizards—PowerPoint 4.0 adds a number of unique features.

The AutoContent Wizard

Word and Excel have Wizards, but PowerPoint's AutoContent Wizard is special. This Wizard conducts a brief interview with you and then creates your entire presentation for you—almost. Just add your text and any graphic objects you need and change the look with the Pick a Look Wizard, and your presentation is complete.

The Pick a Look Wizard

The Pick a Look Wizard guides you through the formatting of your presentation so you'll end up with a presentation that looks professionally designed.

The ClipArt Gallery

The ClipArt Gallery provides a new, easier way to add the expanded collection (more than 1,000 pieces) of included graphics to your presentations. Just pick from the groups of thumbnail sketches.

Free Rotate

You can now freely rotate text and other objects 360 degrees. You can also edit rotated text and objects.

Freehand Drawing

As you give electronic presentations on your computer screen, you can now use the freehand drawing tool to add temporary annotations to your slides.

Some PowerPoint Terminology

- ✓ *Slides* are the heart of every presentation you create in PowerPoint; they can be presented as overheads, as 35mm slides, or electronically on-screen. Slides can contain text, graphics, charts, and even sound and video.
- ✓ *Outlines* contain the text of your slide presentation. You can enter text for your slides directly on the slides or in the outline.
- ✓ *Speaker's notes* provide the presenter with a page that corresponds to each slide and contains a small image of the slide along with additional notes.

- ✓ *Audience handouts* are printed copies of your presentation. You can have two, three, or six slides per handout page and you can add additional elements, such as other text or graphics. For example, you might want each page of the handout to include your company logo.
- ✓ *Placeholders* let you quickly add the type of element you're likely to want in a particular portion of the slide. When you pick a layout for your presentation, placeholders for such elements as text, graphics, and charts are included. Just click or double-click in the placeholder (depending on the type of placeholder) to add or edit the element.
- ✓ *Objects* are the individual elements that make up presentations. Text elements—such as titles, bulleted lists, graphics, and charts—are individual objects and can be moved, sized, and rotated, and even overlap other objects in a presentation.

Starting PowerPoint

If the Microsoft Office Manager toolbar is available, click on the Microsoft PowerPoint button. If Office Manager isn't running, open the Microsoft Office group in Program Manager and double-click on the Microsoft PowerPoint icon. Figure 17–1 shows the opening PowerPoint screen.

note You don't have to exit any other programs that are running before starting PowerPoint. In fact, having all the Office programs you work with open at the same time can make it faster and easier to switch from one to another .

The Tip of the Day dialog box appears when you first start PowerPoint. It's a good idea to leave this feature activated and read these tips. You'll find many pearls of wisdom and bits of useful information.

FIGURE 17–1 The opening PowerPoint screen

You can see the next tip by clicking on the Next Tip button. If you want to open a help screen of tip categories so you can browse through all the tips, click on the More Tips button. To tell PowerPoint not to bother you with the Tip of the Day when you start PowerPoint, click on the Show Tips at Startup check box in the lower-left portion of the dialog box.

Click on the OK button or press Enter to clear the dialog box. Figure 17–2 shows the opening PowerPoint screen after closing the Tip of the Day dialog box.

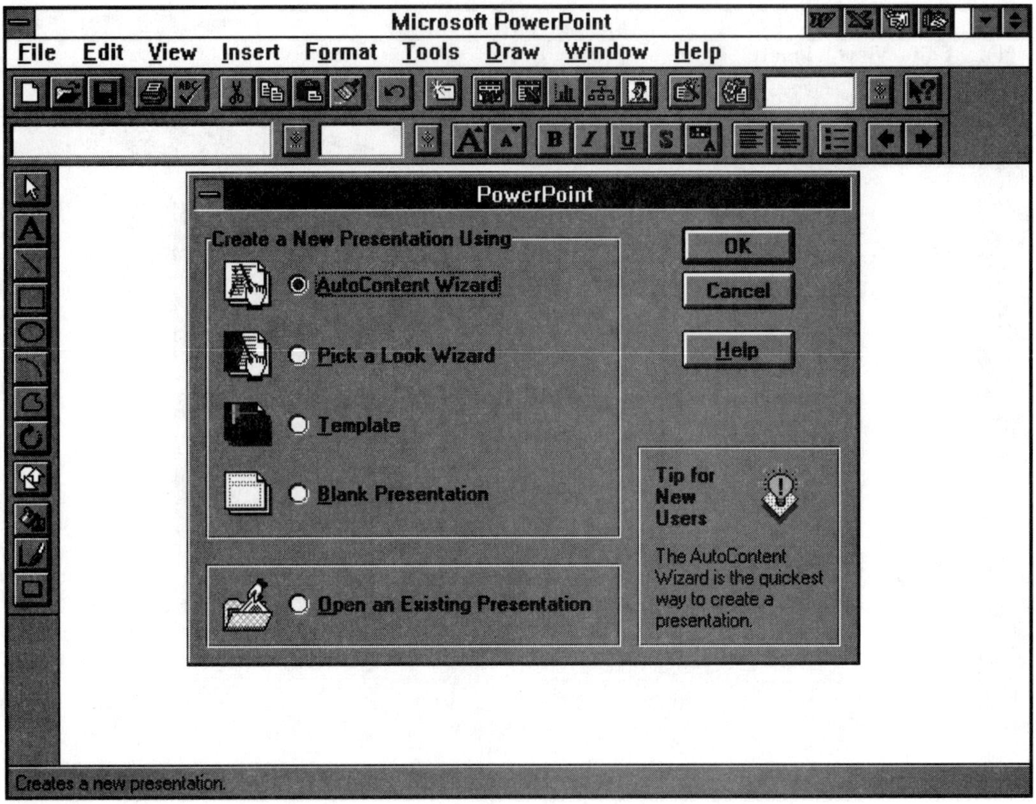

FIGURE 17–2 PowerPoint is ready to create your presentation.

Rather than present you with a blank screen and leave you wondering where to turn first to start creating your presentation, PowerPoint displays a dialog box that offers five option buttons whenever you start PowerPoint, choose File➢New, or click on the New button on the Standard toolbar. Click in the option button next to the path you want to take.

✓ The first option is the AutoContent Wizard. If you are new to the presentation creation process or just can't stand the thought of starting a presentation from scratch, this is the way to go. The AutoContent Wizard guides you through the initial steps of creating and organizing your presentation by asking you a series of questions. You'll learn to put together a presentation using the AutoContent Wizard later in this chapter.

- ✓ The second option is the Pick a Look Wizard. You can use this Wizard to choose from a variety of professional designs, including color schemes and fonts, for your presentation. The options the Pick a Look Wizard gives you are determined by the information you provide, such as whether your presentation will be presented using black-and-white or color overheads, as an electronic presentation on screen, or on 35mm slides. In addition, Pick a Look lets you determine in advance which elements—full-page slides, speaker's notes, audience handouts, and/or outline pages—you want to print.
- ✓ Template lets you choose your presentation's "look" from the included designs. These are the same templates that the Pick a Look Wizard uses. The difference is that Pick a Look narrows your choices based on the information you supply, while Template lets you choose any template you like.
- ✓ Blank Presentation lets you create a presentation without first choosing a design or color scheme. But even this option lets you choose from a variety of presentation layouts, including placeholders for various types of elements, such as charts, clip art, and text. One of the layout options is a truly blank presentation if you really do want to start from scratch.
- ✓ The Open an Existing Presentation option lets you open a presentation that has already been saved, so you can edit or present it.

note You can add elements and change the look of your presentation at any stage of the creation process. In fact, if you use the Pick a Look Wizard to specify a particular look, you can use it again later to specify a different look.

Also, even though the Pick a Look Wizard guides you to the appropriate templates for the type of presentation you are creating, you have access to all of the templates within the Pick a Look Wizard.

Creating Your First Presentation Using the AutoContent Wizard

Planning can be the most difficult part of putting a presentation together. Trying to decide in advance which elements you want to include and how best to organize them can be a daunting task indeed. Fortunately, with PowerPoint, you can approach the presentation creation process with a complete vision of how the presentation should look or with barely a clue.

The AutoContent Wizard is the easiest place to start creating a presentation if you're new to the program or you just want to let PowerPoint create the basic structure and organization of your presentation. In the next chapter, you'll learn to enhance your presentation.

Be sure the AutoContent Wizard button is selected and then click on the OK button to begin creating your presentation. Figure 17–3 shows the first of four AutoContent Wizard dialog boxes.

This first dialog box is just an introduction to the AutoContent Wizard, so just click on the Next button or press Enter to proceed. Figure 17–4 displays the second AutoContent Wizard dialog box, in which you enter the information for the title slide, which is the first slide in the presentation.

Type the main title in the What Are You Going to Talk About? text box. For example, if the presentation is about how to use PowerPoint, the main title might be Getting to the Point with PowerPoint.

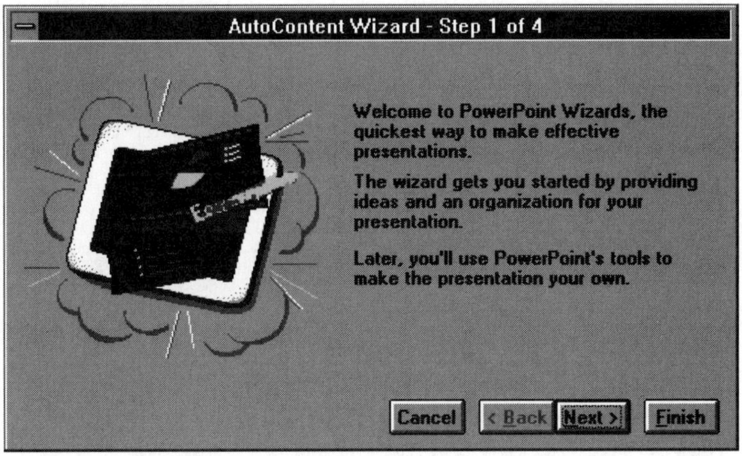

FIGURE 17–3 The first AutoContent Wizard dialog box

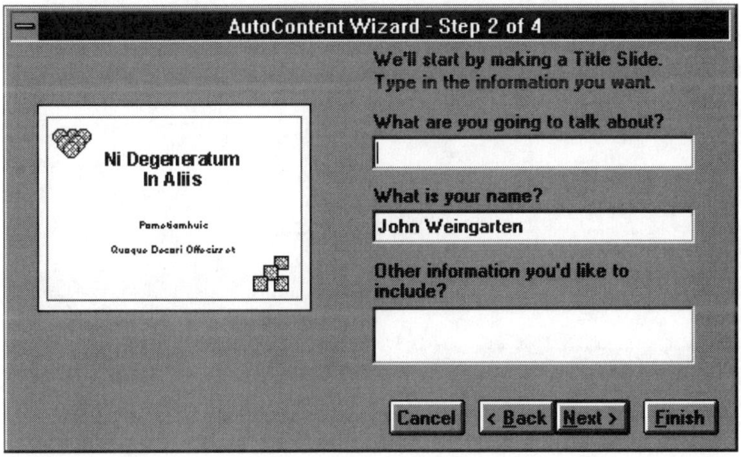

FIGURE 17–4 The second AutoContent Wizard dialog box

The name that was used to install PowerPoint is already entered in the What Is Your Name? text box. You can leave it as is, delete it if you don't want any name to appear on the title slide, or replace it with another name—perhaps the name of your company.

Type any additional text that you want to appear on the title slide in the Other Information You'd Like to Include? text box. You can move between the text boxes by clicking in them or pressing the Tab key.

note Instead of adding your company name as text on the title slide, you may prefer to add your company's logo to the title later.

Don't be too concerned about what you enter or leave out in this dialog box. You can edit the title slide at any time.

After the title slide information is entered the way you want it, click on the Next button. Figure 17–5 shows the third AutoContent Wizard dialog box, in which you specify the type of presentation you'll be creating.

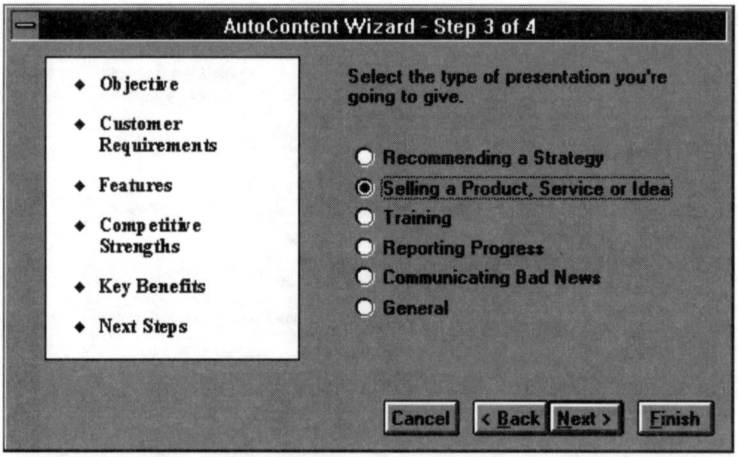

FIGURE 17–5 The third AutoContent Wizard dialog box

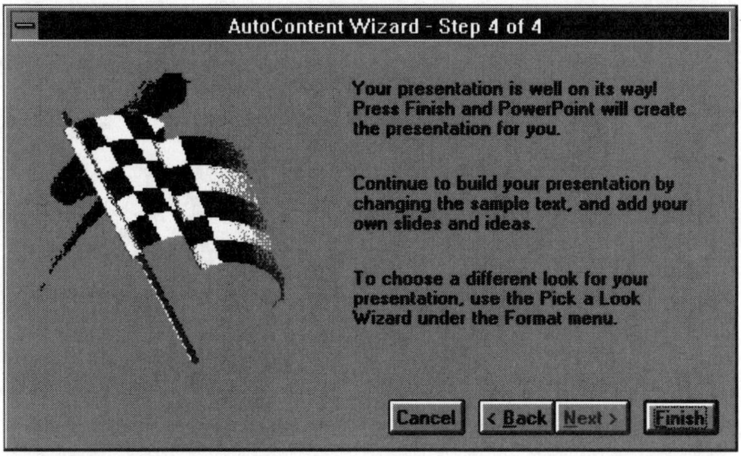

FIGURE 17–6 The final AutoContent Wizard dialog box

Click on the option button next to the type of presentation you're going to give. Choose the General category if none of the other categories describes the presentation subject.

After choosing the presentation type, click on the Next button. Figure 17–6 shows the fourth and final dialog box in the AutoContent Wizard.

Click on the Finish button and, in a few seconds, an outline for your presentation appears, as shown in Figure 17–7.

You may see the Cue Cards help screen sitting on top of your presentation. Cue cards are handy on-line guides for performing various tasks in PowerPoint. Cue cards remain on the screen until you close them or exit PowerPoint. Their persistence can be useful when you are first learning to do something, but it can be annoying once you know what you're doing.

You can close the cue card by clicking on the cue card's Control-menu box and choosing the Close command.

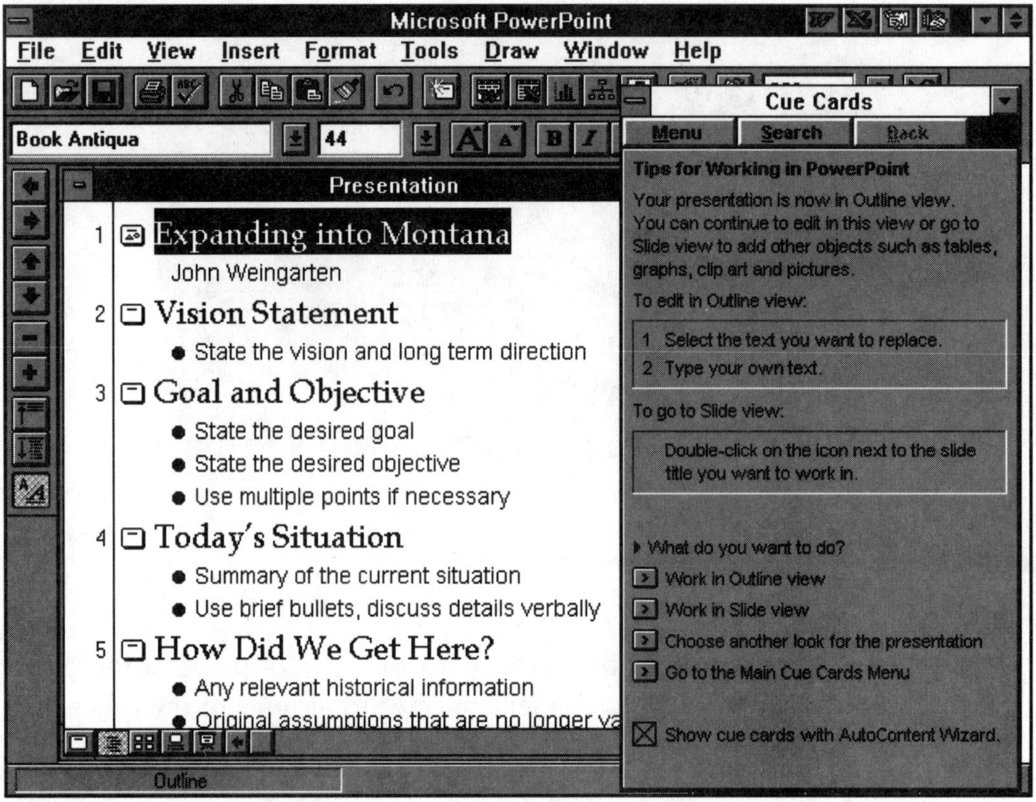

FIGURE 17–7 The beginning of your presentation

If you don't want the cue card to pop up automatically the next time you use the AutoContent Wizard, click in the Show Cue Cards With AutoContent Wizard check box at the bottom of the cue card.

If you want to see what other cue cards are available, click on the Menu button just below the cue card title bar. You can then go the cue card of your choice by clicking on the topic you want. You can open cue cards any time you want by choosing Cue Cards from the PowerPoint Help menu.

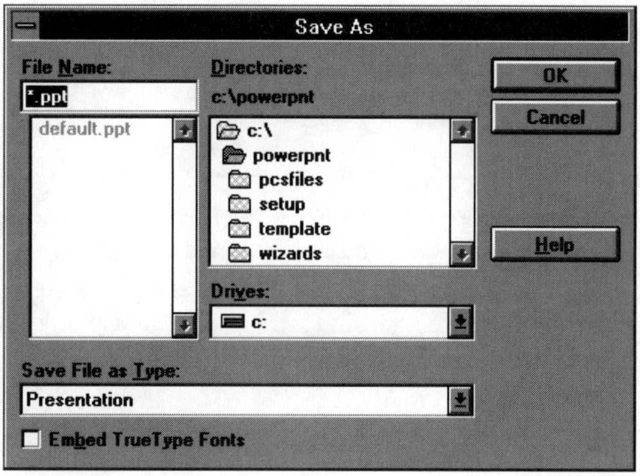

FIGURE 17–8 The Save As dialog box

Before doing any editing or other manipulation of your presentation, it would be a good idea to save it. Saving a presentation is same as saving a Word document or an Excel workbook. Choose File➢Save or press Ctrl-S, and the Save As dialog box appears, as shown in Figure 17–8.

Enter a normal filename of up to eight characters, but let PowerPoint assign the default .ppt extension. If you want the presentation saved on another drive or in a directory other than one of those listed, make the appropriate changes and then click on the OK button. The Summary Info dialog box appears, as shown in Figure 17–9.

tip If this is a presentation that will be run on another computer and you aren't sure whether the other computer has the fonts you have used in the presentation, click on the Embed TrueType Fonts check box in the lower-left portion of the dialog box. Embedding the fonts can make the file considerably larger, so use this option only when necessary.

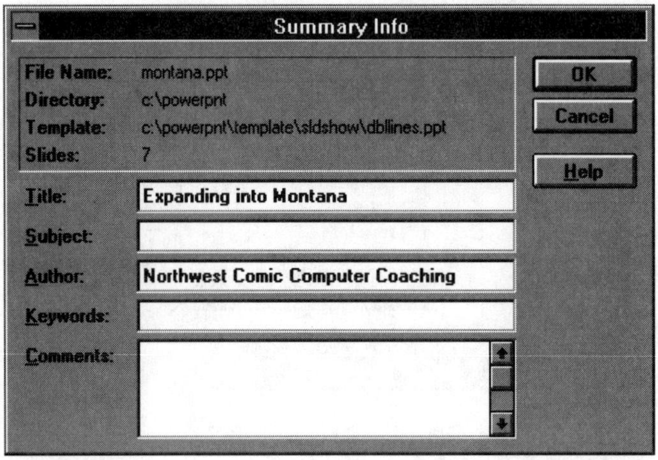

FIGURE 17-9 The Summary Info dialog box

The dialog box contains the presentation's title and your company name. Enter any additional summary information that will help you remember later what this presentation is about. Press Enter when all the summary information has been entered.

PowerPoint's Views

There are several ways to view and edit your presentation. The three primary views are the outline view, the slide view, and the slide sorter view. You can change views by choosing a different view from the View menu or by clicking on one of the view buttons on the left side of the horizontal scroll bar at the bottom of the screen.

Using the view buttons is usually the easiest way to change views, because they are almost always visible and require only a single click. You'll learn to work in the different views in the next chapter.

When the AutoContent Wizard first displays your embryonic presentation, it automatically appears in outline view. Notice that, in outline view, the Drawing toolbar on the left side of the screen is replaced by the Outlining toolbar with buttons that make it easier to work with outlines.

The slide view displays one slide at a time and includes all the slide's graphic elements. Figure 17–10 shows the slide view of a typical slide containing several text and graphic objects.

The slide sorter view lets you see small images of the slides in your presentation. You can't edit the slides directly in slide sorter view, but

FIGURE 17–10 A slide in slide view

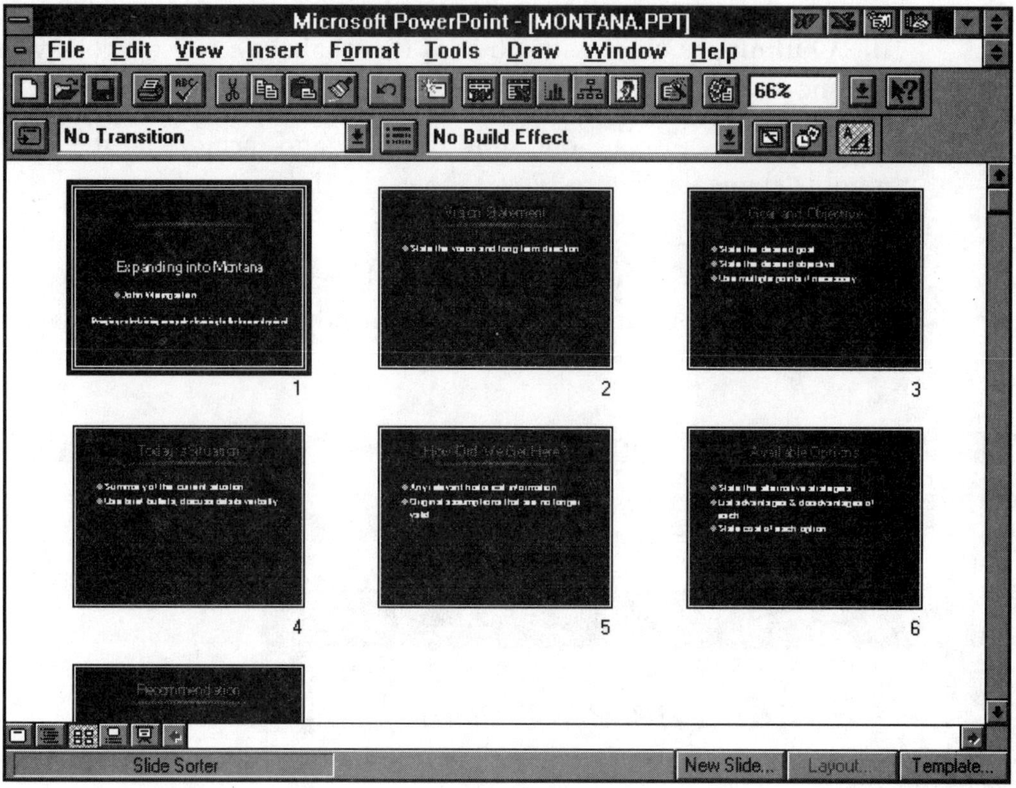

FIGURE 17–11 Slides in the slide sorter view

you can change their order and how they will appear during an on-screen presentation. Figure 17–11 shows slides in the slide sorter view.

It's a good idea to maximize the presentation's document window by clicking on the Maximize button on the right end of the title bar, as was done in Figure 17–11, so you can see as many slides as possible in the slide sorter view.

There is also a Notes Page view, which displays the speaker's notes that go with the slides. This is useful if you are creating speaker's notes.

Exiting PowerPoint

When you are finished working on your presentation, you can exit PowerPoint by choosing File➢Exit. If the presentation has been modified since the last time you saved, a dialog box will ask if you want to save the changes. Click on the Yes button to save the changes and exit PowerPoint.

Summary

This chapter covered some of the basic PowerPoint concepts and how to begin creating a PowerPoint presentation. You also learned to switch among the various views of your presentation.

The next chapter covers how to work in the various views and enhance your presentation.

18

PowerPoint— Editing Presentations

Once the basic structure of your presentation is in place, you'll want to add and edit text, perhaps change the layout, add or change the color scheme, and add or edit graphic elements.

This chapter covers the basics of editing your presentation in PowerPoint's outline, slide, and slide sorter views, as well as creating speaker's notes to go along with the slides. You'll also learn to apply templates and layouts to your presentations.

Editing Your Presentation in Outline View

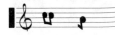

When you want to work with the text of your presentation, the outline view is usually the most direct approach. In outline view, you can see and edit the text in several slides at once. You can also add, delete, and change the order of the slides.

If PowerPoint isn't already running, start PowerPoint and choose Open an Existing Presentation in the first dialog box; then click on the name of the presentation you want to open.

PowerPoint makes it easy to remember which presentation goes with the highlighted filename by showing you a small preview of its title slide in the lower-right corner of the Open dialog box, as shown in Figure 18–1.

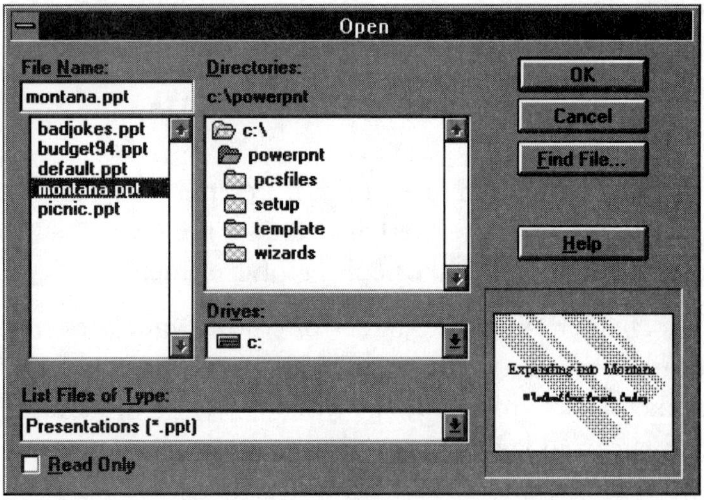

FIGURE 18–1 The Open dialog box with a preview of the title slide

Click on the OK button to open the presentation. If you're not in outline view, switch to outline view by clicking on the outline view button on the left side of the horizontal scroll bar or by choosing View➢Outline from the menu.

The outline displays your presentation's text in outline form with the Outlining toolbar arrayed vertically on the left side of the screen. Outlines can have up to six levels. Titles are always the first (top) level and the levels below the titles are indented.

A slide icon alongside a line of text tells you that that text is the title of a slide. The slide numbers and the slide icons are separated by a vertical line.

In outline view, only text is displayed. You don't see any graphic elements, such as charts or pictures. You can, however, tell if a slide contains graphic elements by looking at the slide icon. Icons for slides that do not have graphic elements appear empty except for a small horizontal line. Icons for slides that include graphic elements have, in addition to the horizontal line, a couple of squiggles that represent a graphic design.

Be aware that text that was added to a slide using the Drawing toolbar is considered a graphic element.

To type your own text in an outline, select the text you want to replace by dragging the mouse over it; then type the new text. You can use most of the selection shortcuts that are available in Word, such as double-clicking to select a word and triple-clicking to select a paragraph.

It's almost the same in PowerPoint's outline view, except that triple-clicking selects a paragraph *and all subordinate outline levels.* So triple-clicking on a slide's title selects all the text in the slide, because, of course, all the text under the title is subordinate to (at least one level lower than) the title. You can also select an entire slide by clicking on its slide icon. This selects all the slide's text and any other objects on the slide that are hidden in the outline view.

As in Word, a paragraph ends when you press Enter. Text in slides usually consists of several short paragraphs—sometimes no more than one line each. To add a new paragraph, position the insertion point at the end of a paragraph and press Enter. The insertion point will be at the beginning of a new line that is at the same outline level as the paragraph above. For example, if you press Enter after a title, you'll be working in a new slide, because there can be only one title-level paragraph per slide.

tip

> To see the greatest amount of text with the least distraction, it's a good idea to display the outline as plain text, without any fancy formatting. To do this, click on the Show Formatting toolbar button at the bottom of the Outlining toolbar. You can click on it again to see the formatting again. Remember, if you're not sure what a button does, just position the mouse pointer over the button to see a ToolTip that tells you what the button does.
>
> Whether the text formatting is displayed in outline view or not has no effect on the way the presentation prints or is displayed on screen in a slide show.

Figure 18–2 shows a presentation in outline view without formatting. Notice the slide icons for slides 3 and 5, which indicate that they contain graphic elements.

Changing Paragraph Levels

To change the level of a paragraph, position the insertion point anywhere in the paragraph and click on the Promote (Indent less) or the Demote (Indent more) button on the Outlining or Formatting toolbar. You can also demote a paragraph by pressing Tab and promote by pressing Shift-Tab.

Another way to promote and demote paragraphs is to drag them left or right with the mouse. To do this, position the mouse pointer just to the left of the paragraph so the pointer becomes a four-headed arrow; then drag left to promote or right to demote. As you drag,

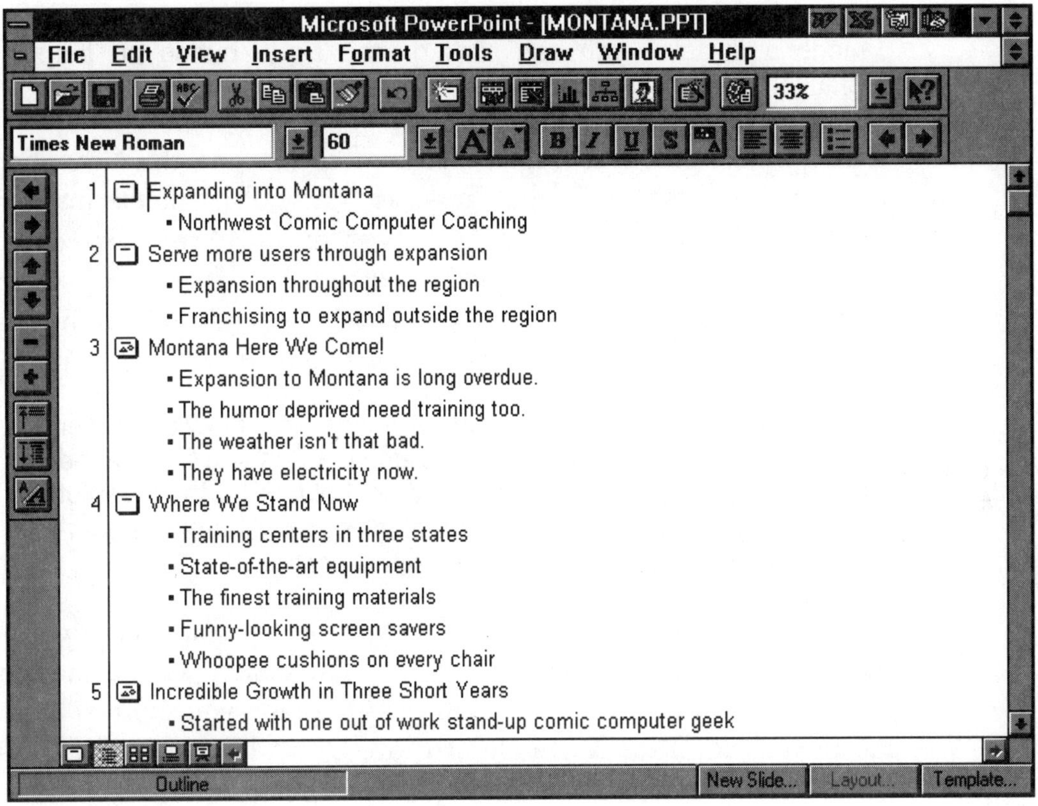

FIGURE 18–2 A presentation in outline view

you'll see a vertical guide that indicates how far you're promoting or demoting.

You can't promote a title, because it is already at the top level. If you demote a title paragraph, it becomes part of the previous paragraph.

CAUTION

If you try to demote the title paragraph in a slide containing graphic elements, including text added via the Drawing toolbar, the slide is deleted and the graphic elements are lost. Of course, PowerPoint displays a warning dialog box so you can cancel such an operation if that was not your intention.

If you do proceed with the demotion and then realize that you made a mistake, you can click on the Undo button on the Standard toolbar or choose Edit➢Undo.

Adding a new slide is a simple matter of clicking on the New Slide button on the right side of the status bar. A new blank slide is inserted below the slide your insertion point was in when you clicked the button. Of course, you can also add a new slide by pressing Enter when your insertion point is at the end of a slide's text and then promoting (indenting less) the level until it is a title with a slide icon next to it.

You may find it preferable to add new slides in slide view rather than outline view. Adding slides in slide view lets you choose the layout of the new slide and include placeholders for the types of elements you want on the new slide. Working with your presentation in slide view is covered later in this chapter.

In addition to changing the level of paragraphs, you may want to rearrange the order of paragraphs or slides. The easiest way to move a paragraph up or down is to click in the paragraph you want to move and then click on the Move Up or Move Down button on the Outlining toolbar. You can also drag a paragraph up or down by positioning the mouse pointer just to the left of the paragraph you want to move and then dragging up or down. You'll see a horizontal guide as you drag.

To move a slide, position the mouse pointer over the slide's icon and drag up or down. You'll see a horizontal guide as you drag. You can also click on the Move Up or Move Down button to move a slide, but dragging is quicker.

Viewing Titles Only in Outline View

Looking at all the text in the slides can obscure the big picture. If each slide has several paragraphs, you may be able to see only a few slides at a time. Displaying only the titles can often give you a better feel for the flow of the presentation.

To display the titles only, click on the Show Titles button on the Outlining toolbar. Figure 18–3 shows a presentation with just the titles displayed. The titles with horizontal lines under them have additional levels of outline text under them.

To expand the outline so all the subordinate levels are visible, click on the Show All button. Displaying just the titles has no effect on the way the presentation prints or displays in an on-screen slide show.

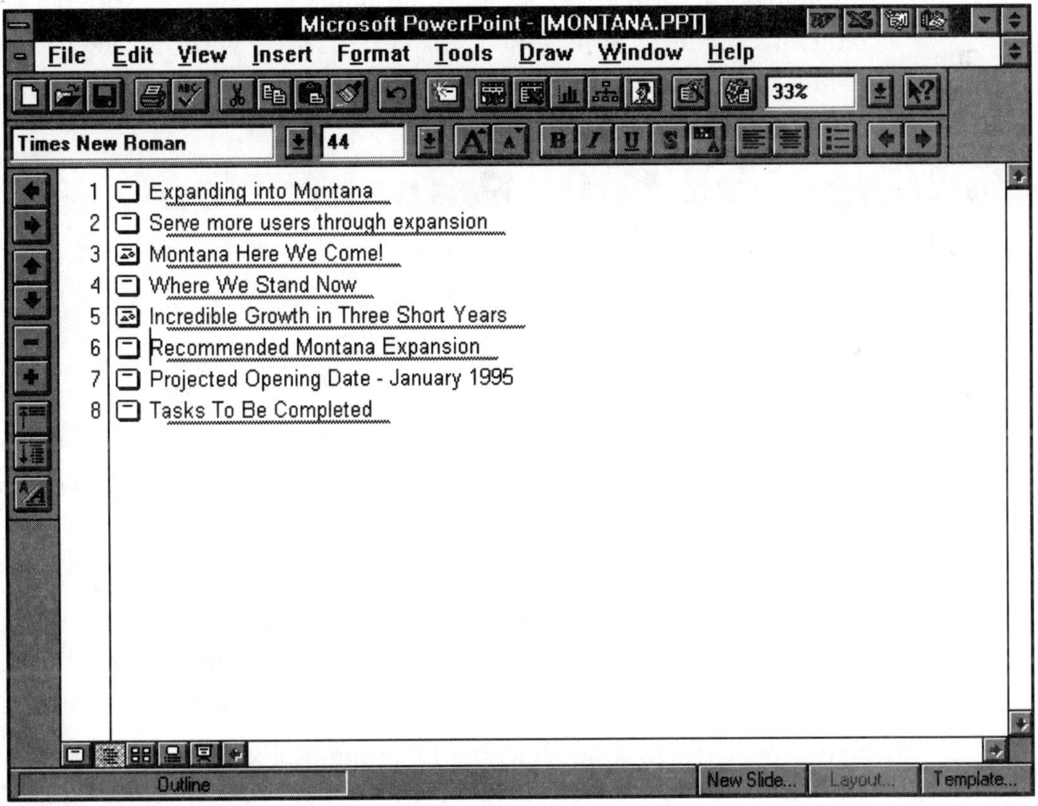

FIGURE 18–3 A presentation in outline view with only titles displayed

You can also expand or collapse the outline for just certain slides instead of expanding or collapsing the entire outline. To expand a single slide, click in that slide's title; then click on the Expand Selection button on the Outlining toolbar. To collapse a slide, click on any of its text, and then click on the Collapse Selection button.

You can use the Show All and Show Titles buttons with the Collapse Selection and Expand Selection buttons. For example, you might click on the Show Titles button to hide all the subordinate text and then expand one or two of the slides whose lower-level text you want to see. Conversely, you could click on the Collapse Selection button to hide lower-level text for a few slides while leaving the other slides expanded. Figure 18–4 shows a presentation with a few slides expanded and a few collapsed.

Working with Your Presentation in Slide View

Outline view is great for working with the text in your presentation, but it doesn't let you see what the slides will look like when printed or displayed on screen. To see—and be able to edit—individual slides the way they actually look, use the slide view.

To switch to slide view, double-click on the slide icon for the slide you want to work with. You can also switch to slide view by choosing View➢Slides or by clicking on the Slide View button on the left side of the horizontal scroll bar. Figure 18–5 shows a slide in slide view.

When you switch to slide view, the Drawing toolbar replaces the Outlining toolbar on the left side of the screen. You'll learn to add drawing objects and other graphic elements to your slides in the next chapter.

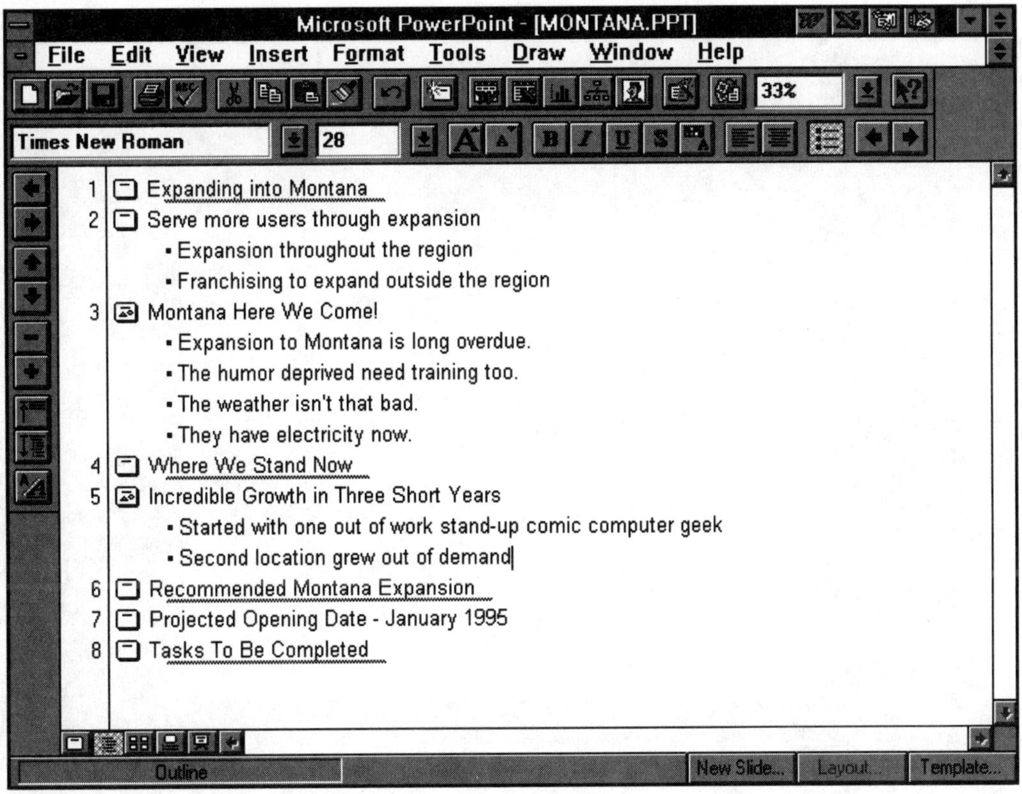

FIGURE 18–4 A presentation with a few slides expanded

You can move from slide to slide in slide view in several ways. You can click on the Previous Slide or Next Slide button below the vertical scroll bar or press the Pg Up or Pg Dn key. Perhaps the easiest way is to drag the scroll box (sometimes called the Elevator in PowerPoint) up or down. When you drag the scroll box in slide view, you can tell which slide will appear when you release the mouse button because the slide number appears to the left of the outline of the scroll box as you drag it.

Editing text in slide view requires positioning the insertion point where you want to add or edit text or selecting the text you want to

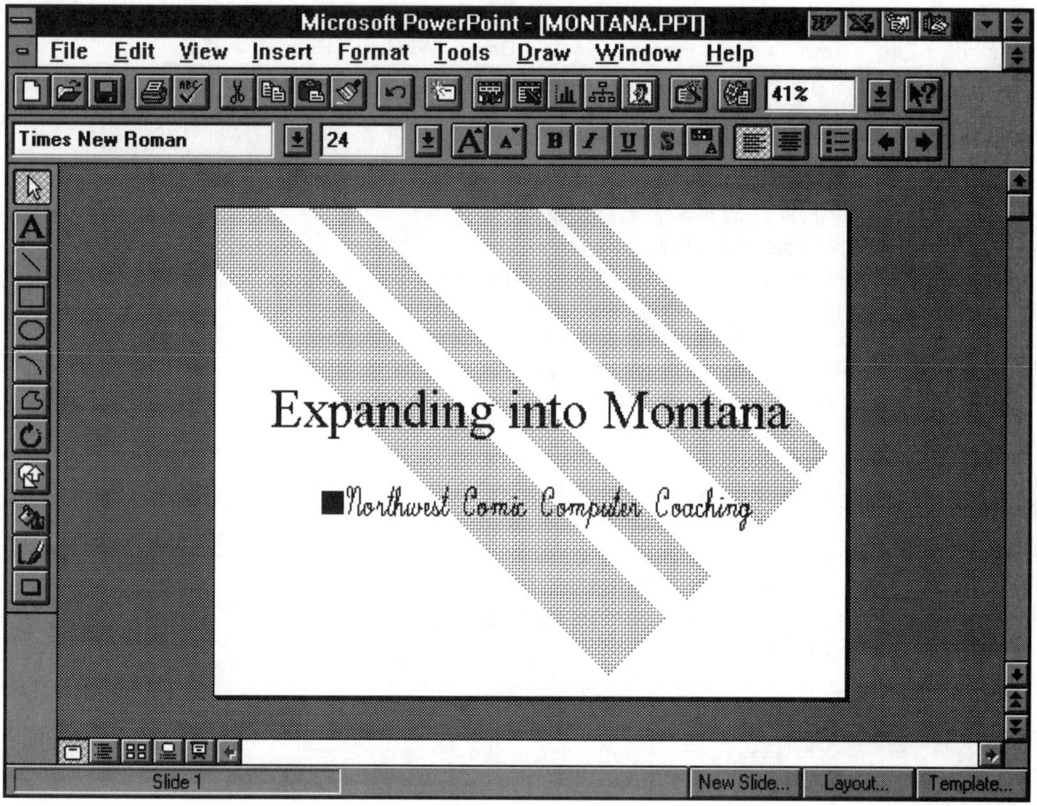

FIGURE 18–5 The title slide in slide view

edit and then typing. Text, along with graphic elements in the slide, is in a placeholder.

You can see the border surrounding the placeholder by clicking on or selecting the text you want to edit. You can move the placeholder on the slide by positioning the mouse pointer over one of the placeholder's borders and dragging it to a new position.

You can resize the placeholder and its contents by clicking on the placeholder's border, again causing eight small handles to appear on

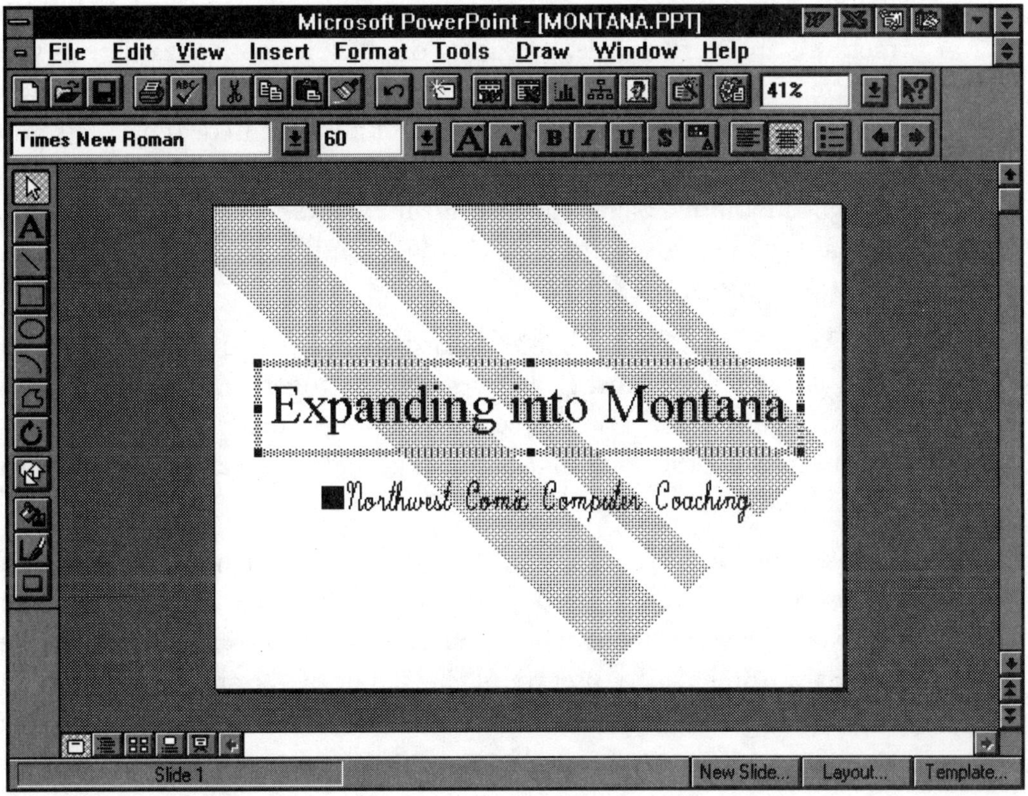

FIGURE 18–6 The title placeholder with sizing handles

the border. Then position the mouse pointer on one of the handles so it assumes the shape of a double-headed arrow and drag. Figure 18–6 shows the title placeholder with its sizing handles.

Changing Your Presentation's Look

You can change your presentation's look by making font changes and adding colors to various portions. The easiest—and safest—way to change the look, however, is to use one of PowerPoint's professionally designed templates.

You can apply templates directly or use the Pick a Look Wizard. Both methods are quite simple, but using the Pick a Look Wizard gives you a better shot at picking an appropriate template, because it requires you to specify how the presentation will be presented. It also lets you choose which portions of the presentation—slides, speaker's notes, audience handout pages, and/or outline pages—you'll be printing as well as whether you want a name, date, and page number to appear on each of the printed pages.

You can use the Pick a Look Wizard to begin your presentation or after you've started putting the presentation together. The choices you make in the Pick a Look Wizard are applied to your entire presentation, not just the slide that happens to be on screen when you start the Wizard.

To use the Pick a Look Wizard when creating a new presentation, choose Pick a Look Wizard from the dialog box that appears when you start PowerPoint or when you click on the New button on the Standard toolbar. To use the Pick a Look Wizard to modify an existing presentation, click on the Pick a Look Wizard on the Standard toolbar or choose Format➢Pick a Look Wizard. The first Pick a Look Wizard dialog box appears, as shown in Figure 18–7.

Click on the Next button to proceed to the second dialog box, as shown in Figure 18–8.

Click on the option button next to the method you plan to use for giving this presentation. For example, if you plan to use black-and-white overheads, click on the Black and White Overheads option button. Then click on the Next button to proceed to the third dialog box, as shown in Figure 18–9.

Choose the template you want to use by clicking on the appropriate option button. There are no right or wrong choices here. Try clicking on each of the option buttons to see what each template looks like. If none of the choices strikes your fancy, click on the More button to open the Presentation Templates dialog box. Click on the filenames

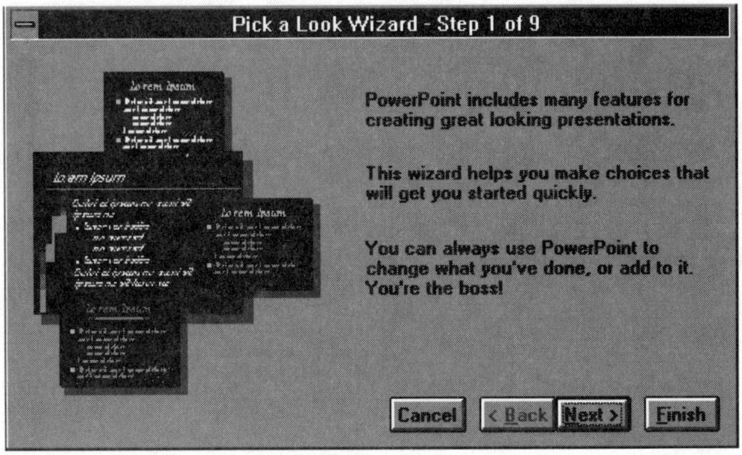

FIGURE 18–7 The first Pick a Look Wizard dialog box

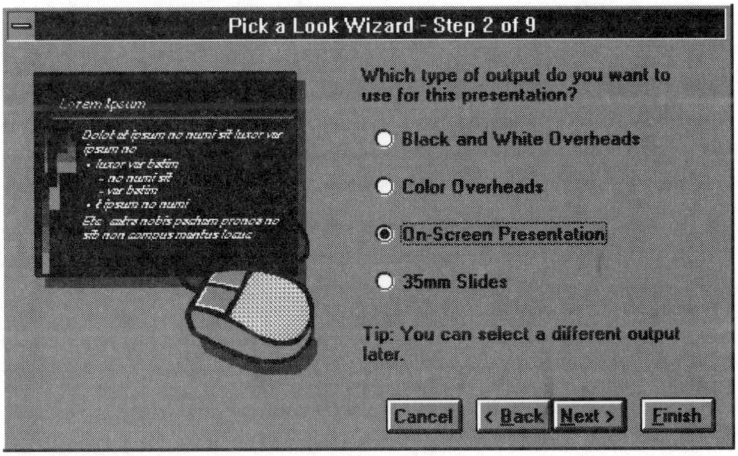

FIGURE 18–8 The second Pick a Look Wizard dialog box

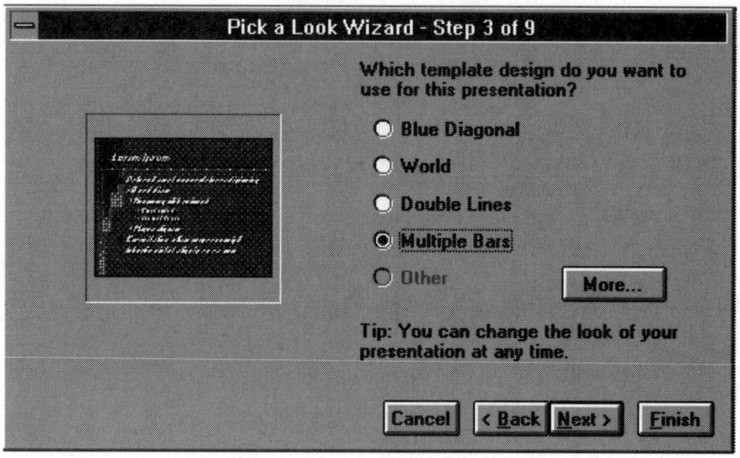

FIGURE 18–9 The third Pick a Look Wizard dialog box

you find there until a sample you like appears in the lower left portion of the dialog box, as shown in Figure 18–10; then click on the Apply button.

note You can change your presentation's template at any time by clicking on the Template button on the right side of the status bar while in slide, slide sorter, or notes pages view. You can't change the template while in outline view.

Click on the Next button to move to the fourth Pick a Look Wizard dialog box, as shown in Figure 18–11.

Click in the check boxes next to any of the items that you don't want to print. For example, if you don't want to print audience handout pages, click in the Audience Handout Pages check box to remove the check mark. Then click on the Next button to proceed to the Pick a Look Wizard – Slide Options dialog box, as shown in Figure 18–12.

If you want some text, such as your name or company name, to appear at the bottom of each slide, click in the Name, Company or

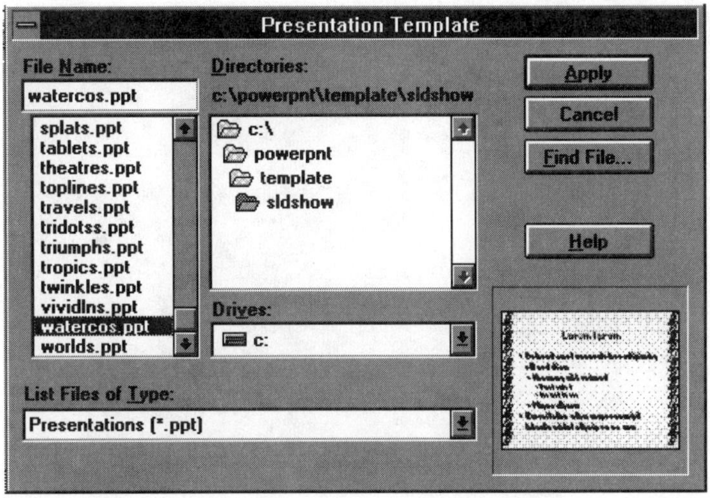

FIGURE 18–10 The Presentation Templates dialog box with a template highlighted

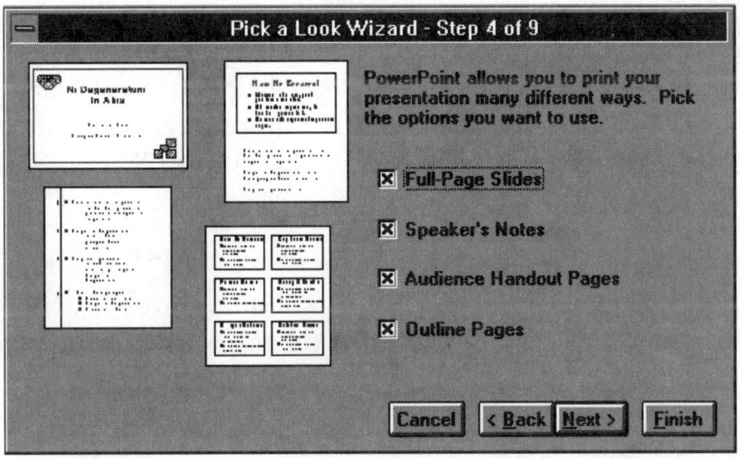

FIGURE 18–11 The fourth Pick a Look Wizard dialog box

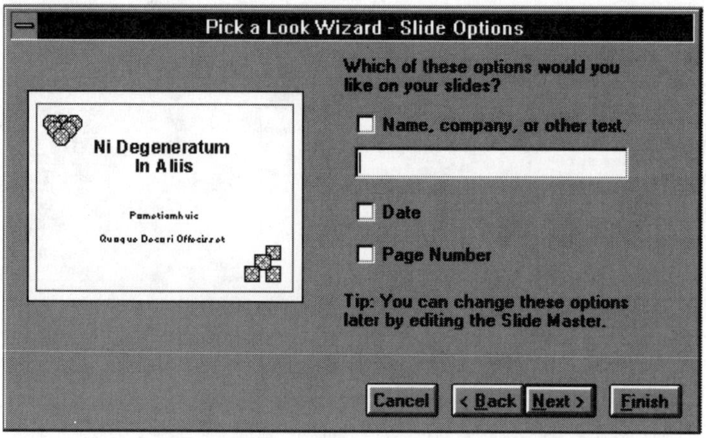

FIGURE 18–12 The Pick a Look – Slide Options dialog box

Other Text check box and then type the text in the text box. If you want the date and/or page number to appear at the bottom of each slide, click in the Date and/or the Page Number check box. Then click on the Next button.

If you told PowerPoint that you wanted to print all portions of the presentation, you will see three more Options dialog boxes exactly like this one—for speaker's notes, audience handout pages, and outline pages. After selecting the options you want, click on the Next button to proceed to the final Pick a Look Wizard dialog box, as shown in Figure 18–13.

Click on the Finish button to complete the Pick a Look Wizard and apply your choices to the presentation. Figure 18–14 shows the title slide we were working with using the formatting from the Pick a Look Wizard.

Adding a New Slide

Adding a new slide in slide view gives you the opportunity to choose a layout for the new slide. Layouts determine which placeholders are

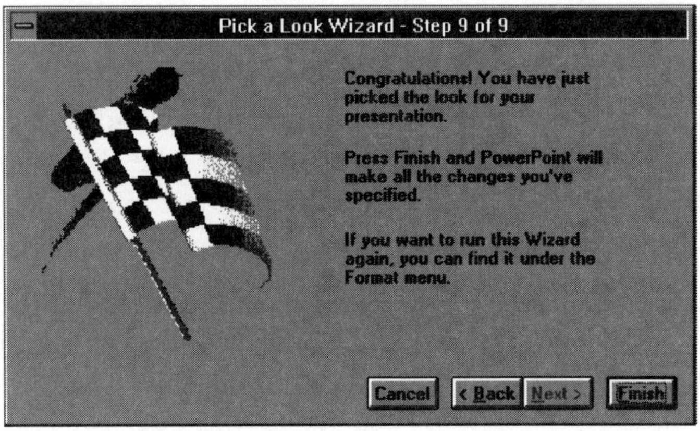

FIGURE 18–13 The final Pick a Look Wizard dialog box

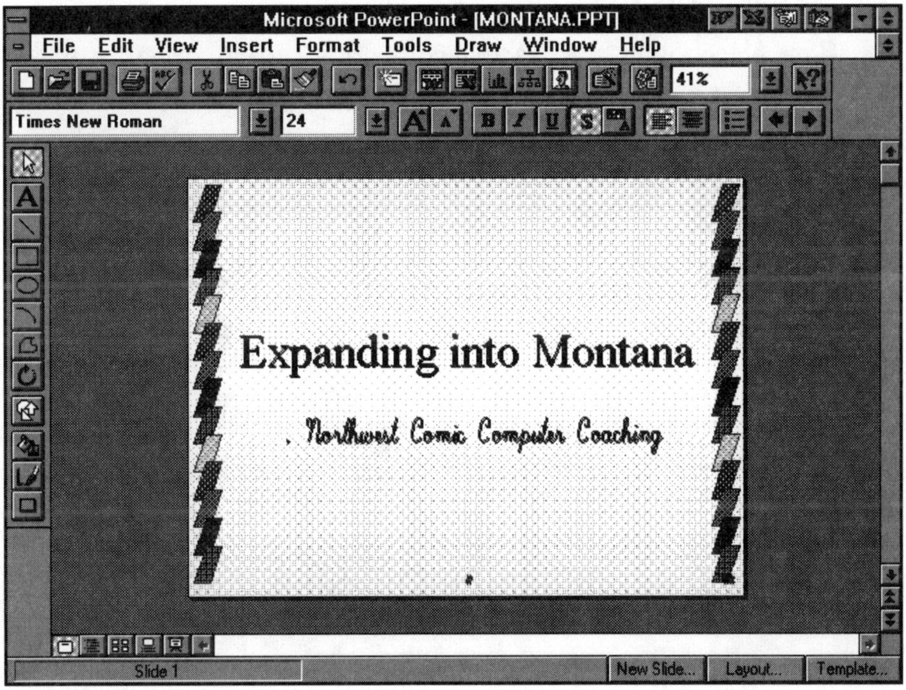

FIGURE 18–14 The reformatted title slide

included in the slide and where they are located. The placeholders determine what type of elements appear on the slide.

Of course, you can change placeholders and add other elements to a slide, regardless of which layout you choose. But choosing a layout that matches what you want to put on the slide as closely as possible makes the job of filling in the slide's elements much easier.

To add a new slide in slide view, click on the New Slide button on the right side of the status bar or choose Insert➢New Slide. The New Slide dialog box appears, as shown in Figure 18–15.

This dialog box presents all the available AutoLayouts. The highlighted layout is the layout of the previous slide. Click on another layout to choose a different placeholder or a differently arranged placeholder. You may want to use the scroll bar in the dialog box to see other layouts.

The placeholder that each layout adds should be fairly self-explanatory, but a description of the highlighted layout appears in the box in

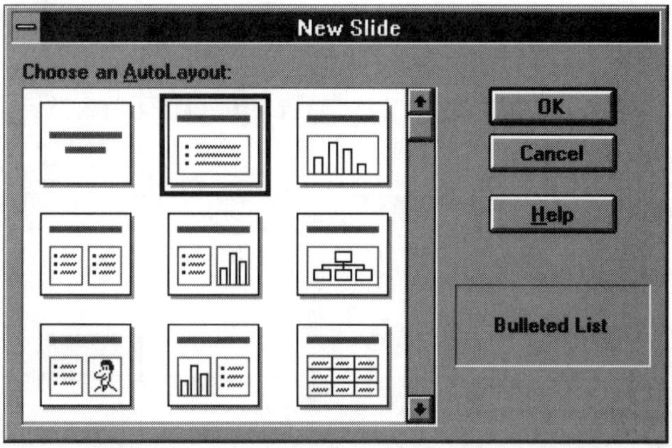

FIGURE 18–15 The New Slide dialog box

the lower-right portion of the dialog box anyway. After choosing the layout you want, click on the OK button. A new slide with the placeholder for the chosen layout appears, as shown in Figure 18–16.

New placeholders are easy to use because they tell you what to do to add the appropriate element. Notice in Figure 18–16 that the placeholders tell you click or double-click to add elements. For example, the title placeholder says "Click to add title." When you click anywhere inside the title placeholder, that message disappears and you

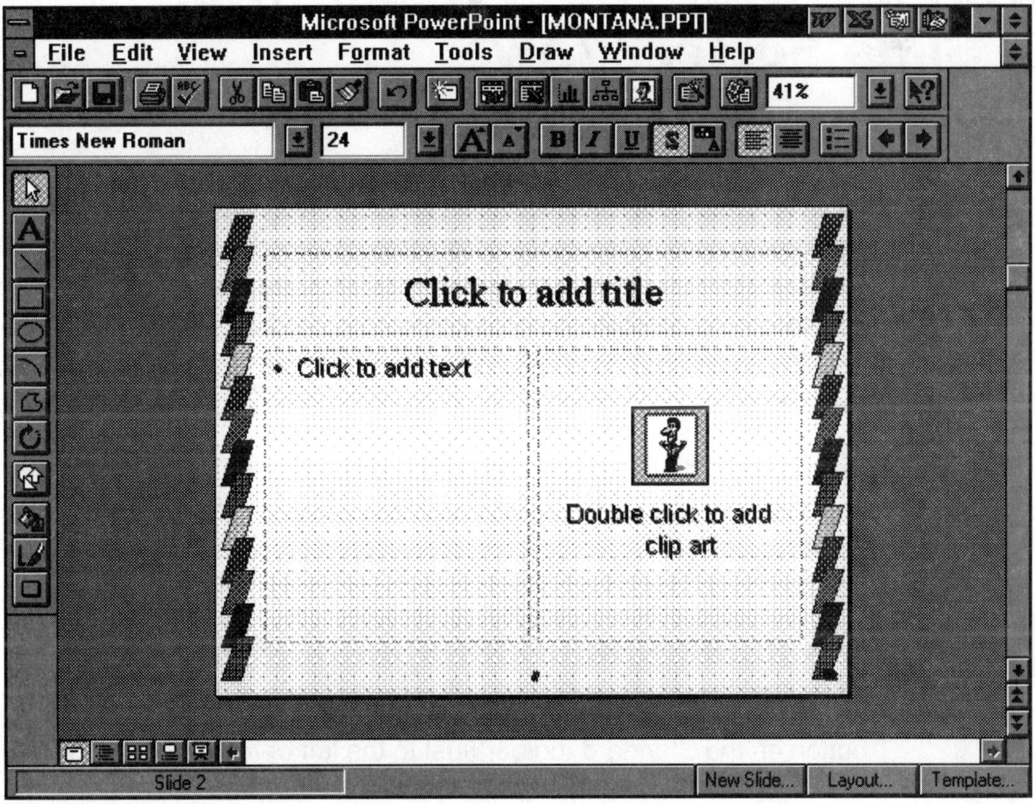

FIGURE 18–16 A new slide with placeholders for the elements to be added

can just start typing the slide's title. When you finish with the title, click or double-click in one of the other placeholders. You'll learn to add graphic elements to your slides in the next chapter.

tip You can change an existing slide's layout by choosing Format➢Slide Layout and then choosing the layout to apply. All of the slide's existing elements remain, although some outline text elements may be rearranged. Placeholders for new elements are added to the slide to facilitate adding the new elements.

Working with Your Presentation in Slide Sorter View

The slide sorter view is the what-you-see-is-what-you-get version of the outline view. Click on the Slide Sorter View button to the left of the horizontal scroll bar or choose View➢Slide Sorter to switch to slide sorter view. In slide sorter view, your slides look just as they do in slide view, except that you can see several of them at once, as shown in Figure 18–17.

In slide sorter view, the Slide Sorter toolbar replaces the Formatting toolbar. You'll learn about the functions of this toolbar in the next chapter.

note The number of slides you see on the screen is determined by the zoom percentage. The default zoom percentage is 66 percent, which lets you see about six slides at once. You can change the zoom percentage by clicking on the Zoom Control button on the Standard toolbar (just to the left of the Help button) and then clicking on the percentage you want to use.

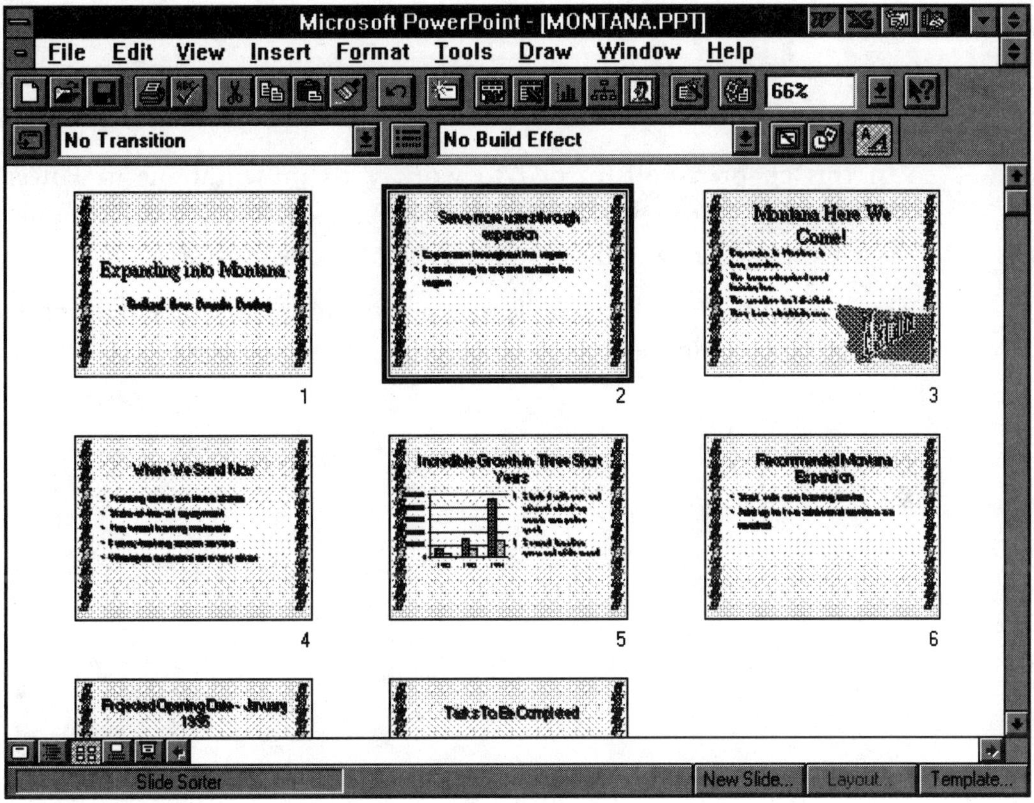

FIGURE 18–17 A presentation in slide sorter view

You can't edit the elements of an individual slide in slide sorter view, but you can double-click on a slide to jump quickly to slide view. What you normally do in slide sorter view, as the name implies, is sort the slides. If you want to move a slide to a new position, just drag it there. That's all there is to it.

If you're finished working with your presentation for now, don't forget to save it so you won't lose any changes you've made.

Summary

In this chapter, you learned to work with presentations in PowerPoint's different views and to use the Pick a Look Wizard. You also learned to add new slides using the AutoLayout feature.

In the next chapter, you'll learn to enhance your presentations by inserting graphic elements and using the drawing tools.

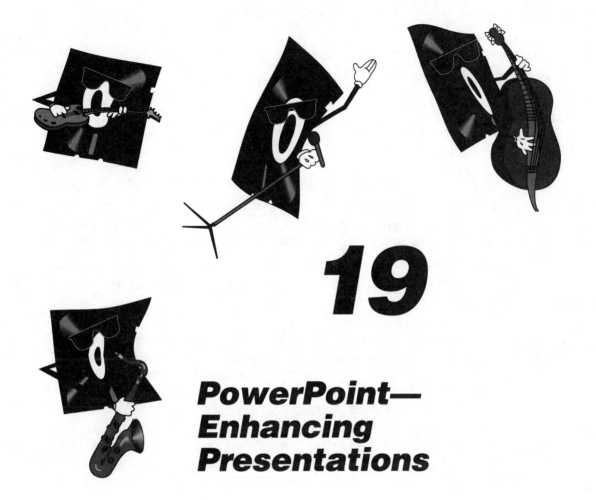

19

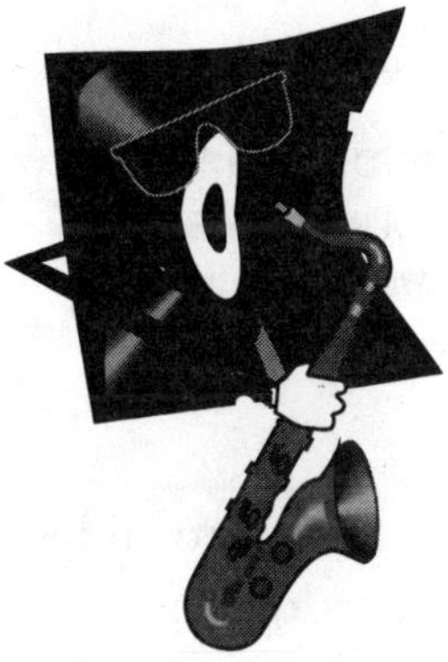

PowerPoint—Enhancing Presentations

Adding graphic elements, in addition to text and background color schemes, can give your presentations the impact they need to drive your point home. Some graphic elements simply add interest, a fact that should not be underestimated, because if you can't keep the attention of your audience, your presentation will be ineffective. Other graphic elements, such as graphs, can support your points by helping the audience to visualize your numbers.

Adding Clip Art to Your Presentation

If a picture is worth a thousand words, PowerPoint includes more than a million words worth of clip art images for you to include in your presentations. Collections of graphic images, such as pictures and drawings, are called *clip art,* because the images can be clipped and placed in your documents. If you need more clip art, you can purchase addition clip art collections to meet just about any need or whim.

note PowerPoint doesn't restrict the graphics you can use to enhance your presentations to clip art. You can also include a wide variety of graphic images and other types of objects created in other programs. You'll learn to insert "foreign" objects into PowerPoint presentations later in this book.

As you learned in the last chapter, many elements are added to slides by clicking or double-clicking on a placeholder that is added using a layouts.

If PowerPoint isn't already running, start PowerPoint and open a presentation or start creating a new one. Make sure you're in slide view and add a new slide using the AutoLayout with a clip art placeholder (it's the one with the drawing of a funny-looking guy in it). If you don't want to add a new slide, you can apply this layout to an existing slide by clicking on the Layout button on the right side of the status bar. Figure 19–1 shows a slide with a clip art placeholder.

Just as it says, double-click anywhere within the clip art placeholder to add clip art. The Microsoft ClipArt Gallery dialog box appears, as shown in Figure 19–2.

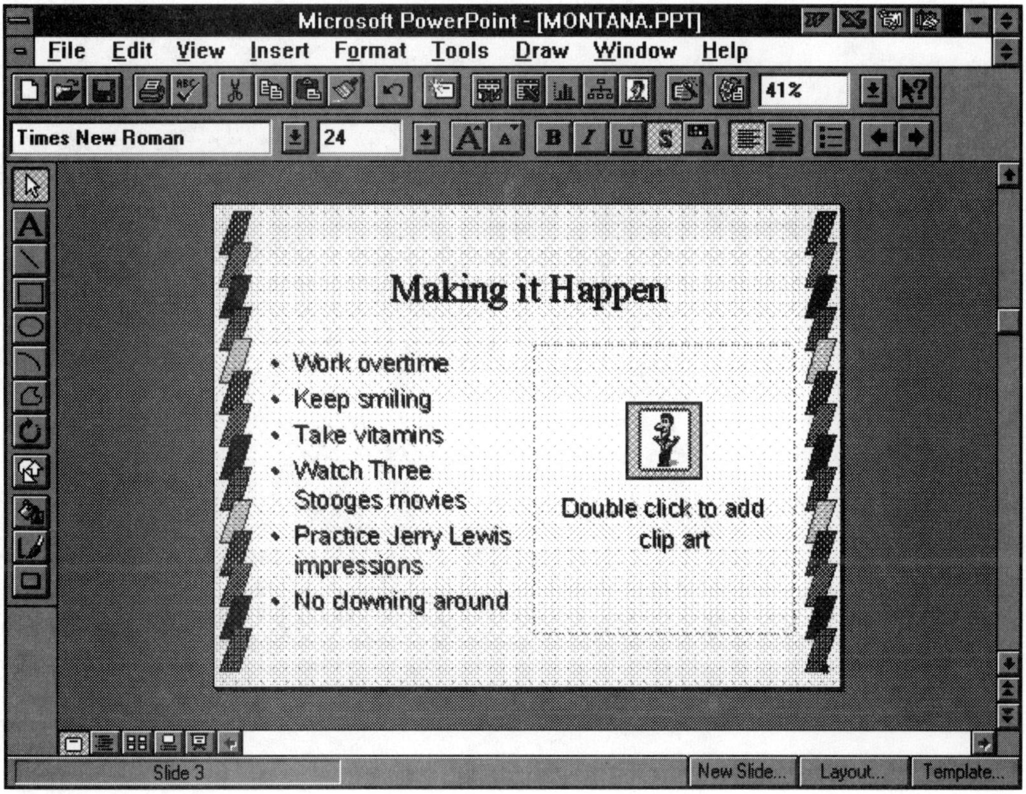

FIGURE 19–1 A slide with a clip art placeholder

note

If this is the first time you've used PowerPoint's clip art, you'll see a dialog box asking if you want to add the images to your ClipArt Gallery. Click on the Yes button and be patient while PowerPoint gathers the clip art images into the ClipArt Gallery.

Be prepared for this process to take a few minutes. The actual time depends on the speed of your computer and the number of groups of images you have told PowerPoint to install on your computer.

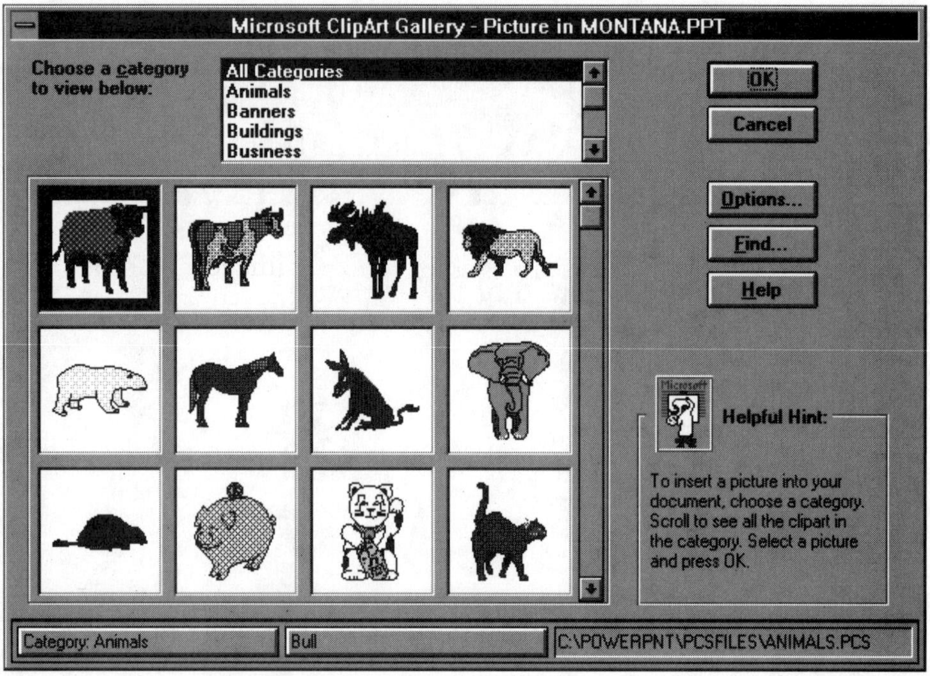

FIGURE 19–2 The Microsoft ClipArt Gallery dialog box

If PowerPoint was installed using the Typical installation, you didn't tell PowerPoint which groups of images to install. If you don't find the images you're looking for, you can add other groups of images at any time. The appendix on installing PowerPoint covers adding and deleting segments of PowerPoint.

When the ClipArt Gallery dialog box first appears, All Categories is selected, and all the images are available. But trying to find the image you want by sifting through the entire collection of images can be like trying to find the proverbial needle in a haystack. That's why the ClipArt Gallery groups the images into categories.

Scroll through the list of categories at the top of the dialog box to find the group you think is most likely to contain a useful image and then click on the category name. For example, click on Cartoons to see—surprise—cartoon images. Then use the scroll bar next to the images to find an image in the group that you want to use.

Click on an image to display its description at the bottom of the dialog box. These descriptions can be particularly useful in categories such as Flags, Landmarks, and Maps. After selecting an image, click on the OK button or double-click on the image. The image appears in the clip art placeholder, as shown in Figure 19–3.

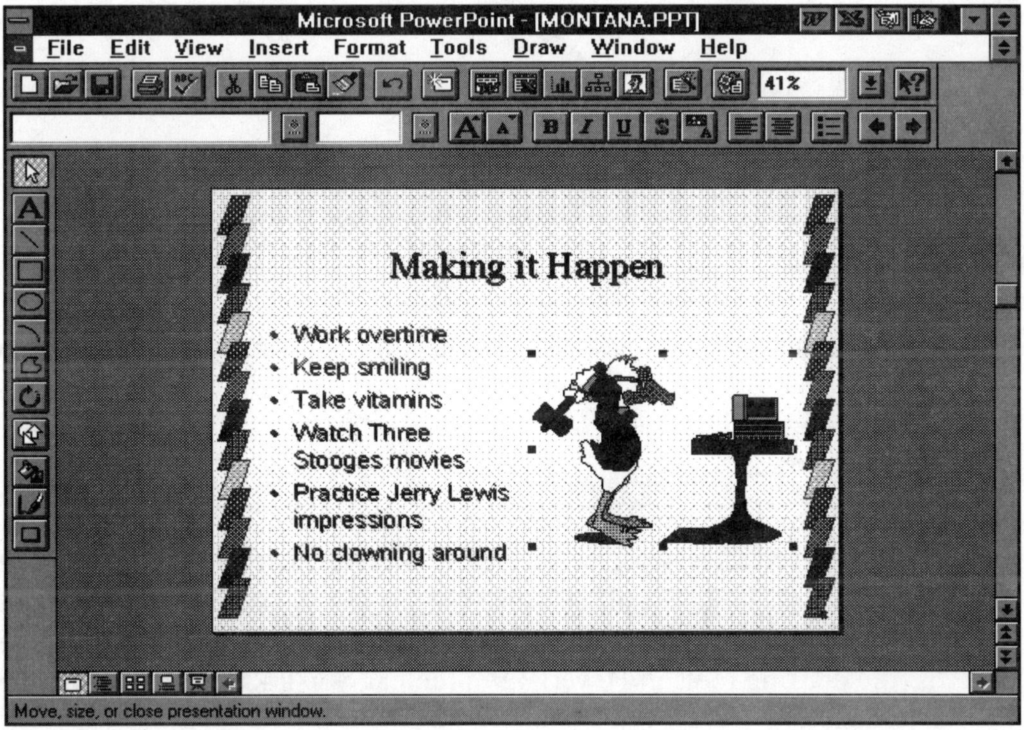

FIGURE 19–3 An image from the ClipArt Gallery inserted into a slide

note You can insert clip art into a slide or other portion of a presentation even if there is no clip art placeholder. Just choose Insert➢Clip Art. The ClipArt Gallery dialog box pops up, and you choose a clip art image the same way you would if you had a clip art placeholder.

After the image is inserted, you may have to resize and reposition it. Resize it by positioning the mouse pointer over one of the six handles surrounding the image so the pointer becomes a two-headed arrow; then drag. Reposition the image by pointing anywhere inside the image and dragging. You can use this technique to resize and move an image whether it was inserted into a predefined placeholder or not.

Using the Drawing Toolbar

The Drawing toolbar lets you add a virtually unlimited variety of text, shapes, and freehand drawings to your presentations. To use the Drawing toolbar, you must be in slide or notes page view. Drawings can't be added in outline or slide sorter view.

The other Office programs have Drawing toolbars that work in much the same way as the Drawing toolbar in PowerPoint. Each program's Drawing toolbar has a few buttons that aren't available in the other programs.

For example, PowerPoint's Drawing toolbar has a Text Tool button for adding text that isn't part of the outline, but neither Word nor Excel has a Text Tool button, because you can always add text wherever you are in those programs. Despite the differences, once you learn to use the drawing tools in PowerPoint's toolbar, you'll know how to use the others.

Lets look at some of the most often-used buttons in the Drawing toolbar.

Adding Text to Slides

The Drawing toolbar's Text Tool button—the one with the letter A on it—lets you put text that isn't part of the presentation's outline anywhere on a slide or note page.

There are two ways to use the text tool. If you just want to type a single line of text, click on the Text Tool button and then click on the slide and start typing. This lets you type as long a line of text as you want. In fact, if you keep typing, the text will extend beyond the edge of the slide. You can press Enter to start a new line of text, but if you want to type more than one line of text, the best approach is to add text in a text box.

To add text in a text box, click on the Text Tool. Then move the mouse pointer to where you want to begin the text box and drag to the right until the rectangle appears to be about the size you want.

The rectangle appears large enough for only one line of text, but when you type in a text box, the words wrap at the right side of the rectangle just as they do in outline view or in a Word document. Figure 19–4 shows some text in a text box placed under the clip art in a slide.

As with any other object, you can right-click in a text box to see a shortcut menu of options for the object, or you can use options from the toolbars or normal menus.

For example, the default alignment for text is left. If you want the text in the text box to be centered—as might be appropriate for a figure caption—just click on the Center Alignment button on the Formatting toolbar while the text box is selected. When a text box is selected, it has a hashed border around it.

Adding Lines and Shapes

The five buttons below the Text Tool button are for adding lines and shapes. Using these tools is easy because, after you click on one of the

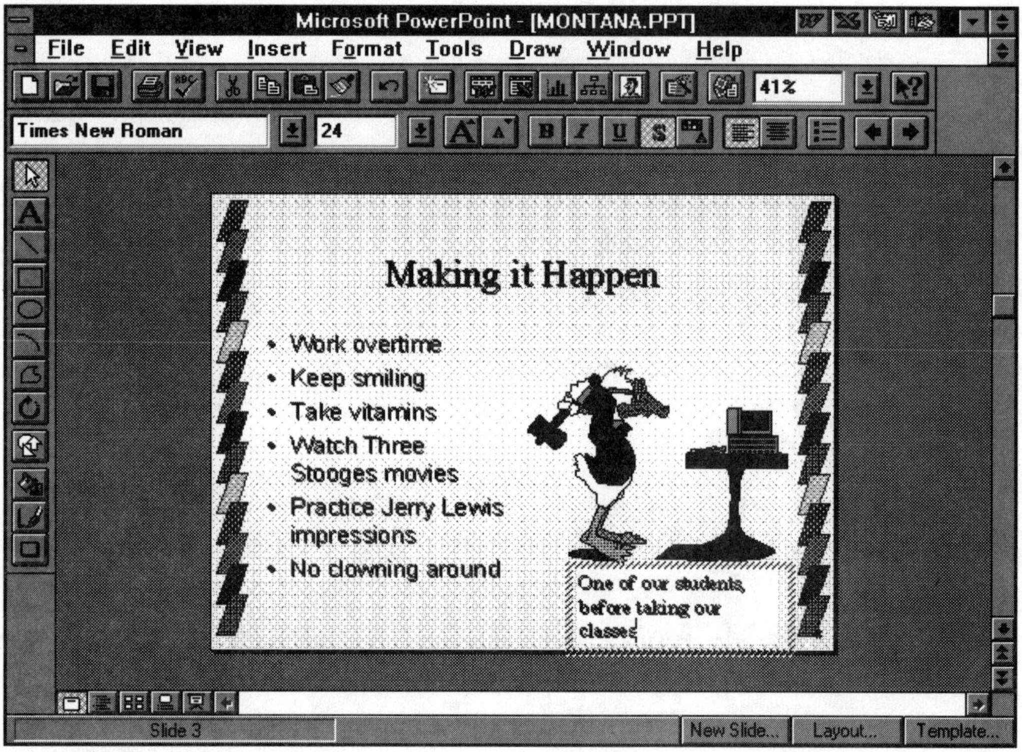

FIGURE 19–4 Text in a text box

buttons and move the mouse pointer into the slide area, the left side of the status bar tells you what do. For example, if you click on the Line Tool button, the status bar tells you to "Drag to draw a line, press Shift key to constrain angle."

So if you just drag the mouse, you draw a line of any angle. The line length is determined by how far you drag before releasing the mouse button. If you press the Shift key as you start dragging, the line can only be rotated in 45-degree increments.

The Rectangle Tool works pretty much the same as the Line Tool. To draw a rectangle, click on the Rectangle Tool; then drag to create a rectangle. If you want a perfect square, hold the Shift key down while you drag.

The Ellipse Tool lets you draw an ellipse when you drag, unless you hold the Shift key down, in which case it draws a circle.

The Arc Tool lets you draw a curved line. If you hold the Shift key down while dragging, you draw a circular arc.

The Freeform Tool lets you draw a polygon or draw freehand as though using a pencil on the screen. To draw a polygon, click on the Freeform Tool; then click on the slide where you to begin the first line, move the mouse to where you want to begin the next line, and click. Repeat the process until you have all the lines you want and then double-click.

To draw freehand, click on the Freeform Tool and move to where you want to begin drawing; then hold the mouse button down as you draw. When the mouse button is pressed while using the Freeform Tool, the mouse pointer takes the shape of a pencil.

tip Text, lines, and shapes can overlap. This can be useful if, for example, you want to put some text inside a circle or combine several rectangles to create a more complex design.

Rotating Objects

In addition to moving and sizing objects, you can rotate objects by using the Drawing toolbar. And you aren't limited to objects created with the Drawing toolbar; you can also rotate outline text.

To rotate an object, select the object by clicking on it. If you are selecting an outline text placeholder, you'll have to click in the placeholder and then click on its border so the handles appear. Then click on the Free Rotate Tool and move the mouse pointer over one to the object's handles so the pointer becomes a four-sided arrow. Finally, drag the mouse until the object is at the desired angle. If you hold the

[Shift] key down while rotating, the object can only be rotated in 45-degree increments.

note You can't rotate clip art, pictures, or objects brought in from other programs, such as Word documents or Excel worksheets. In some cases, however, the other program you use to create an object will have the ability to rotate or manipulate the object before bringing it into PowerPoint.

Using AutoShapes

For creating a simple rectangle or ellipse, the Rectangle and Ellipse tools on the Drawing toolbar work just fine. When you want to create more complex shapes, however, the AutoShapes feature is a dream come true.

AutoShapes is a palette of shapes you can use by simply clicking on the shape you want and then dragging on the slide. Actually, the Rectangle and Ellipse tools are AutoShapes tools that appear on both the Drawing toolbar and the AutoShapes palette.

To use AutoShapes, click on the AutoShapes button on the Drawing toolbar. The AutoShapes palette appears, as shown in Figure 19–5.

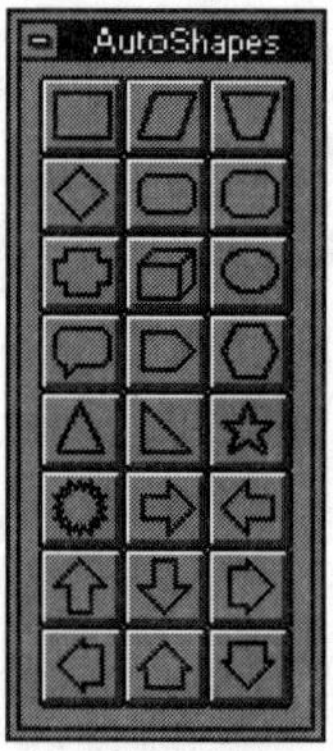

FIGURE 19–5 The AutoShapes palette

Click on the shape you want and then drag on the slide where you want the shape to appear. Use the Shift key to create shapes with proportional dimensions. Figure 19–6 shows some of the AutoShapes.

If having the AutoShapes palette right next to the Drawing toolbar obscures some of your slide, you can move it to a new location by dragging it by its title bar. The AutoShapes palette remains on the screen until you close it by clicking on the close box in the upper-left corner.

You can change any AutoShape to any other. For example, you could change a circle to a star or a cube to an arrow. Select the shape you

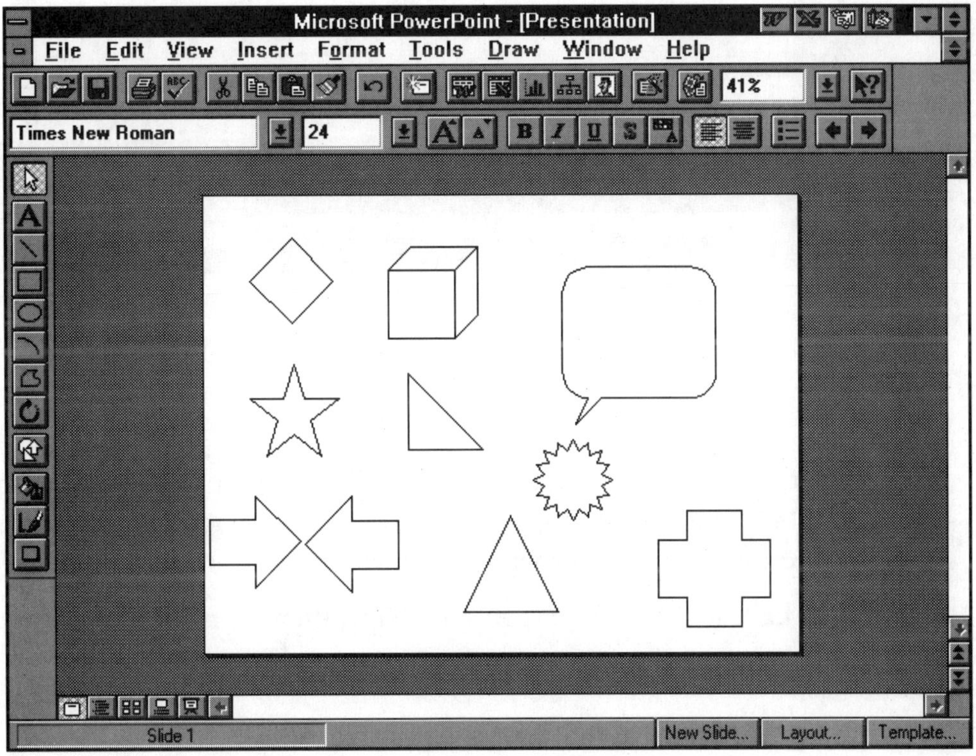

FIGURE 19–6 Some AutoShapes

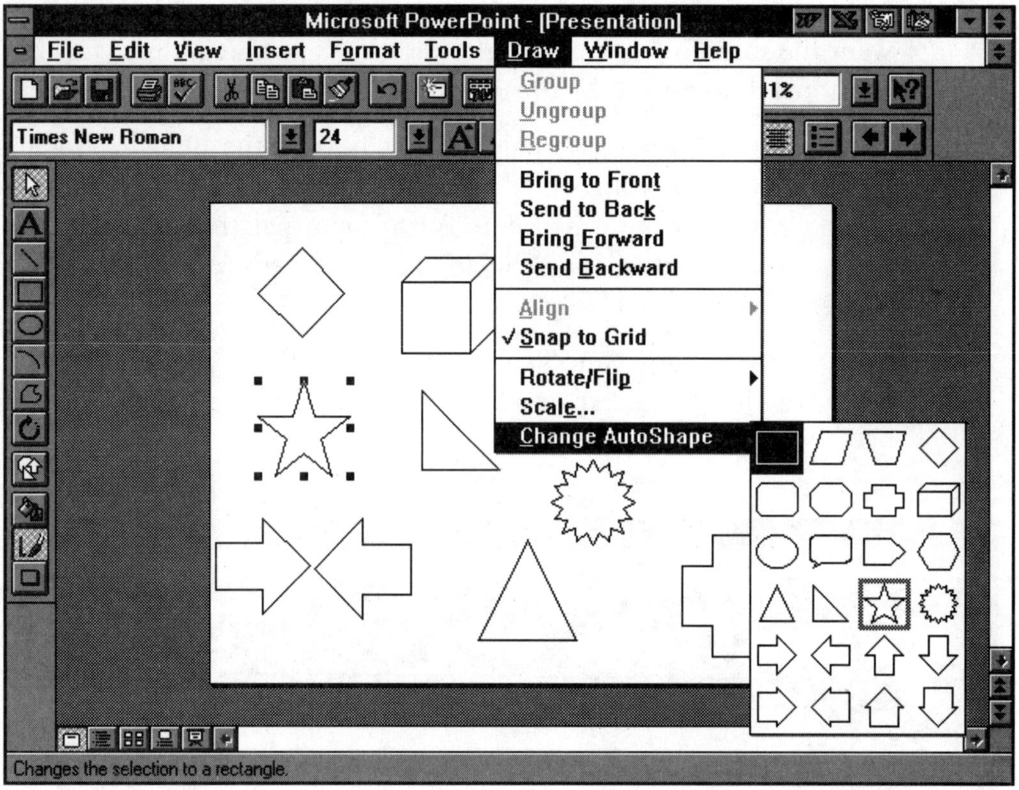

FIGURE 19–7 The AutoShapes palette for changing shapes

want to change by clicking on it so its handles appear; then choose Draw➢Change AutoShape. A palette of AutoShapes appears with a box around the selected shape, as shown in Figure 19–7.

If you have selected more than one shape, there won't be a box around any of the shapes on the palette.

Changing Colors and Lines

One of the options you'll probably want to experiment with is changing the colors and lines for various objects. To change the colors

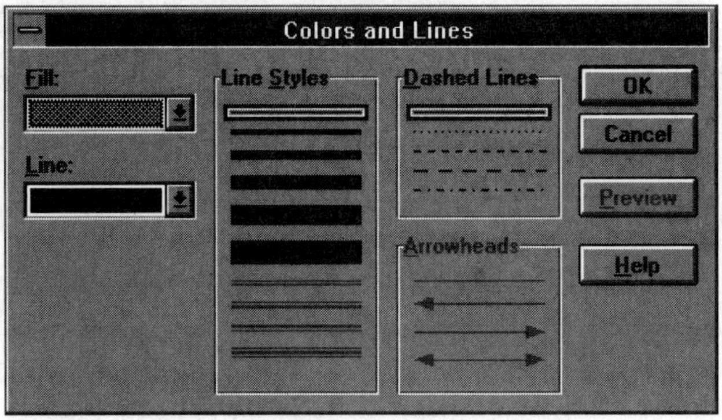

FIGURE 19–8 The Colors and Lines dialog box

and lines, select the object or objects you want to change, right-click on the object, and choose Colors and Lines from the shortcut menu or choose Format➢Colors and Lines. The Colors and Lines dialog box appears, as shown in Figure 19–8.

Click on the drop-down arrows to change the Fill and Line colors. Click on the Line Style width you want and, if you want dashed lines, click on one of the Dashed lines. After making your selections, click on the OK button.

Presenting Your Presentation

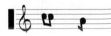

After making enhancements to your presentation, you're ready to print it, have 35mm slides created, or display it on screen. If you're going to be showing the presentation on screen, there are a few other steps you may wish to take to specify the transition from one slide to the next.

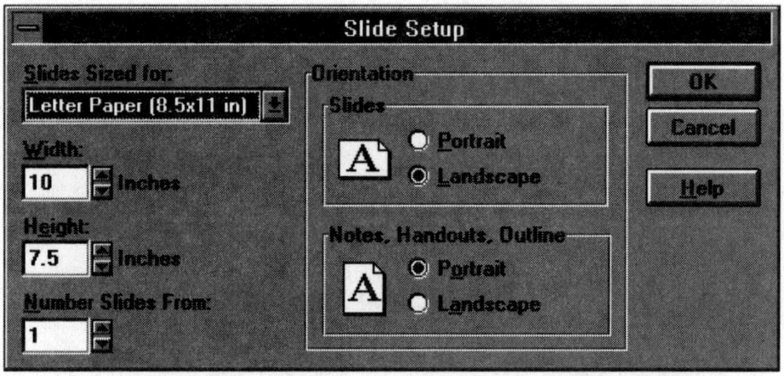

FIGURE 19–9 The Slide Setup dialog box

Even if you're going to be using 35mm slides or showing the presentation on screen, you'll want to print out certain portions of the presentation, such as audience handouts and speaker's notes.

If you're printing the presentation, the first thing you'll want to do is make sure the format is correct for the way the slides will be presented. If you used the Pick a Look Wizard, you should be all set, because the Pick a Look Wizard asks what type of presentation you'll be giving. If you're not sure, open the presentation and choose File➢Slide Setup. The Slide Setup dialog box appears, as shown in Figure 19–9.

If the specification in the Slides Sized For box isn't correct, click on the drop-down arrow and then click on the correct one. You can also choose whether your slides, notes, handouts, and outlines will be printed in a portrait (vertical) or landscape (horizontal) orientation. After making your choices, click on the OK button.

To print your presentation, choose File➢Print. The Print dialog box appears, as shown in Figure 19–10.

Click on the drop-down arrow next to Print What if you want to print a portion of the presentation other than what is currently in the

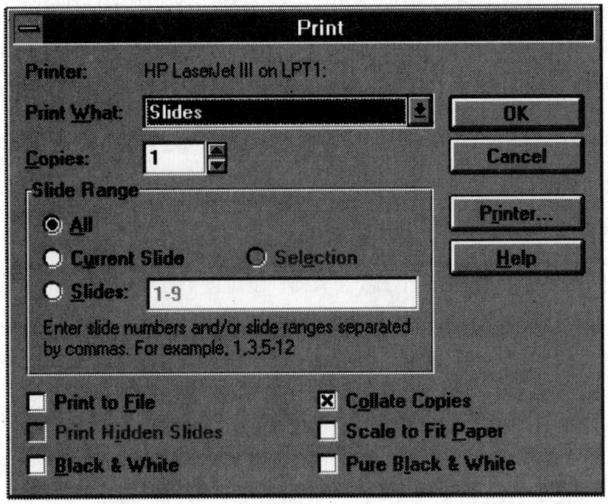

FIGURE 19–10 The Print dialog box

Print What box. Make any other changes you want, such as whether to print all the slides or just a range of slides, and then click on the OK button.

note Creating 35mm slides usually requires sending or taking your presentation file to a production service company. Microsoft recommends the Genigraphics Corporation, a company that can produce not only 35mm slides but color overheads, large prints, and even posters. You can contact them at 800-638-7348. You'll find additional information about Genigraphics services in the PowerPoint package.

Setting Up for On-Screen Presentations

If you'll be giving your presentation on screen, you can add professional effects, such as transitions and builds, to your slides.

Transitions let you specify how the next slide appears as the previous slide leaves the screen. Transition effects include dissolves and fades.

Builds—sometimes called *progressive disclosures*—cause the main text in a slide to appear one point at a time. You can also specify whether the previous point dims when the next point appears.

Adding transitions and builds is most easily done in slide sorter view, because you can work with all your slides at once.

Open the presentation you'll be giving and switch to slide sorter view, if you're not already in it. Then click on the first slide for which you want to create a transition or build.

tip You can add transitions and builds to groups of slides by selecting multiple slides before adding the effects. For example, you might want to use the dissolve transition effect for every other slide. You can select multiple slides by holding down [Shift] while clicking on the slides you want to select. If you want to select all the slides, press [Ctrl]-[A]. Then add the effects just as you would if only one slide were selected.

To add a transition, click on the Transition button on the Slide Sorter toolbar, choose Transition from the shortcut menu, or choose Tools➢Transition. The Transition dialog box appears, as shown in Figure 19–11.

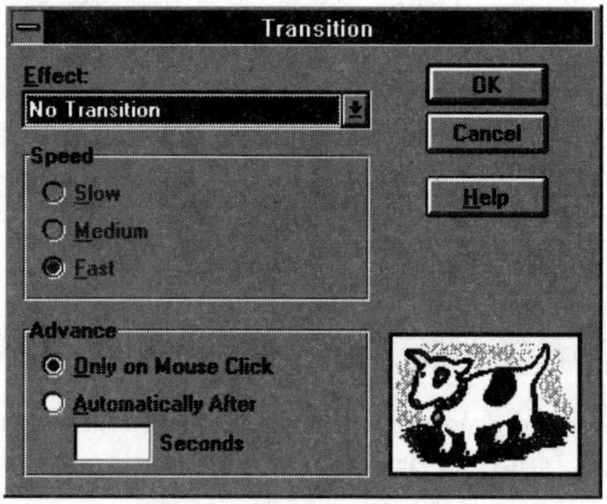

FIGURE 19–11 The Transition dialog box

The default transition is No Transition, which means there won't be any special effects when this slide appears on the screen. To add a transition effect, click on the drop-down arrow and then click on one of the effects listed in the drop-down list. As soon as you click on an effect, the sample slide in the lower-right portion of the dialog box demonstrates how the effect will look.

Next, click on one of the speed option buttons. Again, the sample in the lower-right demonstrates the transition at the selected speed.

Finally, choose the method you want to use to advance from this slide to the next. If you click on the Only On Mouse Click option button, the only way you can advance to the next slide is to click the mouse. The arrow keys, Spacebar, and Pg Up and Pg Dn keys also work.

If you click on the Automatically After button, you can specify how many seconds the slide will remain on screen before the presentation proceeds. The number of seconds you specify will appear under the slide after you close the dialog box. If you choose this timing option, you can still use a mouse click to move to the next slide in the presentation at any time. After making your transition choices, click on the OK button.

tip

A small icon of a slide with a right arrow appears under each slide that has a transition assigned to it. If you want to test the transition, click on the icon. The previous slide appears and makes the transition to the slide whose transition icon you clicked on. If the slide you're checking is the first slide, the slide goes black before proceeding.

To create a build slide, click on a slide and then click on the Build button on the Slide Sorter toolbar. The Build dialog box appears, as shown in Figure 19–12.

Click on the Build Body Text check box. If you want the previous points dimmed as the new points appear, click in the Dim Previous Points check box. You can click on the drop-down arrow below the

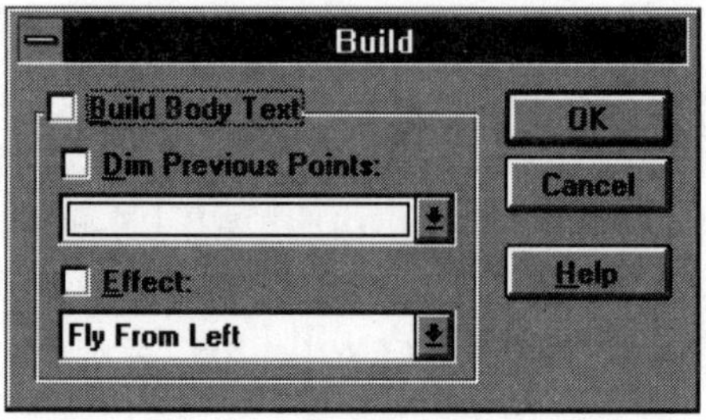

FIGURE 19–12 The Build dialog box

Dim Previous Points check box to specify a color or shade to use for the dimmed points.

If you want to use effects to build from one point to the next, click on the Effect check box; then click on the drop-down arrow below the Effect check box and choose one of the effects.

After making your build choices, click on the OK button. A small icon representing three bulleted lines appears below the slide. Figure 19–13 shows the transition and build icons as well as the timings for the slides in the slide sorter view.

To start the slide show on screen from the selected slide, click on the Slide Show button on the left of the horizontal scroll bar. This is a good, quick way to see what your slide show will look like. But if you want to specify a range of slides to show or you want the slides to repeat continuously, you'll have to start your slide show from the Slide Show dialog box.

To open the Slide Show dialog box, choose View➢Slide Show. Figure 19–14 shows the Slide Show dialog box.

If you want to show only a range of slides, type the number of the slide you want to start with. The From option button is automatically filled in when you enter a slide number. If you want the slide show to end before the last slide, press Tab and enter the number of the slide you want to end with.

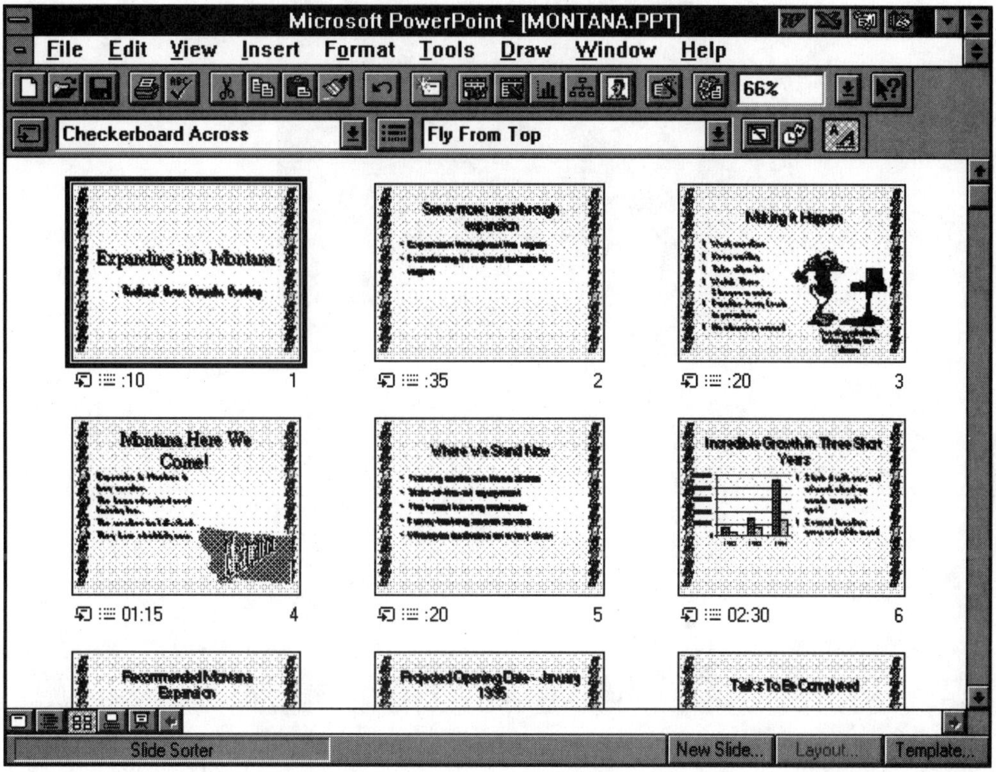

FIGURE 19–13 The slide sorter view with the icons for builds and transitions and the timing numbers

Choose Manual Advance➢Use Slide Timings or, if you want to run through your presentation to see how long it takes, choose Rehearse New Timings. If you want the slide show to run continuously—as you would in an unattended demonstration at a trade show, for example—click in the Run Continuously Until 'Esc' box. After making your presentation choices, click on the OK button to start the slide show. Figure 19–15 shows a slide from an on-screen slide show.

tip You might want to quit the Microsoft Office Manager, if it is running, before starting the presentation. This will prevent the

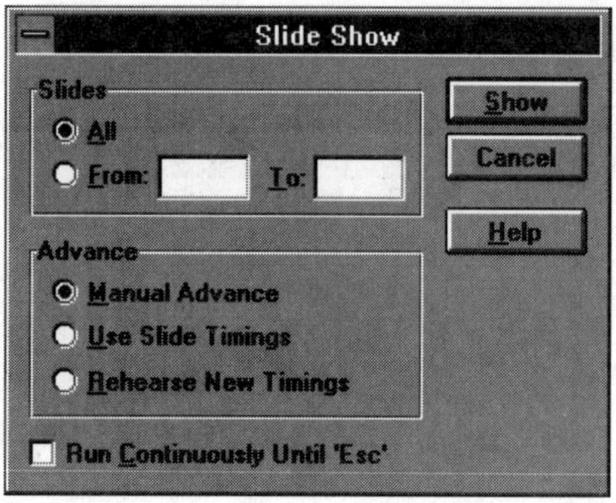

FIGURE 19–14 The Slide Show dialog box

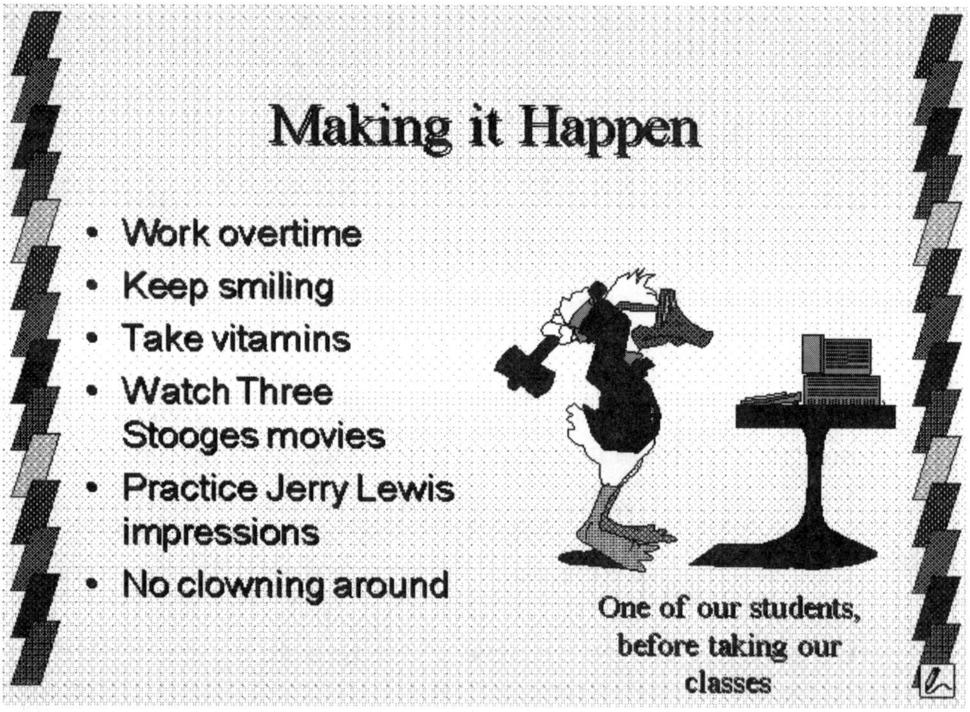

FIGURE 19–15 A slide show slide filling the screen

Microsoft Office Manager toolbar from appearing in the upper-right corner of the screen during the presentation.

To turn off the Microsoft Office Manager, press Ctrl-Esc to open the Task List. Click on Microsoft Office in the list and then on the End Task button.

You can add temporary freehand drawings to a slide as it's being presented to highlight important points. To do this, click on the pencil icon in the lower-right corner of the slide. The mouse pointer turns into a pencil shape. Drag to draw. Click on the pencil icon again to stop drawing. The drawing isn't added permanently to the presentation. Figure 19–16 shows a slide with a circle drawn around an important point.

FIGURE 19–16 Drawing on screen during a presentation

tip You can give your presentation to other people to run on other computers, even if they don't have PowerPoint. Just copy the PowerPoint Viewer disk and provide it, along with your presentation file, to the other user. Don't worry, this is perfectly legal.

The other user will have to set up the Viewer by running VSETUP.EXE from the copy of the Viewer disk while in Windows.

Summary

In this chapter, you learned to enhance and present your PowerPoint presentations by adding transitions, builds, and freehand drawings to your slides as they are presented.

The next section gives you an overview of the Access database program for manipulating complex data management tasks.

Section VI

Database Power with Access

20

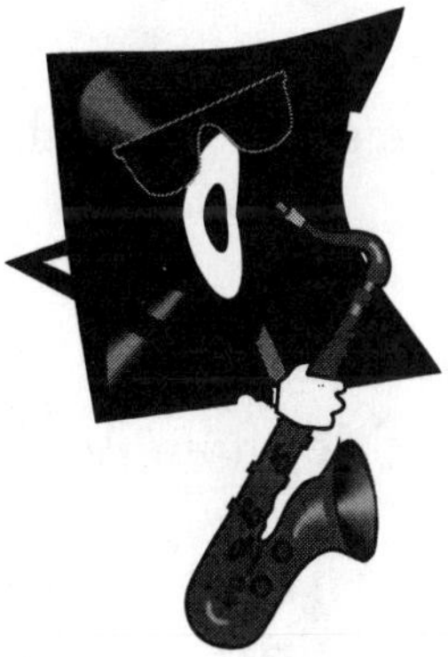

The Basics

You learned about Word databases in Chapter 10 and Excel databases in Chapter 15. With all these database facilities in the other Office programs, why on earth do we need Access? Access provides power and capabilities for more complex database tasks than Word or Excel can handle. With Access, you can facilitate data entry by creating an electronic form that resembles the paper form you use now. Access lets you create elaborate reports, including groupings, calculations, and a virtually unlimited array of other options, using the information in your database.

The most compelling reason to use Access, however, is to take advantage of its relational capabilities, which you'll learn about later.

Overview of New Features in Access 2.0

Version 2.0 of Access takes a giant leap forward in both power and ease of use. Version 1.1 could be cumbersome, particularly for those who wanted to create complex database applications without resorting to programming, but version 2.0 changes all that and allows even the database neophyte to develop powerful databases.

Input Masks and Input Mask Wizard

Access now makes it easier to enter data by allowing you to specify patterns for the data to follow.

Automatic Merge of Access Data with Word

The Word 6.0 Mail Merge Wizard lets you insert fields from Access tables directly into Word documents.

Table Wizard

The new Table Wizard makes creating new tables a snap by providing predefined sample tables and fields.

Graphic Definition of Relationships

The relationships, or links, between tables can now be defined graphically using the Relationships window. This capability makes understanding and working with a relational database much easier.

Automatic Forms and Reports

Access 2.0 has AutoForm and AutoReport buttons to make the creation of forms and reports unbelievably easy.

Access Database Concepts

Before covering database concepts specific to Access, I'll recap some database fundamentals. A database is a collection of related facts that are organized and stored in a systematic manner. Databases are everywhere. A telephone directory, for example, is a database that contains the names and phone numbers of the residents in a community.

A computer database lets you store, maintain, and retrieve facts (data) so you can generate useful information more easily and quickly than by manual means. Isn't that what computers do best—make tasks faster and easier?

Imagine trying to look through a telephone directory to find all the residents whose phone numbers have the same exchange (the first three digits of a phone number, e.g., 555 in the number 555-4444). It would be quite a job. But this would be a relatively painless task if the data was properly organized and stored in a computer database.

In Access, data is stored in tables. A table organizes related facts into rows and columns. The rows in a table are called *records* and the columns are called *fields.* A record is a line of related facts, such as a name (say, Joe Smith) and the person's phone number (say, 555-2345). In this example, Joe Smith occupies one field in the record and 555-2345 occupies another. When you create a table in Access, you specify a field name for each field. The field names appear as column headings in a table.

So far, this is all pretty much the same as the way you work with databases in Word or Excel. Access, however, is a *relational* database program. A relational database is nothing more than a collection of tables that can be connected to make a larger database.

At least one of the tables that are to be linked in a relational database must have a *primary key.* The data entered in fields defined as primary key fields must be unique. For example, if the Name field in a table is set as a primary key, no duplicate entries are allowed; you can't have more than one Joe Smith. Because it is possible that you will have more than one Joe Smith, a Name field usually isn't set as a primary key. As you'll see when we start working with Access, a counter field that simply identifies the number of the record is often the best choice for the primary key.

note In addition to allowing table linking, primary keys allow Access to create an index for faster data retrieval. Don't worry. You don't have to do a thing. Access creates these indexes on its own when you specify primary keys.

The tables that are to be linked must also have at least one field that is common to both tables. Fields that are often used to link tables are item numbers in inventory tables and customer numbers in customer tables. These are good fields to use for linking because duplicate entries in these fields are unlikely.

This is all pretty interesting, but why store data in multiple tables? Why not just throw all the information into one large table. The simple answer is: to avoid redundant data entry. Suppose you want to create a simple database to schedule classes. Each record needs the student's name, address, and phone number, as well as the information about the classes he or she is signing up for.

The first time Joe Smith signs up for a class, no problem. You enter all the pertinent information into the table, where it's stored for future recall. But suppose Joe decides to sign up for a second class. Now you have to enter Joe's information all over again, wasting time and effort and risking data entry errors.

In addition to those problems, keeping redundant entries in a table makes it much more difficult to update as the data changes. If Joe's address changes, you have to change the information in the record for each class Joe is taking. If, instead, you had a separate customer table from which the class table could draw data, you would have to change Joe's address in only one record. Access handles everything else for you.

Starting Access

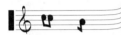

If the Microsoft Office Manager toolbar is available, click on the Microsoft Access button to start Access. If the Office Manager isn't running, open the Microsoft Office group icon in Program Manager and then double-click on the Microsoft Access icon. Figure 20–1 displays the opening Access screen.

Access uses cue cards the same way PowerPoint does to guide you through a variety of tasks. When you first start Access, the Welcome

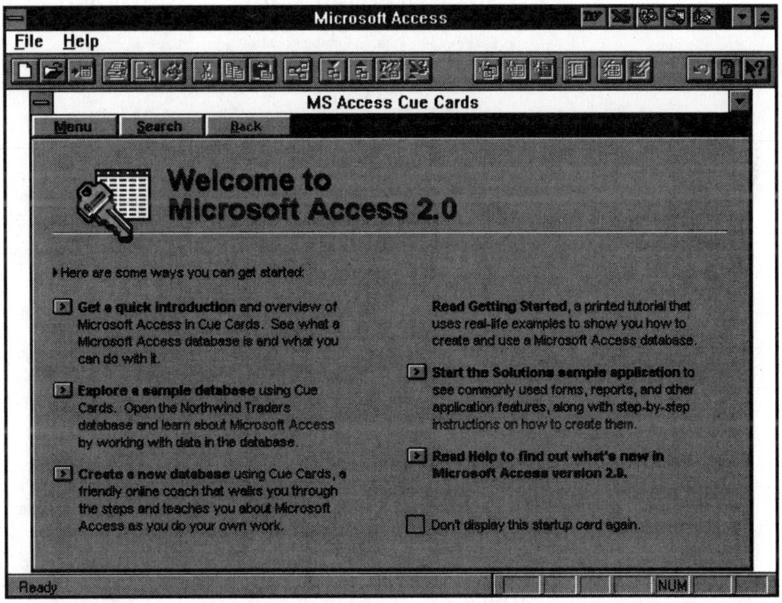

FIGURE 20–1 The opening Access screen

to Microsoft Access 2.0 cue card sits on top of the screen. You can use the startup cue card to give you a guided tour of Access, explore a sample database, guide you through creating a new database, explore a sample application (a complete database system set up to make it easier for others to use), or read the Help screen explaining what's new in this version of Access.

If you don't want to see this cue card when you start Access in the future, click in the check box in the lower-right portion of the cue card next to the text that says "Don't display this startup card again."

To clear the cue card for this session, double-click in its Control-menu box.

Generally, the next step in using Access is either to create a new database or open and work with an existing database. The easiest way to perform either of these tasks is by clicking on the New Database or Open Database button. When you click on the New Database button, the New Database dialog box appears, as shown in Figure 20–2.

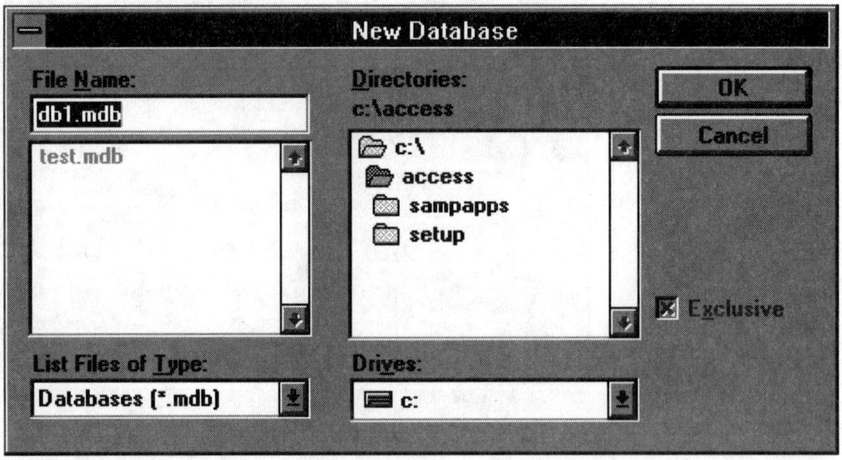

FIGURE 20–2 The New Database dialog box

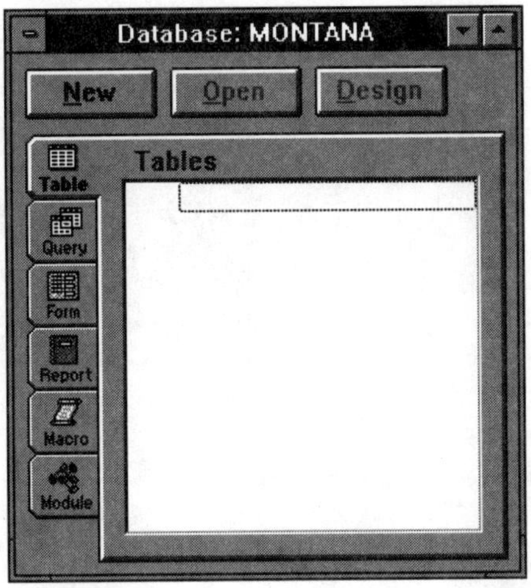

FIGURE 20–3 The Database window

Switch to the directory you want to use for your new database in the Directories list; then type a name for your new database and click on the OK button. Don't add an extension to your database name—Access adds the MDB extension for you. The Database window appears, as shown in Figure 20–3.

The Database window lets you create, open, and change the design of objects in the database. As discussed earlier, tables are the fundamental objects upon which databases are built. You must create at least one table before you can create and manipulate other objects in the database.

To create a new table, click on the Table object button and then click on the New button. The New Table dialog box appears, as shown in Figure 20–4.

You can create a table from scratch or let the Table Wizard help you out. If you know exactly which fields and field types you want to use for your table, it's actually easier to create the table from scratch. The

FIGURE 20–4 The New Table dialog box

Table Wizard can help, however, if you know the purpose of the table but aren't sure which fields to use.

We'll use the Table Wizard, so click on the Table Wizards button to display the first Table Wizard dialog box, as shown in Figure 20–5.

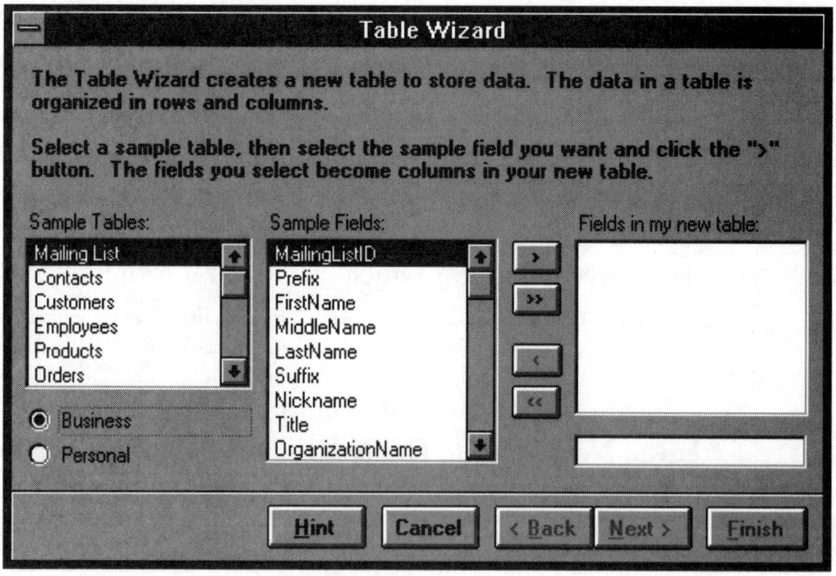

FIGURE 20–5 The first Table Wizard dialog box

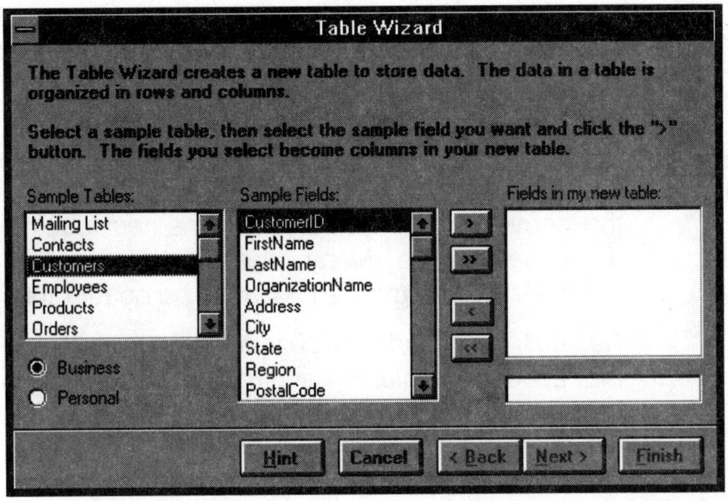

FIGURE 20–6 The Table Wizard lists the sample fields for the Customers table.

The first thing to do is determine the table's category. If you're creating a table for business purposes, be sure the Business option button in the lower-left portion of the dialog box is selected. Otherwise, click on the Personal option button so the Sample Tables list displays table categories for personal and home use.

Next, look in the Sample Tables list for the name of the table type that most closely matches the purpose you have in mind for your table and click on it. The field names in the Sample Fields list change, depending on your sample table selection, as shown in Figure 20–6.

You choose which of the sample fields you want to include in the table by clicking on the field name in the Sample Fields list and then clicking on the right arrow button (>), or you can just double-click on the field name. The field name will appear in the Fields in My New Table list. If you accidentally add a field you don't want in the table, click on the left arrow button (<). You can add all the sample fields by clicking on the double arrow (>>) button.

tip If you want to change the name of a sample field, edit it in the text box below the Fields in My New Table list and then press the [Tab] key.

note You may notice that there are no spaces between words in the sample field names. You can edit field names to add spaces (see the above tip), but running field names together is a standard database practice. Many other database programs don't allow spaces in field names, so you may be better off not using spaces.

As you'll see shortly, Access lets you provide alternate captions that appear as column headings in the table. Even if your actual field names don't have spaces, the column headings can have spaces or even different text.

After you add all the fields you want in your table, click on the Next button to move to the second Table Wizard dialog box, which is shown in Figure 20–7.

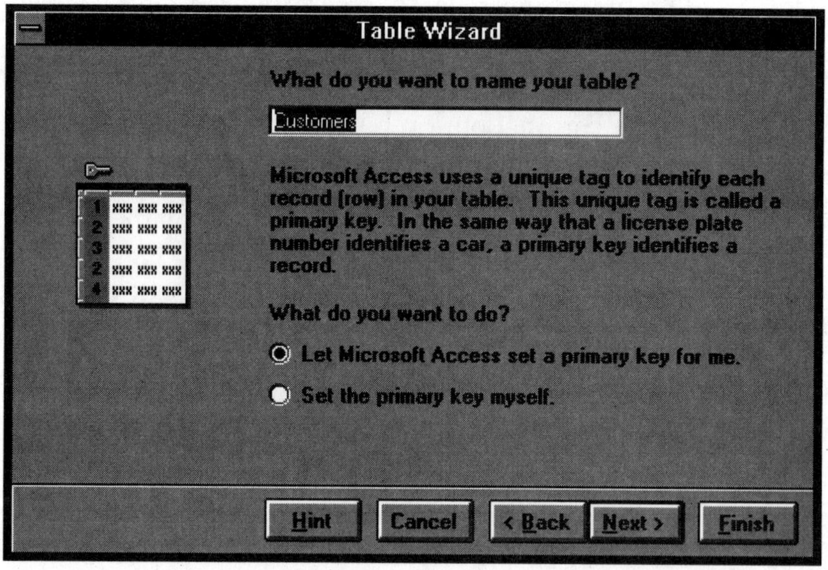

FIGURE 20–7 The second Table Wizard dialog box

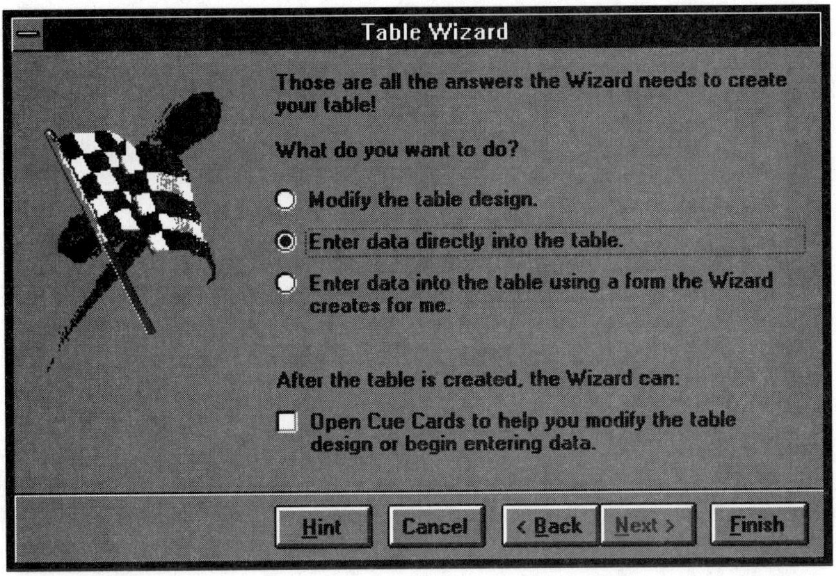

FIGURE 20–8 The final Table Wizard dialog box

In this dialog box, you can change the proposed table name by typing a new name. You can also choose whether to let Access set the primary key or specify it yourself. Remember, you cannot have duplicate entries in a primary key field. In the example Customers table, the CustomerID field makes sense as a primary key because each customer can have a unique ID. Access is clever enough to know this and specify the CustomerID field as the primary key.

Click on the Next button to move to the third, and final, Table Wizard dialog box, which is shown in Figure 20–8.

In the final dialog box, you can choose to modify the table design, start entering data directly into the table, or enter data into an automatically created form. We'll be covering modifications to the table design and working with forms in the next chapter, so we'll choose to enter data directly into the table.

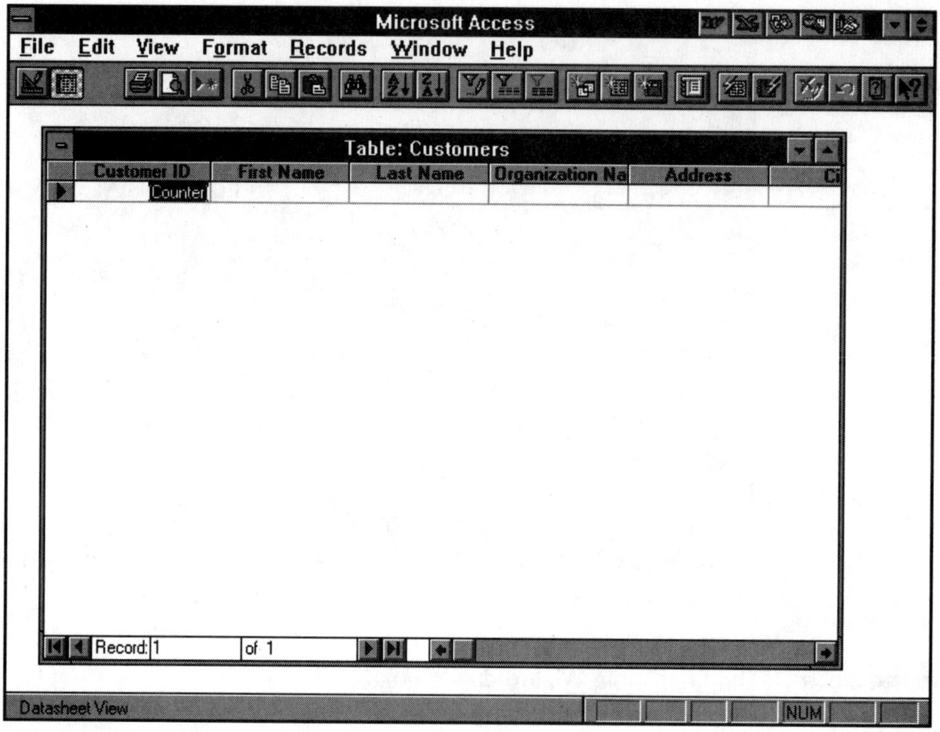

FIGURE 20–9 The table without any records entered

Be sure the Enter Data Directly into the Table option button is selected and then click on the Finish button. The finished table appears, as shown in Figure 20–9.

When the table first appears, it is in Datasheet view, which allows you to enter data and change the view of the data. You can't change the underlying design of the table in Datasheet view, however. You'll learn to modify the table design using Design view in the next chapter.

Notice the word *Counter* in the Customer ID field. A counter field is used to increment records automatically. Access made the Customer ID field a counter field when it set it as the primary key. As you enter records, you'll see how this works. The Customer ID field for the first record will be number 1, the second will be number 2, and so on.

CAUTION

Although a Counter field could be used to link two tables, it's usually not the best choice, because the field entries are automatic. If you use a Counter field for a customer ID, for example, you wouldn't be able to use the same customer IDs in a related table.

Entering Data in a Table

Entering data in a table is simply a matter of typing it in the appropriate fields. Because counter fields are filled in automatically, you begin the first record by pressing the Tab key and typing the data. As soon as you begin typing, the counter moves down to the next row and a 1 appears in the Customer ID field of the first record, as shown in Figure 20–10.

Also notice the pencil symbol in the row heading just to the left of the first record. This indicates that the record contains data that hasn't been saved. You don't have to do anything to save the data in a record. It is saved automatically (and the pencil will disappear) when you finish the data entry and move to the next record. If you want to save the data before moving to the next record, choose File ➢ Save Record or press Shift-Enter.

After you finish entering the data in a field, move to the next field by pressing the Tab key or clicking in the next field. You can then enter the data for that field. When you enter the data for the last field in the record, press Tab or Enter to move to the next record.

note

One of the options that can make data entry easier is the input mask. An input mask is a pattern to which the data for a particular field must conform. For example, the Phone Number field in the example table is assigned an input mask that places the area

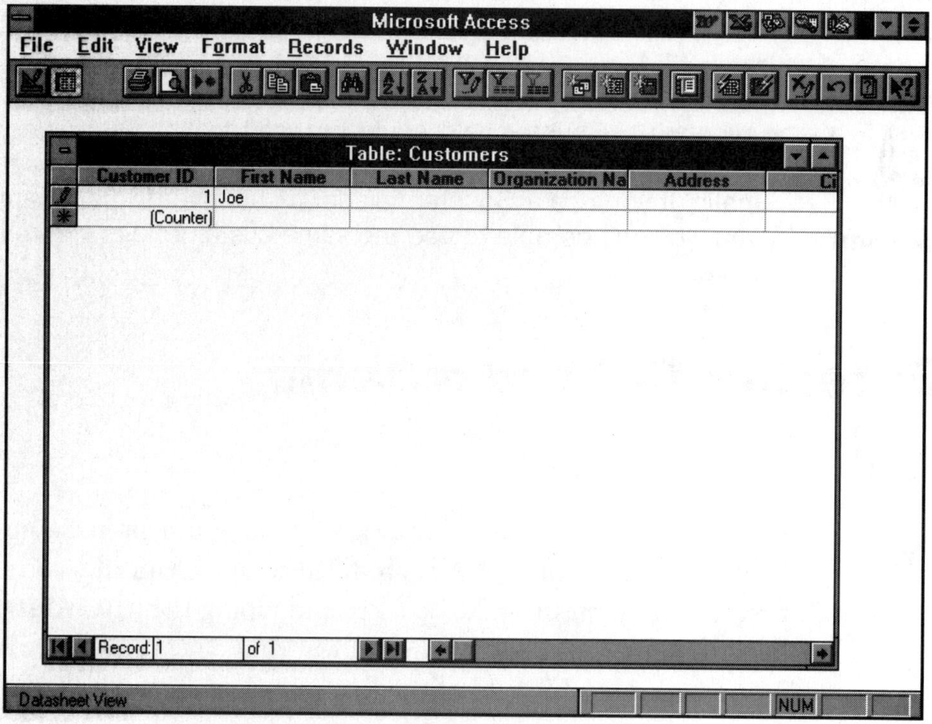

FIGURE 20–10 Data in the first two fields of the first record

code in parentheses and a hyphen after the first three numbers. You'll learn more about input masks in the next chapter.

tip As you enter a series of records, you'll often find that several records have the same data in one or more of their fields. For example, you might enter a long list of customers from the same city and state. Fortunately, there's no need to retype the repetitive data. With the cursor in the field that contains the common data, just press Ctrl- ' (apostrophe), and the data from the previous record will be entered.

When you have finished your data entry session, you can close the table by choosing File➢Close or double-clicking on the table's

FIGURE 20–11 The Database window lists the name of the new table.

Control-menu box. You will be returned to the Database window, where the table will be listed, as shown in Figure 20–11.

If you don't plan to move on to the next chapter now, you can exit Access by choosing File ➢Exit.

Summary

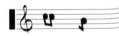

This chapter covered the basic concepts that underlie Access, and you learned to create a table and enter data.

The next chapter covers modifying a table design and the use of forms to make working with data even easier.

21

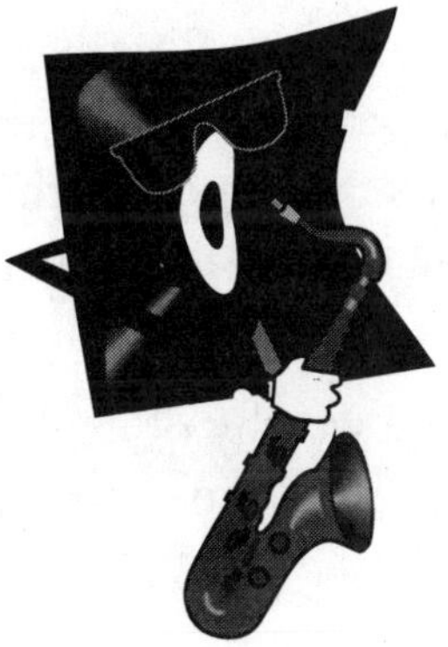

Modifying Tables and Using Forms

You will rarely get a table set up exactly the way you want it the first time. For this reason, the next step you'll want to take after creating a table is modifying it. Later in the chapter, you'll learn to create forms and enter records using forms.

Modifying a Table

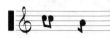

You can specify a wide variety of attributes for your tables either when you first create them or after the fact. You may have noticed in Chapter 20 that the final Table Wizard dialog box provided an option for modifying the table design after it finished creating the table for you. Even if you don't use this option, you can make modifications at any time by moving from the Datasheet view to the Design view.

We'll explore some of the ways to modify tables. Start Access (if it isn't running), clear the Cue Card, and click on the Open Database toolbar button. The Open Database dialog box appears, as shown in Figure 21–1. (If the table you want to modify is already open in the Datasheet view, click on the Design View toolbar button to display the table in Design view, as shown in Figure 21–2.)

Several options in the Open Database dialog box are worthy of explanation. If the Read Only check box is checked, you can open a

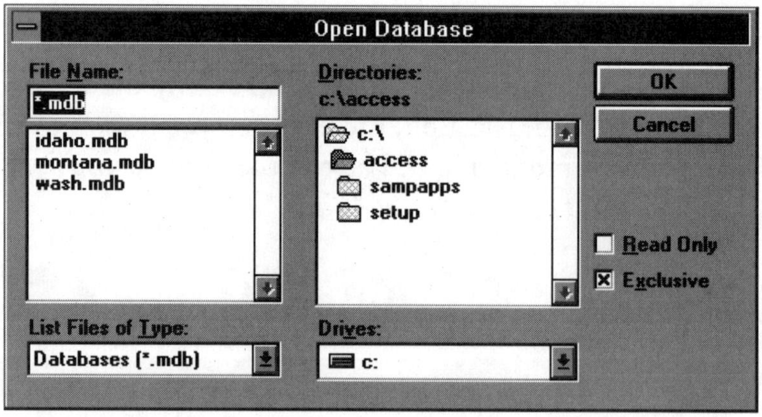

FIGURE 21–1 The Open Database dialog box

database, but you can't add or modify data or modify objects. This might be a good choice when you want to search for some data in the database but don't want to run the risk of messing it up.

The Exclusive check box, which is checked by default, lets you modify the database but won't let anyone else on a network use the database at the same time. Obviously, this is relevant only if you are working on a network.

Double-click on the name of the database you want to open in the File Name list. When the Database window appears, click on the name of the table you want to modify and click on the Design View button. The table's structure appears in Design view, as shown in Figure 21–2.

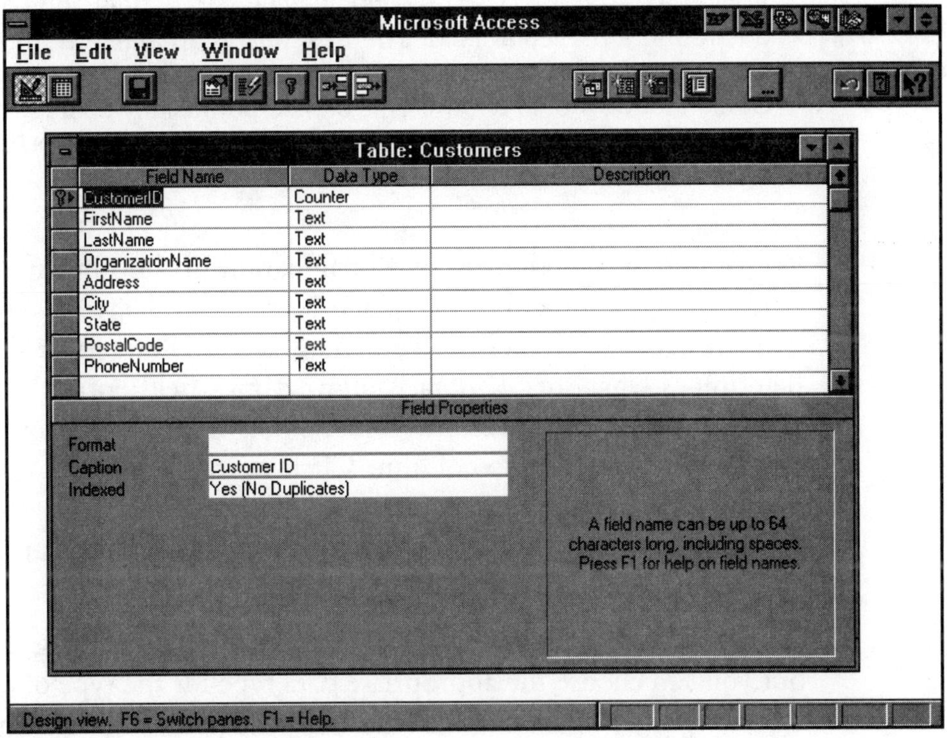

FIGURE 21–2 A table in Design view

The top half of the window in Design view shows the table's field names in the first column, the data types in the second column, and the descriptions, if any, in the third column. Notice that the CustomerID field is selected in Figure 21–2. The bottom half of the Design view window displays the field properties of the selected field.

You can change a field name, data type, or description entry by editing the data. For example, to change the name of the OrganizationName field to CompanyName, just select OrganizationName by double-clicking on it and type **CompanyName**. To enter a description for a field, click in the Description column for that field and type a description.

tip Adding a description can help clarify what sort of data should be entered in a particular field. The description appears on the left side of the status bar when you move to the field in the Datasheet view or in a form. This can be particularly useful when others, who might not be as familiar with the fields as you are, are doing the data entry.

You can use your judgment and imagination in choosing appropriate field names and descriptions. When it comes to data types, however, you must use one of eight types that Access allows. The data type determines what sort of data is allowed in a field entry. When you click in the Data Type column for a field, a drop-down arrow appears on the right side of the column. Click on the drop-down arrow to display the list of allowable data types. Figure 21–3 shows the drop-down list of data types for the FirstName field. The field's properties appear at the bottom of the window.

Access chose the Text data type for this field when creating the table, but you can choose the appropriate data type for the type of data you intend to enter in the field. For example, a field with the name DollarAmount would probably use the Currency data type. A field

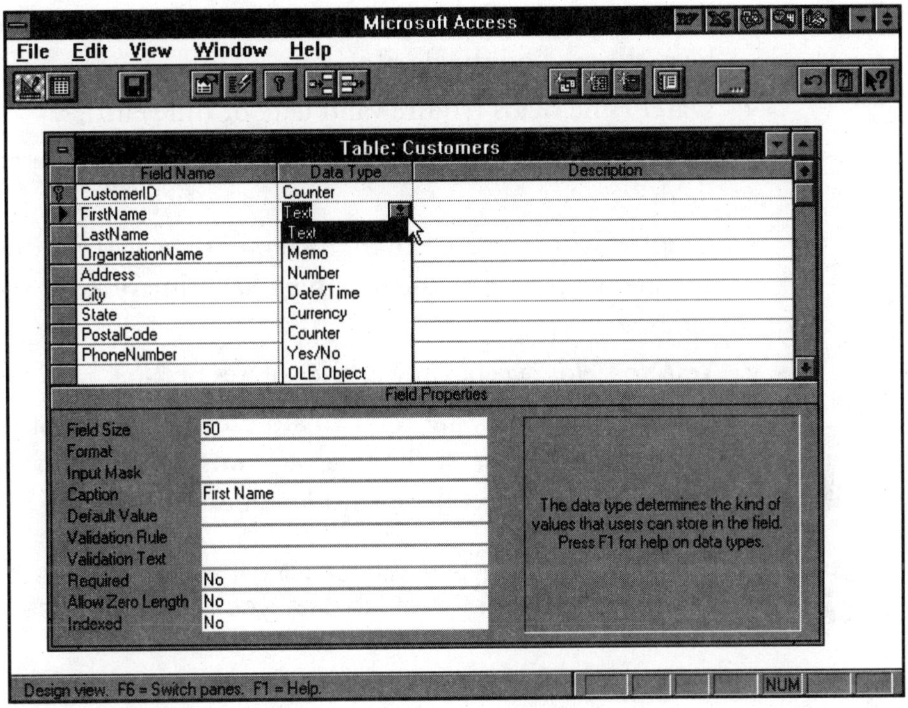

FIGURE 21–3 The drop-down list of data types

named PreviousCustomer? would normally use the Yes/No data type. The following is a brief description of the available data types.

- ✓ **Text** is used for data up to 255 characters. Text and numbers can be entered in a Text field, but calculations cannot be performed on the numbers.
- ✓ **Memo** is used for fields that might need larger amounts of text—up to 64,000 bytes (virtually unlimited). This data type might be used for adding comments of several sentences or paragraphs. Keep in mind that memo fields cannot be indexed.

- ✓ **Number** fields will accept only numeric data. Calculations can be performed on the data.
- ✓ **Date/Time** fields require valid date or time entries.
- ✓ **Currency** is used when dollars and cents will be entered in the field.
- ✓ **Counter** fields are used to increment records automatically and are often used as the data type for primary keys, which are indexed.
- ✓ **Yes/No** fields accept only entries of Yes or No.
- ✓ **OLE Object** fields are used to store objects from other Windows applications, such as Excel worksheets, clip art, and graphs. OLE Object fields can't be indexed.

tip You can specify data types without using the drop-down list by just typing the first letter or two of the data type you want to use.

CAUTION Although you can change data types, you must be very careful when doing so in a table that already has data entered, because this is a very easy way to lose data. For example, if you change a Number field to a Text field, the values will be converted to text and you will no longer be able to perform calculations on them.

Notice some of the field properties that have been set in the bottom portion of the window shown in Figure 21–3. The Field Size property allows you to specify the number of characters to allow in a field. The FirstName field has been set at 50, which means that the longest entry can be a maximum of 50 characters. That should be more than enough for a first-name field.

tip To conserve disk space, keep your field lengths as short as possible. If a field is set for 50 characters, Access reserves 50 characters of space for that field in every record in the database, whether the actual entry for a given record is 50 characters or just one.

A Caption property has been entered for each field. In the example table, the captions are just the field names with spaces added to make them easier to read when they appear as column headings. You can use any text you like for the captions.

The Input Mask property lets you specify a pattern to follow for the data entered in that field. In the example table, the PhoneNumber and PostalCode fields use input masks. The easiest way to add an input mask is with the Input Mask Wizard.

To use the Input Mask Wizard, click in the Data Type column next to the field in which you want to apply the input mask so its field properties are displayed. Next, click on Input Mask in the Field Properties portion of the window and then click on the button that appears to the right of the Input Mask text box. A dialog box telling you that you must save the table first will appear. Click on the Yes button to save the table. The first Input Mask Wizard dialog box appears, as shown in Figure 21–4.

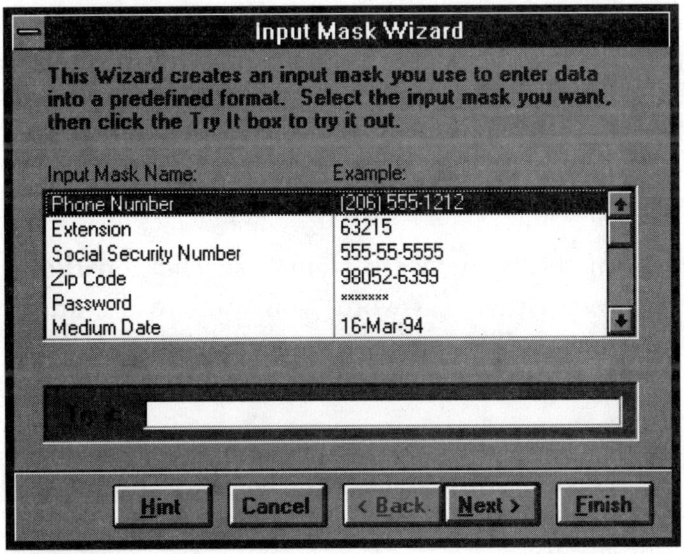

FIGURE 21–4 The first Input Mask Wizard dialog box

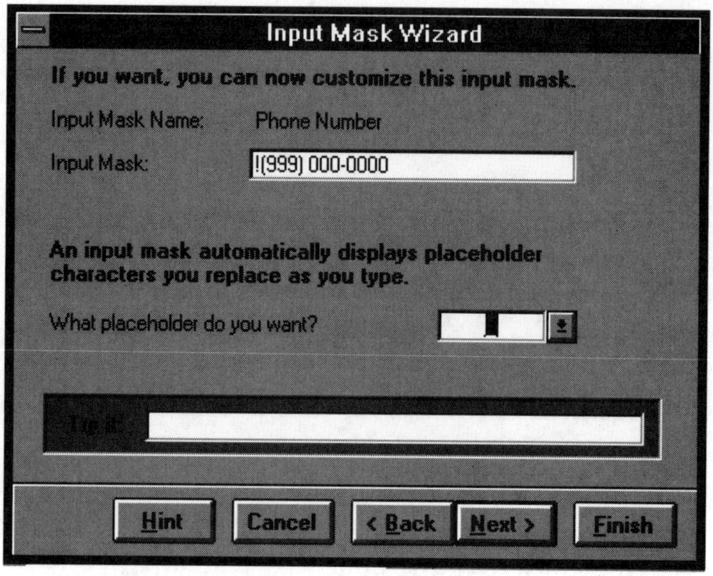

FIGURE 21-5 The second Input Mask Wizard dialog box

note One of the input masks—Password—is not really an input mask but a way of concealing the data you enter from prying eyes. If you choose the Password input mask, the data you enter in the specified field is displayed as asterisks (*****). This does not affect the underlying data.

In the Input Mask Name list, click on the name of an input mask (other than Password) you want to use and then click on the Next button. The second Input Mask Wizard dialog box appears, as shown in Figure 21–5.

In this dialog box you can customize the input mask. Click on the Next button to display the third Input Mask Wizard dialog box, which is shown in Figure 21–6.

Here you can choose whether the data is stored with the symbols in the mask or as straight text or numbers. After making the choice, click

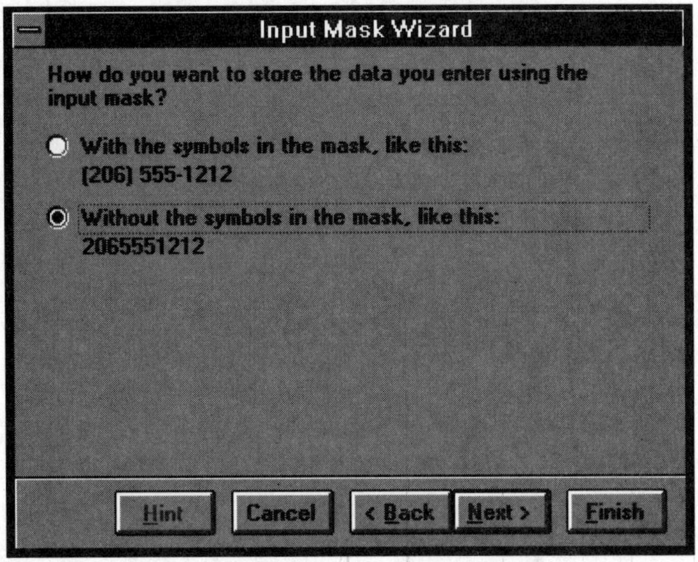

FIGURE 21–6 The third Input Mask Wizard dialog box

on the Next button to display the fourth, and final, Input Mask Wizard dialog box, which is shown in Figure 21–7. Click on Finish to complete the input mask.

note When you specify an input mask, it will be used in all areas of Access, including forms and queries. If you just want to use an input mask for forms, for example, you can specify the input mask as a form property.

The Default Value field property can facilitate data entry by entering the data in the field automatically. You might want to use this feature when most of the entries in a particular field will be the same. If most of your customers live in Montana, for example, you might want to use MT as the default value for the State field.

The Validation Rule and Validation Text properties let you specify certain criteria the field entries must meet. For example, you could

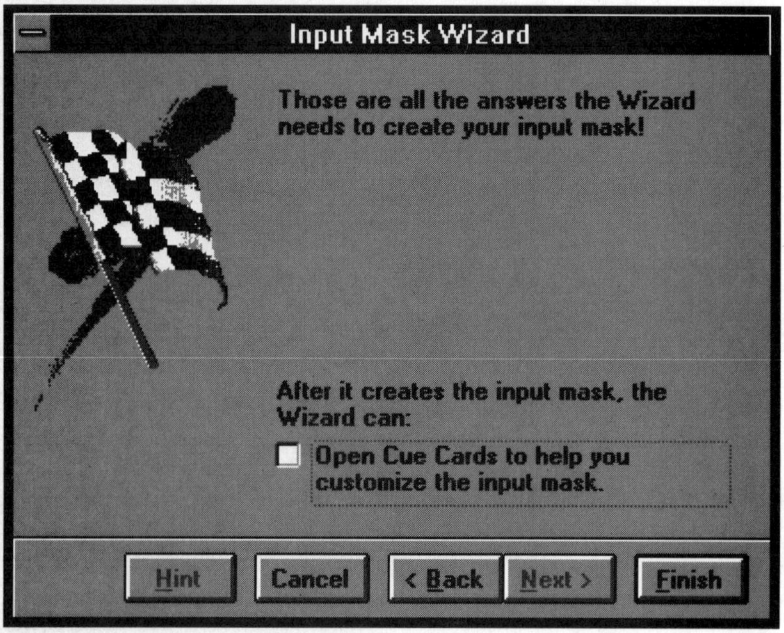

FIGURE 21–7 The final Input Mask Wizard dialog box

specify that the zip code be within a specified range. For information on how to implement the validation rules property, click on the Help toolbar button and then on Validation Rule in the Field Properties portion of the window.

Use the Required property to ensure that data is entered in a field for every record. Your options are Yes (for required) or No.

After you finish modifying the table, close it by double-clicking on its Control-menu box. When the dialog that tells you that you must save the table appears, click on the OK button. If some of the changes you made could affect the data in the table, you'll be presented with a dialog box asking you if you want Access to check the integrity of the data against the new rules, as shown in Figure 21–8.

Using Forms

It's often easier to enter data using a form. Forms can resemble paper forms and can be more aesthetically pleasing than the Datasheet view.

The easiest way to create a new form is to click on the name of the table on which you want to base the form in the Database window and then click on the AutoForm button. Access creates a form with the fields arranged vertically, as shown in Figure 21–9.

note You can use the Forms Wizard to create forms or start with a blank form and add the objects you want. To perform either of these tasks, click on the Form tab in the Database window and then click on the New button. A dialog box, giving you the choice of using the Forms Wizard or creating a blank form, will appear.

The table name, which appears in the title bar, is also used as the form header. You can edit data in a record by selecting the contents of a field and typing new data. You can move from record to record by pressing the Pg Up and Pg Dn keys or by clicking on the arrows at the bottom of the form. The arrows let you move one record at a time.

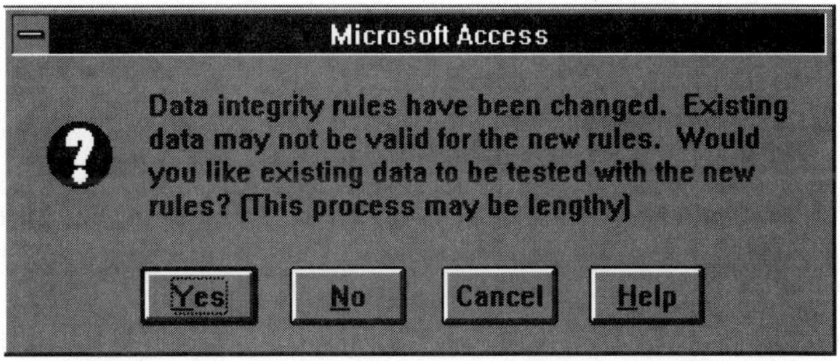

FIGURE 21–8 This dialog box asks if you want to check the integrity of the data in the table.

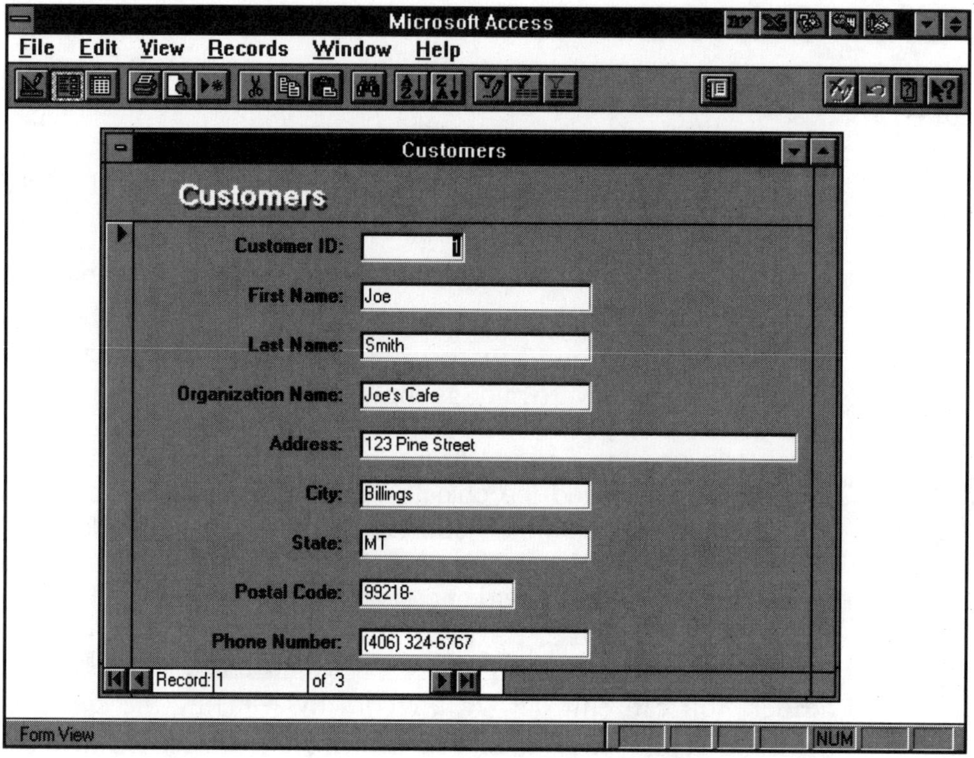

FIGURE 21-9 The new form displayed in Form view

The arrow that has a vertical line to its left moves you to the first record and the one that has a line to its right moves you to the last record. You'll learn how to find specific records in the next chapter.

To add a new record, click on the New toolbar button. A blank record appears, and you can start entering data just as though you were in a Datasheet view.

tip You can easily switch between Form view and Datasheet view by clicking on the Datasheet view or Form view button on the toolbar.

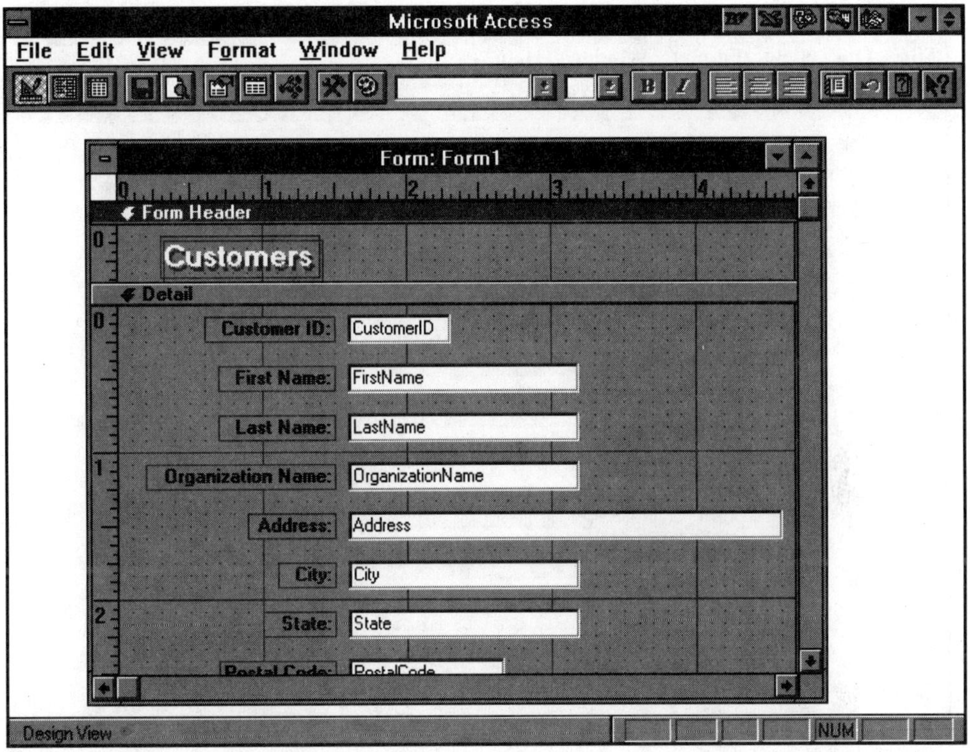

FIGURE 21–10 The form in Design view

To change the design and layout of the form, click on the Design View toolbar button. The form appears in Design view, as shown in Figure 21–10.

In Design view you can move the objects around, and you can change their properties. To move a field, simply position the mouse pointer over the object you want to move; then drag it to the desired location and release the mouse button. If you use this method to move a field, the text box and accompanying label will move together. You can resize an object by positioning the mouse pointer over one of the size handles and dragging.

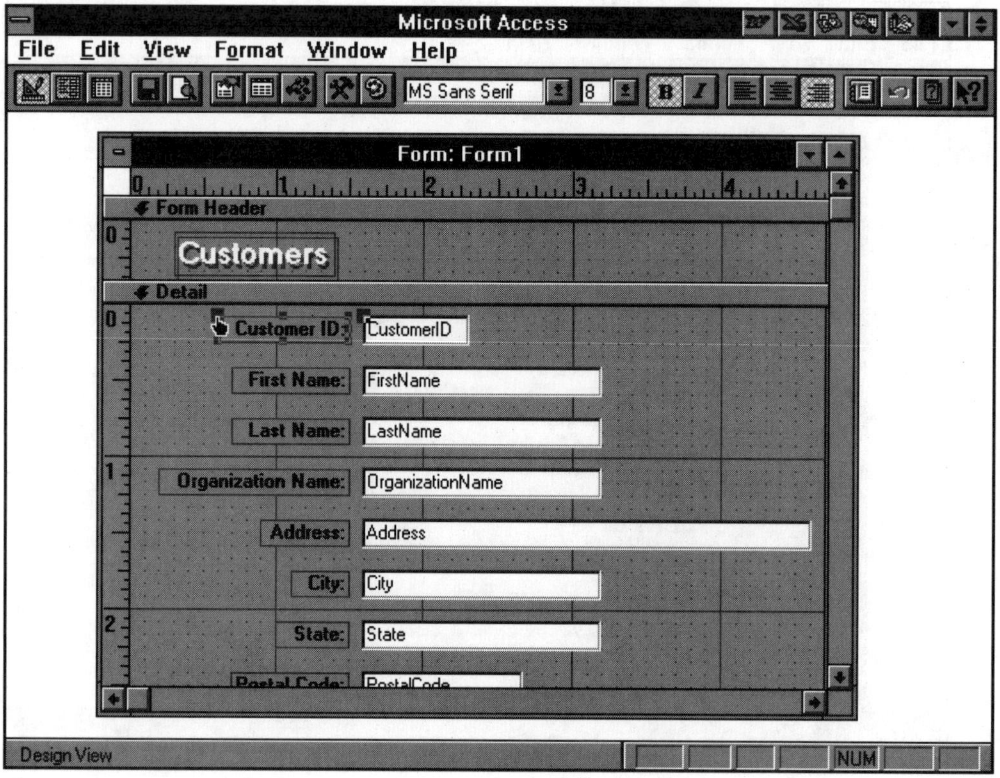

FIGURE 21–11 The mouse pointer over the Move handle of the Customer ID label

If you want to move a text box or a label independently, click on the field and position the mouse pointer over the Move handle for the part of the object you want to move; then drag it to the new location. Figure 21–11 shows the Customer ID field selected with the mouse pointer positioned over the Move handle of the field label.

tip

You can move or size several objects simultaneously by selecting all the objects you want to move or size at once. Do this by holding down the Shift key as you select the second and succeeding objects. You can also select multiple objects by dragging the mouse over the objects to be selected.

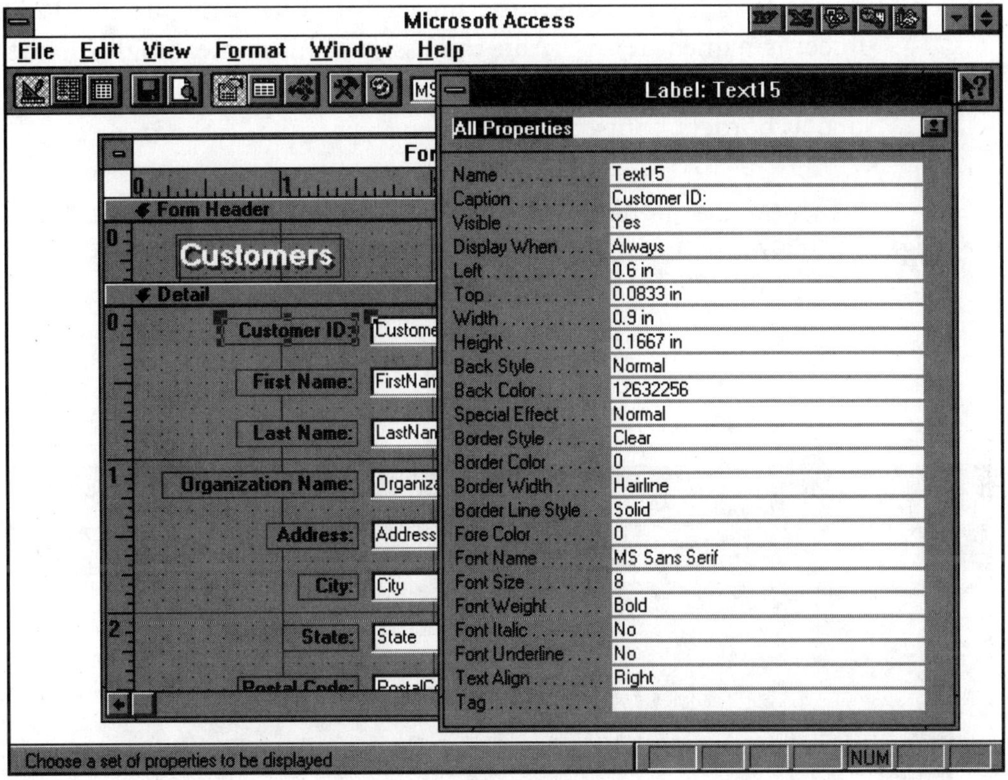

FIGURE 21–12 The Properties window for the Customer ID label

As you rearrange the objects in the form, notice the guides that appear on the horizontal ruler at the top of the form and the vertical ruler on the left side of the form. These guides can help you position objects more precisely.

To change the properties of an object on a form, double-click on the object to display its Properties dialog box. Figure 21–12 shows the Properties window for the Customer ID label. I've resized the window to display all the properties for this object. Of course, you can use the scroll bars to see portions of the list of properties that aren't currently visible.

Notice that Access names the object for you. In Figure 21–12, the object is named Text15. You can assign a more meaningful name in the Properties window. You can also change appearance attributes, such as borders, fonts, and alignment.

tip To view the properties of another object, leave the Properties window open and click on that object in the form. Its properties will appear in the Properties window.

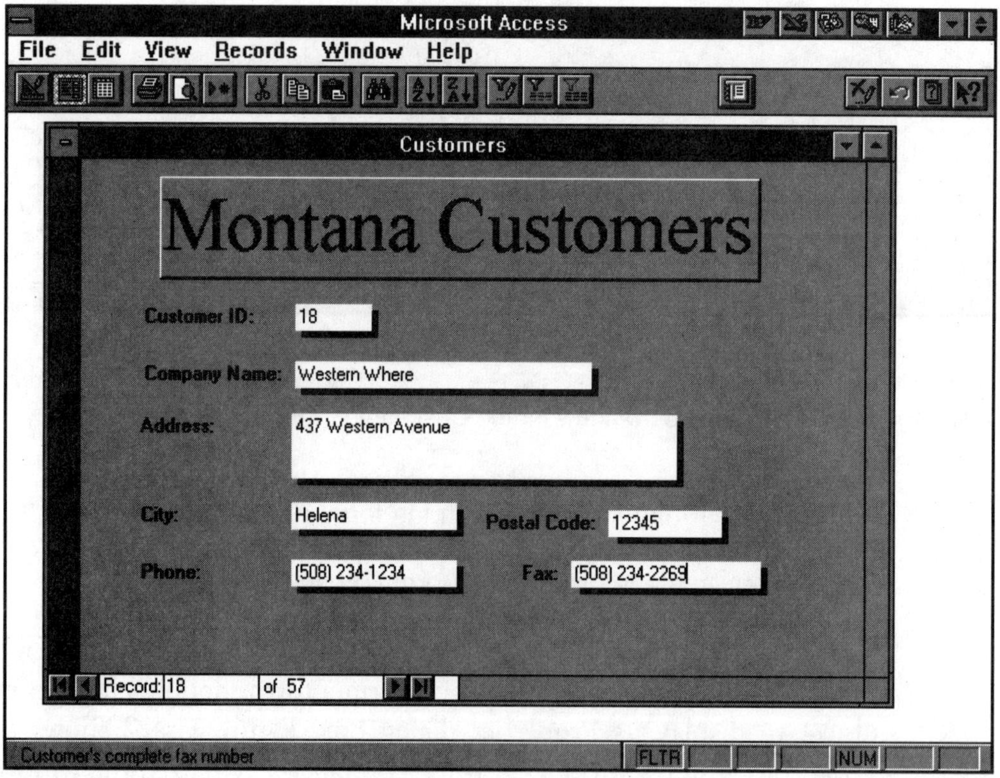

FIGURE 21–13 An example of a presentable form

After modifying the form to your liking, you can close the form or move to the Datasheet view. Either way, you'll be asked if you want to save the form and given an opportunity to name the form.

Once the form is created and saved, it will appear in the list of forms when you click on the Forms tab in the Database window.

There are far more options for modifying forms than we can discuss in detail here. You would be wise to explore all of them to see how each affects the form's appearance and data.

Figure 21–13 shows an example of a form with several of its properties modified to make it more effective and attractive.

Summary

In this chapter, you learned how to modify tables and how to create and modify forms.

The next chapter covers finding specific data and creating reports.

22

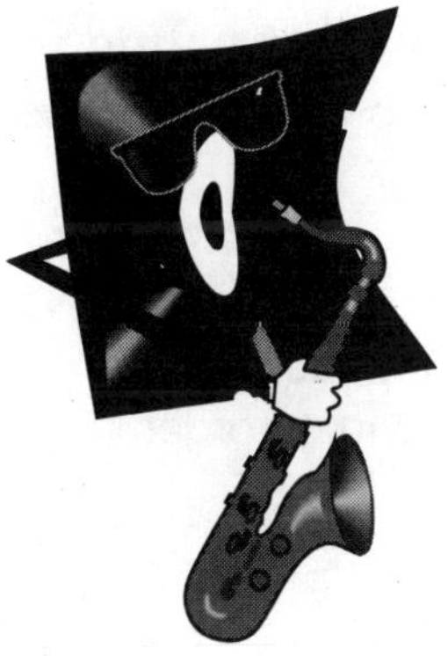

Finding Data and Creating Reports

Knowing how to put data into tables and forms is all well and good, but it won't do much for you if you can't find the data you're looking for when you need it.

Creating reports gives you a way to print compilations of data from a database in a more organized fashion than can usually be accomplished by printing out a bunch of forms or a table listing.

Sorting Data

One way to make it easier to find data is to sort the records in alphabetical or numerical order. For example, sorting the customer table in alphabetical order by customer's last name would make it quite easy to find a particular customer's record quickly.

To sort the contents of a table, have the table open in Datasheet view and click in the column that contains the field you want to base the sort on. For example, click in the Last Name field if you want to sort by last name. Finally, click on the Sort Ascending toolbar button to sort by last name from A through Z. If you want to sort in reverse order, from Z through A, click on the Sort Descending button. Figure 22–1 shows our Customers table sorted by last name.

tip If you have a counter field, you can quickly restore your table to its original order by sorting on the counter field in ascending order. You knew that counter field would come in handy, didn't you?

Finding Data

If you have a very large table containing many records, sorting may not be the most efficient way to find the records you want. When you want to zero in on records that meet certain criteria, the Find feature may be your best bet.

To find records, click in the field you want to search and click on the Find toolbar button. (If you want to search for data that could be in any field, it doesn't matter which field you start with.) The Find in Field dialog box appears, as shown in Figure 22–2.

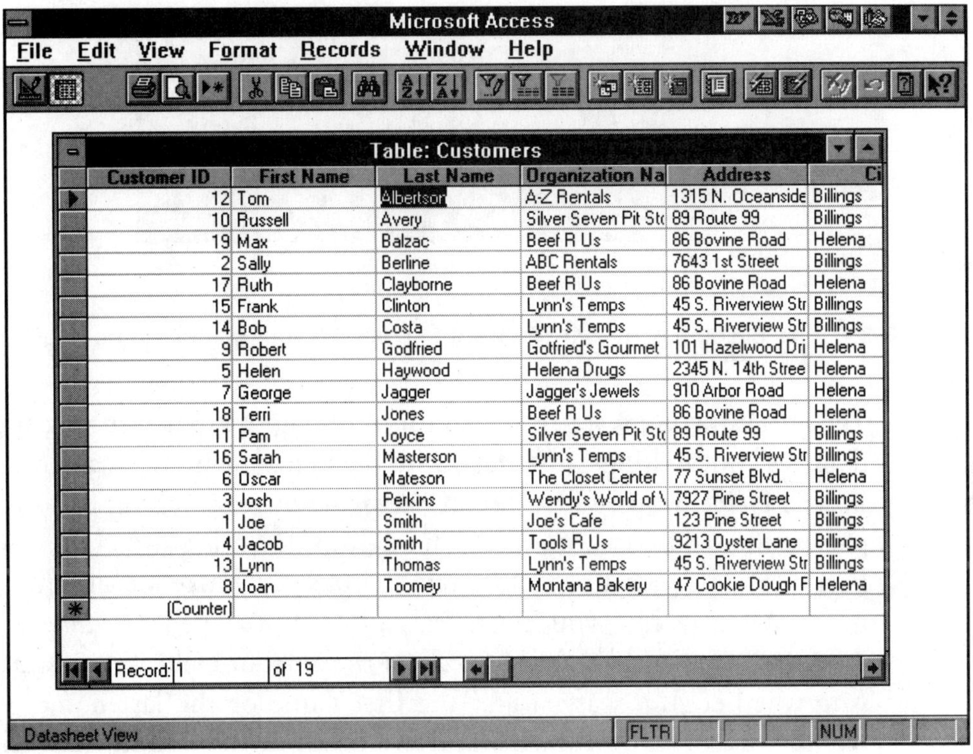

FIGURE 22–1 The sorted Customers table

FIGURE 22–2 The Find in Field dialog box

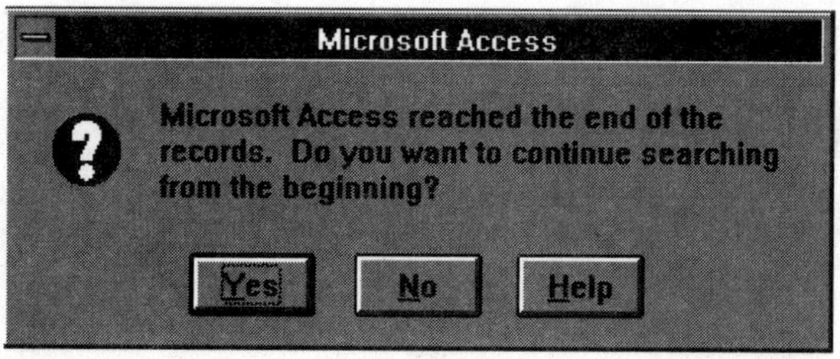

FIGURE 22–3 This dialog box asks if you want to continue your search at the beginning of your file.

Type the data you want to search for in the Find What text box. If the data you're searching for is the entire field entry, you can leave Match Whole Field in the Where list. If the data you're searching for is only part of the field entry, use the Where drop-down list and choose Any Part of Field or Start of Field. For example, say you're looking for the name *Mateson* but you can't remember if it's spelled *Mateson* or *Matason.* You would search for *Mat* at the Start of Field. If you weren't sure whether *Mat* was part of the first name or the last name, you would click on the All Fields option button in the Search In portion of the dialog box.

To start searching from the current record down, be sure the Down option button is selected in the Direction portion of the dialog box. Click on the Find Next button, and the next record that matches your search criteria will be selected. Click on Find Next again to find the next match. When you reach the last record that matches your criteria, Access displays a dialog box asking if you want to continue searching from the beginning, as shown in Figure 22–3.

Filtering Data

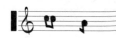

Filtering is a great alternative to just sorting or searching. When you filter a table's data, only the records that meet the filter criteria appear.

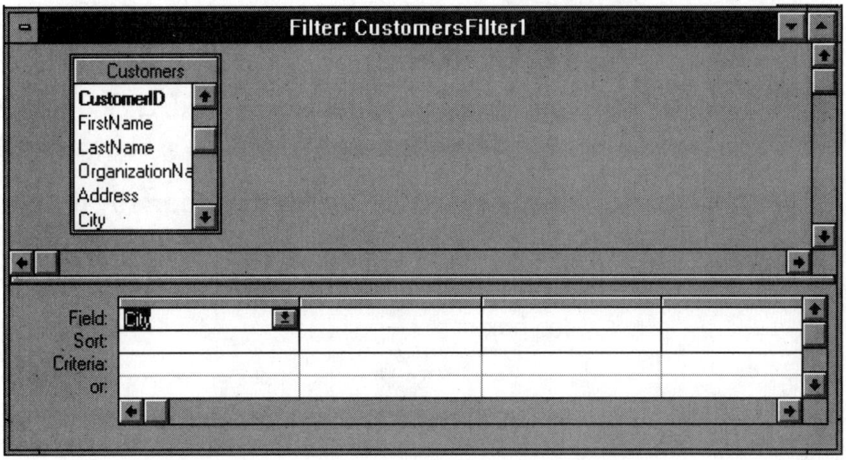

FIGURE 22–4 The Filter dialog box

Suppose you want to find all the customers in Helena. If you filter the table, you won't have to be distracted by the records of customers in other towns.

To create a filter, click on the Edit Filter/Sort toolbar button. The Filter dialog box appears, as shown in Figure 22–4.

Double-click on the name of the first filter field you want to use in the representation of the table in the top portion of the dialog box. You can sort the table while filtering. If you don't want the data sorted or you want it sorted in descending order, click in the sort box; then click on the sort drop-down arrow and choose Not Sorted or Descending.

Type your criteria in the Criteria box. For example, if you want only records with Helena entered in the City field, type **Helena**. If you want Helena or Billings, type **Helena** in the Criteria row and **Billings** in the Or row. You can also filter based on more than one field.

If you want records with Helena in the City field *and* Smith in the LastName field, click in the second column of the field row and use the drop-down arrow to choose LastName from the drop-down list. Then type **Smith** in the Criteria row of the second column.

When you have all the filter criteria entered, click on the Apply Filter/Sort toolbar button. The filtered table appears, as shown in Figure 22–5.

Filtering is usually used as a way to temporarily change the way data is displayed. When you want to see all the records again, just click on the Show All Records toolbar button.

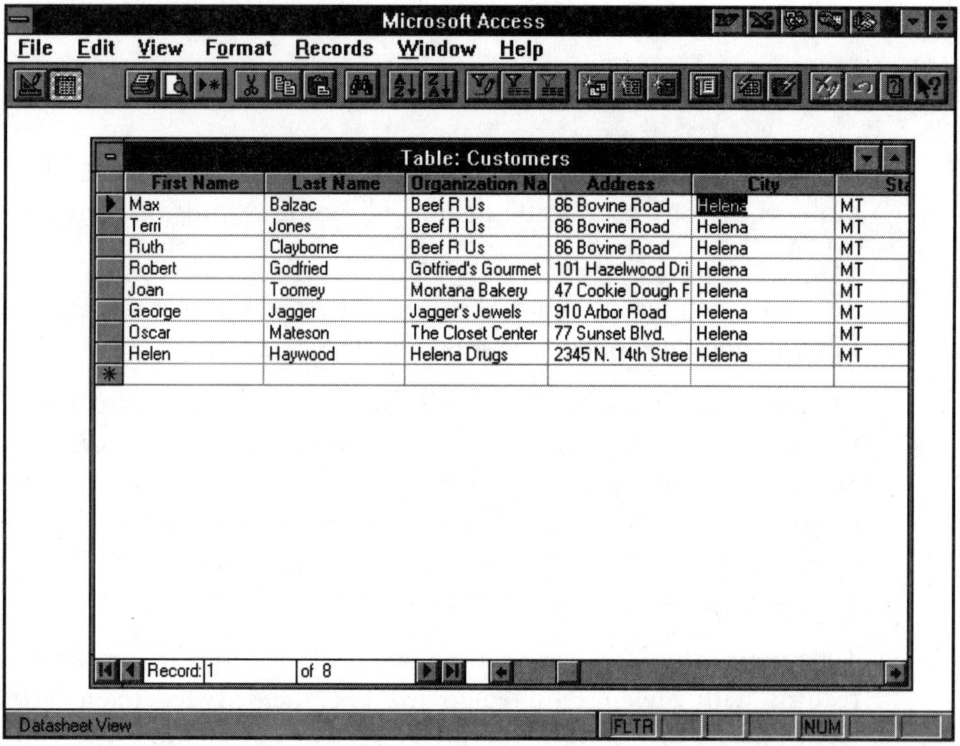

FIGURE 22–5 The filtered table

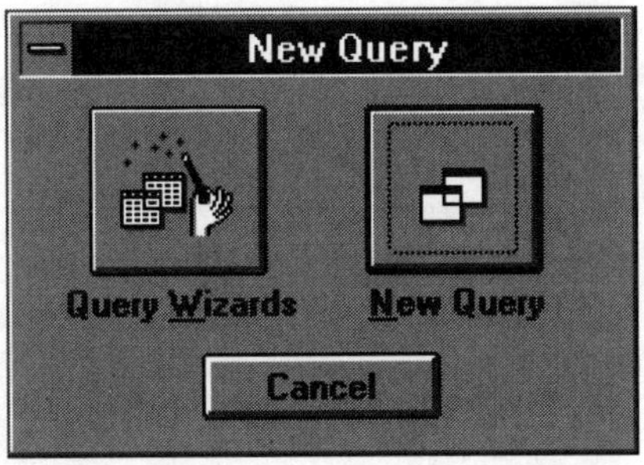

FIGURE 22–6 The New Query dialog box

Creating a Query

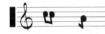

Queries are used for more complex searches, particularly when you want to combine data from more than one table. It's usually easiest to create a new table from the Database window. In the Database window, click on the Query button and then click on the New button. The New Query dialog box appears, as shown in Figure 22–6.

Click on the New Query button to display the Add Table dialog box on top of the Select Query dialog box, as shown in Figure 22–7.

All the tables in your database are listed in the Add Table dialog box. Add any tables that contain data that you want to retrieve with the query. To add a table to the query, double-click on its name or click on it and then click on the Add button. After you add the needed tables to the query, click on the Close button of the Add Table dialog box. The added tables appear in boxes at the top of the Select Query dialog box, as shown in Figure 22–8.

Notice the line connecting the CustomerID field in the Customers table with the CustomerID field in the Classes table. Access was clever

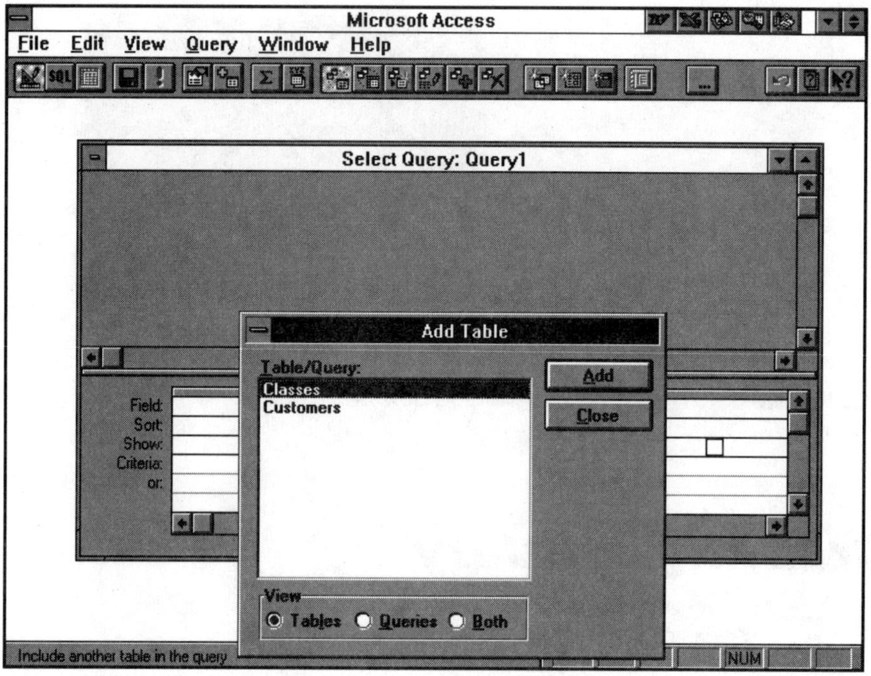

FIGURE 22–7 The Add Table and Select Query dialog boxes

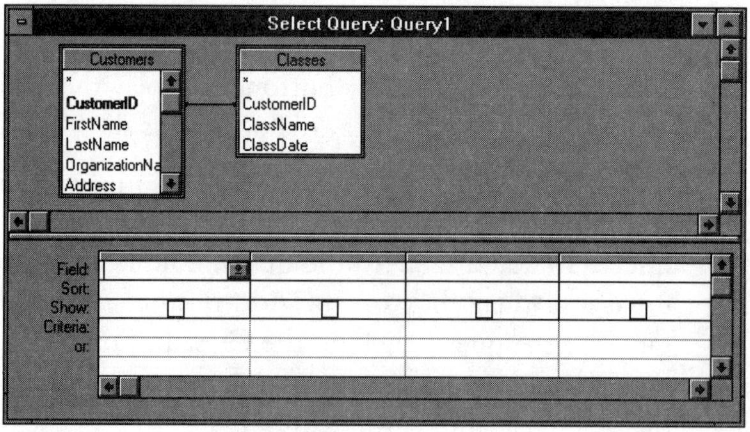

FIGURE 22–8 The tables to be used in the query

enough to figure out on its own that these two fields contain the same sort of data and are the logical basis for a relationship.

If Access can't figure out how you intend to relate the tables, you can tell it by dragging a field from one table to another.

note Don't forget, the fields you use to link tables must have the same data type. If they don't the query won't work.

Once the tables are linked, you can start to enter your query specifications. Entering query specifications is similar to the process used for filtering tables discussed in the previous section. Notice that the bottom portion of the Select Query window has one additional row—Show. You use the Show row to determine which fields you want displayed in the result of the query.

There will be many times when you'll want to use a field as part of the query criteria but won't want that field displayed in the result. For example, suppose you want to display the names and addresses of the customers signed up for Access classes. You would have to include the ClassName field as part of the query criteria, but you wouldn't want to include the class name in the resulting table.

To add a field for the query, double-click on its name in the top portion of the Select Query window. The field name appears in the Field row in the bottom portion of the window, with the Show check box checked. If you don't want that field's contents included in the query results, click in the Show check box under the field name to remove the check.

Add query criteria in the rows under the Show row just as you entered filter criteria. For example, if you want to find all the records with Access in the ClassName field type **Access** in the Criteria row. Figure 22–9 shows the filled in Select Query window.

Notice the quotation marks surrounding the criteria text. You don't have to add these; Access adds them automatically. Also notice that the line linking the two tables appears to be pointing to the Title bar

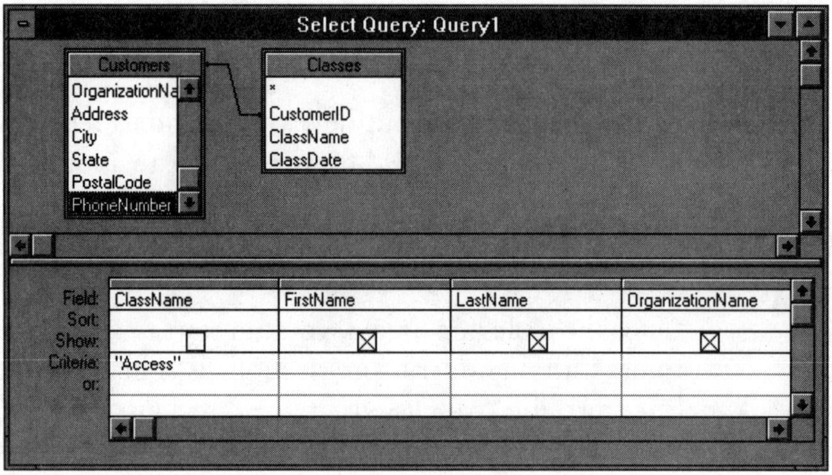

FIGURE 22–9 A completed Select Query window

of the first table in the figure. This just means that the joined field isn't currently visible.

After filling in the query specifications, click on the Run toolbar button to execute the query. Figure 22–10 shows the table that results from the example query.

If you change the data in the tables the query is based on, you can click on the Datasheet view button to re-query the database.

With the table that results from the query, you can do anything that you can with any other table; you can create forms and reports and even make queries.

When you're finished with the query, double-click on its Control-menu box to close it. A dialog box asks if you want to save the query, as shown in Figure 22–11.

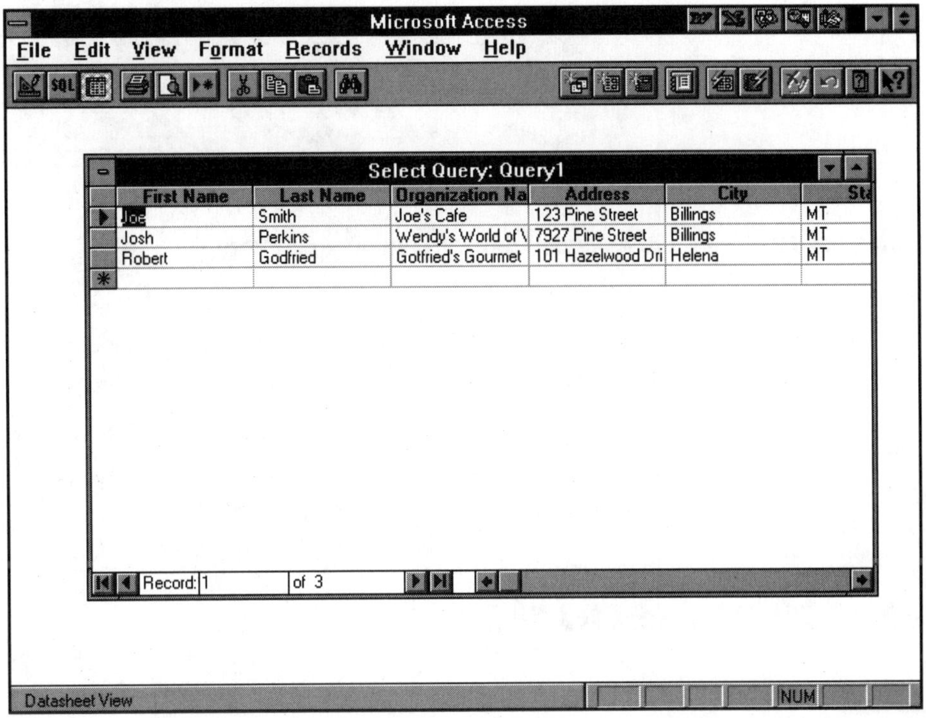

FIGURE 22–10 The result of the query

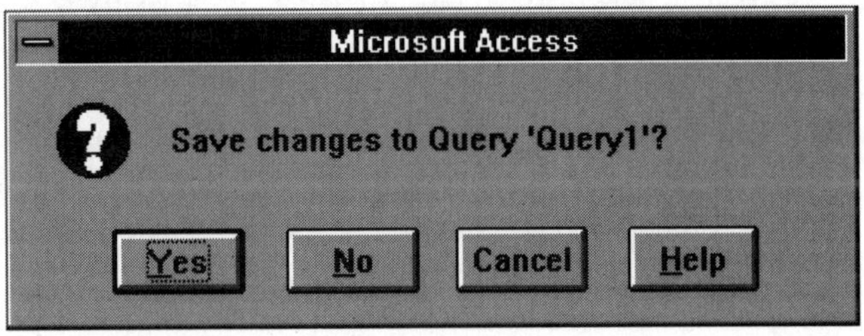

FIGURE 22–11 This dialog box asks if you want to save the query.

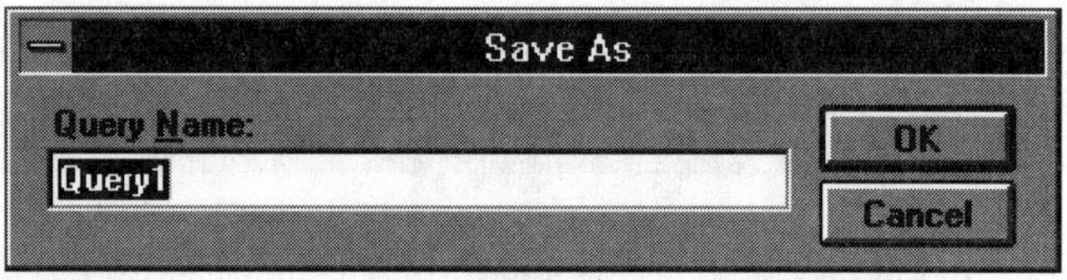

FIGURE 22-12 The Save As dialog box for naming your query

Click on the Yes button if you intend to use the query again. The Save As dialog box appears, as shown in Figure 22–12.

Enter a name for your query and click on the OK button. When you want to use the query again, you'll find it in the Database window by clicking on the Query button.

Creating Reports

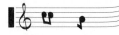

Reports are used to print data from databases in a variety of formats. Using the Access report capabilities, you can add headers and footers to print repeating information at the top and bottom of each report page. You'll also use reports to create and print mailing labels.

Suppose you want to print out a simple customer list, including names and phone numbers, grouped by city. We'll use the Report Wizard to see how easily this report can be created.

From the Database window, click on the Report button; then click on the New button. The New Report dialog box appears, as shown in Figure 22–13.

Click on the drop-down arrow below Select A Table/Query and click on the name of the table or query you want to base the report on; then click on the Report Wizards button. The Report Wizards dialog box appears, as shown in Figure 22–14.

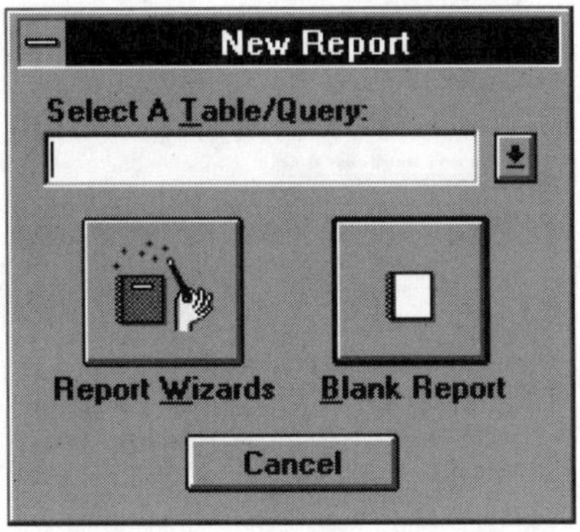

FIGURE 22–13 The New Report dialog box

Click on the name of the Report Wizard you want to use; then click on the OK button. For the example report, we'll use the Groups/Totals wizard. The Groups/Totals Report Wizard dialog box is shown in Figure 22–15.

In this dialog box, you choose which fields you want on the report and specify the order in which you want them to appear in your report. To add fields, click on the field name and then the right-

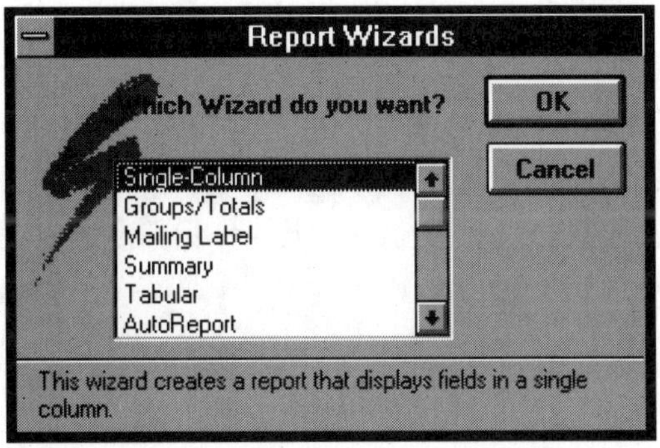

FIGURE 22–14 The Report Wizards dialog box

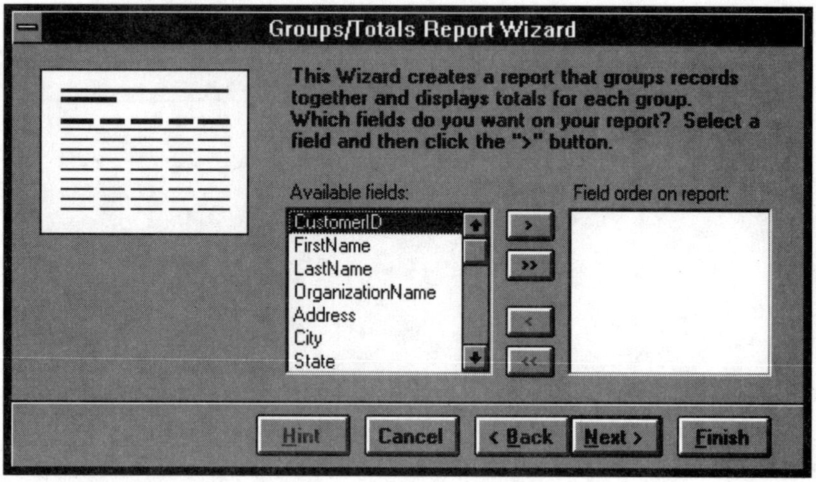

FIGURE 22–15 The first Groups/Totals Report Wizard dialog box

pointing arrow (>), or just double-click on the field names in the order in which you want them to appear. For example, if you want the LastName field to appear before the FirstName field, double-click on LastName; then double-click on FirstName.

After you have added all the desired fields, click on the Next button to display the second Report Wizard dialog box, which is shown in Figure 22–16.

In this dialog box, you choose which fields you want the report grouped by. You can group by up to four fields. In our example we'll just group by the City field. Double-click on the names of the fields you want to group by; then click on the Next button to display the third Report Wizard dialog box, which is shown in Figure 22–17.

Click on the Next button to accept the Normal grouping, and move to the next Report Wizard dialog box, which is shown in Figure 22–18.

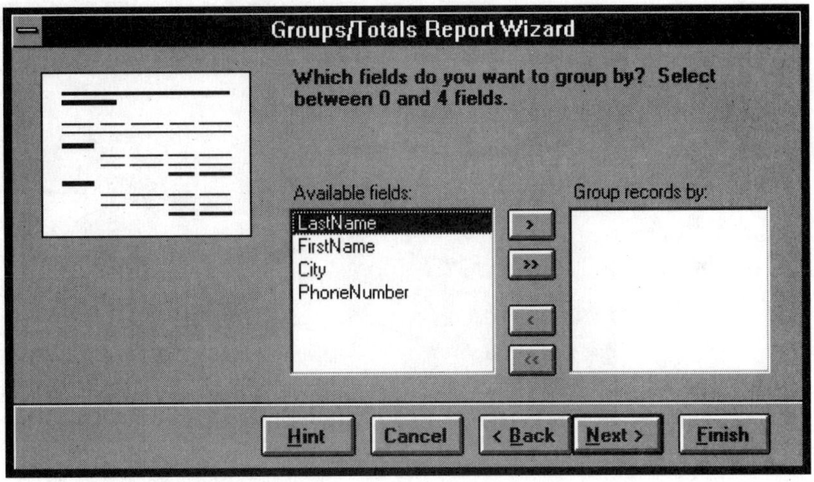

FIGURE 22–16 The second Groups/Totals Report Wizard dialog box

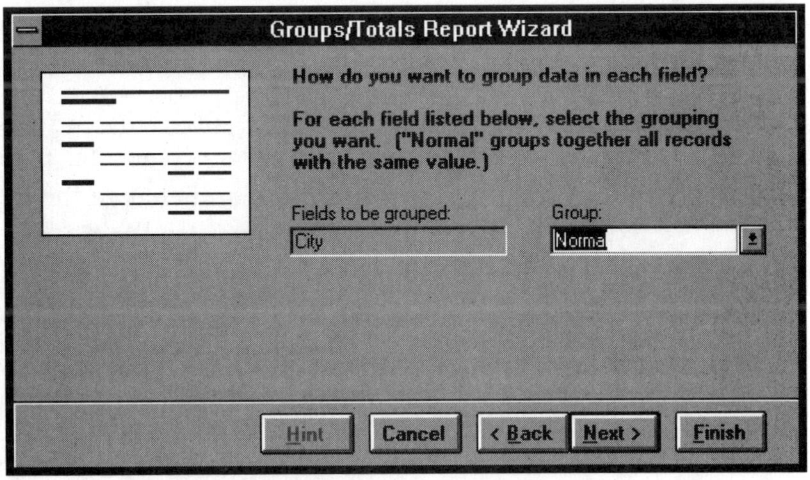

FIGURE 22–17 The third Groups/Totals Report Wizard dialog box

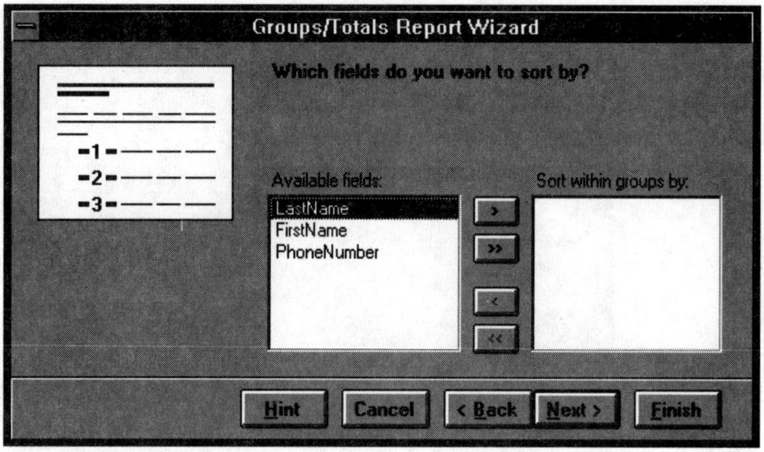

FIGURE 22–18 The fourth Groups/Totals Report Wizard dialog box

In this dialog box, you choose which fields you want to sort by. We'll sort by last name. After selecting the fields to sort by, click on the Next button to display the fifth Report Wizard dialog box, which is shown in Figure 22–19.

In the fifth dialog box, you choose the style you want for your report, specify whether to print it in Portrait (normal page orientation) or Landscape (sideways) orientation, and change the line spacing if necessary. Click on the Next button to display the final Report Wizard dialog box, which is shown in Figure 22–20.

Enter a title for your report if you wish. Access uses the name of the table or query the report is based on by default. You can also choose to have all fields appear on each page and to calculate percentages of the total. After making your choices, click on the Finish button. The finished report appears in a Print Preview window, as shown in Figure 22–21. I've maximized the report window to show more of the report.

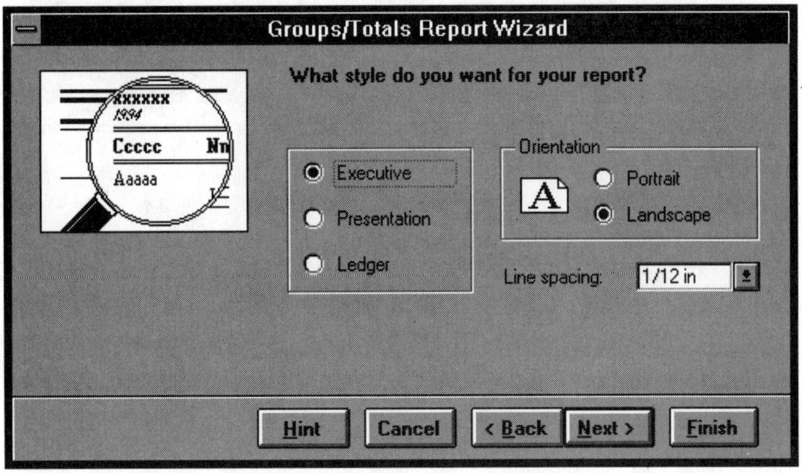

FIGURE 22–19 The fifth Groups/Totals Report Wizard dialog box

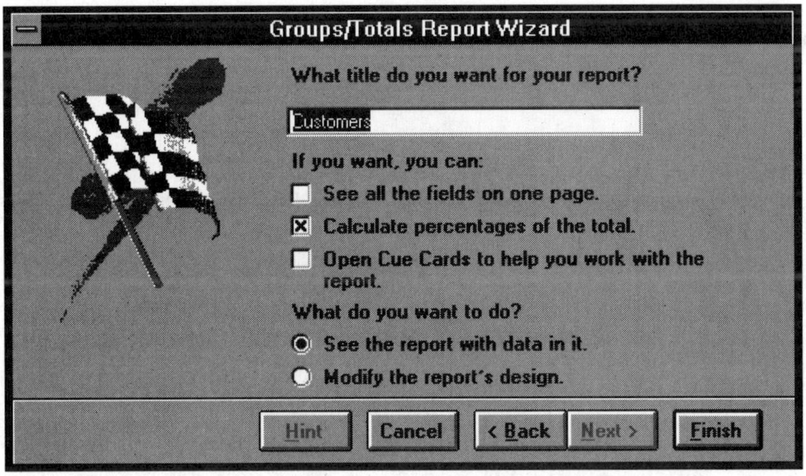

FIGURE 22–20 The final Groups/Totals Report Wizard dialog box

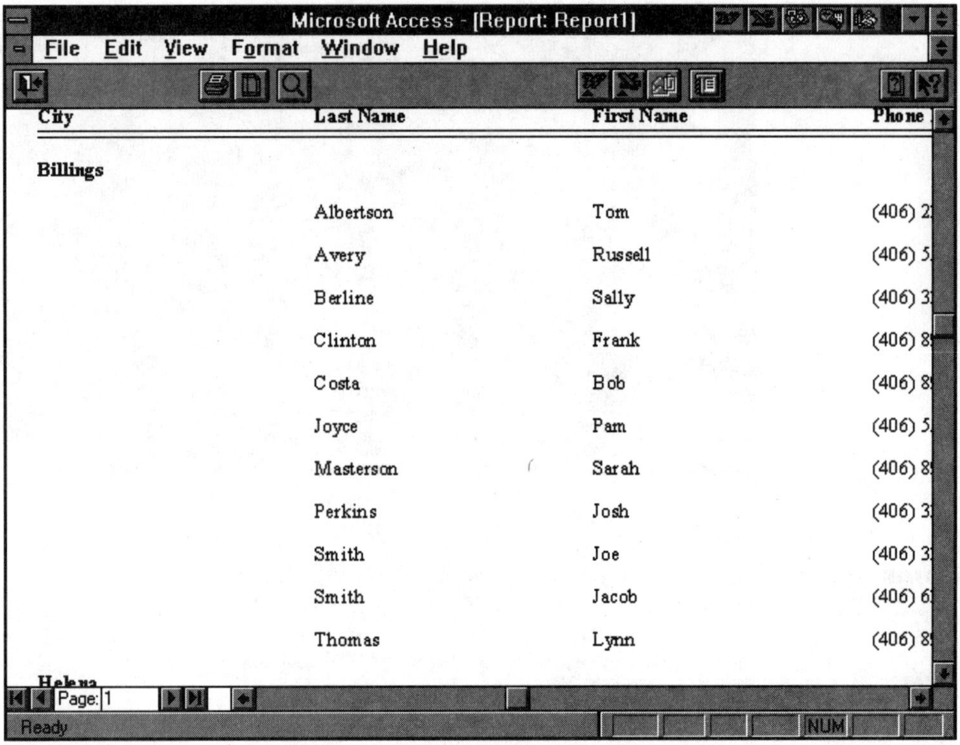

FIGURE 22–21 The finished report

tip Notice the two toolbar buttons for sending the report to other Office programs. The first, Publish It with MS Word, sends the report to a Word document, where you can use Word's extensive formatting capabilities to polish its appearance. The second, Analyze It with MS Excel, sends the report to an Excel worksheet, where you can use Excel's tools to manipulate it.

The mouse pointer assumes the shape of a magnifying glass. By clicking anywhere on the report you can zoom out to see the entire page, as shown in Figure 22–22.

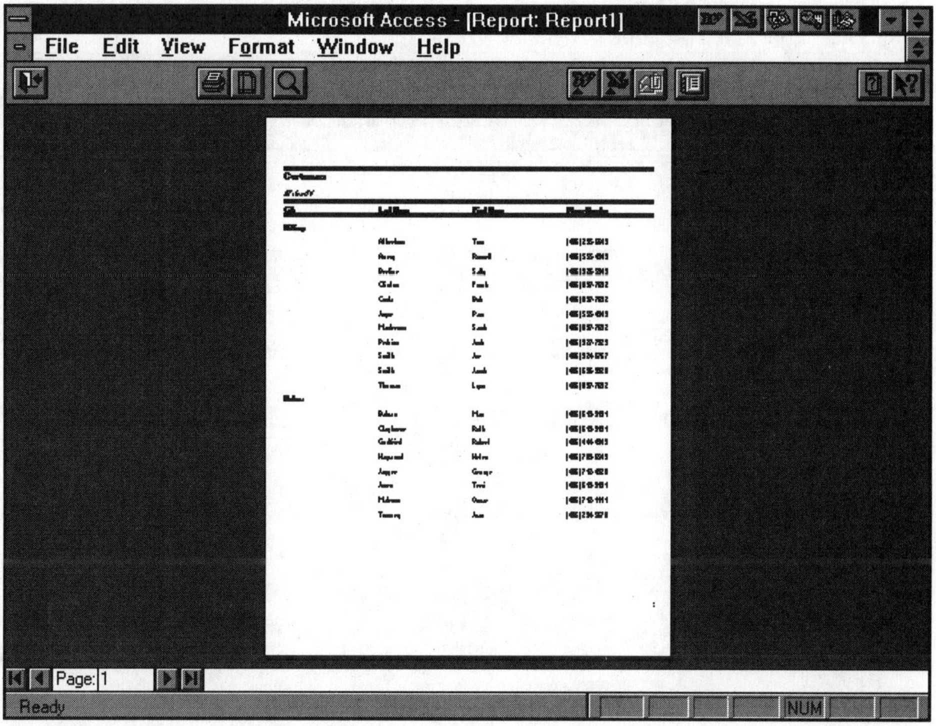

FIGURE 22–22 The preview of an entire page of the report

To print the report, click on the Print toolbar button and then click on the OK button when the Print dialog box appears. When you finish examining the report, click on the Close Window button. The report appears in Design view with the Toolbox toolbar open, as shown in Figure 22–23. For the figure, I dragged the Toolbox toolbar to the middle of the screen so it wouldn't obstruct the report.

The Design view of the report lets you see how the report is constructed. You can change the elements of reports in much the same way you change the elements of forms. For more information about

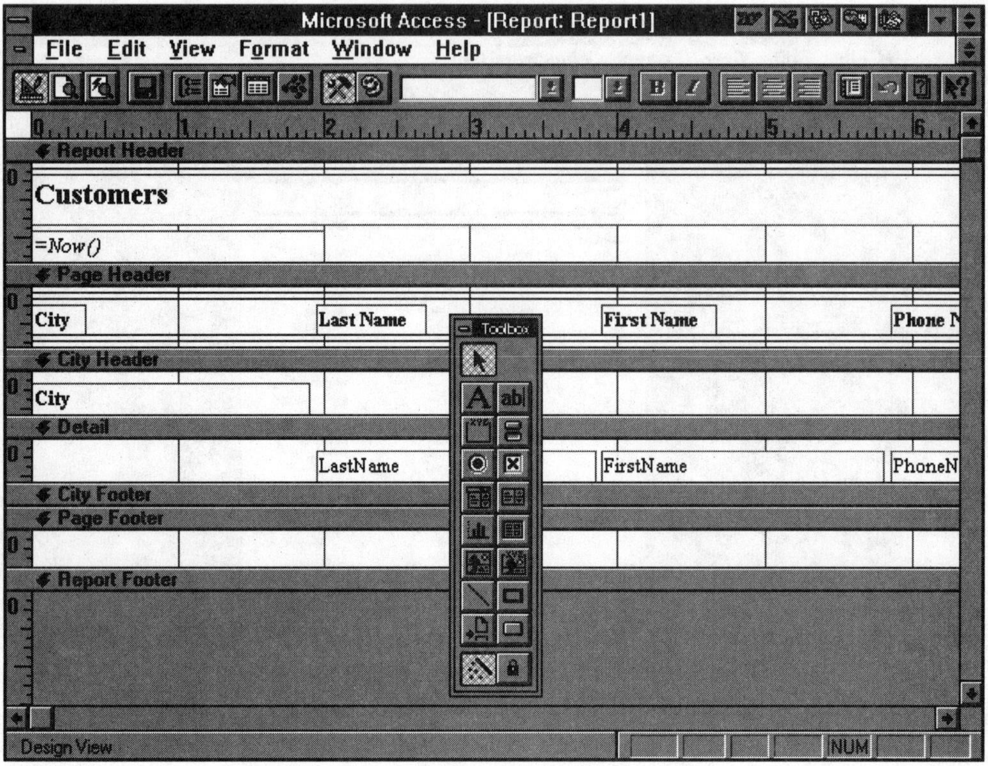

FIGURE 22–23 The report in Design view

customizing reports, press F1 and use the Access help facility to guide you through the elements of the report.

When you have finished with the report, double-click on its Control-menu box. Click on the Yes button in the dialog box that asks if you want to save the report. Then enter a name for the report in the Save As box and click on OK.

The report will be available in the Database window.

Summary

In this chapter, you learned to use Find, Filter, Sort, and Query to get to the data you're looking for in your database. You also learned to create simple reports to print data in an organized fashion.

The remaining chapters cover how to use the Office programs in combination. You'll learn to move information from one Office application to another and to add objects to the main applications from the shared applications.

Section VII

Putting It All Together

23

The Application Shuffle

As great as each of the individual Office programs is, using them in combination enhances their usefulness dramatically. In this chapter, you'll learn how to run two or more of the Office programs—as well as other Windows programs—simultaneously. You'll also learn to switch from one to another.

Running Multiple Applications

In previous chapters, I have alluded to the fact that you don't have to quit one program before starting another. But there are several ways to accomplish this feat.

You can start a program by opening its group in the Program Manager and then double-clicking on its icon. Once two or more programs are running, you can use the Alt-Tab combination to switch from one to another. If you hold down Alt, each time you press Tab the name of the next running program and its icon appears in a box in the middle of the screen—unless you do this from a DOS program, where the program name appears in a bar at the top of the screen. Release Alt when the name of the program you want appears.

tip Pressing Alt-Tab once and then releasing both keys is a quick way to switch back and forth between the last two running programs.

You can also use the Microsoft Office Manager, discussed in previous chapters, as well as the Windows Task list to switch between programs.

Using the Microsoft Office Manager

If you installed Microsoft Office in the normal manner, the Microsoft Office program starts automatically when you start Windows, and its Microsoft Office toolbar appears in the upper-right corner of the screen.

Don't confuse the Microsoft Office program with the programs that come with Microsoft Office. The Office program merely launches the Microsoft Office Manager toolbar, which provides easy access to the Office programs.

To start or switch to any of your Office programs using the Microsoft Office Manager toolbar, just click on the button that represents that program. If the program isn't already running, it may take a while to start. If the program is already running, clicking on its Microsoft Office Manager toolbar button will switch you to that program almost instantly.

tip Remember, if you don't know which Microsoft Office Manager toolbar button belongs to which program, position the mouse pointer over the button to see a ToolTip for the button that tells you the name of the program.

The Microsoft Office Manager is so convenient that I recommend that you keep it running, except, perhaps (as noted in Chapter 19), when you are giving on-screen PowerPoint slide show presentations.

tip If the Microsoft Office Manager doesn't start automatically when you start Windows, copy the Microsoft Office icon into the StartUp group in the Windows Program Manager.

You may have to move some windows out of the way before you can perform this operation. Refer to Chapter 2 if you need a refresher on repositioning windows. Then do the following:

- Press Ctrl-Esc to open the Task List; then double-click on Program Manager. Double-click on the group icon that contains the Microsoft Office program icon (usually the Microsoft Office 4.2 group) to open it. Make sure the StartUp group icon is visible.

- Hold down Ctrl and drag the Microsoft Office icon onto the StartUp group icon. You can tell when the Office icon is positioned correctly over the StartUp group icon because it turns from a circle with a diagonal line through it into the normal Microsoft Office icon. The next time Windows starts, Microsoft Office will start automatically.

This technique also works for any program you want to start automatically when you start Windows. For example, if you spend most of your time working in Word, you may find it convenient to copy the Microsoft Word icon into the StartUp group.

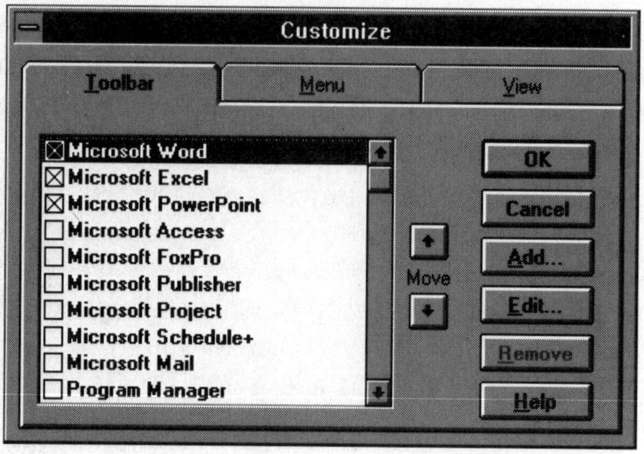

FIGURE 23–1 The Microsoft Office Customize dialog box

If the Microsoft Office Manager toolbar doesn't have buttons for some of the programs you use regularly, you can easily add them. You can also delete any buttons you don't want cluttering the toolbar.

To customize the toolbar, click on the Microsoft Office button to display the Microsoft Office menu; then choose Customize. When the Customize dialog box appears, click on the Toolbar tab if it isn't already highlighted. Figure 23–1 shows the Toolbar portion of the Customize dialog box.

As you scroll down the list of items in the dialog box, you'll notice that the items whose check boxes are checked have corresponding buttons on the Microsoft Office Manager toolbar. The list includes all the popular Microsoft programs, as well as many tasks you often perform in Windows. To add a button for an unchecked item, simply click on its check box.

tip As I pointed out in Chapter 3, you probably don't have to use a screen saver to protect your screen. But if you work in an environment where it might be useful to be able to blank out your screen to keep prying eyes from seeing your work, you can add a screen saver button to the Microsoft Office Manager toolbar that will let you do so with a mouse click. Just click on the Screen Saver check box in the Toolbar portion of the Customize dialog box.

Any time you want to start your screen saver, click on the Screen Saver button. To turn off the screen saver, move your mouse or press any key on the keyboard.

Of course, this only works if you've set up a screen saver in the Control Panel's Desktop. Refer to Chapter 3 for more information on the Desktop.

To add a button for an item that isn't on the list, click on the Add button in the Customize dialog box. The Add Program to Toolbar dialog box appears, as shown in Figure 23–2.

Enter the description for the new button in the Description text box. The description will become the ToolTip for the new button. Press Tab and enter the complete path and program name in the Command Line text box.

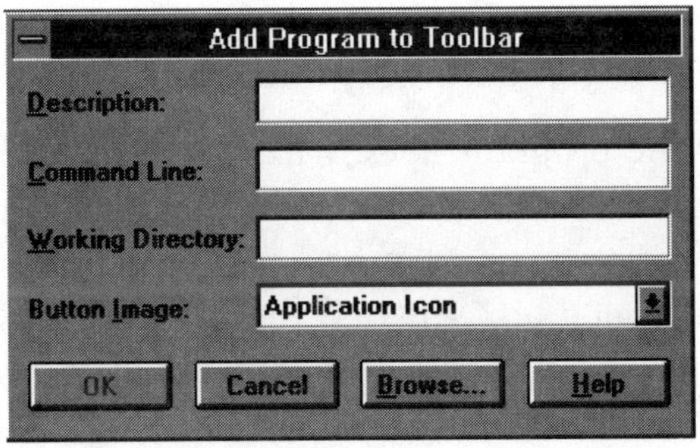

FIGURE 23–2 The Add Program to Toolbar dialog box

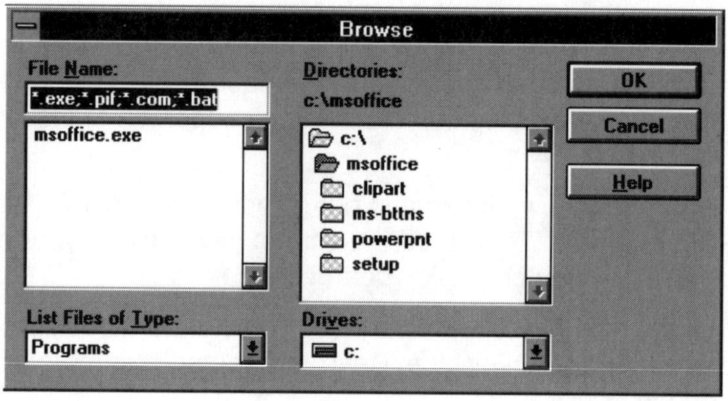

FIGURE 23–3 The Browse dialog box

If you aren't sure of the exact name and path you use to start a particular program, you can use the Browse button to open the Browse dialog box, as shown in Figure 23–3, to find it.

Select the correct drive from the Drives drop-down list; then choose the correct directory in the Directories list. When the program name appears in the File Name list, double-click on it to enter it automatically in the Command Line text box.

Enter a directory name in the Working Directory text box if you want to specify a default document directory for the new program.

Finally, if the program doesn't have its own icon, click on the drop-down arrow next to the Button Image text box and choose one of the available button images. When you click on the OK button in the Customize dialog box, the new button will appear on the toolbar and you will be able to start the program using that button.

Using the Task List

The Task List is more than just another method for switching between programs. The Task List lets you arrange and organize multiple

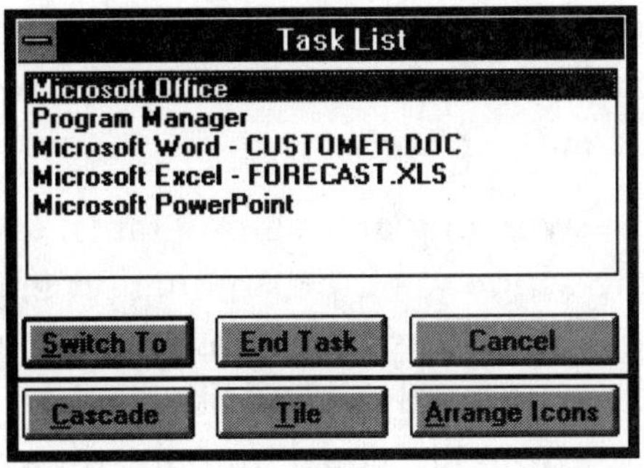

FIGURE 23–4 The Task List

programs that are running at the same time. It's also a convenient way to see a list of all the programs that are currently running.

Just because the Task List lets you arrange your program windows doesn't mean you have to arrange them. You may prefer, as I do, to run them full-screen and switch to another full-screen program when you need it. Trying to work in several cramped windows displaying relatively little information can be far less convenient than switching.

Of course, if you have a large enough screen and run Windows at a higher resolution than the standard 640×480, several on-screen windows can display enough information to give you the best of both worlds.

You can open the Task List by double-clicking on any exposed portion of the desktop or by clicking on an application's Control-menu box and then choosing Switch To. But the best way to open the Task List is to press Ctrl-Esc because it works consistently, no matter what's on your screen at the time. Figure 23–4 shows the Task List with several applications listed.

To switch to one of the programs listed in the Task List, click on it and then click on the Switch To button, or simply double-click on the program name. If you have more programs running than will fit in the list, a scroll bar appears, allowing you to scroll to the programs that aren't currently in view.

In addition to switching among programs, the Task List lets you Tile or Cascade the windows of the running programs, just as the Window menu of most Windows programs gives you the option to Tile or Cascade document windows, as discussed in Chapter 2. Tiling gives each program a roughly equal amount of screen space, as shown in Figure 23–5.

In Figure 23–5, the Program Manager was minimized by clicking on its Minimize button before tiling, and it is represented as an icon in the lower-left portion of the screen. Consider minimizing any programs you don't want to include as tiles. Another option for reducing screen clutter is to exit any application you're not using before you tile.

Cascading places the open windows on top of each other, leaving just the title bar and a bit of the left edge of each window that is are under the first one visible. Figure 23–6 shows the same two program windows cascaded.

note

Although you can have one or more DOS programs running along with your Windows programs, they can't be tiled, cascaded, or moved unless they are running in windows. You can put a DOS program in a window by pressing Alt-Enter. Press Alt-Enter again to return it to full screen.

Many DOS programs don't take kindly to such Windows shenanigans and may actually freeze up if you try to window them. So, if you must try this, use caution and save your work first.

You can also exit a Windows program from the Task List by highlighting its name and then clicking on the End Task button. If an open document in the program you're trying to end has been modified, the program will present you with a dialog box asking if you want to save the document before exiting. Also, you won't be permitted to exit a Windows program if there is a dialog box open.

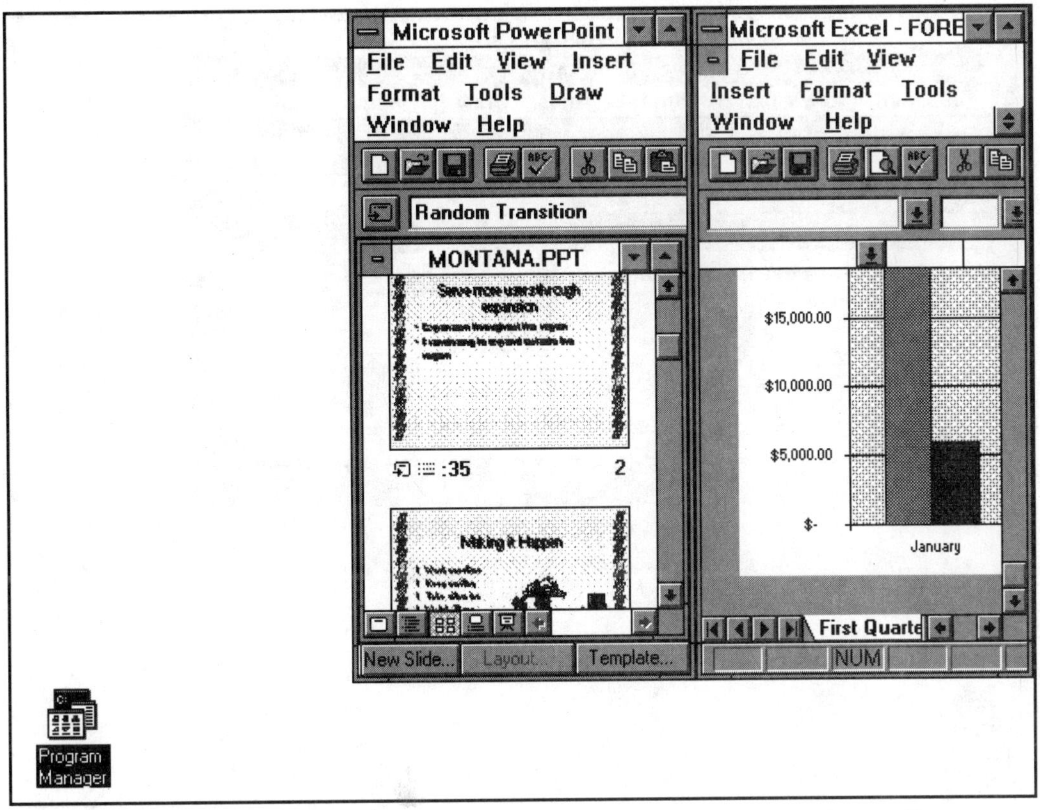

FIGURE 23–5 Two tiled program windows

CAUTION

You can't exit a DOS program from the Task List. If you try to do so, you will see a dialog box telling you that the application is still active and you must quit the application before quitting Windows.

You must switch to the DOS program and use its own method for quitting.

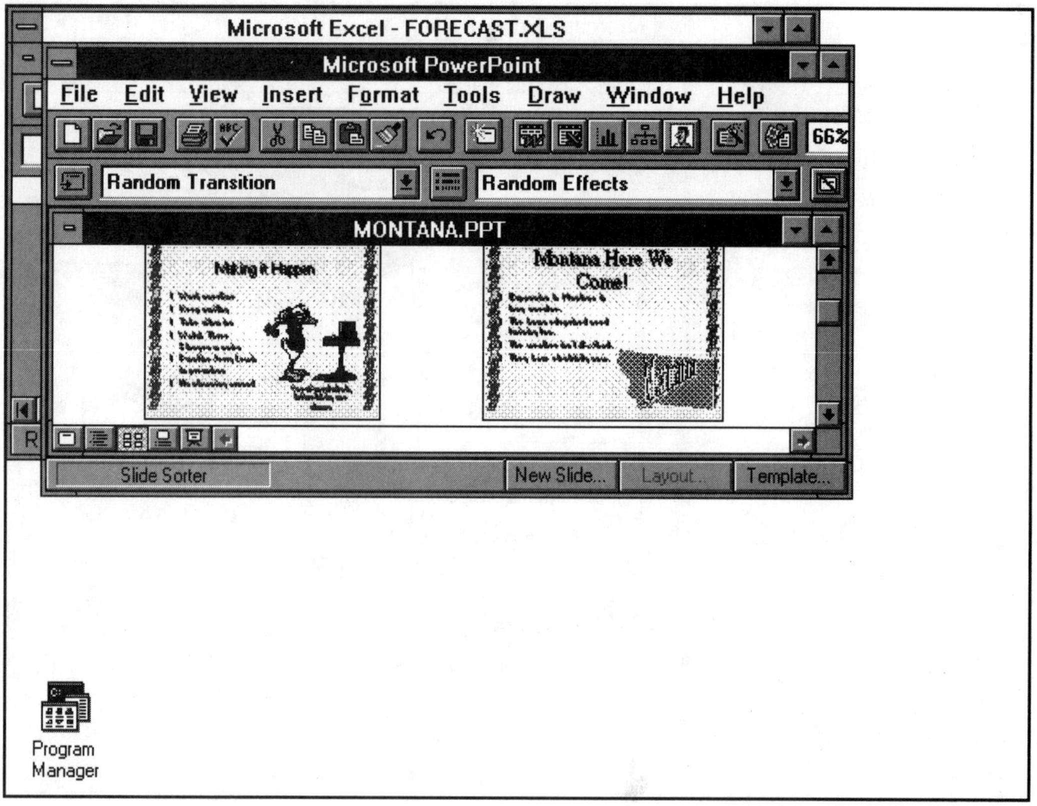

FIGURE 23–6 Cascaded program windows

When multiple programs are visible, the easiest way to switch from one to another is to click on any visible portion of the program you want to switch to.

You may find that neither tiling nor cascading positions or sizes your windows the way you want them. You may want to enlarge the window for the program you're working with most and reduce the size of the other windows. As discussed in Chapter 2, you can resize a window by dragging it by one of it borders, and you can reposition a

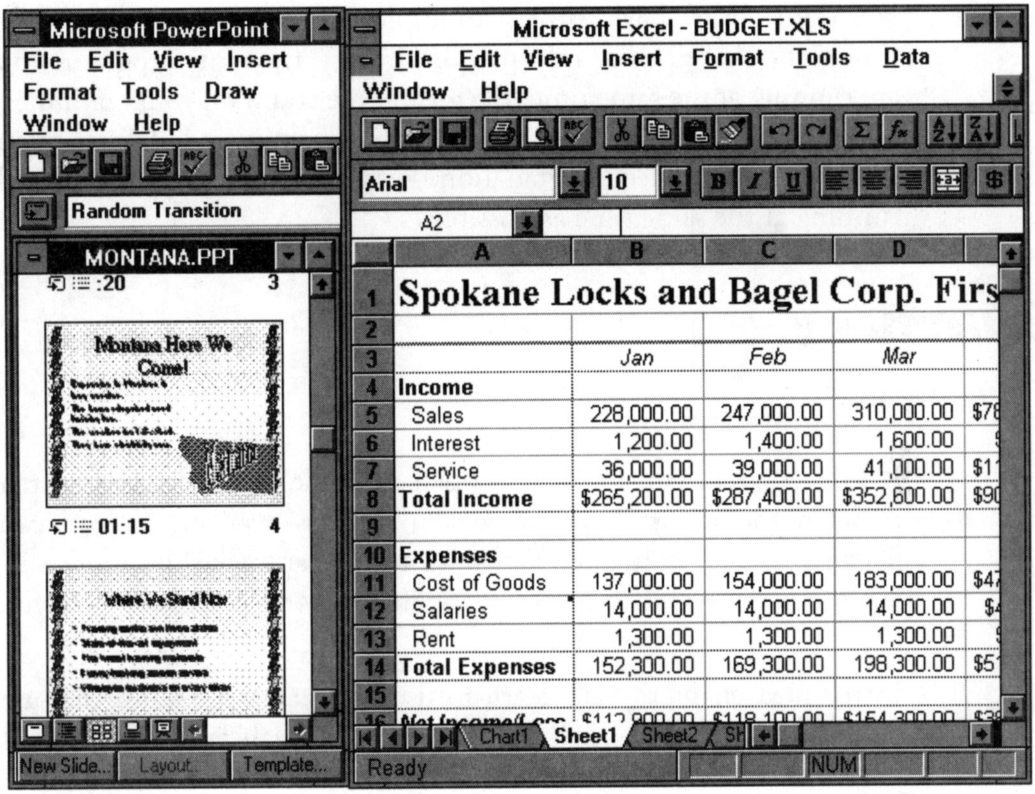

FIGURE 23–7 Two program windows sized to taste

window by dragging it by its title bar. Figure 23–7 shows program windows in two different sizes.

CAUTION

Unless you want the position and size of your icons, Program Manager window, and any open group windows arranged the same way the next time you start Windows, choose Options from the Program Manager's menu and be sure there is no check mark in front of Save Settings On Exit. If there is, click on Save Settings On Exit to remove the check mark.

You don't always have to have multiple programs open at the same time to be able to share information. In fact, the more programs you are running at the same time, the greater the strain on your computer, and performance can suffer. So, unless your computer so fast that you don't notice any speed degradation, keep as few programs open and running at the same time as possible.

Summary

In this chapter, you learned to open multiple programs and switch between them. Just having several programs available so you can instantly switch to the one you want to use can make you more efficient, but being able to move information among them really justifies running multiple programs.

In the next chapter, you'll learn to use the shared programs that are included with Office—including WordArt, Organization Chart, and Graph—to insert objects into any of the main Office programs.

24

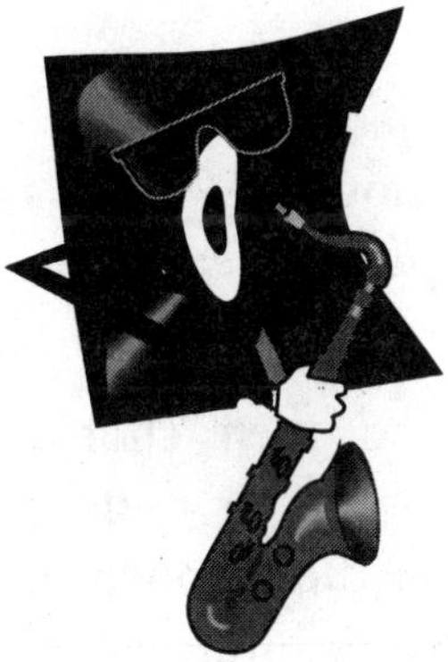

Embedding Objects from Supplemental Applications

The object of this chapter is to teach you about the objects you can create with the supplemental applications that come with Office and how to insert those objects in the main Office programs.

An object is a graph, a picture, or just about any piece of information—usually created in another program—that can be inserted in a document. Office's supplemental programs provide some valuable features and enhancements for your documents and are a good place to start learning about putting information from one program into another.

You worked with one of the supplemental programs—the ClipArt Gallery—in Chapter 19 when you inserted a clip art picture in a PowerPoint presentation.

I'll just hit the highlights of two of the supplemental applications, but you'll get enough of an overview to get started and find your way around in these programs.

Introduction to OLE (Object Linking and Embedding)

There are three ways to insert information from another Windows program in a document. You can *paste* from the *Clipboard*, *embed* an object, or *link* an object.

When you select information in a document and then choose Edit➢Cut or Edit➢Copy (or use a keyboard shortcut or toolbar button to cut or copy), the information is stored on the Clipboard. The Clipboard is a temporary holding area that stores information until you cut or copy something else. The Clipboard holds only the last thing you cut or copied and replaces it with the next thing you cut or copy.

You can retrieve the contents of the Clipboard by positioning your insertion point where you want the information to go—whether in a different location in the same document, a different document in the same program, or even a document in a different program—and then choosing Edit➢Paste.

Cutting or copying and then pasting information is simple and straightforward, but it has some limitations. Typically, the information you paste is treated as ordinary text or graphics that either can't be edited at all or must be edited using the tools available in the program in which you pasted it.

All the Office programs, and many other Windows programs, take advantage of a Windows feature called *Object Linking and Embedding,* or *OLE* (pronounced *oh-lay*) for placing information from one application into another.

The advantages of OLE over ordinary cutting or copying and pasting are dramatic. An OLE object can be edited using all the tools that were available in the application that created it. For example, if you embed some cells from an Excel worksheet in a Word document, you can edit the spreadsheet cell just as if you were in Excel without ever leaving Word.

A linked object is really just a representation of the information in the source document. The link can be updated when the source information changes. For example, if those Excel worksheet cells in the Word document I was just talking about are linked, changes made to the cells' contents in the worksheet will be reflected in the Word document.

If the worksheet cells are embedded, however, changes made in the worksheet (the source document) won't be reflected in Word.

You'll learn more about the wide variety of linking and embedding possibilities in the next chapter, but this chapter will examine the process of embedding objects from Office's supplemental applications.

Using WordArt

The WordArt program lets you create fancy text with a virtually unlimited variety of effects. You can use WordArt to add dazzling titles or to draw the reader's attention to a particular portion of a document.

Technically, WordArt is included with Word. In fact, if you purchase Word separately from the Office package, you'll get WordArt as part of the deal. But WordArt, like all the supplemental Office programs, can be used with any of the Office programs.

You can also use the supplemental programs with other Windows programs that support OLE. And other programs may come with supplemental programs that you can use with your Office programs.

I'll use Word and PowerPoint as the programs in which we'll embed the objects from the supplemental programs. But once you know how to use the supplemental programs with one of the Office programs, you'll know how to use them with all of the others. The procedure is exactly the same, regardless of which program you're using.

note

Although embedding objects from the supplemental programs works exactly the same way in all the Office programs, this isn't necessarily the case when using these supplemental programs with other Windows programs.

Other programs may not support the latest version of OLE (2.0 as of this writing), or they may not support OLE at all. If the program in which you want to embed an object from a supplemental application doesn't operate in exactly the same way as described in this chapter, don't panic. Refer to that program's documentation to see if, and how, it handles OLE objects.

Start Word and open the document in which you want to embed a WordArt object. You can embed the WordArt object in a new document if you like. Position the insertion point where you want the WordArt object to appear. Don't worry about precise positioning, because you can easily reposition and resize the object later.

Choose Insert➢Object. The Object dialog box appears, as shown in Figure 24–1.

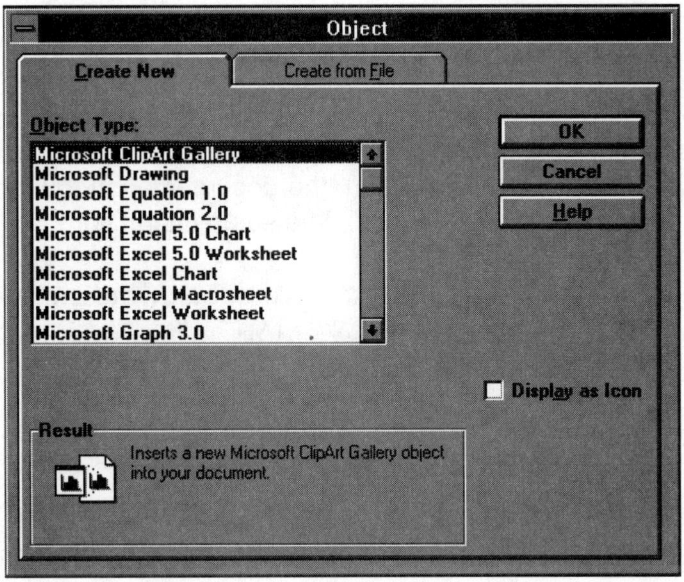

FIGURE 24–1 The Create New tab of the Object dialog box

If the Create New tab of the Object dialog box isn't displayed, click on the Create New tab. You'll learn about creating objects from files in the next chapter.

The names in your Object Type list may differ from those in the figure, depending on how your Office programs were installed and what other programs are installed on your computer.

You'll also notice a check box for Display as Icon in the lower-right portion of the dialog box. This option lets you display a small icon representing the type of embedded object. You'll learn more about this option in the next chapter.

Scroll down the list to Microsoft WordArt 2.0 and click on it. The Result portion of the dialog box shows you what will happen if you choose this object type. Click on the OK button.

note If Microsoft WordArt 2.0 doesn't appear in your list, you may have to run the Word setup program to install the application. Start Word Setup by double-clicking on the Word Setup icon in Program Manager group that contains your Office icons. The screen prompts tell you what to do to add to your installation. If you want further instruction, the documentation that comes with the Word program has complete setup instructions.

The title bar still says Microsoft Word, but Word's menus and toolbars have been replaced by the WordArt menus and toolbar. Also, the WordArt text entry box appears on the screen, as shown in Figure 24–2.

The first step in creating a WordArt object is to type your own text. All you have to do is start typing, replacing the text in the text entry box that says Your Text Here (unless of course you want your text to be Your Text Here). For example, you might type a title for your document, such as New Product Unveiling at Monday Meeting.

The text you type in the text entry box doesn't replace the WordArt text above the dialog box until you apply an effect or attribute or click on the Update Display button in the WordArt text entry box.

After typing your text, you can use the menus and toolbar buttons to specify how your text should look by selecting fonts and font attributes, curves and shapes, alignment, and shadows. Unlike the main Office programs, WordArt does not make all the toolbar functions accessible from the menus and vice versa, so you may have to use both menus and toolbar buttons.

note Because the WordArt toolbar doesn't provide ToolTips as the toolbars in the main programs do, Figure 24–2 shows each of the buttons' actions.

One of the first things you might want to alter is the shape of the text. Click on the Line and Shape toolbar button (the one next to the box that says Plain Text) to see the shapes available, as shown in Figure 24–3.

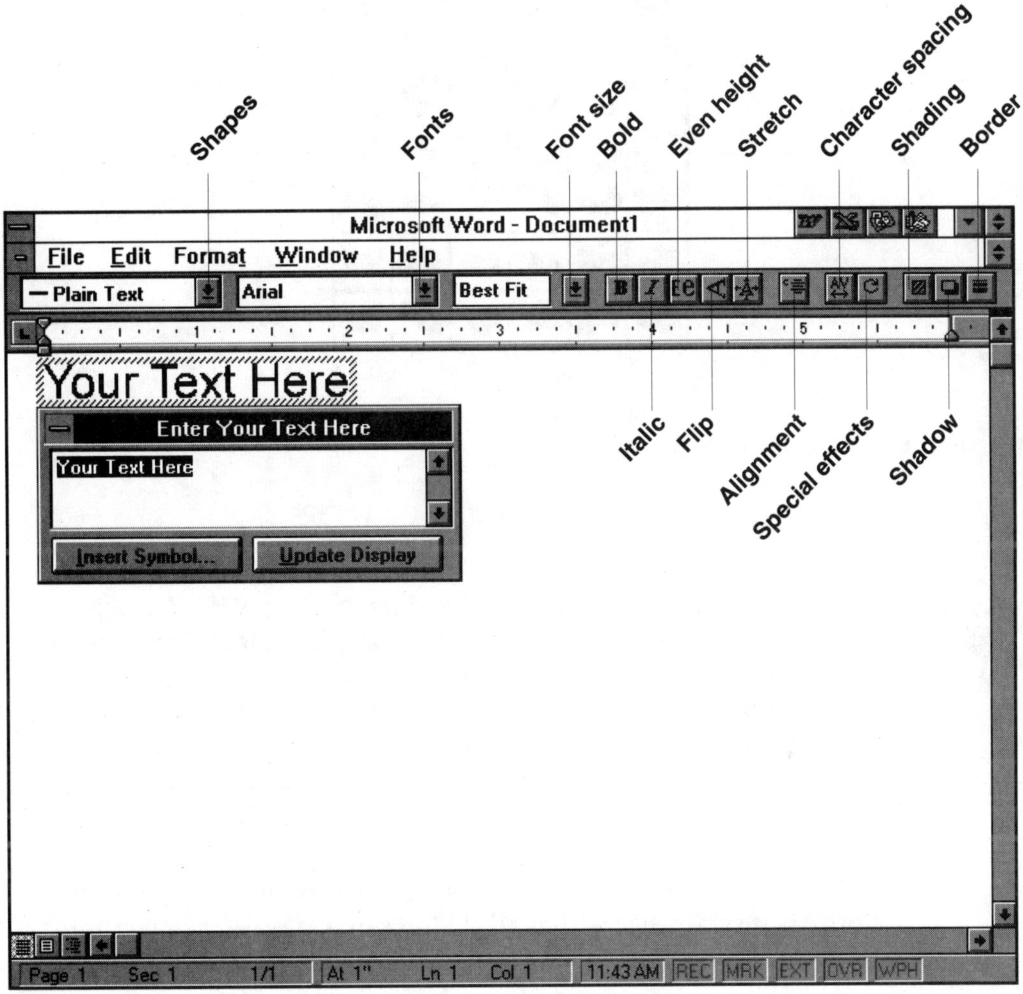

FIGURE 24–2 The WordArt menus, toolbar, and dialog box in Word

As soon as you choose one of the line and shape effects, the text above the text entry box displays the text you entered with the effect you chose. Experiment with the shapes to find one that suits you. Figure 24–4 shows three lines of text in the Button shape.

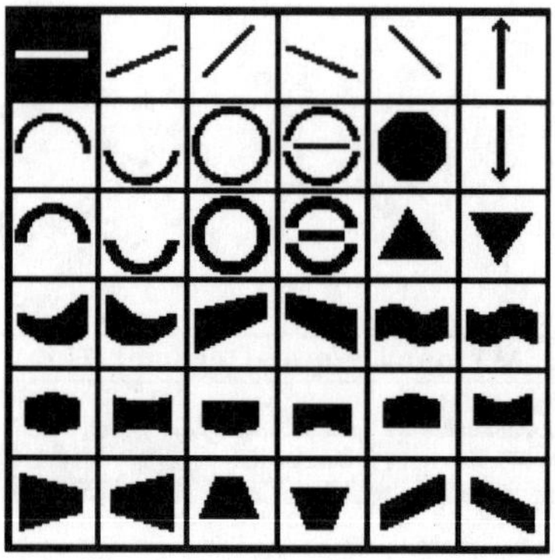

FIGURE 24–3 The palate of shapes

note You can have any amount of text you want in a WordArt object, but some of the shapes require two or three lines of text to be displayed properly. For example, the Button shape requires three lines—one for the top curve, one for the middle line, and one for the bottom curve, as shown in Figure 24–4. You could use just one line for this shape, but you would have only the top curve, which would defeat the purpose of choosing this shape.

You can click on the Font button to choose another font for your WordArt text. Be aware that all the text in a WordArt object must use the same font and size as well as other attributes. You can't have a single word bold, for example. If you select the bold attribute, all the text is bold.

tip Although you can choose a specific point size for your WordArt text, the Best Fit option is often the best. If you use Best Fit, you can change the size of the WordArt object, and the text will adjust to the new size. If you choose a particular point size and then change the object size, the text will remain the specified size, which may no longer be appropriate.

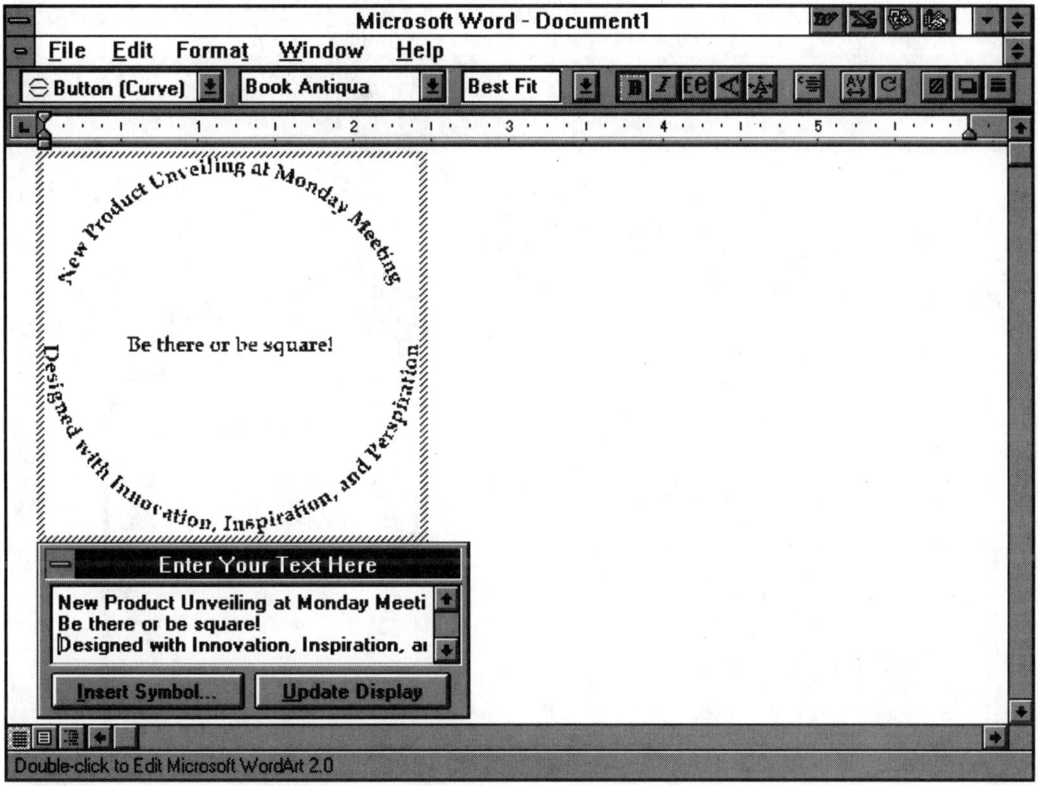

FIGURE 24–4 Button-shaped text

Use the Shading, Shadow, and Border buttons to add shading, shadows, and borders to your text. These options affect only the text, not the box that surrounds the text.

To edit the text, select the portion you want to change or position the insertion point where you want to type in the WordArt text entry box. If you've already added the attributes you want to the text, click on the Update Display button. Figure 24–5 shows some examples of what you can do with WordArt.

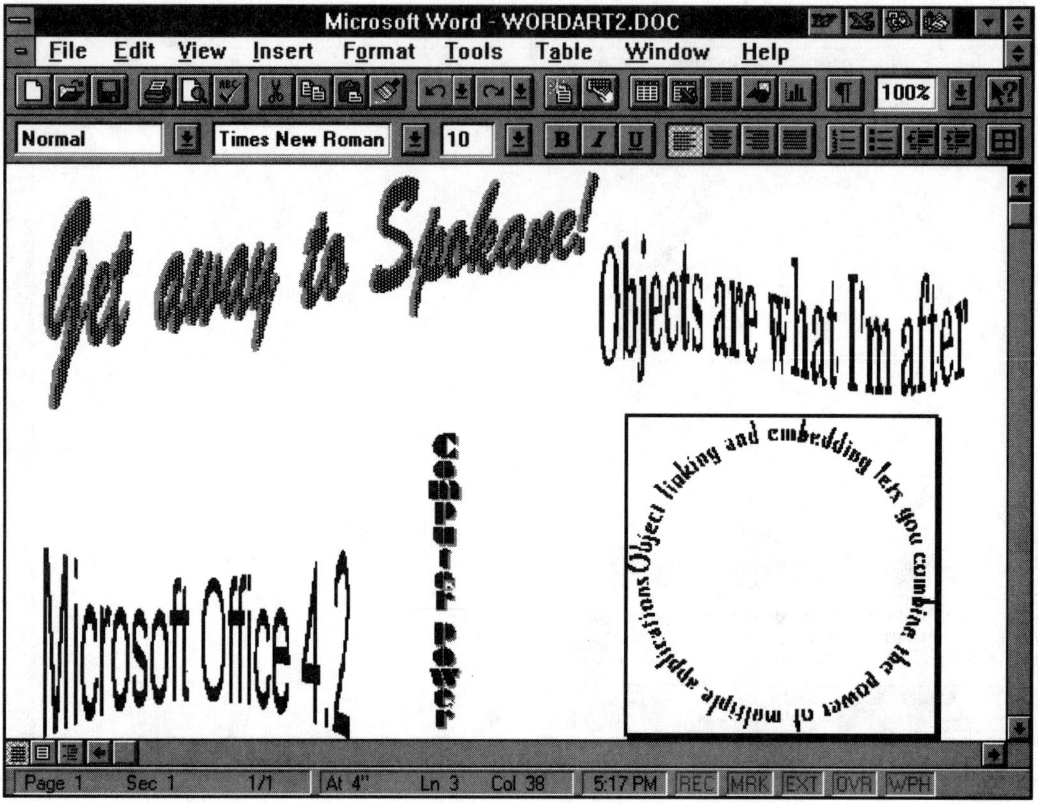

FIGURE 24–5 Examples of effects created with WordArt

After your WordArt text looks the way you want it to, you can click anywhere on the document outside the text entry box and the WordArt text. The Word menus and toolbars that were present before you started using WordArt reappear, and your WordArt object becomes part of your Word document.

You can resize the object by using the handles surrounding it. You can move it to another part of an existing document by positioning the mouse pointer inside the object and dragging.

If you want to edit the WordArt text after you have left WordArt, double-click in the WordArt object or choose Edit WordArt 2.0 from its shortcut menu, and the text entry box and WordArt menus and toolbars will reappear.

If you want to add a border to the area surrounding the text—as was done to the circle-shaped text in the lower-right corner of Figure 24–5—you'll have to use the tools available in the program you're putting the object in. In Word, you can right-click in the object and then choose Borders and Shading from the shortcut menu.

If you choose Open WordArt 2.0 from a WordArt object's shortcut menu, a WordArt dialog box that contains all the tools for editing the WordArt text appears, as shown in Figure 24–6.

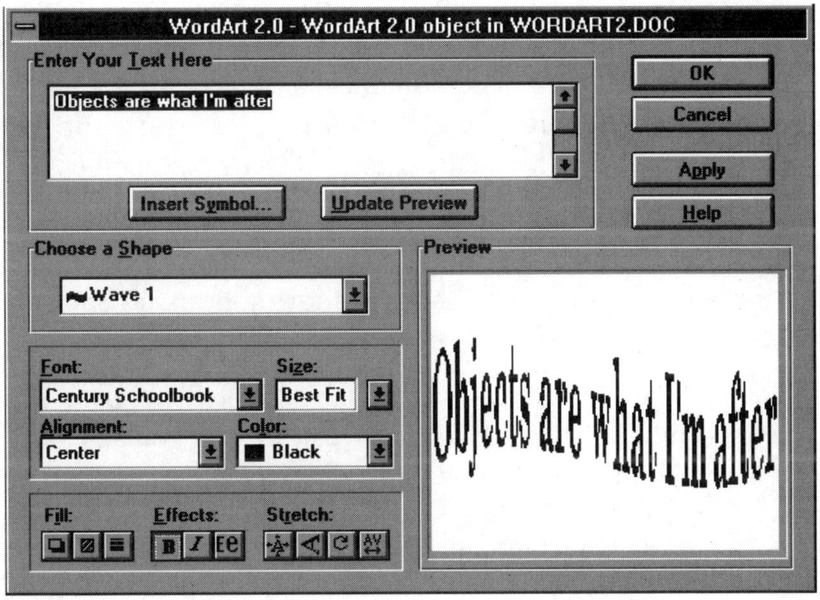

FIGURE 24–6 The WordArt 2.0 dialog box

You may find it more convenient to do your editing in the WordArt dialog box since it puts everything in one place. Use whichever method seems more comfortable.

Using Microsoft Organization Chart

We'll work with Organization Chart in PowerPoint since that is the program it comes with. But, like the other supplemental programs, Organization Chart can be used with any of the Office programs.

There are several ways to place an organization chart in a presentation. You can, of course, choose Insert➢Object and then choose Microsoft Organization Chart. This is the method you would use to create an organization chart in a program other than PowerPoint. The second method is to click on the Insert Org Chart button on the Standard toolbar and then click on the slide you want. Finally, you can create a new slide that has an org chart placeholder, as shown in Figure 24–7, and then double-click in the placeholder.

No matter how you start Microsoft Organization Chart, the Microsoft Organization Chart window appears, as shown in Figure 24–8.

Unlike WordArt, Organization Chart doesn't replace a program's menus and toolbars with its own. Instead, it is available only as a separate program in its own window with its own menus and buttons.

note If you are creating an org chart in a program other than PowerPoint or on a PowerPoint slide that won't have a title, you may want to select the text that says Chart Title and enter a title for your organization chart. On the other hand, if you are creating the org chart on a PowerPoint slide that has, or will have, its own title, you may want to just select the Chart Title text and press

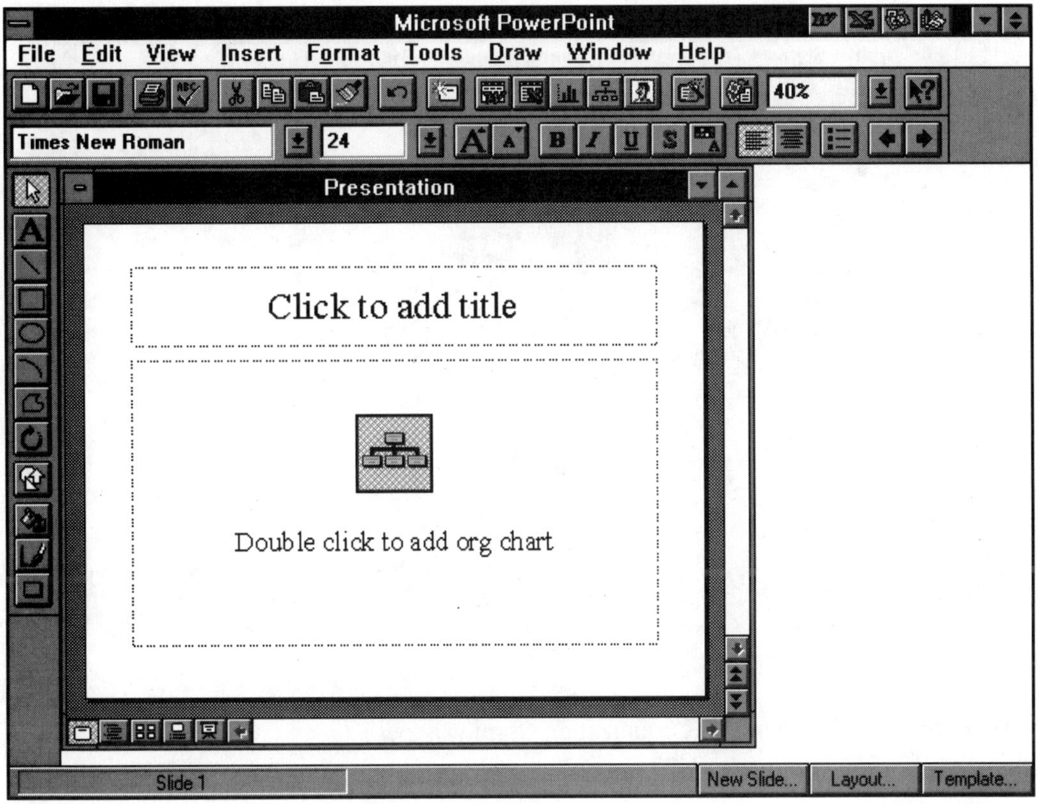

FIGURE 24–7 A PowerPoint slide with an org chart placeholder

> Delete to get rid of it. You'll then have to click on a box in the chart to start entering your data.

The top box is highlighted and ready to accept your information. Just start typing to enter the name of the person at the top of the chart—usually the head of the company or department for which you are creating the chart. Notice that, as soon as you start typing, the box opens

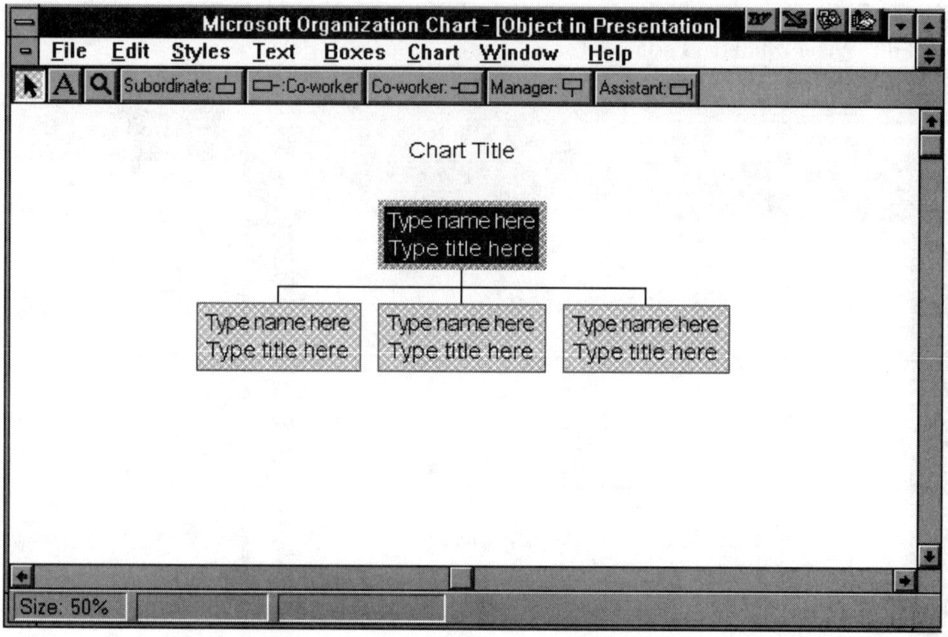

FIGURE 24–8 The Microsoft Organization Chart window

to reveal Comment 1 and Comment 2 in angle brackets, as shown in Figure 24–9.

After typing the person's name, press Enter. The text that says Type Title Here is highlighted so you can type the person's title. If you aren't going to enter a title for this person, press Delete so the box doesn't end up saying Type Title Here. After typing the title, either press Enter and type a comment or click on the next box you want to fill in.

If you aren't going to use the comment fields, you don't have to delete them. They won't show up in the final org chart unless you enter text in them.

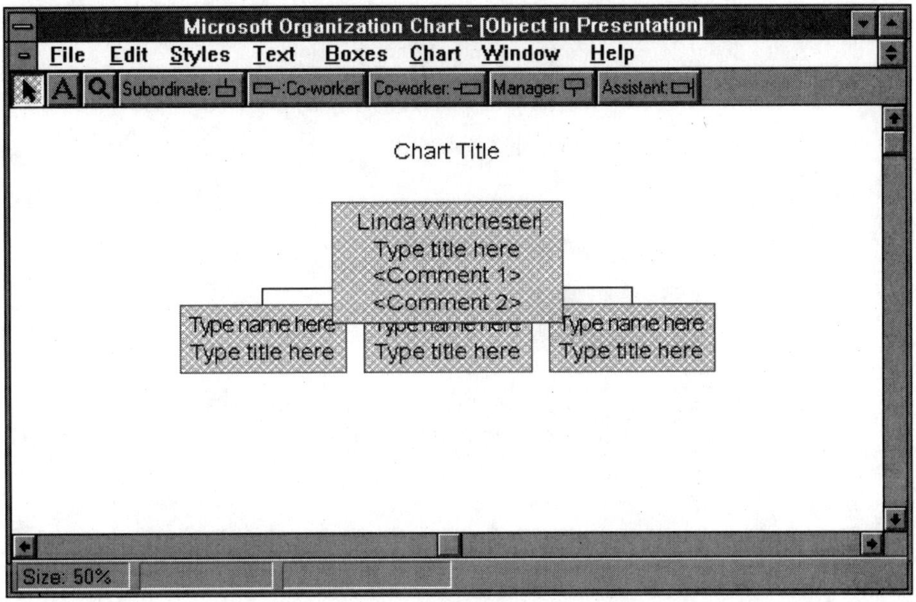

FIGURE 24–9 An org chart box with the Comment fields visible

After entering the names and titles and any comments you want in the four initial boxes, you will probably want to add additional boxes. To add a box for another person in the organization, click on one of the buttons under the menu bar labeled Subordinate, Co-worker, Manager, and Assistant and then click on the box you want to attach it to.

For example, if the head of the company has an assistant you want to include, click on the Assistant button and then click on the top box. The assistant's box is added, as shown in Figure 24–10.

Enter the information in the new box just as you did in the other boxes.

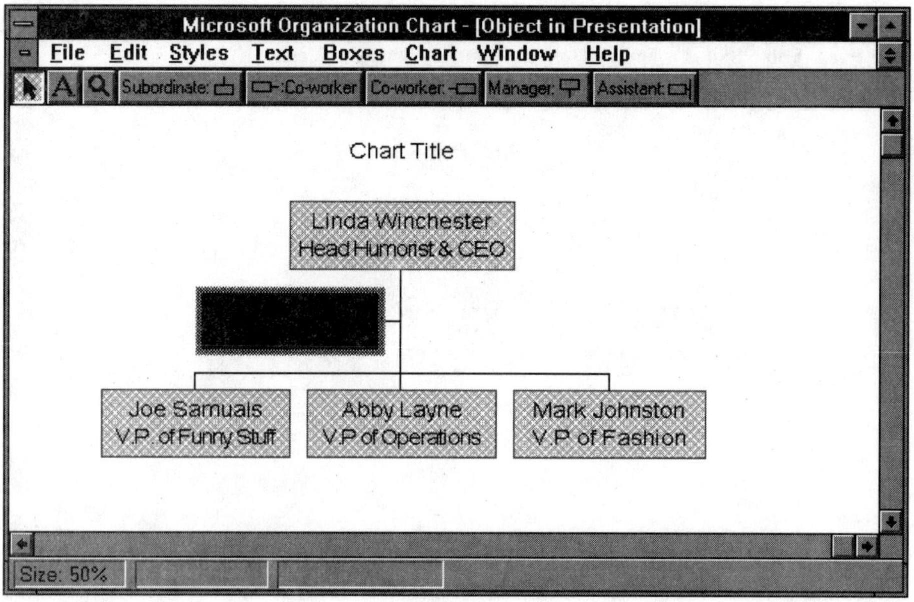

FIGURE 24–10 A new box represents the assistant to the head honcho.

tip You can create multiple boxes of the same type by clicking multiple times on the button for the type of boxes you want and then clicking on the box.

You can use the menus to change the border, the color and shading, the arrangement of groups of boxes, the text in the boxes, and the size of the overall chart. You can also drag a box to a new location in the chart by holding down Shift while dragging.

After the chart is set up the way you want it, choose File➢Exit and Return to Presentation. A Microsoft Organization Chart dialog box appears, telling you that the object has been changed and asking if you want to update the object before proceeding, as shown in Figure 24–11.

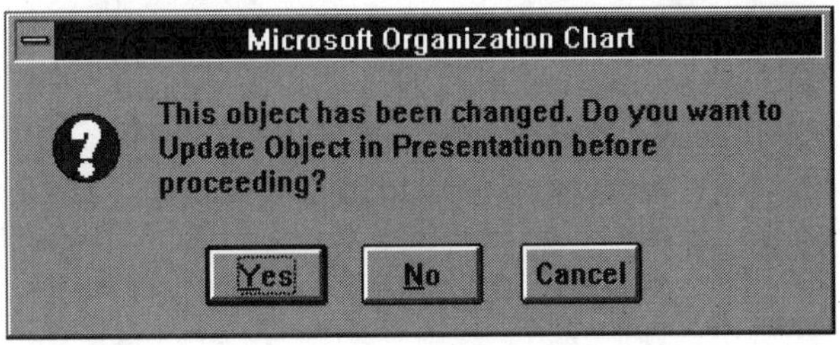

FIGURE 24–11 The dialog box asks if you want to update.

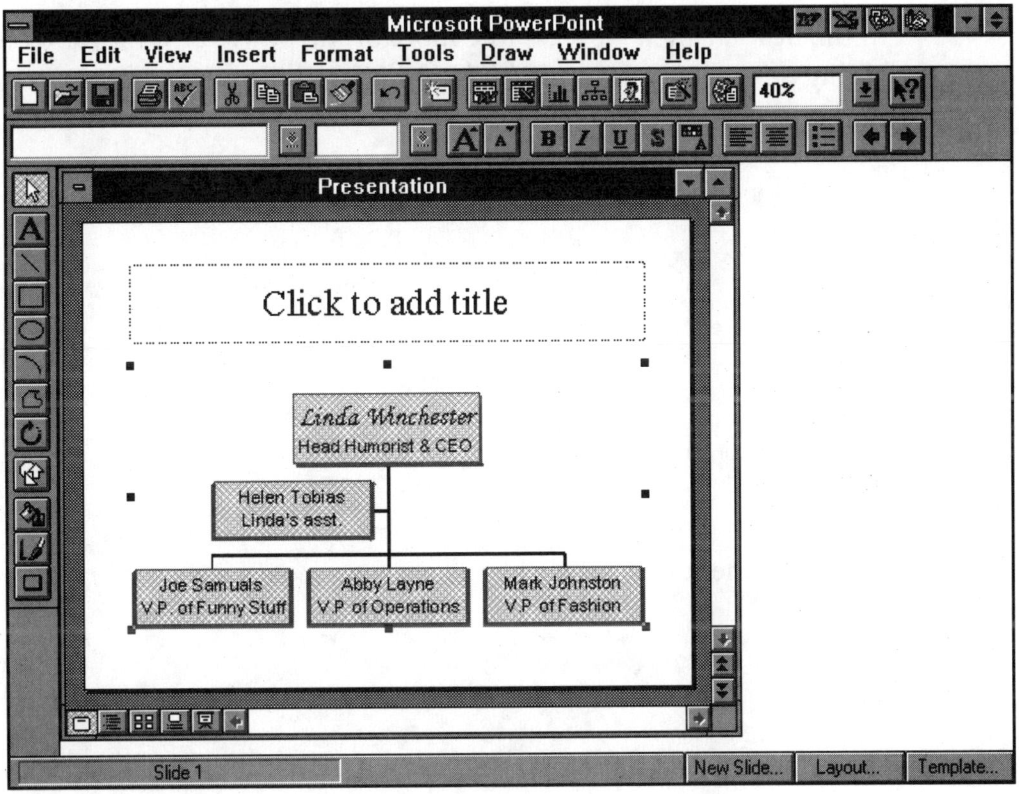

FIGURE 24–12 The org chart in a slide

Click on the Yes button so the org chart will appear in the presentation slide. The chart will appear in place of the slide's placeholder, as shown in Figure 24–12. To edit the org chart, double-click on it to open the Organization Chart program.

Summary

In this chapter you learned how to embed objects from the WordArt and Organization Chart programs that come with Office.

In the next chapter, we'll explore more of the power of OLE for combining information from multiple Office applications.

25

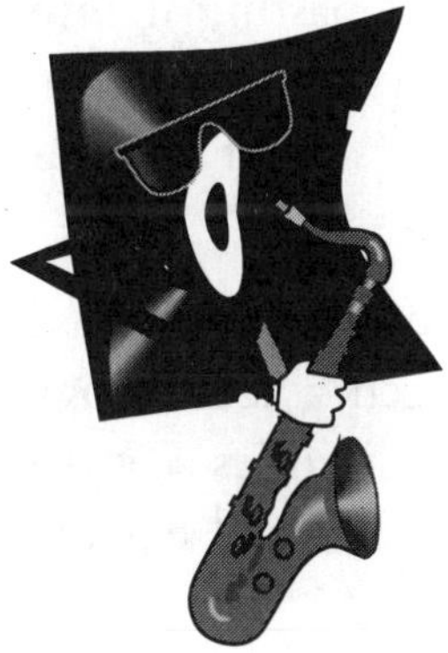

Getting It Together—Using the Office Programs in Concert

The previous chapter gave you an introduction to OLE (Object Linking and Embedding) using the supplemental programs to embed objects in the main Office programs. When it comes to taking advantage of using the Office programs in concert, however, that is only the beginning.

The first version of Windows to accommodate the integration of data between applications allowed only simple cut-and-paste operations. That certainly made sharing data easier than it had been, but editing the data once it was pasted into its new location was difficult or impossible. Updating the pasted data often required that you go through another copy-and-paste routine. Not very efficient, to say the least.

Windows and Compound Documents

For as long as people have been creating paper documents, they have been adding bits and pieces of various types of information together—cutting out a picture from one place and pasting it into another, cutting out a chart here and pasting it into a report there. In computer jargon, documents that include pieces from several applications are called *compound documents.*

The technology to create computerized compound documents has been like the Holy Grail—very elusive. Finding such a technology promised far greater computer productivity. The possibilities seemed endless, but the search for a means to accomplish it seemed equally staggering.

Dynamic Data Exchange—Baby Steps

With Windows 3.0, a technology called DDE (Dynamic Data Exchange), which enabled users to create truly compound documents, was introduced. Not only could these compound documents include information from multiple applications, but the data could be updated as the source data changed. DDE was a step in the right direction but hardly a panacea.

Creating compound documents with DDE could be intimidating, often requiring that the user write a bit of programming code, and dangerous as well. It was common for DDE documents to cause applications, and Windows itself, to crash. With DDE, you learned to save your work often or suffer the consequences.

OLE 1.0—The Holy Grail? Not Quite

The first implementation of OLE 1.0 after the release of Windows 3.1 removed many of the obstacles to creating compound documents. Using OLE, embedded data was more easily edited, and linked data was less likely to cause system crashes. Also, for the first time, you could create useful compound documents without a degree in rocket science.

OLE isn't really a separate technology from DDE, it is just an evolutionary progression. In fact, OLE is based on the technology underlying DDE. It has just added a friendlier interface and additional features.

As wonderful as OLE 1.0 was, it suffered from some of the same instability problems that plagued DDE. It was more stable, but not stable enough. Links to source data were still easily broken. And, while it made embedding data easy, editing embedded data still had to be done in the source application, away from the document in which the object was embedded.

OLE 2.0—The Genuine Article

OLE 2.0, the latest version of OLE, which is supported by all the main Office applications, has everything computer users have been searching for—almost. Links created using OLE 2.0 are much more stable. You won't have nearly as many lost links or system crashes as you once had to put up with.

Perhaps best of all is the way you can edit embedded objects. Embedded objects can now be edited in place, a process that is sometimes called *visual editing.* With in-place editing, you edit the object right in the document in which it's embedded, surrounded by the other parts of the document. This way, you can see your edits in context, which greatly enhances efficiency.

When you edit an embedded object, the menus and toolbars of the application in which the object was created usually replace the menus and toolbars of the application in which the object is embedded. You can edit the embedded object without leaving the document.

You saw how in-place editing works with WordArt in the previous chapter. You'll see more examples later in this chapter.

About the only difficulty with OLE 2.0 is finding Windows programs that support it. It takes time for companies to design programs to take advantage of software innovations. OLE 2.0 is still a fairly new technology and a complex one to implement.

The good news is that there are quite a few programs that do support OLE 2.0, and more are appearing all the time. The really good news is that Microsoft Office 4.2 is the first suite of programs that supports OLE 2.0. Lucky you! It makes sense that Office is the first OLE 2.0-compatible suite. After all, it was Microsoft that developed OLE 2.0.

CAUTION

Documents that take advantage of OLE require more of your computer's resources than simple documents created in one application. If you have an older computer with relatively little memory, you may be better off avoiding OLE. Trying to create compound documents with a weakling computer may take more time and patience than it's worth.

On second thought, the benefits of OLE are so compelling that you would probably be wise to upgrade or replace your computer so you have enough muscle to make working with OLE bearable.

Linking or Embedding? That's the Question

When creating a compound document, the first decision you have to make is whether to link the data to or embed the data in the document. Let's take a look at the differences.

Linking places a representation of the data from one document in another. The primary advantage is that the data in the representation is updated when the data in the source document is updated.

Linking would be the right choice if you were putting a portion of an Excel worksheet, such as a budget, into a Word document and you wanted to be certain that the Word document always reflected the latest budget numbers.

One disadvantage of linking is that linked data isn't quite as easy to edit as embedded data. You don't have the advantage of in-place editing. When you double-click on the linked data, the source document appears in its original application. It's not a big problem, just a bit less convenient.

Another disadvantage to consider is that the document containing the source data must be available in order for you to edit the linked data. If you delete the source document, you won't be able to edit the linked data.

Choose embedding if you don't have to update the data from a source document. A graphic image, such as clip art or an object created in WordArt, doesn't usually have to be updated and is a perfect candidate for embedding.

Embedding makes editing easier by allowing in-place editing. The menus and toolbars are replaced by the menus and toolbars of the application in which the embedded document was created. In the example of an Excel worksheet in a Word document, the Word menus and toolbars would be replaced by the Excel menus and toolbars, allowing you to edit the worksheet data in the context of the Word document using Excel's tools.

The primary disadvantage of embedding is that it makes the document larger by roughly the size of the source document. For example, if you embed a 15K Excel worksheet in a 15K Word document, the result is a Word document of about 30K. Linking, on the other hand, adds very little to the size of the document.

tip

PowerPoint has several buttons on its Standard toolbar for embedding objects from other applications. The Insert Microsoft Word Table and Insert Microsoft Excel Worksheet buttons let you embed empty rows and columns that you can edit using Word or Excel tools. PowerPoint also has Insert Graph, Insert Org Chart, and Insert Clip Art buttons for embedding those objects.

Word also has an Insert Microsoft Excel Worksheet button for embedding blank rows and columns. Using the buttons is the easiest way to embed these objects in PowerPoint and Word documents.

OLE Examples

The best way to learn how to use OLE is to look at some practical examples. For the remainder of the chapter, we'll examine some examples that will show you how to link and embed a variety of data.

Linking an Entire Excel Worksheet to a Word Document

You can link or embed an entire document or just a portion of it into another document. There are fewer steps involved in linking or embedding the entire document, so that's where we'll start.

Start Word and open the document you want the Excel worksheet linked to; then position your insertion point where you want the worksheet data to appear. Next, choose Insert➢Object and click on the Create from File tab. Figure 25–1 shows the Create from File tab of the Object dialog box.

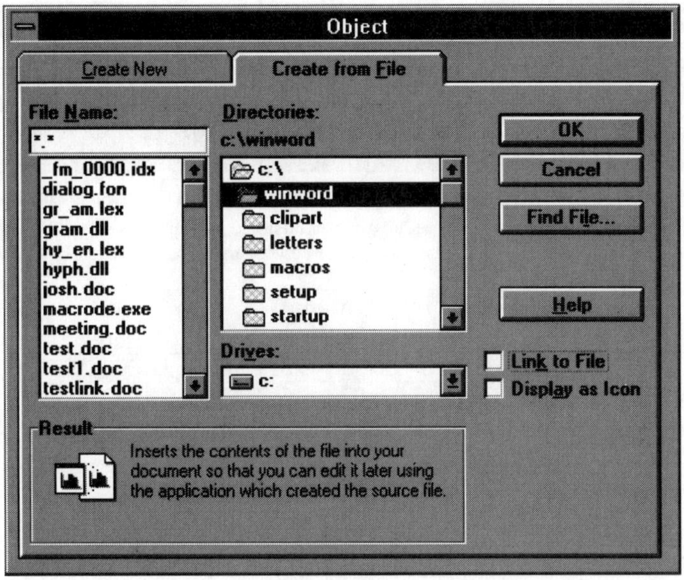

FIGURE 25–1 The Create from File tab of the Object dialog box

Click on the Link to File check box in the lower-right portion of the dialog box. This check box tells Word to create a link to the file rather than embed it. The Result portion of the dialog box tells you what will happen when you click in the Link to File dialog box.

Change to the drive and directory in which the Excel worksheet is stored, click on the worksheet's name in the File Name list, and then click on the OK button.

note Excel doesn't have to be running to link or embed a worksheet. It does, of course, have to be available to run.

After a while (it could be several minutes if you have a slow computer), the worksheet appears in the Word document, as shown in Figure 25–2.

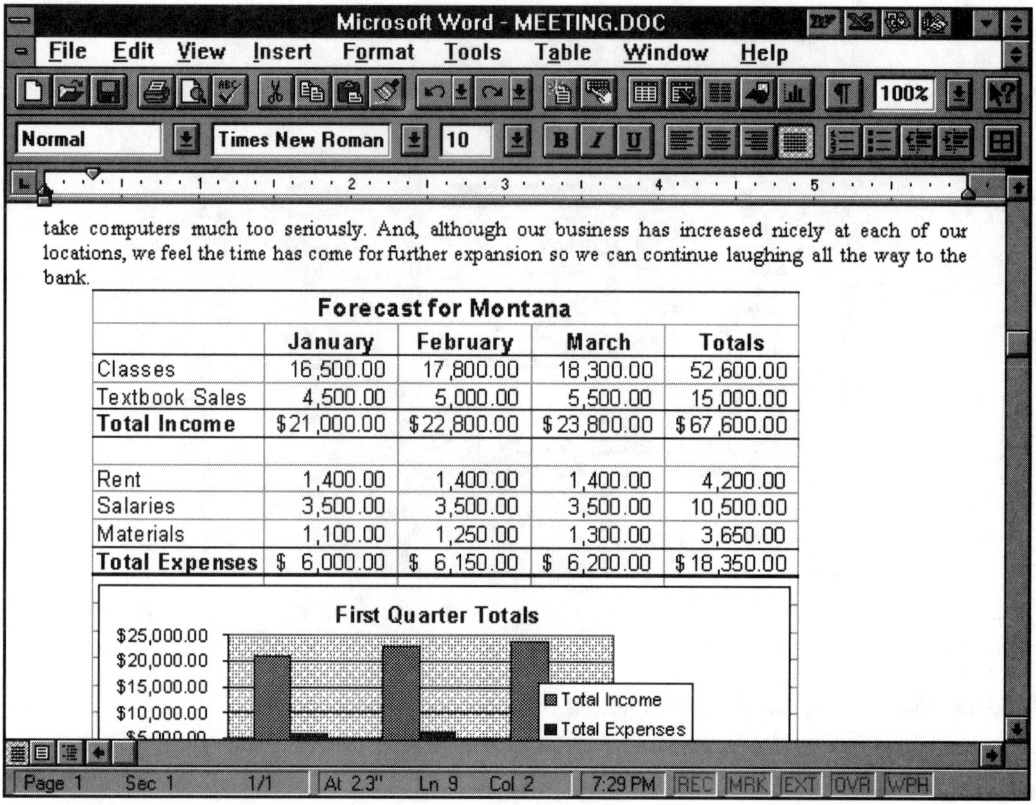

FIGURE 25–2 An Excel worksheet in a Word document

The worksheet is now an object in the Word document, and it can be moved and sized. To move the worksheet click on it so handles appear surrounding the object; then position the mouse pointer anywhere in the object and drag. To resize it, position the mouse pointer over one of the handles so it becomes a double-headed arrow and then drag.

To edit the worksheet data, double-click on the object. The worksheet will appear in a separate Excel window. You don't have to exit Excel to see the results of any changes you make. Just switch back to Word to see that the data is updated. Don't forget to save any changes you make to your worksheet data in Excel.

You can see the problem with inserting an entire worksheet. It can take over the whole document, leaving little room for the surrounding text. For this reason, you may choose to insert just selected cells rather than the entire worksheet. There is a way to insert an entire worksheet or a large portion of a worksheet without having it overwhelm the document. You can insert the worksheet as an icon.

To insert a worksheet as an icon, follow the above steps, but click on Display as Icon in the Create from File dialog box. After the file is linked, it appears as an icon, as shown in Figure 25–3.

The icon lets the reader know that there is additional information available. To see the worksheet, simply double-click on the icon. The worksheet appears in Excel just as if it were a normal, non-icon link.

CAUTION

The Display as Icon option is a good idea only if the intended reader of the document will be reading it on a computer that has Excel (and the document) available. If you print a document with a linked file displayed as an icon, the icon prints just as it appears on the screen. If the reader views the document on a computer that doesn't have Excel, of course, the data won't be visible.

Linking Selected Cells of an Excel Worksheet to a Word Document

Usually, when I use linking or embedding, I find that I want to link or embed only a portion of a document. Here's how to link just selected Excel worksheet cells to a Word document.

Start Excel and open the worksheet that contains the cells you want to insert in the Word document. Select the cells and choose Edit➢Copy or click on the Copy button on the Standard toolbar.

Switch to Word (or start it if it isn't running) and open the document in which you want to insert the worksheet cells. Position the insertion

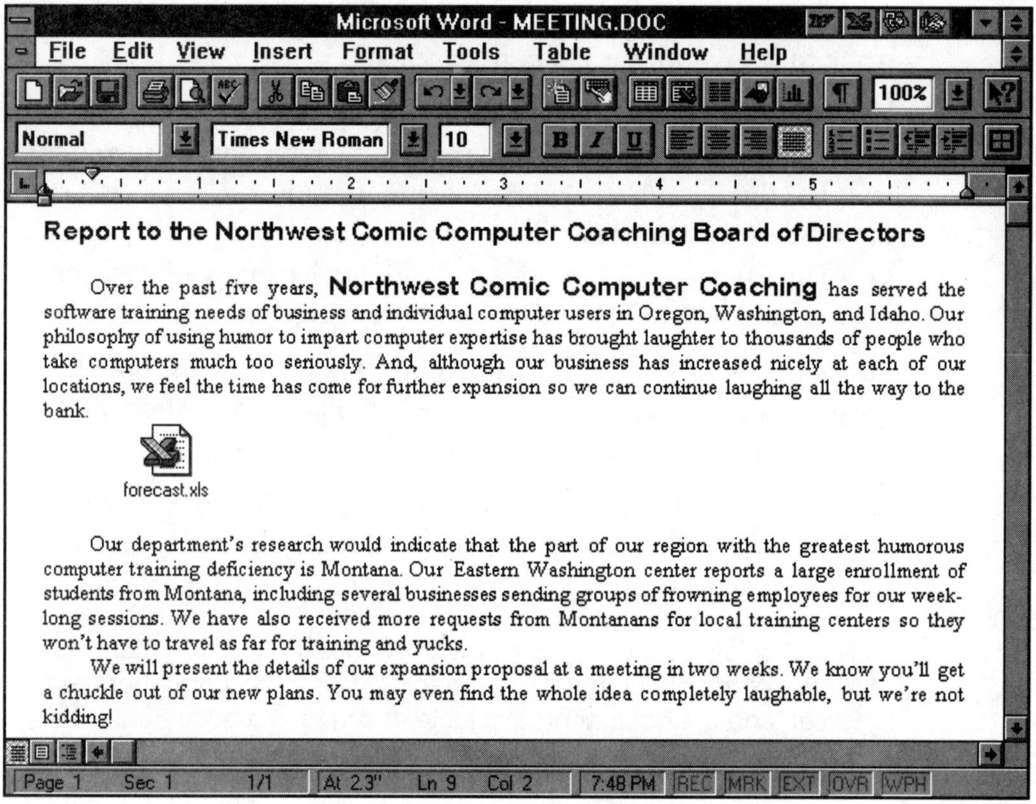

FIGURE 25–3 A linked worksheet displayed as an icon

point where you want the cells to appear and choose Edit➢Paste Special. The Paste Special dialog box appears, as shown in Figure 25–4.

Click on the Paste Link option button and then click on Microsoft Excel 5.0 Worksheet Object in the As list. If you wanted to display the selected cells as an icon, you would click on the Display as Icon check box. Finally, click on the OK button. The selected cells appear in the Word document, as shown in Figure 25–5.

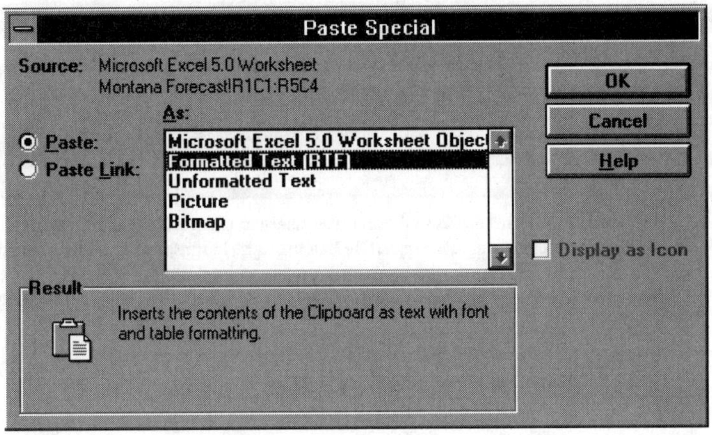

FIGURE 25–4 The Paste Special dialog box

To edit the cells, double-click on them. The worksheet that contains them will appear in an Excel window. To size or move the object in the Word document, click on the object so the handles appear and drag inside the object to move it or by one of the handles to size it.

Embedding Selected Excel Worksheet Cells in a Word Document

Embedding is the way to go if you don't need the data updated and want to be able to edit the data within the context of the document. Here's how to embed selected Excel worksheet cells in a Word document.

Start Excel and open the worksheet that contains the cells you want to insert in the Word document. Select the cells and choose Edit➢Copy or click on the Copy button on the Standard toolbar.

Switch to Word (or start it if it isn't running) and open the document into which you want to insert the worksheet cells. Position the

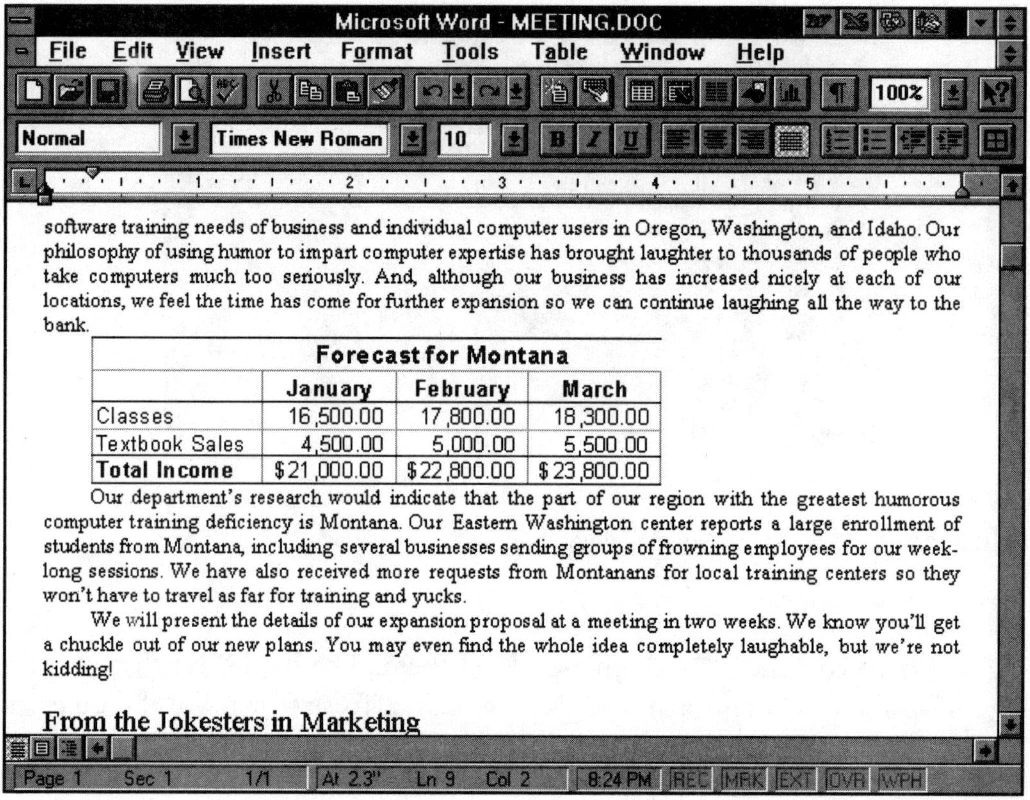

FIGURE 25–5 Selected Excel worksheet cells in a Word document

insertion point where you want the cells to appear and choose Edit➢Paste Special.

Be sure the Paste and not the Paste Link option button is selected and then click on Microsoft Excel 5.0 Worksheet Object in the As list. Click on the OK button.

The selected cells appear in the Word document, just as they appeared when linked. You'll see the difference when you edit the cells. Double-click on the cells to edit them.

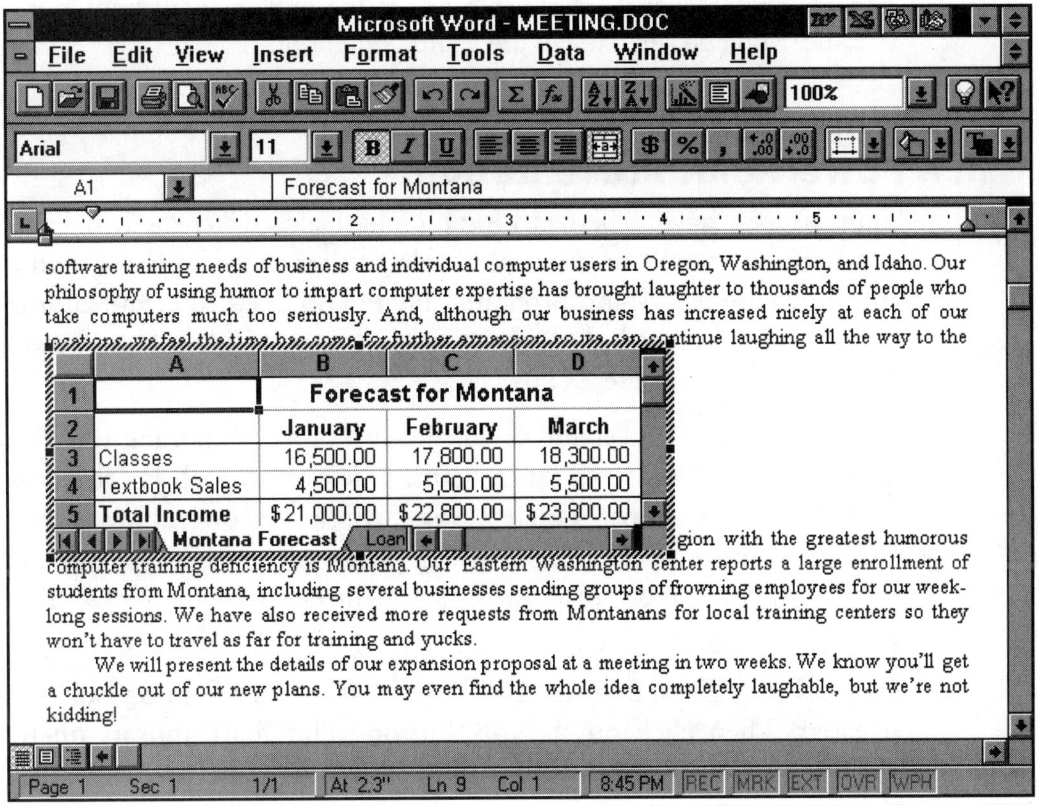

FIGURE 25–6 Selected Excel worksheet cells in a Word document

The cells are surrounded by the familiar row and column headings, and the Excel menus and toolbars have replaced Word's. You can edit the cells and add rows, formulas, and functions, just as if you were in Excel. When you finish editing, click outside the Excel object and the Word menus and toolbars will return.

note Don't forget, the data in these cells isn't linked. Any changes you make to the data in the Word document won't affect the original worksheet. Likewise, changes made to the original worksheet in Excel won't be reflected in the Word document.

Embedding an Excel Chart Sheet in a PowerPoint Presentation

Suppose you have a perfectly usable chart already created in Excel. Furthermore, you're more comfortable editing charts in Excel than in the supplemental Graph program. There's no need to create another chart. Just embed or link the existing chart into a slide in your PowerPoint presentation. Here's how.

Start or switch to Excel and open the workbook containing the chart sheet you want to use in PowerPoint. Click on the tab for the chart sheet and then choose Edit➢Copy. Switch to PowerPoint and, in slide view, move to the slide in which you want to insert the chart. If you want, you can create a new slide for the chart.

Choose Edit➢Paste Special. Be sure Microsoft Excel 5.0 Chart Object is highlighted in the As list and that the Paste option button is selected. Then click on the OK button. The chart appears on the slide, as shown in Figure 25–7.

note

Objects can be imbedded by dragging them from one application window to another. As in other drag and drop operations, you can *copy* an object by holding down Ctrl while dragging. If you don't press Ctrl while dragging, the object is moved from one application to another.

I find it cumbersome to use drag and drop for embedding. Both applications must be on-screen, and dragging an object from one window to another can be tricky. It is a matter of personal preference, of course, so use the method that suits you best.

You can resize the chart object in the slide by dragging one of the handles. You can move the object by dragging inside it. To edit the chart, double-click in the chart object on the slide. You may have to

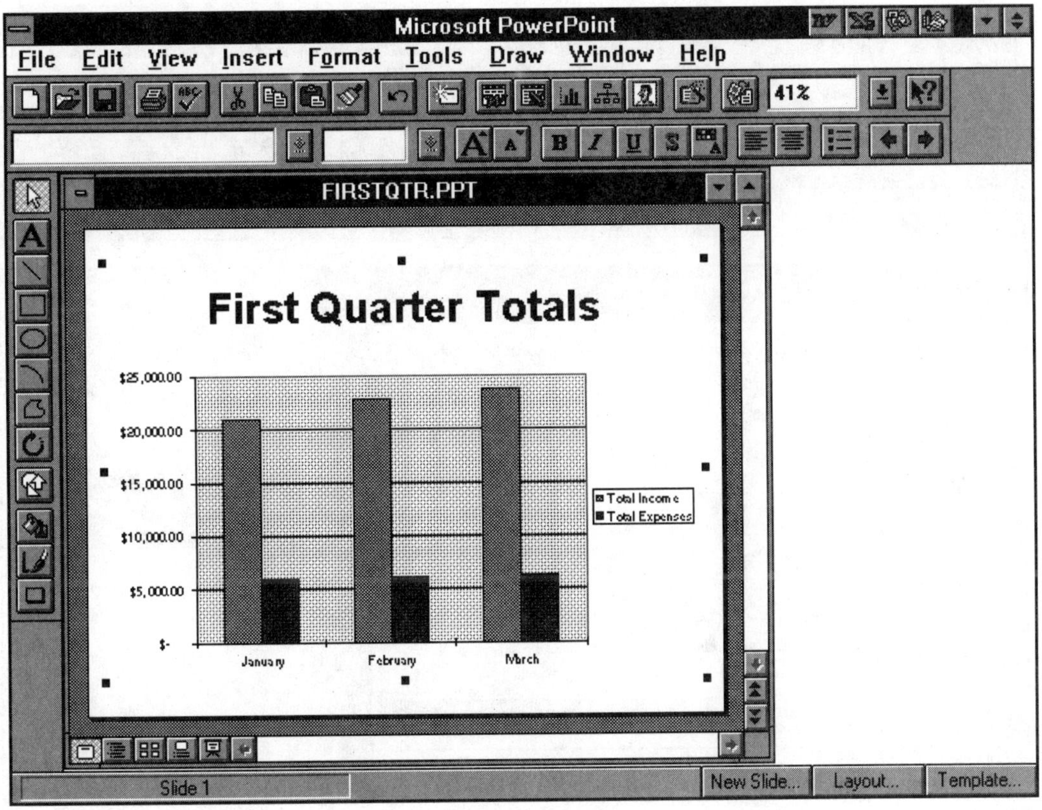

FIGURE 25–7 An Excel chart in a PowerPoint slide

resize the object to edit it after double-clicking on it. Notice that the Excel menus and toolbars replace the PowerPoint menus and toolbars, as shown in Figure 25–8.

After following along with these examples, you should have no problem linking or embedding any document or portion of a document from one Office program into another.

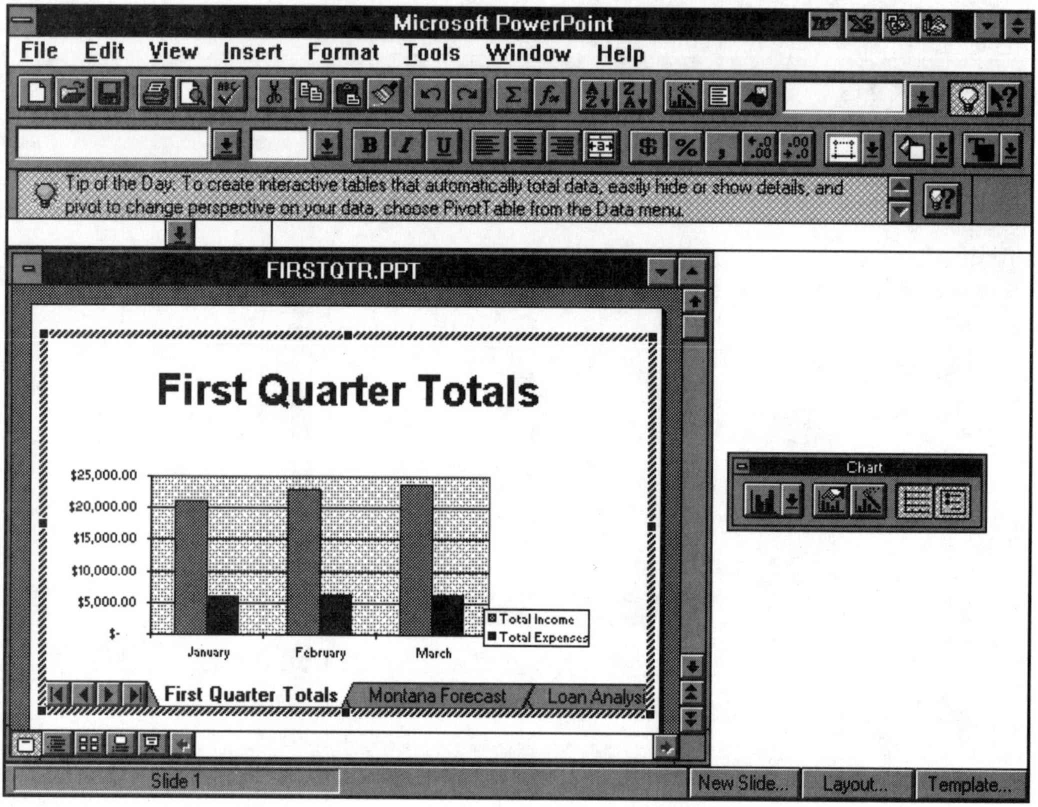

FIGURE 25–8 The embedded chart ready for editing in PowerPoint

Editing Links

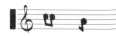

Most of the housekeeping is handled automatically when you create links, but there will be occasions when you will want to alter the way

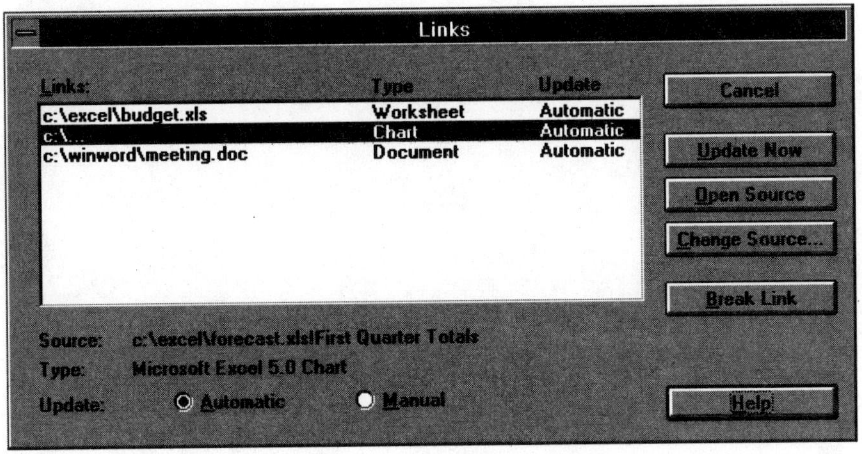

FIGURE 25–9 The Links dialog box

the links are handled. For example, suppose you linked the Excel chart in the previous example instead of embedding it, so that changes in the underlying data would be reflected in the presentation.

Furthermore, suppose you have made several other links back and forth between this presentation and other applications. You might find that waiting for all your links to be updated when you start the presentation is disconcerting. One of the link options is to have the links update only when you tell them to.

To edit your links, open the document that contains the links and choose Edit➢Links. The Links dialog box appears. Click on the first link in the Links list that you want to edit. For example, the link to the chart is shown in Figure 25–9.

Appendix

Microsoft Mail Overview

Microsoft Mail is an *electronic mail* (e-mail) program that runs on a network. If your computer isn't part of a local area network (LAN), you can save yourself some time and stop reading right now.

Microsoft Mail is listed on the Office package as one of the included programs. Well, it's not exactly *included.* If you look at the fine print, you'll see that what's actually included is a small instruction booklet and a license to use Mail on your networked computer. Before you start feeling shortchanged, read this overview to see why Microsoft took this approach.

The main Mail program and all the mailboxes and the mail in them aren't stored on your personal computer the way the other Office programs can be. Instead, Mail is stored on a central network computer, called a *server,* to which all users have access.

Only enough of the Mail program is stored on your computer to allow you to connect to your mailbox on the server, create messages, and read mail retrieved from the server. The portion of Mail that has to be installed on your computer is copied to your personal computer from the Mail server—no floppy disks are used for the setup, which is why Microsoft doesn't include Mail disks in the Office package.

Electronic mail lets users on a network send messages to other users or groups of users on the network. A mailbox is assigned to each user on the network who has a mail license, and a user name and password are required for access to each mailbox.

You don't have to know any special mailbox addresses to send messages. Address lists are available on the server, and you can simply select a recipient from the list.

You can create your own personal lists of mailbox addresses for people you frequently send mail to. You can also create your own group names and add as many addresses to a group as you like. Then, when you send a message to the group, every user on the list receives the message.

Your lists of addresses can be sorted in a variety of ways to make it easy to find the person or group you want to receive a message.

In addition to sending normal text messages, you can attach any type of file to a message. For example, you could send a message to the sales department and attach an Excel worksheet containing last month's sales figures. Mail also supports OLE, so objects from other Office applications and other OLE-compatible Windows programs can be inserted in your Mail messages.

> **tip** Although the Office package includes instructions for setting up Mail on your computer, in practice this is something that your network system administrator will probably do for you. Most companies that provide electronic mail service, whether Microsoft Mail or another e-mail program, take care of all the setup and training for all users.

After setting up Mail for your computer, you'll be able to start Mail by double-clicking on a Microsoft Mail icon—the same way you start other Windows programs. You can also add a Microsoft Mail button to the Microsoft Office Manager toolbar by clicking on the Microsoft Office button, choosing Customize, and then clicking on the Microsoft Mail check box in the Toolbar tab of the Customize dialog box.

If you need more help using Mail than your company provides, check out the on-line help system and demonstrations that are included with Mail.

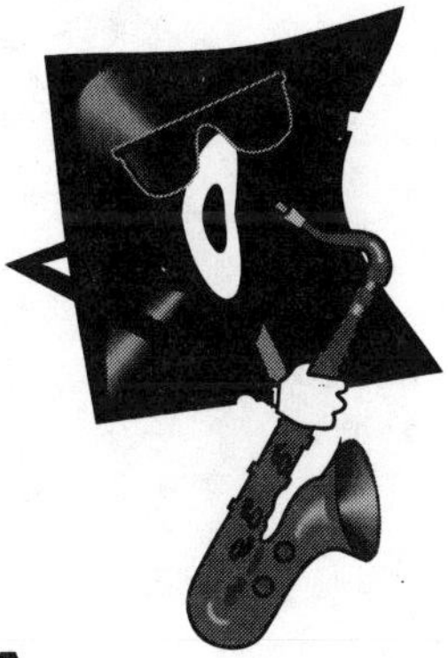

Index

A

B

C

D

K

L

M

N

O

P

R

S

T

U

V

W

Excel 5 for Windows: The Visual Learning Guide

Grace Joely Beatty & David C. Gardner

The Fastest Way to Learn Excel 5 for Windows!

Learning experts Grace Joely Beatty and David C. Gardner apply their tested teaching techniques to the latest Excel 5 for Windows. The unique graphical approach of Prima's Visual Learning Guides takes you through the basics of spreadsheet design and creation in a way that makes it virtually impossible for you to get lost or confused.

Compressed text and goal-oriented tasks, combined with hundreds of screen shots and graphics, allow you to move from beginning concepts to importing graphics and using dynamic data exchange (DDE) features in the shortest time possible. Full-color screen shots let you see the screens just as you see them on your monitor.

Drs. Beatty and **Gardner** are faculty members of Boston University and have served as consultants to major corporations that have undergone system-wide computer conversions.

272 pages	$19.95
7⅜"×9¼"	Paperback
1-55958-392-4	Available now

Windows 3.1: The Visual Learning Guide

David C. Gardner & Grace Joely Beatty

The Fastest Way to Get Started in Windows 3.1!

If you've hesitated to move to Windows or to upgrade to version 3.1, wait no longer! Gardner and Beatty are here to smooth out the learning curve with their beautiful, full-color learning guides. Hands-on examples guide you through specific tasks that lead to general principles. Master a task, and the text asks you what you want to do next. Accomplish your goals immediately. The graphical approach, with screen shots on every page, lends itself perfectly to the graphical Windows environment. The Visual Learning Guides set a new standard in computer book publishing.

> *"The Gardner Beatty Group's documentation expertise is unparalleled. Their combination of learning psychology, computer training experience, and popular writing skills always produces a superior product."*
>
> *—Michael Torre, First Vice President, Dean Witter Reynolds, New York*

Drs. Gardner and **Beatty** are licensed psychologists who specialize in computer software training and documentation design. They live near San Diego, California.

288 pages	$19.95
7⅜"×9¼"	Paperback
1-55958-182-4	Available now

Prima Computer Books You Can Order Directly

1-2-3 for Windows: The Visual Learning Guide	$19.95
WINDOWS Magazine Presents: Access from the Ground Up	$19.95
Adventures in Windows	$14.95
Computing Strategies for Reengineering Your Organization	$24.95
CorelDRAW! 4 Revealed!	$24.95
Create Wealth with Quicken	$19.95
DOS 6: Everything You Need to Know	$24.95
DOS 6.2: Everything You Need to Know	$24.95
WINDOWS Magazine Presents: Encyclopedia for Windows	$29.95
Excel 4 for Windows: The Visual Learning Guide	$19.95
Excel 5 for Windows: The Visual Learning Guide	$19.95
Free Electronic Networks	$24.95
WINDOWS Magazine Presents: Freelance Graphics for Windows: The Art of Presentation	$27.95
Harvard Graphics for Windows: The Art of Presentation	$27.95
Improv 2.1 Revealed! (with 3½" disk)	$27.95
Microsoft Works for Windows By Example	$24.95
NetWare 3.x: A Do-It-Yourself Guide	$24.95
Novell NetWare Lite: Simplified Network Solutions	$24.95
PageMaker 5 for Windows: Everything You Need to Know	$19.95
PC DOS 6.1: Everything You Need to Know	$24.95
QuickTime: Making Movies with Your Macintosh	$24.95
WINDOWS Magazine Presents: The Power of Windows and DOS Together, 2nd Edition	$24.95
Smalltalk Programming for Windows (with 3½" disk)	$39.95
Superbase Revealed!	$29.95
Think THINK C!	$39.95
Windows 3.1: The Visual Learning Guide	$19.95
Windows for Teens	$14.95
WinFax PRO: The Visual Learning Guide	$19.95
Word for Windows 2: The Visual Learning Guide	$19.95
Word for Windows 2 Desktop Publishing By Example	$24.95
Word for Windows 6: The Visual Learning Guide	$19.95
WordPerfect 5.1 for Windows Desktop Publishing By Example	$24.95
WordPerfect 6 for DOS: The Visual Learning Guide	$19.95
WordPerfect 6 for Windows: The Visual Learning Guide	$19.95
Your FoxPro for Windows Consultant (with 3½" disk)	$39.95